VALIANT

Peter Cuneo
Chairman

Dinesh Shamdasani
CEO and Chief Creative Officer

Gavin Cuneo
CFO and Head of Strategic Development

Fred Pierce
Publisher

Warren Simons
VP Executive Editor

Walter Black
VP Operations

Hunter Gorinson
Director of Marketing, Communications
and Digital Media

Atom! Freeman
Sales Manager

Travis Escarfullery
Production and Design Manager

Alejandro Arbona
Associate Editor

Josh Johns
Assistant Editor

Peter Stern
Operations Manager

Robert Meyers
Operations Coordinator

Ivan Cohen
Collection Editor

Steve Blackwell
Collection Designer

Rian Hughes/Device
Trade Dress and Book Design

Russell Brown
President, Consumer Products,
Promotions and Ad Sales

Jason Kothari
Vice Chairman

Valiant Masters Rai®: From Honor to Strength. Published by
Valiant Entertainment, LLC. Office of Publication: 424 West
33rd Street, New York, NY 10001. Compilation copyright ©2013
Valiant Entertainment, Inc. All rights reserved. Contains materials
originally published in single magazine form as Rai® #1-8.
Copyright ©1992 Valiant Entertainment, Inc. All rights reserved. All
characters, their distinctive likeness and related indicia featured in
this publication are trademarks of Valiant Entertainment, Inc. Solar,
Magnus and Turok are registered trademarks of Classic Media, Inc.
The stories, characters, and incidents featured in this publication
are entirely fictional. Valiant Entertainment does not read or accept
unsolicited submissions of ideas, stories, or artwork. Printed in the
U.S.A. First Printing.
ISBN: 9781939346070.

RAI

FROM HONOR TO
STRENGTH

DAVE MICHELINIE | JOE ST. PIERRE | PETER GRAU

CONTENTS

Special thanks to Dan Moler & Iggy Cheung

FOREWORD

David Letterman has a catch phrase that seems uniquely appropriate to the situation I faced when first assigned to write the ongoing *Rai* series for Valiant Comics: "I wouldn't give this guy's troubles to a monkey on a rock!"

In the four-part miniseries that introduced Rai – as a flip-book in *Magnus, Robot Fighter* #5-8 – Jim Shooter had established a world of conflict and catastrophe, of hard choices and tragic repercussions.

In the year 4001, Japan, traditionally an advocate of cultural isolation, had become physically distanced as well. Entirely encapsulated in an artificial shell, the island had evolved into a totally self-sufficient entity, maintained and regulated by a computer intelligence called "Grandmother." And for forty generations the one person Grandmother empowered to be the physical protector of the millions of people under her care was known as "Rai" – meaning "spirit" – and was infused with a mysterious energy that gave him superhuman abilities.

The current Rai, 90-something Rentaro Nakadai, was ready to hand over the mantle of responsibility to his son, Tohru, but there was a slight glitch: Tohru didn't want to be the new Rai. A dedicated husband and father, Tohru sought only to live a normal life, and to keep his infant son from what he considered to be the forced servitude of becoming another Rai after him.

But as mentioned earlier, this was a tale of hard choices. And when Earth was attacked by spider-like aliens, a threat Rentaro in his aged form was unable to counter, Tohru felt obligated to take on the Rai energy in a last-ditch effort to save the world. The invasion

was turned back, but in the culminating battle Japan was launched into space, to become an artificial moon orbiting its former home. In the end, Tohru's attitude had caused a breach with his father. Accepting his destiny as spirit guardian had estranged him from his wife. And his first actions as the new Rai had resulted in his country becoming more truly alone than anyone could ever have imagined.

This was the setting I inherited when the scripting chores were handed over to me with a jaunty, "Okay, Dave – take it!"

Gee. Thanks, Jim.

But a challenge is a challenge, and so I faced it like I face all major difficulties in this uncertain life: I curled up in a corner and wept. Unfortunately, that didn't work. (It rarely does.) So I sighed, sat down at my desk and urged myself to think. The Valiant Universe had been founded on reality – real people reacting in believable ways to strange circumstances. And so I focused on Tohru Nakadai as an actual person; if I were in his place, what would I do?

And out of those musings came a saga of isolation, both societal and individual; of freedom versus duty, responsibility versus patriotism, of alienation and the struggle to keep hope alive. On the surface, the theme was that of civil war, a battle of words and violence between two factions vying for control of the new Japan: the Humanist government that championed self-determination, a world guided by humans, imperfect but theirs; and the Restoration Underground, fighting just as vehemently for a return to a computer-controlled Utopia. But behind this clash, at the heart of every chapter, was always the personal journey

of Tohru Nakadai, a man caught between his sense of responsibility to Grandmother's legacy, and loyalty to a wife who now fought for the underground Healers; a man desperately trying to do the right thing in a chaotic world where the definition of "right" seemed to change on a daily basis.

But even though *Rai* was set in the far future, it was important to make the series relatable to 20th century audiences. Guest appearances by the likes of Magnus, Solar, the Eternal Warrior, and others helped keep *Rai* connected to the Valiant Universe. Couching familiar problems in fresh frameworks helped future conflicts resonate with contemporary readers. One such example was the introduction of a new designer drug called "neopium," a seemingly harmless yet sinister serum that could sway addicts' political viewpoints. This allowed us to touch upon such universal topics as the danger of too much government control, and the right of individuals to decide what's best for themselves. Another angle was explored with the introduction of Rai's first super-villain: Icespike, an apparently ego-driven maniac whose true motivation was far more subtle: anonymity. As a solitary citizen in a society of fifty billion, he felt unimportant, unnoticed, unappreciated. And how many of us, today, haven't in our lives felt the passing sting of being ignored?

In my relatively short run on *Rai*, I was blessed to be teamed with such then-and-future superstars as Joe St. Pierre, Sal Velluto, Charles Barnett III, Peter Grau, and others. Covers that graced those issues were drawn by enduring luminaries like Frank Miller, Walter Simonson, and Bob Layton. The artistic and storytelling expertise of those amazing illustrators being added to my scripts was (if

you'll forgive the butchered cliché) sweet icing on a many-layered cake. The job of taking an ancient culture and projecting it two millennia into the future, keeping the flavor of traditional Japan while infusing it with the high-tech wonder of tomorrow, wasn't exactly a walk in the park. And I only had to attempt it with written words, while the artists were tasked with imagining the visuals for every detail, from environments to clothing to what a baby's crib would look like in 4001! And they did it month after month. Kudos are well-deserved.

So that's the background for the stories in this collection: issues #1-8 of Valiant's first Asian solo hero. They form a closed narrative arc in themselves, while establishing a foundation on which future versions of Rai could be based. I was flattered and honored to be allowed to script these tales, and I'm proud of what was accomplished by everyone involved, from editors to artists, from colorists and letterers to all the unsung behind-the-scenes craftsmen (and women) who worked hard to make these stories happen. Our common goal was to entertain, and if you find yourself swept away, drawn into new worlds and grand adventure, then we've succeeded. But here's a suggestion to perhaps make the experience even more interesting: while reading these stories ask yourself, if you were Rai... what would you do?

David Michelinie
October 2013

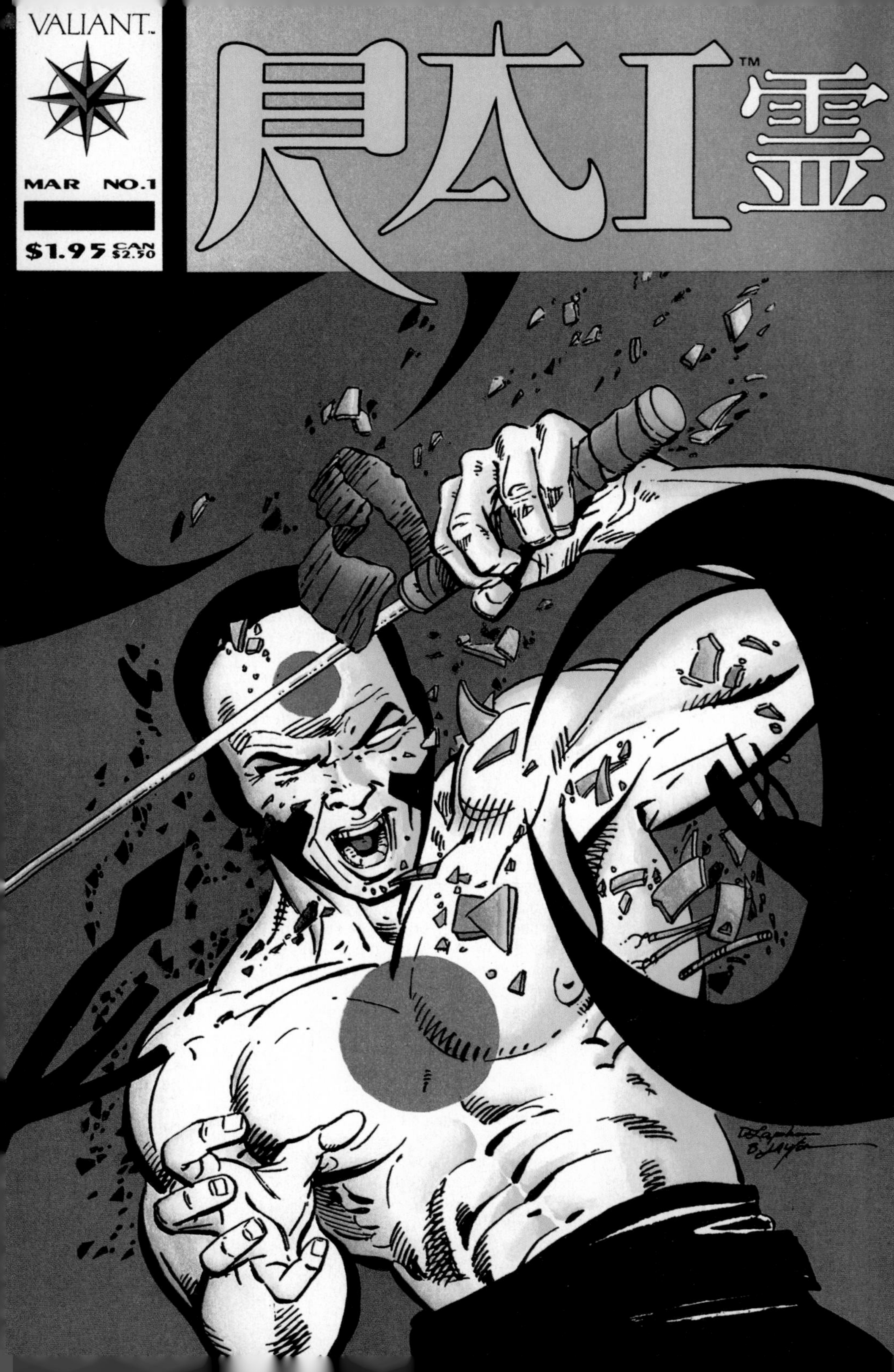
VALIANT™
MAR NO.1
$1.95 CAN $2.50
RAI™ 霊

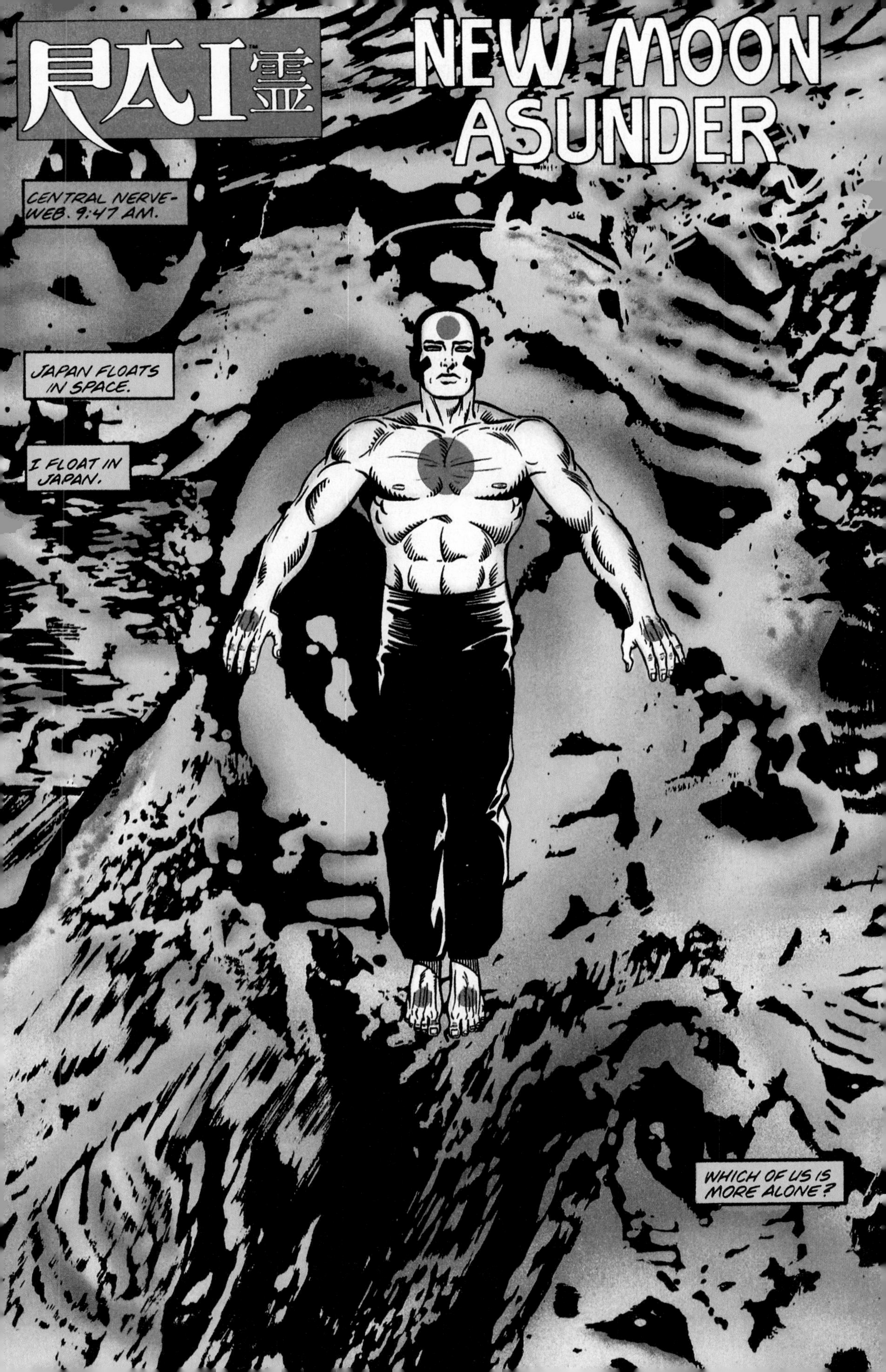
RAI 霊
NEW MOON ASUNDER
CENTRAL NERVE-WEB. 9:47 AM.
JAPAN FLOATS IN SPACE.
I FLOAT IN JAPAN.
WHICH OF US IS MORE ALONE?

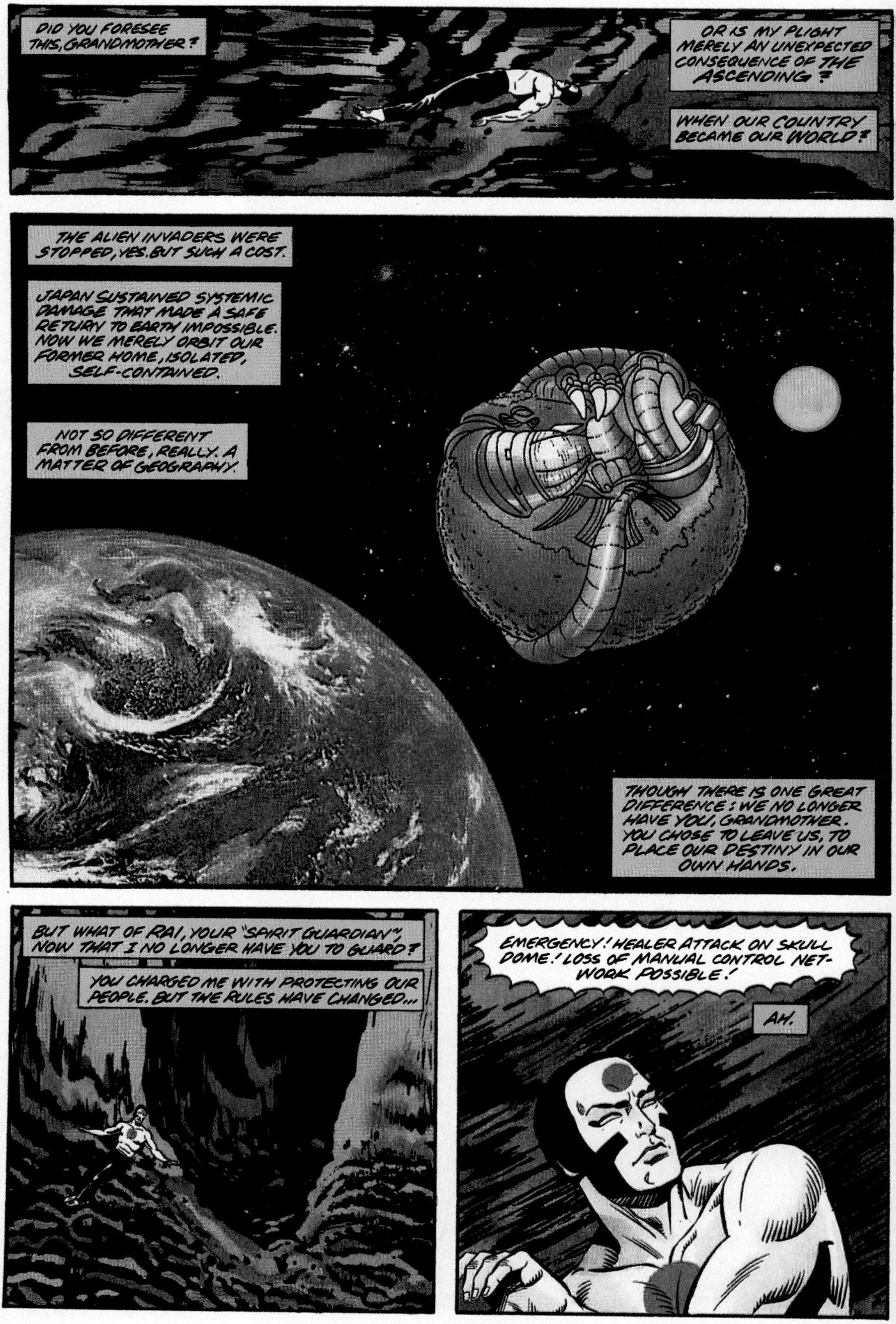
DID YOU FORESEE THIS, GRANDMOTHER?
OR IS MY PLIGHT MERELY AN UNEXPECTED CONSEQUENCE OF THE ASCENDING?
WHEN OUR COUNTRY BECAME OUR WORLD?
THE ALIEN INVADERS WERE STOPPED, YES. BUT SUCH A COST.
JAPAN SUSTAINED SYSTEMIC DAMAGE THAT MADE A SAFE RETURN TO EARTH IMPOSSIBLE. NOW WE MERELY ORBIT OUR FORMER HOME, ISOLATED, SELF-CONTAINED.
NOT SO DIFFERENT FROM BEFORE, REALLY. A MATTER OF GEOGRAPHY.
THOUGH THERE IS ONE GREAT DIFFERENCE: WE NO LONGER HAVE YOU, GRANDMOTHER. YOU CHOSE TO LEAVE US, TO PLACE OUR DESTINY IN OUR OWN HANDS.
BUT WHAT OF RAI, YOUR "SPIRIT GUARDIAN", NOW THAT I NO LONGER HAVE YOU TO GUARD?
YOU CHARGED ME WITH PROTECTING OUR PEOPLE. BUT THE RULES HAVE CHANGED...
EMERGENCY! HEALER ATTACK ON SKULL DOME! LOSS OF MANUAL CONTROL NET-WORK POSSIBLE!
AH.

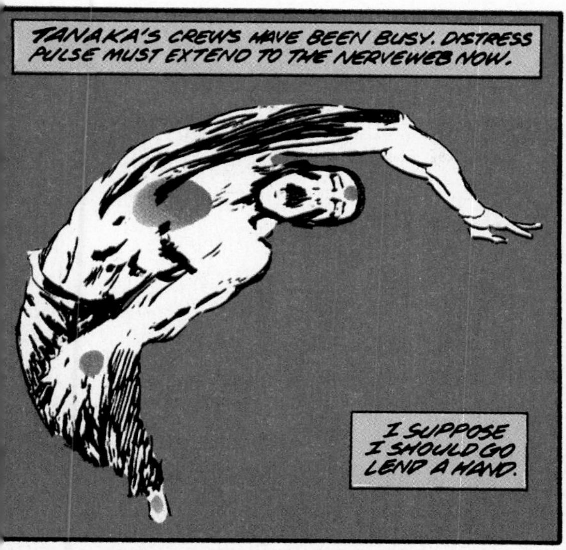
TANAKA'S CREWS HAVE BEEN BUSY. DISTRESS PULSE MUST EXTEND TO THE NERVEWEB NOW.
I SUPPOSE I SHOULD GO LEND A HAND.
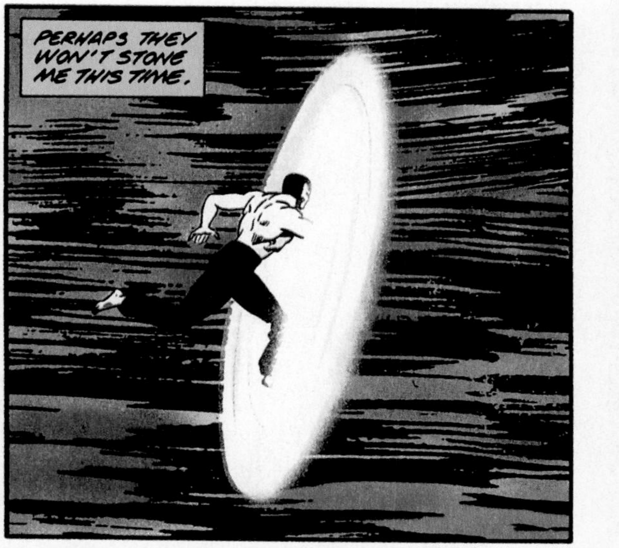
PERHAPS THEY WON'T STONE ME THIS TIME.
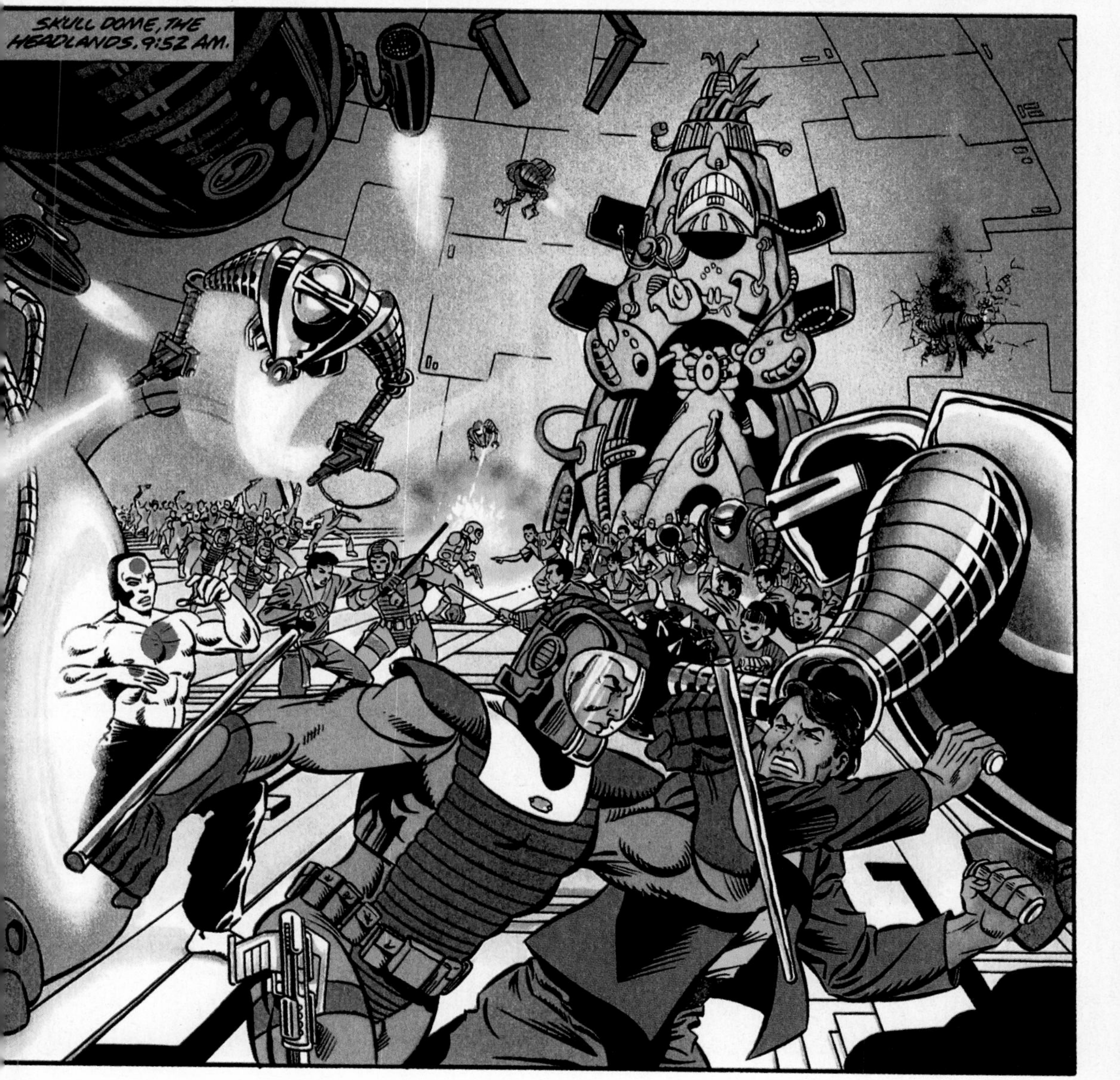
SKULL DOME, THE HEADLANDS. 9:52 AM.

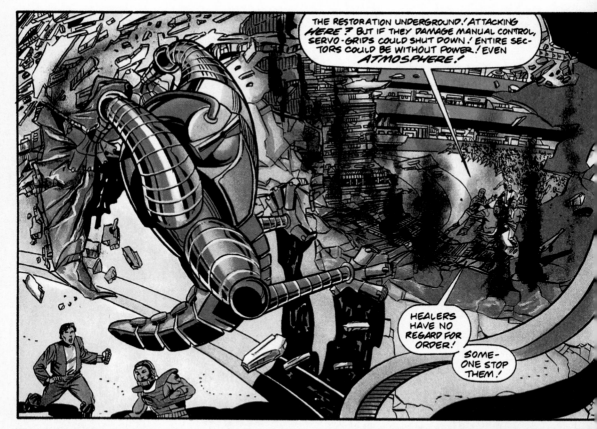

THE RESTORATION UNDERGROUND! ATTACKING *HERE*? BUT IF THEY DAMAGE MANUAL CONTROL, SERVO-GRIDS COULD SHUT DOWN! ENTIRE SECTORS COULD BE WITHOUT POWER! EVEN *ATMOSPHERE*!

HEALERS HAVE NO REGARD FOR ORDER!

SOMEONE STOP THEM!

ALL RIGHT.

LOOK! IT'S RAI!

TRAITOR! WORK LOVER!

HEALERS HATE ME. THINK I ALLOWED GRANDMOTHER TO LEAVE, HELPED PUT TANAKA'S HUMANISTS IN POWER.

DO THEY FORGET I ONCE PROTECTED GRANDMOTHER FROM SUCH ANTI-GRANNIES?

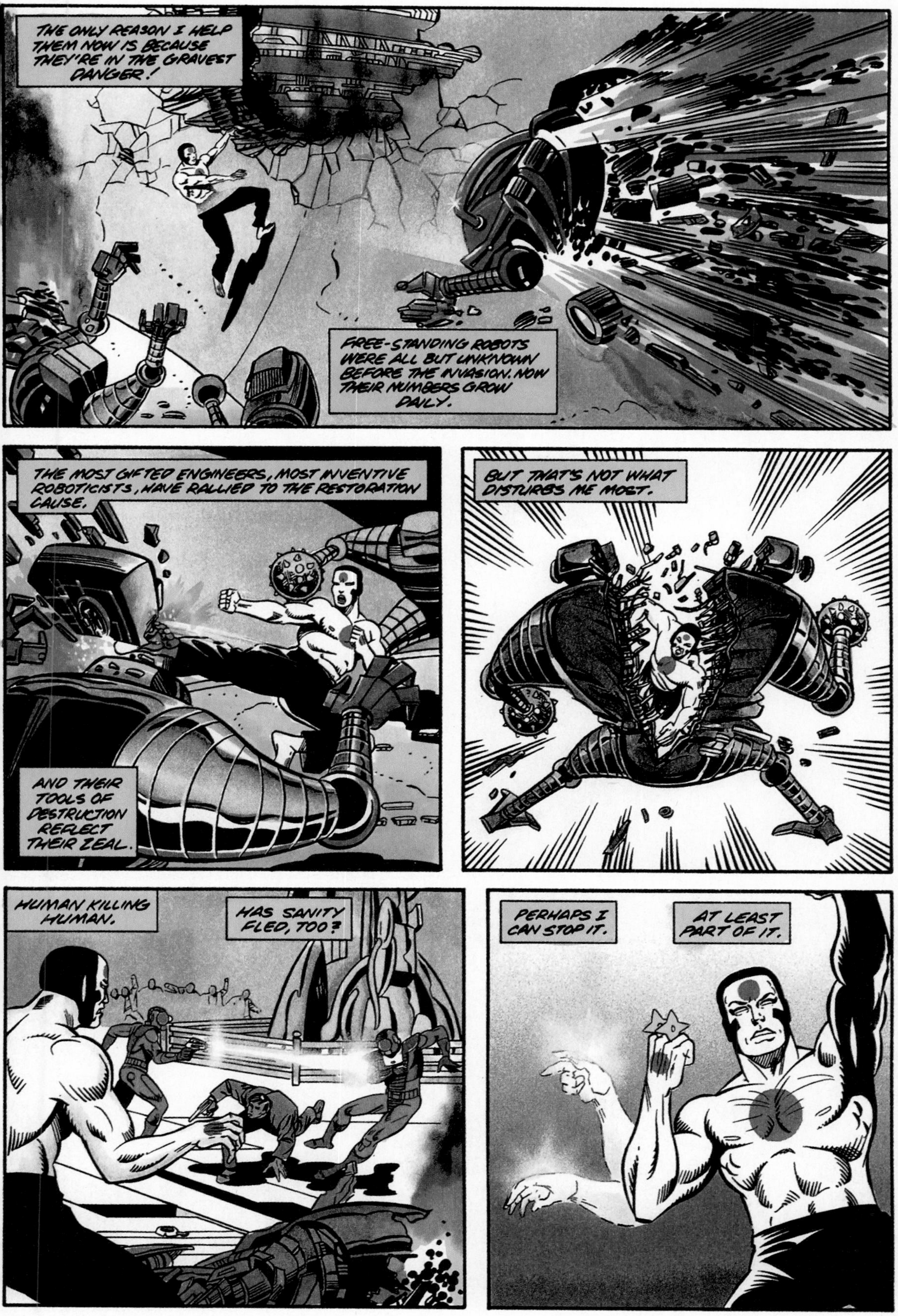
THE ONLY REASON I HELP THEM NOW IS BECAUSE THEY'RE IN THE GRAVEST DANGER!
FREE-STANDING ROBOTS WERE ALL BUT UNKNOWN BEFORE THE INVASION. NOW THEIR NUMBERS GROW DAILY.
THE MOST GIFTED ENGINEERS, MOST INVENTIVE ROBOTICISTS, HAVE RALLIED TO THE RESTORATION CAUSE.
AND THEIR TOOLS OF DESTRUCTION REFLECT THEIR ZEAL.
BUT THAT'S NOT WHAT DISTURBS ME MOST.
HUMAN KILLING HUMAN.
HAS SANITY FLED, TOO?
PERHAPS I CAN STOP IT.
AT LEAST PART OF IT.

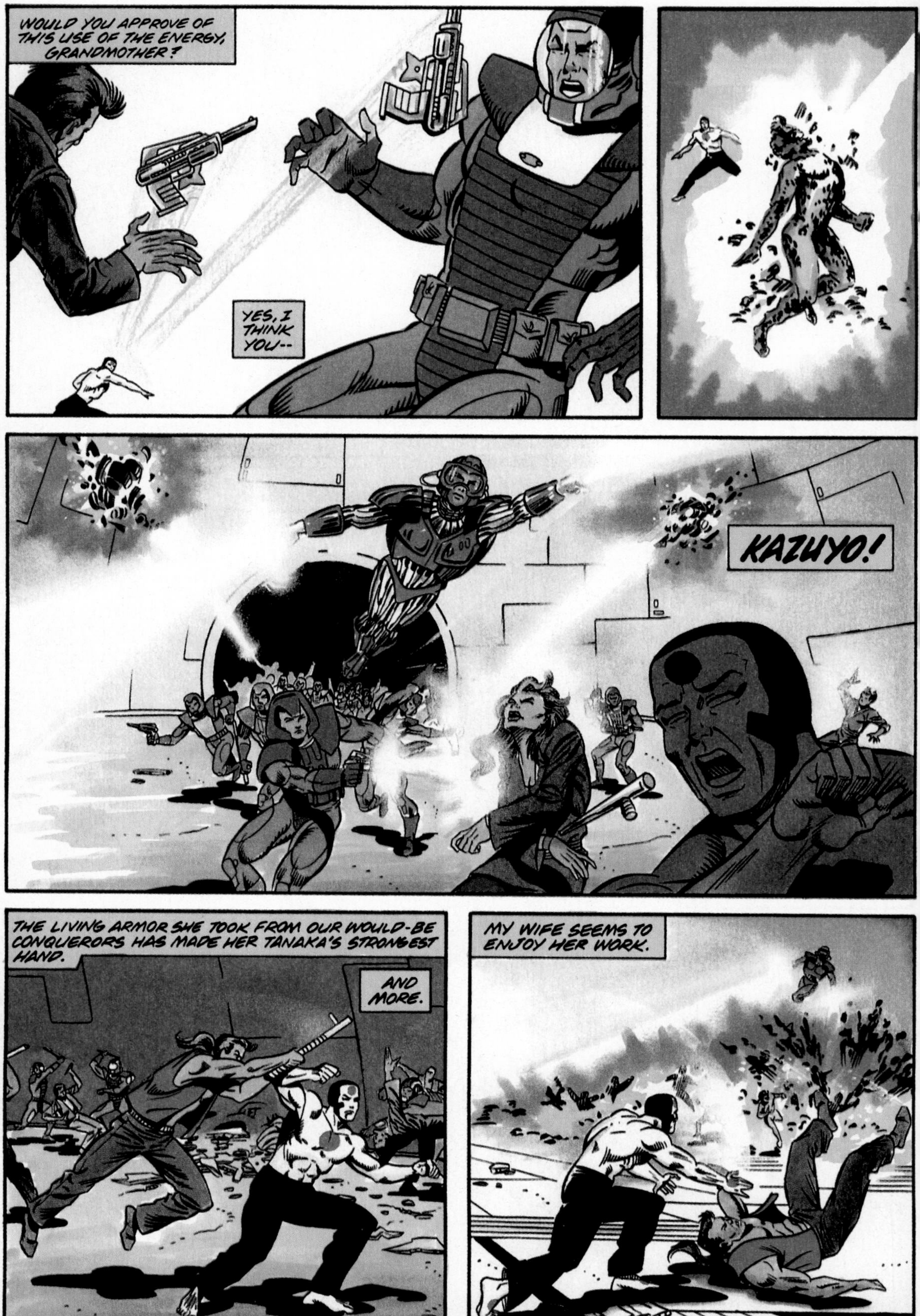

WOULD YOU APPROVE OF THIS USE OF THE ENERGY, GRANDMOTHER?
YES, I THINK YOU--
KAZUYO!
THE LIVING ARMOR SHE TOOK FROM OUR WOULD-BE CONQUERORS HAS MADE HER TANAKA'S STRONGEST HAND.
AND MORE.
MY WIFE SEEMS TO ENJOY HER WORK.

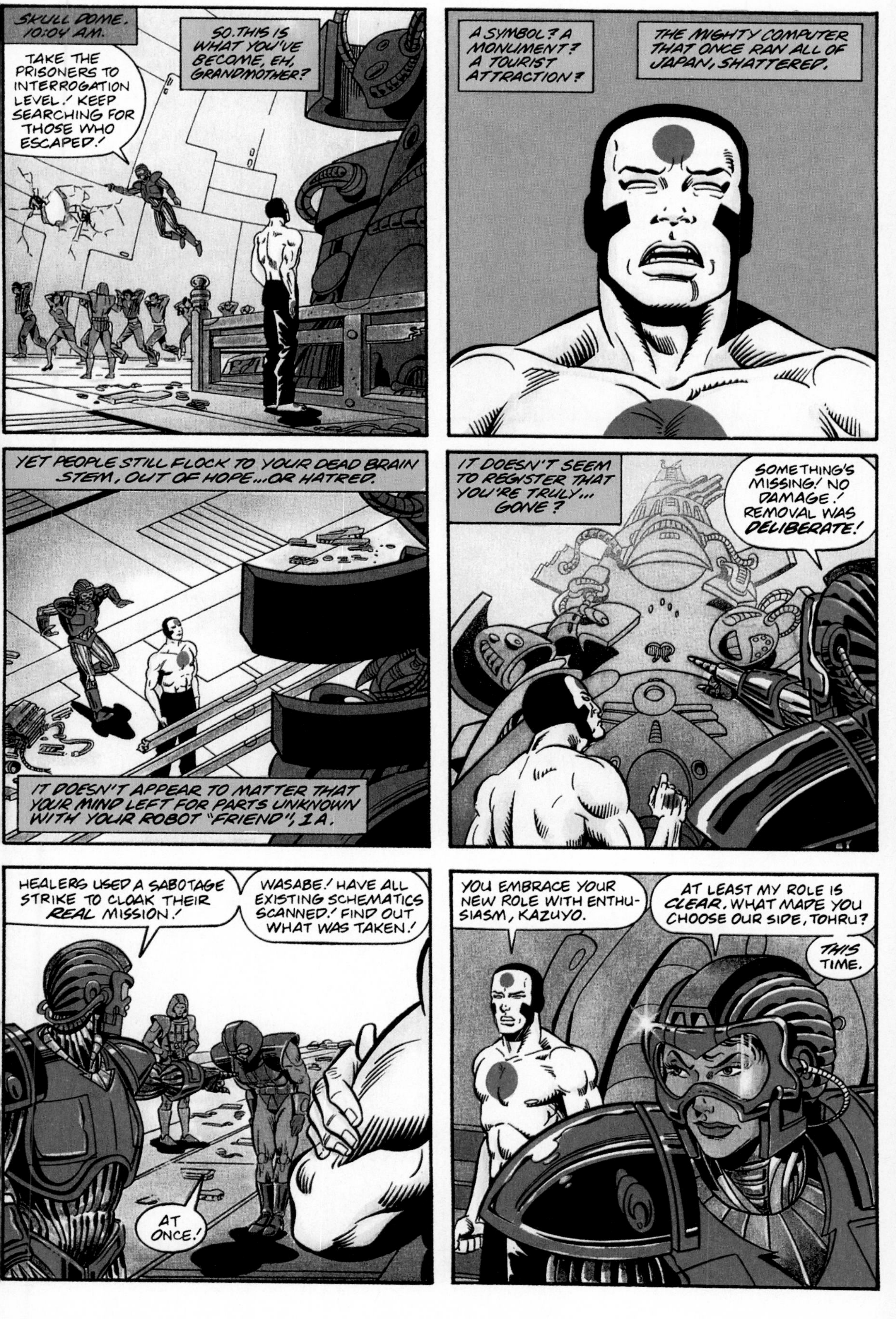
SKULL DOME. 10:04 AM.
SO. THIS IS WHAT YOU'VE BECOME, EH, GRANDMOTHER?
TAKE THE PRISONERS TO INTERROGATION LEVEL! KEEP SEARCHING FOR THOSE WHO ESCAPED!
A SYMBOL? A MONUMENT? A TOURIST ATTRACTION?
THE MIGHTY COMPUTER THAT ONCE RAN ALL OF JAPAN, SHATTERED.
YET PEOPLE STILL FLOCK TO YOUR DEAD BRAIN STEM, OUT OF HOPE...OR HATRED.
IT DOESN'T APPEAR TO MATTER THAT YOUR MIND LEFT FOR PARTS UNKNOWN WITH YOUR ROBOT "FRIEND", 1A.
IT DOESN'T SEEM TO REGISTER THAT YOU'RE TRULY... GONE?
SOMETHING'S MISSING! NO DAMAGE! REMOVAL WAS DELIBERATE!
HEALERS USED A SABOTAGE STRIKE TO CLOAK THEIR REAL MISSION!
WASABE! HAVE ALL EXISTING SCHEMATICS SCANNED! FIND OUT WHAT WAS TAKEN!
AT ONCE!
YOU EMBRACE YOUR NEW ROLE WITH ENTHUSIASM, KAZUYO.
AT LEAST MY ROLE IS CLEAR. WHAT MADE YOU CHOOSE OUR SIDE, TOHRU?
THIS TIME.

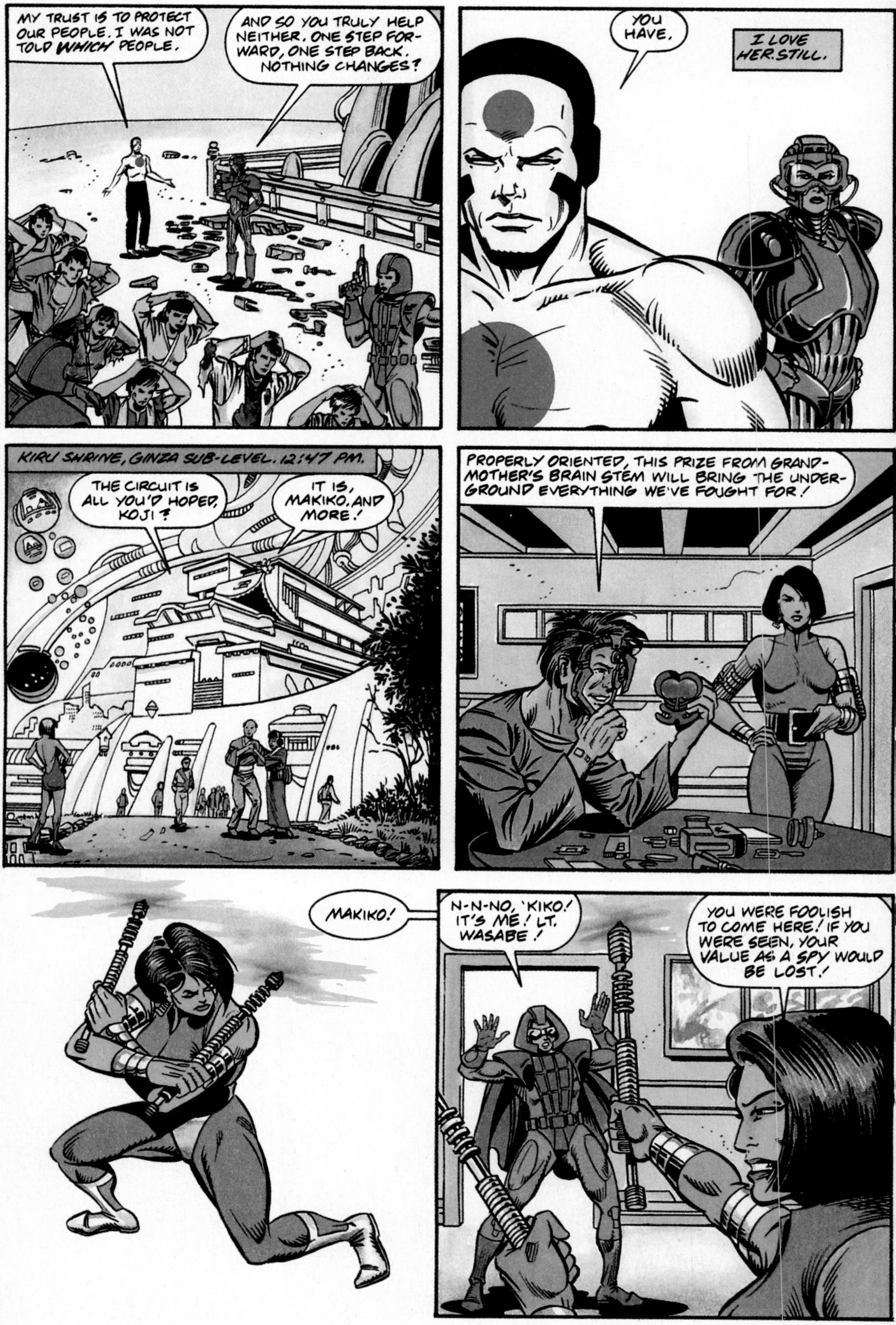
MY TRUST IS TO PROTECT OUR PEOPLE. I WAS NOT TOLD WHICH PEOPLE.
AND SO YOU TRULY HELP NEITHER. ONE STEP FORWARD, ONE STEP BACK. NOTHING CHANGES?
YOU HAVE.
I LOVE HER STILL.
KIRU SHRINE, GINZA SUB-LEVEL. 12:47 PM.
THE CIRCUIT IS ALL YOU'D HOPED, KOJI?
IT IS, MAKIKO, AND MORE!
PROPERLY ORIENTED, THIS PRIZE FROM GRANDMOTHER'S BRAIN STEM WILL BRING THE UNDERGROUND EVERYTHING WE'VE FOUGHT FOR!
MAKIKO!
N-N-NO, 'KIKO! IT'S ME! LT. WASABE!
YOU WERE FOOLISH TO COME HERE! IF YOU WERE SEEN, YOUR VALUE AS A SPY WOULD BE LOST!

A NECESSARY RISK! I COULDN'T TRUST TRANS-MISSION, EVEN ON OUR SCAN-SHIELDED WAVE-LENGTHS! AND THIS IS VITAL!

I WAS UNABLE TO DISGUISE THE REMOVAL IN TIME! TANAKA'S TROOPS KNOW OF THE MISSING CIRCUIT!

THERE'LL BE AN INVESTIGATION! IF THEY DISCOVER THIS MODULE'S TRUE PURPOSE, ALL WILL BE LOST!

NO! PROJECT: HOMECOMING IS TOO IMPORTANT! IT MUST BE PROTECTED!

EVEN IF DRASTIC MEASURES NEED BE TAKEN,

RAI GLOBE, WESTERN EXTERIOR. 1:32 P.M.

HOME,

I MIGHT HAVE BEEN HAPPY HERE, ONCE.

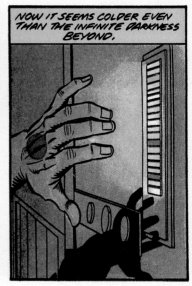

NOW IT SEEMS COLDER EVEN THAN THE INFINITE DARKNESS BEYOND.

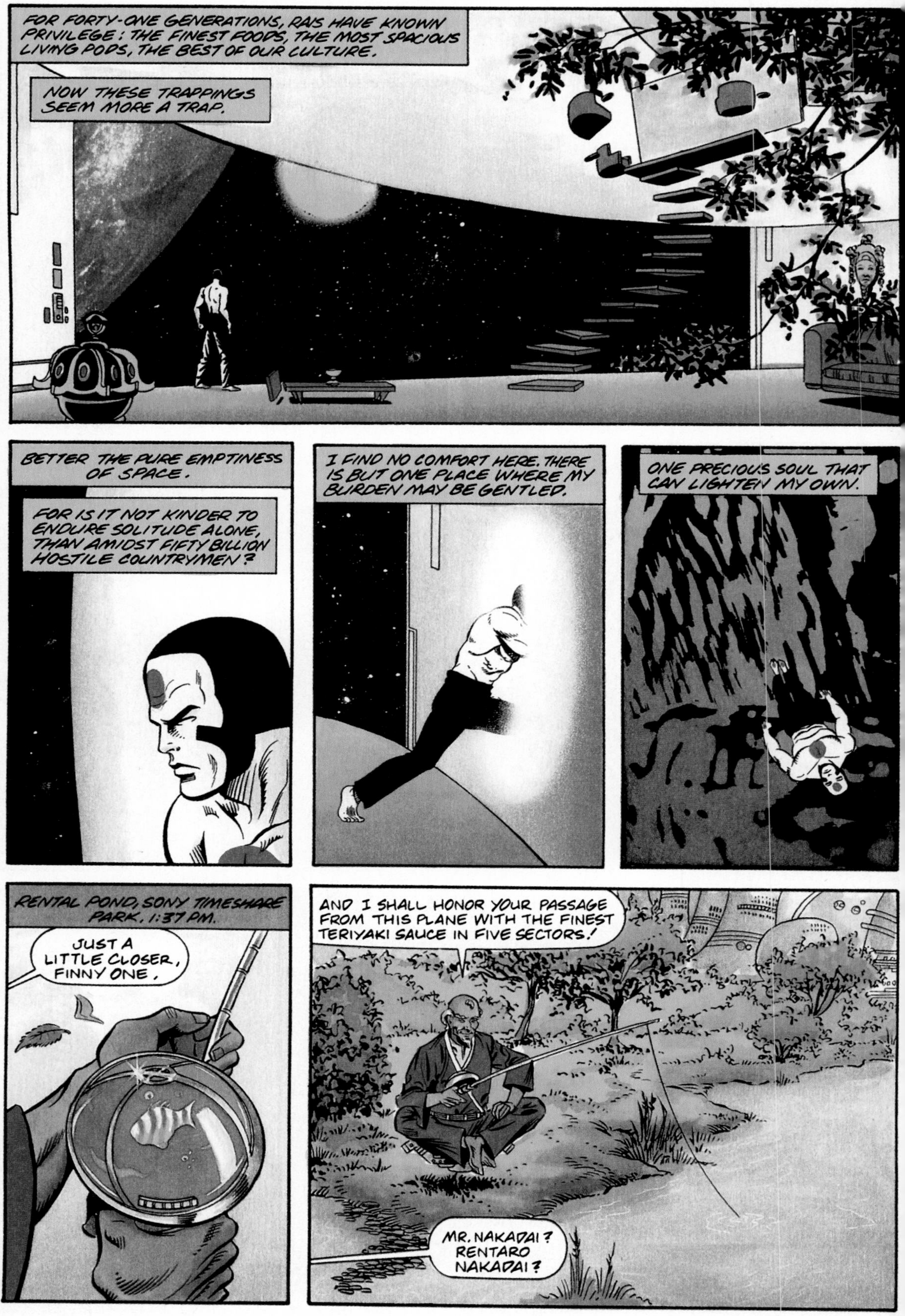
FOR FORTY-ONE GENERATIONS, RAIS HAVE KNOWN PRIVILEGE: THE FINEST FOODS, THE MOST SPACIOUS LIVING PODS, THE BEST OF OUR CULTURE.
NOW THESE TRAPPINGS SEEM MORE A TRAP.
BETTER THE PURE EMPTINESS OF SPACE.
FOR IS IT NOT KINDER TO ENDURE SOLITUDE ALONE, THAN AMIDST FIFTY BILLION HOSTILE COUNTRYMEN?
I FIND NO COMFORT HERE. THERE IS BUT ONE PLACE WHERE MY BURDEN MAY BE GENTLED.
ONE PRECIOUS SOUL THAT CAN LIGHTEN MY OWN.
RENTAL POND, SONY TIMESHARE PARK, 1:37 PM.
JUST A LITTLE CLOSER, FINNY ONE.
AND I SHALL HONOR YOUR PASSAGE FROM THIS PLANE WITH THE FINEST TERIYAKI SAUCE IN FIVE SECTORS!
MR. NAKADAI? RENTARO NAKADAI?

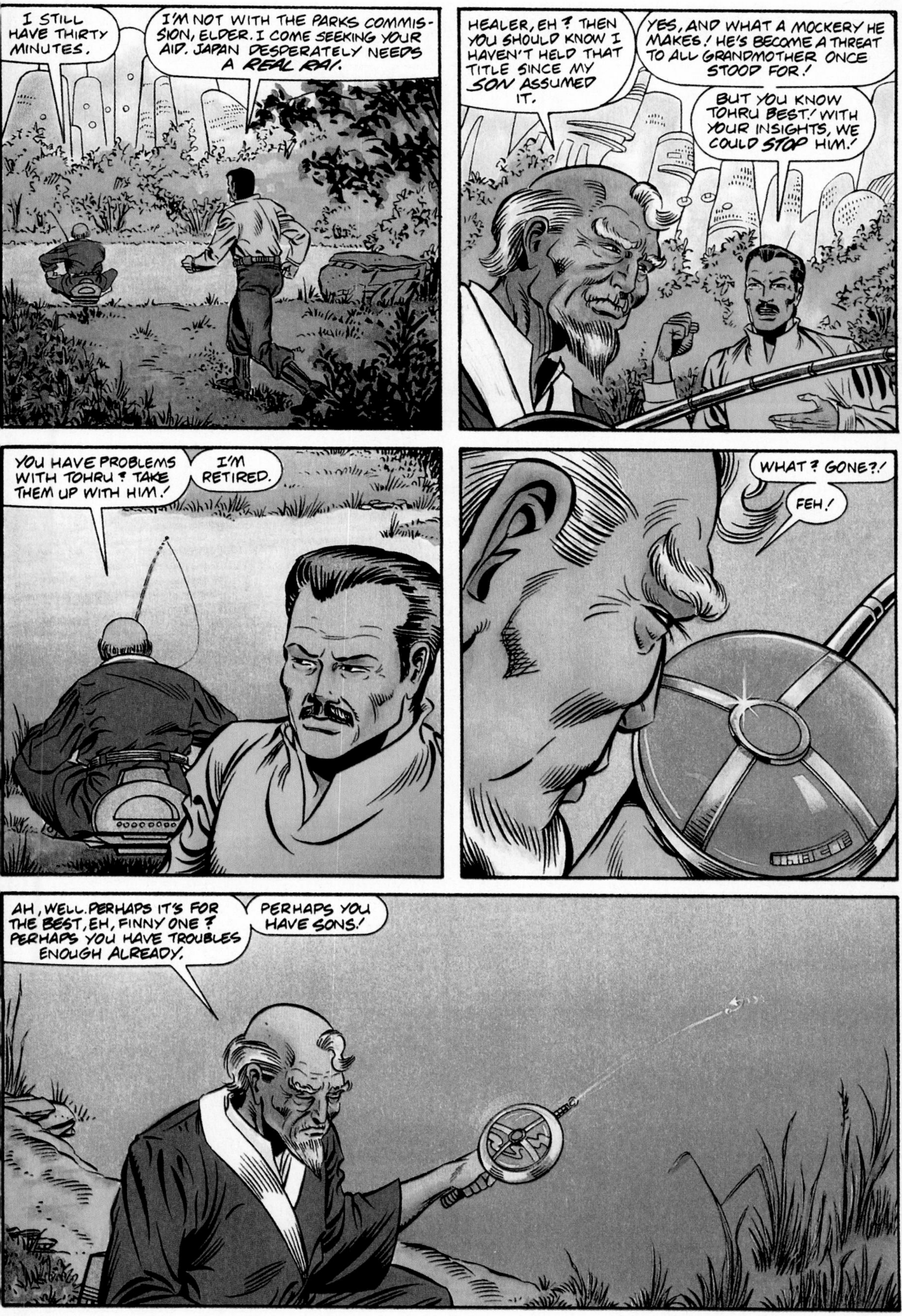
I STILL HAVE THIRTY MINUTES.
I'M NOT WITH THE PARKS COMMISSION, ELDER. I COME SEEKING YOUR AID. JAPAN DESPERATELY NEEDS A REAL RAI.
HEALER, EH? THEN YOU SHOULD KNOW I HAVEN'T HELD THAT TITLE SINCE MY SON ASSUMED IT.
YES, AND WHAT A MOCKERY HE MAKES! HE'S BECOME A THREAT TO ALL GRANDMOTHER ONCE STOOD FOR!
BUT YOU KNOW TOHRU BEST! WITH YOUR INSIGHTS, WE COULD STOP HIM!
YOU HAVE PROBLEMS WITH TOHRU? TAKE THEM UP WITH HIM!
I'M RETIRED.
WHAT? GONE?!
FEH!
AH, WELL. PERHAPS IT'S FOR THE BEST, EH, FINNY ONE? PERHAPS YOU HAVE TROUBLES ENOUGH ALREADY.
PERHAPS YOU HAVE SONS!

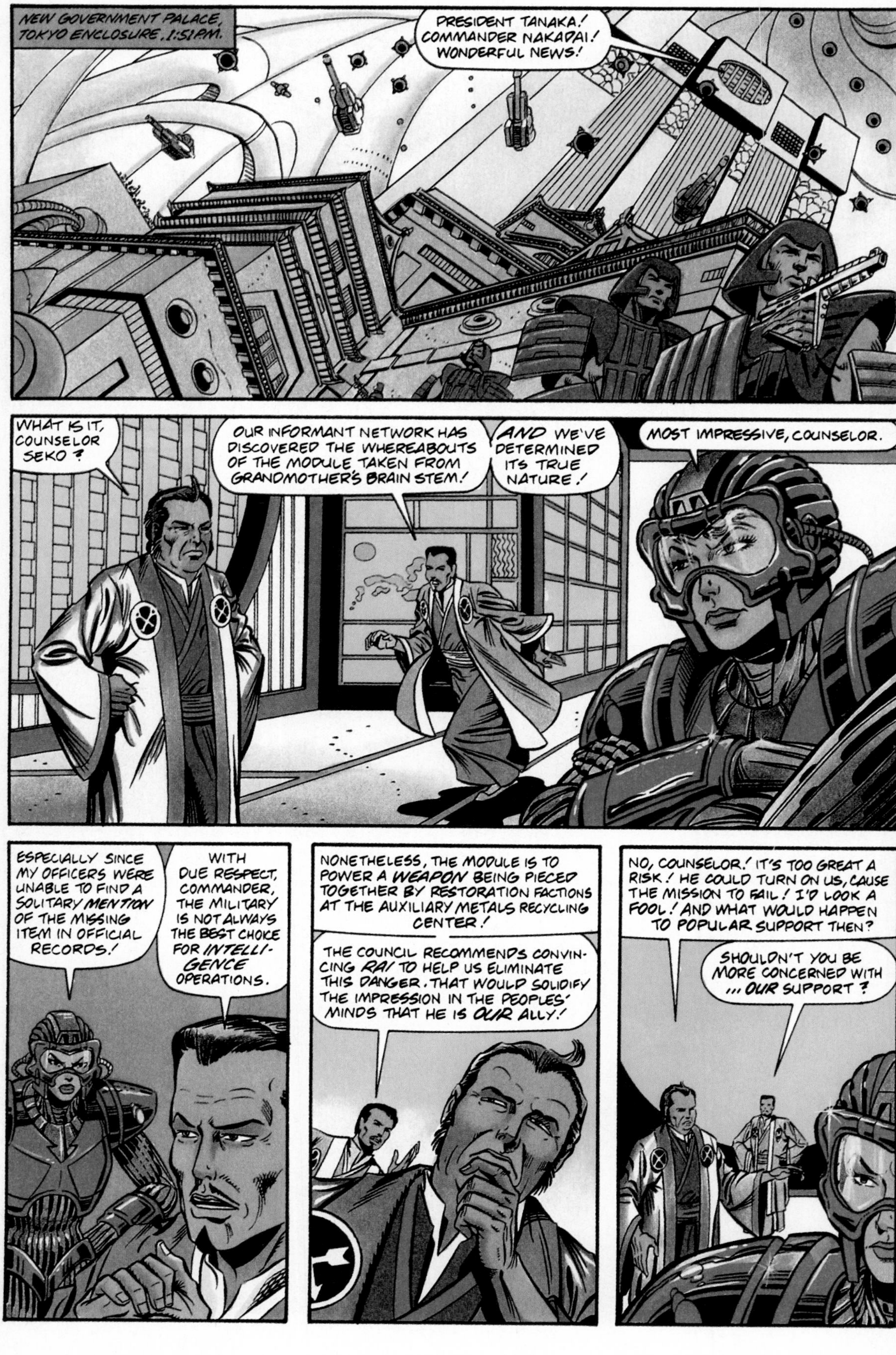
NEW GOVERNMENT PALACE, TOKYO ENCLOSURE. 1:51 P.M.
PRESIDENT TANAKA! COMMANDER NAKADAI! WONDERFUL NEWS!
WHAT IS IT, COUNSELOR SEKO?
OUR INFORMANT NETWORK HAS DISCOVERED THE WHEREABOUTS OF THE MODULE TAKEN FROM GRANDMOTHER'S BRAIN STEM!
AND WE'VE DETERMINED ITS TRUE NATURE!
MOST IMPRESSIVE, COUNSELOR.
ESPECIALLY SINCE MY OFFICERS WERE UNABLE TO FIND A SOLITARY MENTION OF THE MISSING ITEM IN OFFICIAL RECORDS!
WITH DUE RESPECT, COMMANDER, THE MILITARY IS NOT ALWAYS THE BEST CHOICE FOR INTELLIGENCE OPERATIONS.
NONETHELESS, THE MODULE IS TO POWER A WEAPON BEING PIECED TOGETHER BY RESTORATION FACTIONS AT THE AUXILIARY METALS RECYCLING CENTER!
THE COUNCIL RECOMMENDS CONVINCING RAI TO HELP US ELIMINATE THIS DANGER. THAT WOULD SOLIDIFY THE IMPRESSION IN THE PEOPLES' MINDS THAT HE IS OUR ALLY!
NO, COUNSELOR! IT'S TOO GREAT A RISK! HE COULD TURN ON US, CAUSE THE MISSION TO FAIL! I'D LOOK A FOOL! AND WHAT WOULD HAPPEN TO POPULAR SUPPORT THEN?
SHOULDN'T YOU BE MORE CONCERNED WITH ... OUR SUPPORT?

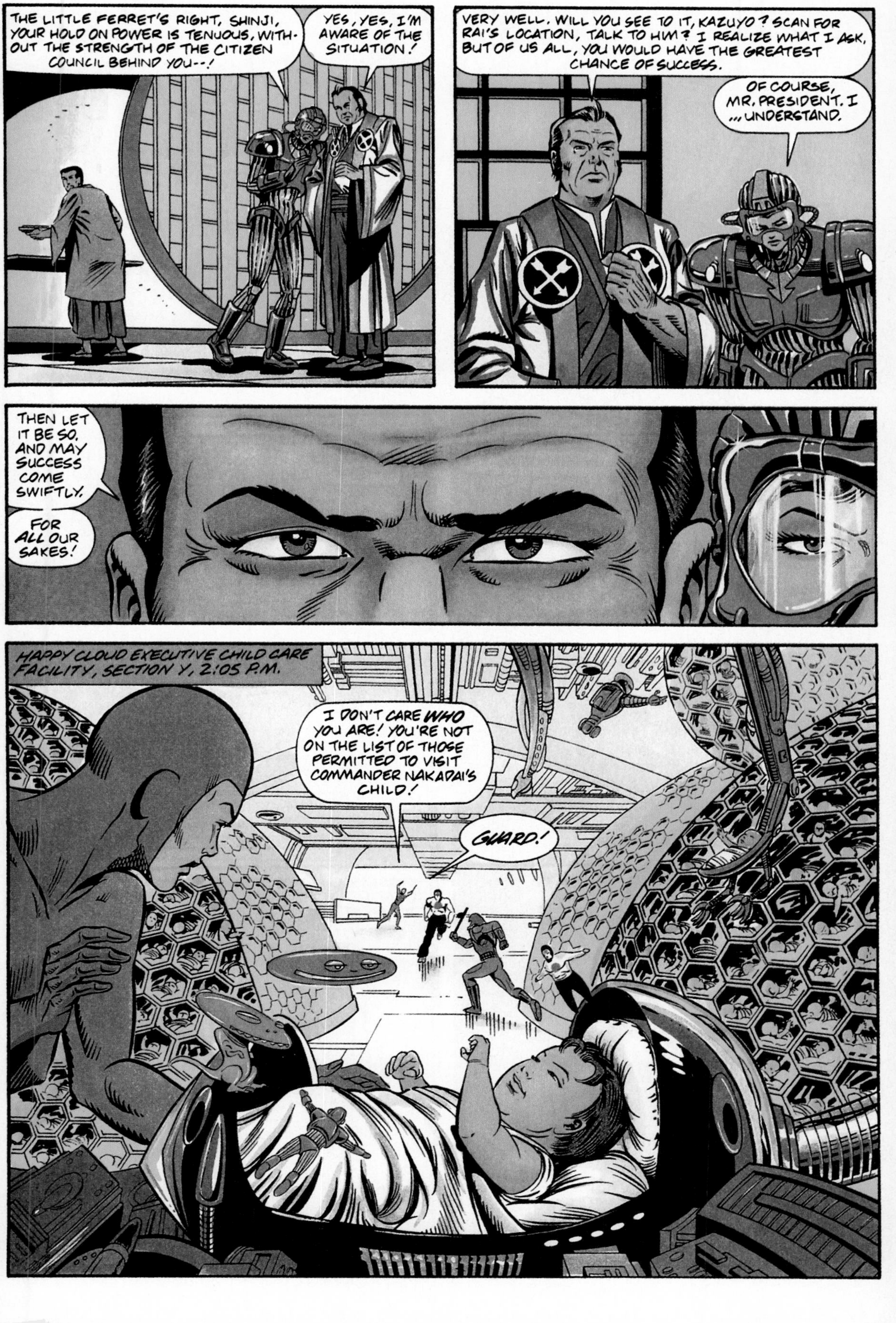
THE LITTLE FERRET'S RIGHT, SHINJI, YOUR HOLD ON POWER IS TENUOUS, WITHOUT THE STRENGTH OF THE CITIZEN COUNCIL BEHIND YOU--!
YES, YES, I'M AWARE OF THE SITUATION!
VERY WELL. WILL YOU SEE TO IT, KAZUYO? SCAN FOR RAI'S LOCATION, TALK TO HIM? I REALIZE WHAT I ASK, BUT OF US ALL, YOU WOULD HAVE THE GREATEST CHANCE OF SUCCESS.
OF COURSE, MR. PRESIDENT. I ... UNDERSTAND.
THEN LET IT BE SO, AND MAY SUCCESS COME SWIFTLY.
FOR ALL OUR SAKES!
HAPPY CLOUD EXECUTIVE CHILD CARE FACILITY, SECTION Y, 2:05 P.M.
I DON'T CARE WHO YOU ARE! YOU'RE NOT ON THE LIST OF THOSE PERMITTED TO VISIT COMMANDER NAKADAI'S CHILD!
GUARD!

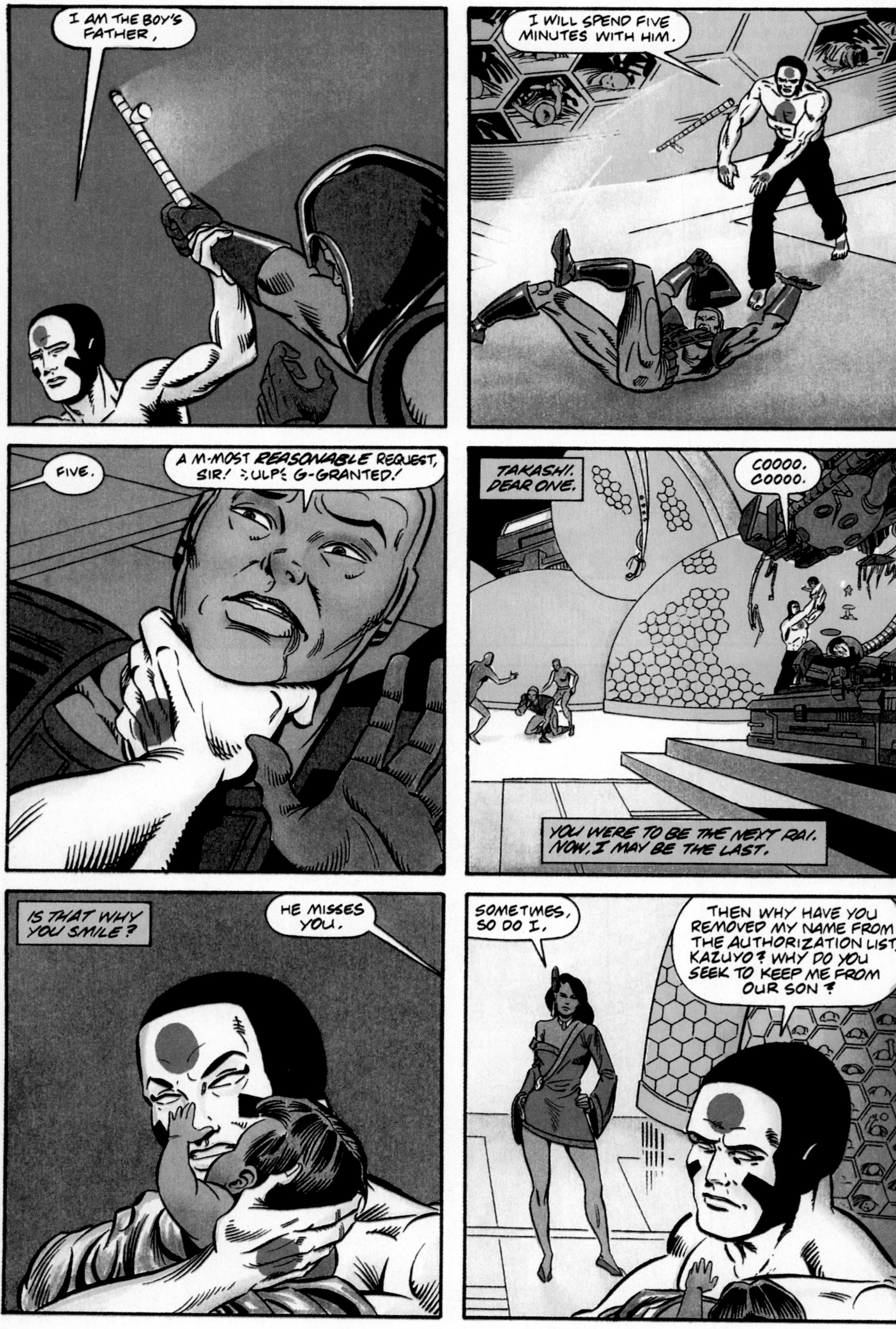

I AM THE BOY'S FATHER,
I WILL SPEND FIVE MINUTES WITH HIM.
FIVE.
A M-MOST *REASONABLE* REQUEST, SIR! ULP G-GRANTED!
TAKASHI. DEAR ONE.
COOOO. COOOO.
YOU WERE TO BE THE NEXT RAI. NOW, I MAY BE THE LAST.
IS THAT WHY YOU SMILE?
HE MISSES YOU.
SOMETIMES, SO DO I.
THEN WHY HAVE YOU REMOVED MY NAME FROM THE AUTHORIZATION LIST, KAZUYO? WHY DO YOU SEEK TO KEEP ME FROM OUR SON?

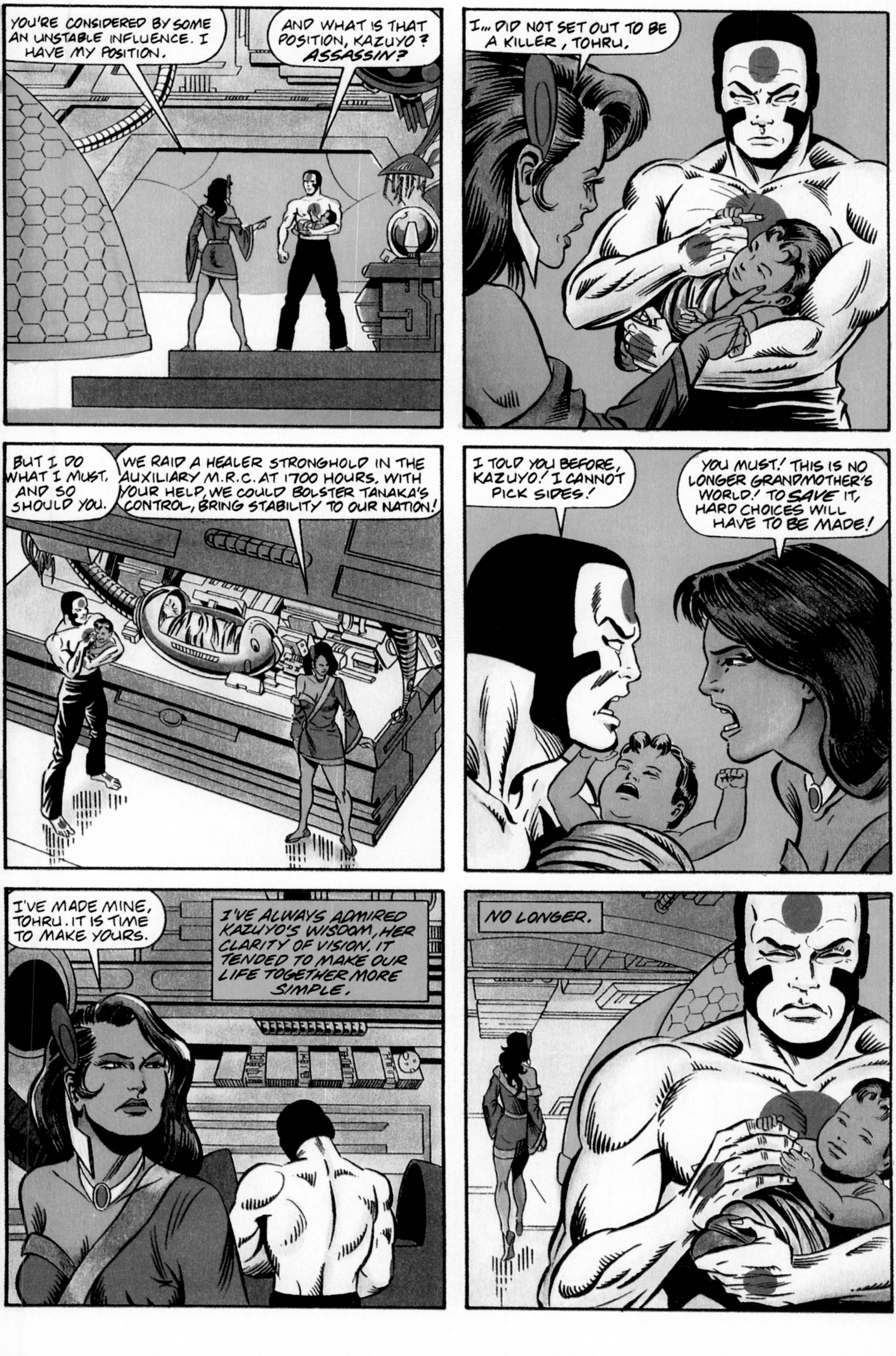
YOU'RE CONSIDERED BY SOME AN UNSTABLE INFLUENCE. I HAVE MY POSITION.
AND WHAT IS THAT POSITION, KAZUYO? ASSASSIN?
I... DID NOT SET OUT TO BE A KILLER, TOHRU.
BUT I DO WHAT I MUST. AND SO SHOULD YOU.
WE RAID A HEALER STRONGHOLD IN THE AUXILIARY M.R.C. AT 1700 HOURS. WITH YOUR HELP, WE COULD BOLSTER TANAKA'S CONTROL, BRING STABILITY TO OUR NATION!
I TOLD YOU BEFORE, KAZUYO! I CANNOT PICK SIDES!
YOU MUST! THIS IS NO LONGER GRANDMOTHER'S WORLD! TO SAVE IT, HARD CHOICES WILL HAVE TO BE MADE!
I'VE MADE MINE, TOHRU. IT IS TIME TO MAKE YOURS.
I'VE ALWAYS ADMIRED KAZUYO'S WISDOM, HER CLARITY OF VISION. IT TENDED TO MAKE OUR LIFE TOGETHER MORE SIMPLE.
NO LONGER.

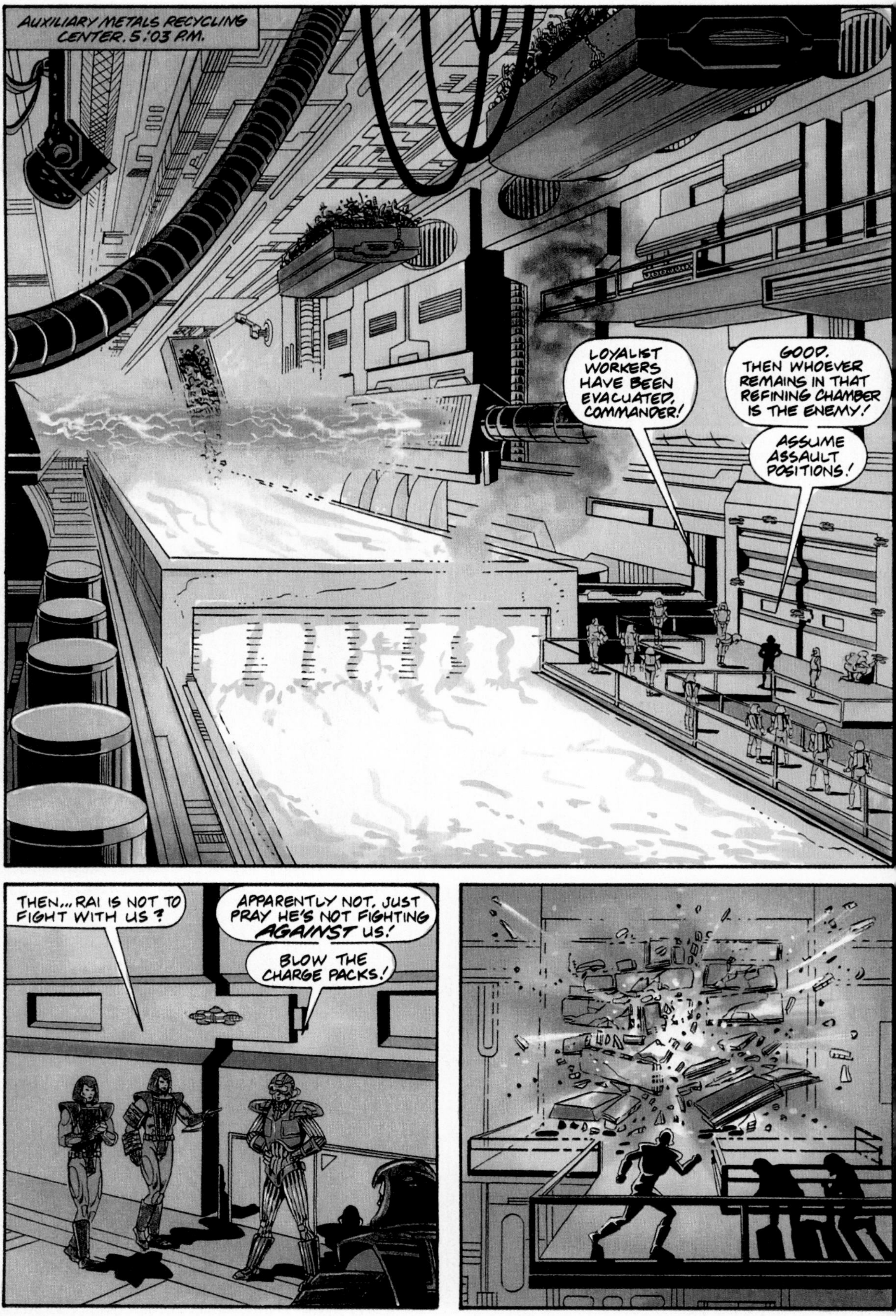
AUXILIARY METALS RECYCLING CENTER. 5:03 P.M.
LOYALIST WORKERS HAVE BEEN EVACUATED, COMMANDER!
GOOD. THEN WHOEVER REMAINS IN THAT REFINING CHAMBER IS THE ENEMY!
ASSUME ASSAULT POSITIONS!
THEN... RAI IS NOT TO FIGHT WITH US?
APPARENTLY NOT. JUST PRAY HE'S NOT FIGHTING AGAINST US!
BLOW THE CHARGE PACKS!

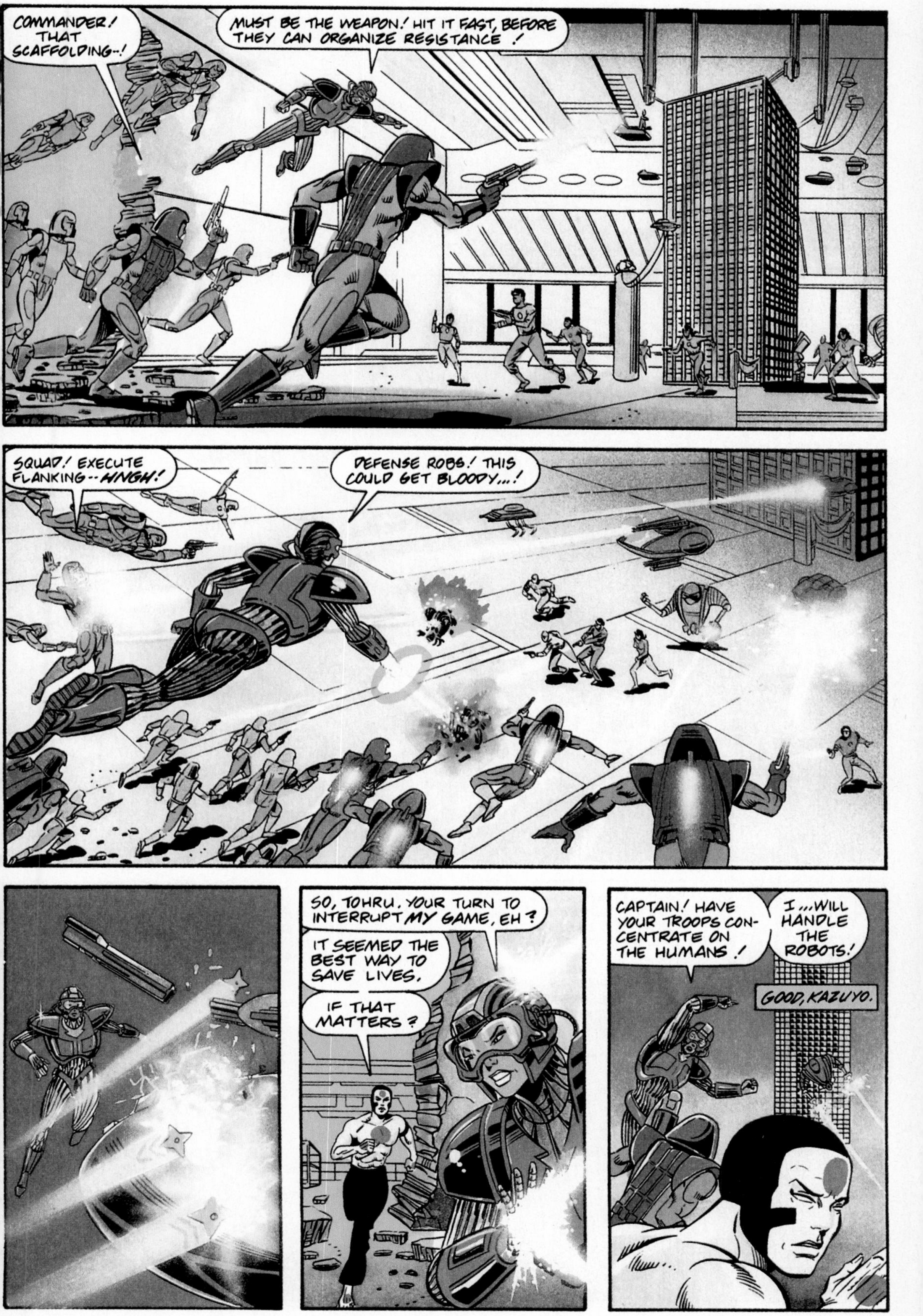
COMMANDER! THAT SCAFFOLDING--!
MUST BE THE WEAPON! HIT IT FAST, BEFORE THEY CAN ORGANIZE RESISTANCE!
SQUAD! EXECUTE FLANKING--HNGH!
DEFENSE ROBS! THIS COULD GET BLOODY...!
SO, TOHRU. YOUR TURN TO INTERRUPT MY GAME, EH?
IT SEEMED THE BEST WAY TO SAVE LIVES.
IF THAT MATTERS?
CAPTAIN! HAVE YOUR TROOPS CONCENTRATE ON THE HUMANS!
I...WILL HANDLE THE ROBOTS!
GOOD, KAZUYO.

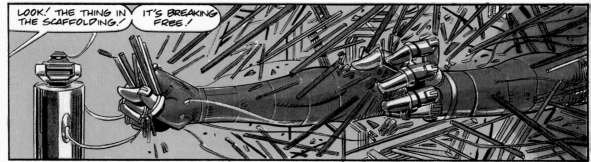

LOOK! THE THING IN THE SCAFFOLDING!

IT'S BREAKING FREE!

NO!

GRAND-MOTHER?

HOW BETTER TO DESTROY TANAKA'S FORTRESS?

WE APPROPRIATED PIECES OF THE DRONES RAI DISMEMBERED, THE ONES GRANDMOTHER CREATED WHEN SHE WAS ATTACKED BY THE ALIEN CANCER!

THEN WE USED THEM TO CONSTRUCT HER ULTIMATE *PROTECTOR*!

WITH CIRCUITRY STOLEN FROM HER BRAIN STEM, WE'VE ADDED A DEFLECTION FIELD THAT CAN RESIST EVEN A *TRAITOR'S* BLOWS!

IT... IT'S JUST A SHELL! IT CAN'T BE THE REAL--

Rai? Young spirit, why do you deny me?

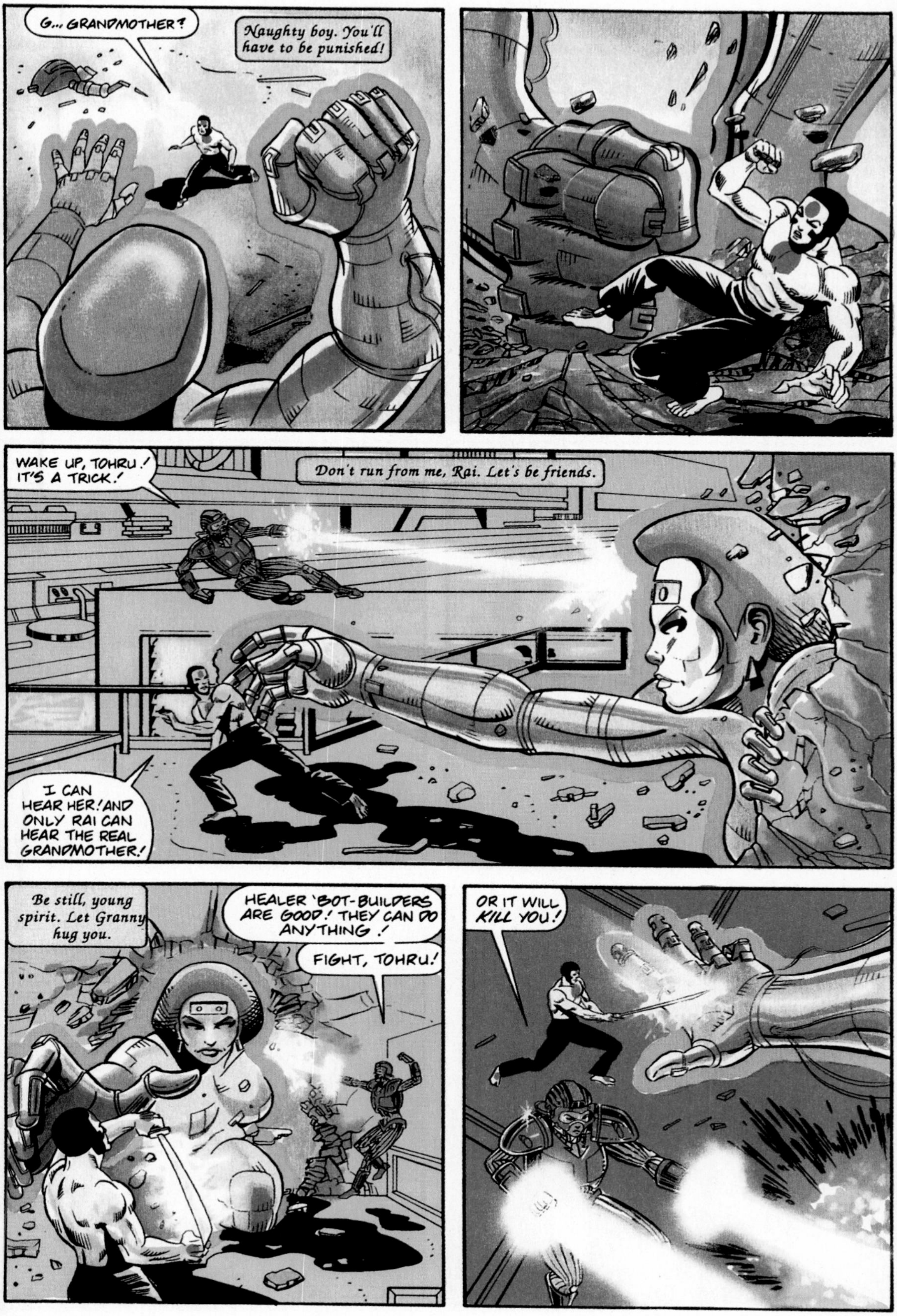
G... GRANDMOTHER?
Naughty boy. You'll have to be punished!
WAKE UP, TOHRU! IT'S A TRICK!
Don't run from me, Rai. Let's be friends.
I CAN HEAR HER! AND ONLY RAI CAN HEAR THE REAL GRANDMOTHER!
Be still, young spirit. Let Granny hug you.
HEALER 'BOT-BUILDERS ARE GOOD! THEY CAN DO ANYTHING!
FIGHT, TOHRU!
OR IT WILL KILL YOU!

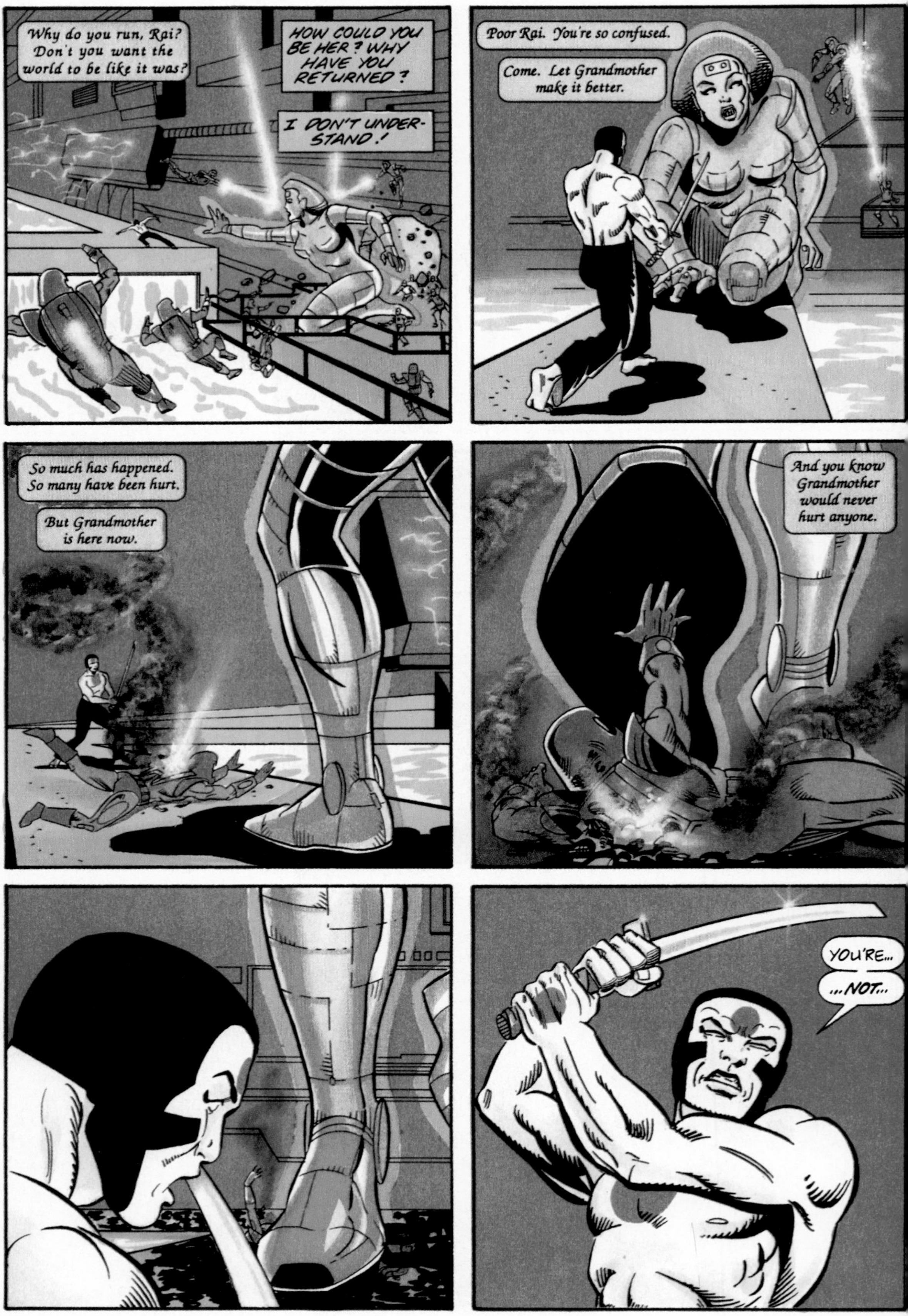
Why do you run, Rai? Don't you want the world to be like it was?
HOW COULD YOU BE HER? WHY HAVE YOU RETURNED?
I DON'T UNDER-STAND!
Poor Rai. You're so confused.
Come. Let Grandmother make it better.
So much has happened. So many have been hurt.
But Grandmother is here now.
And you know Grandmother would never hurt anyone.
YOU'RE...
...NOT...

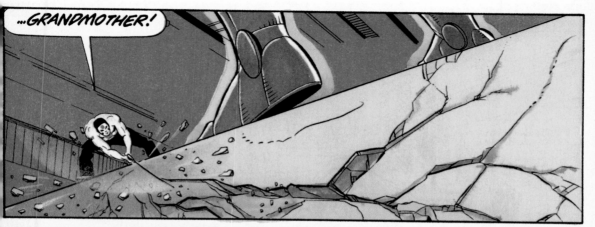

...GRANDMOTHER!

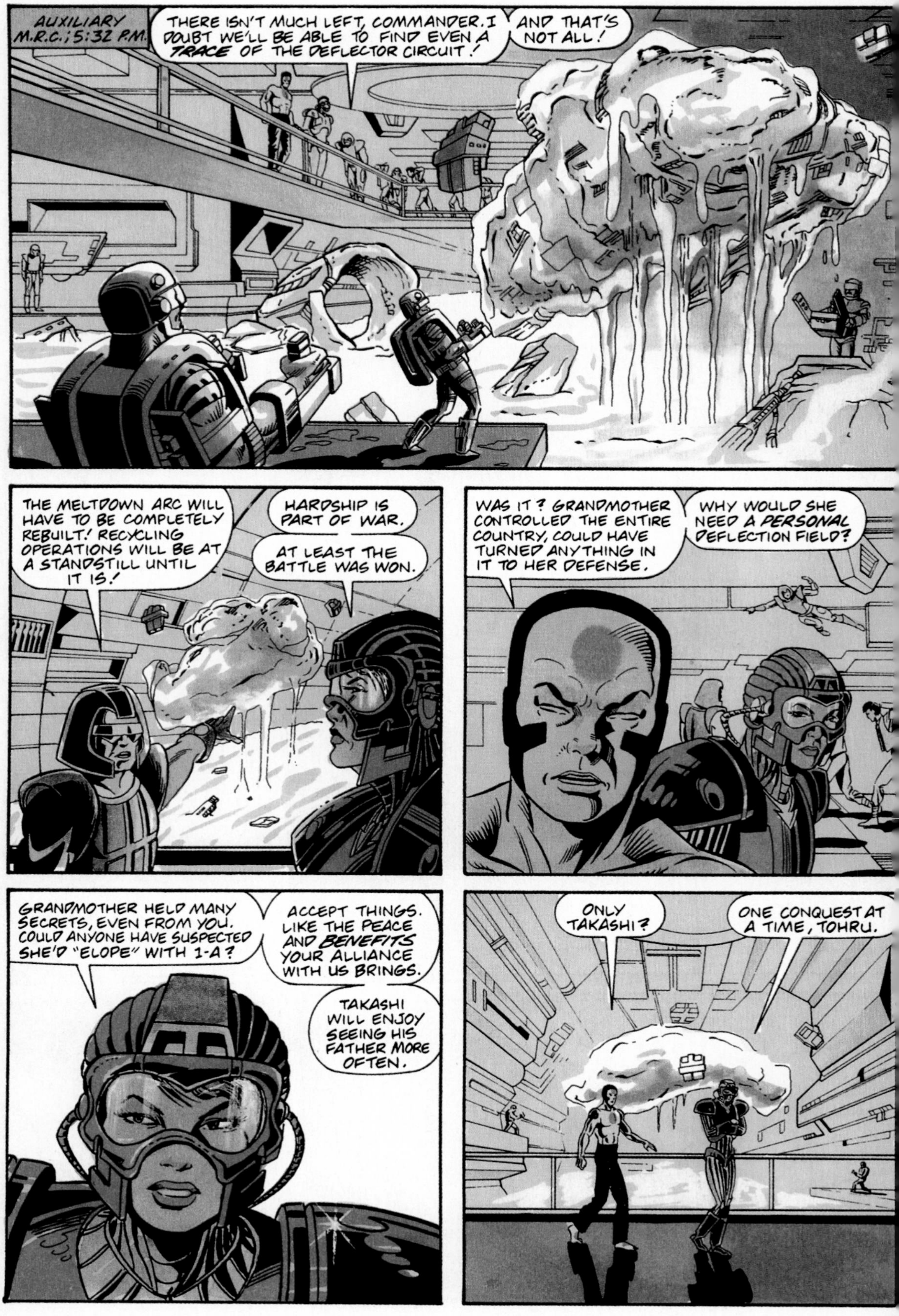
AUXILIARY M.R.C.; 5:32 P.M.
THERE ISN'T MUCH LEFT, COMMANDER. I DOUBT WE'LL BE ABLE TO FIND EVEN A TRACE OF THE DEFLECTOR CIRCUIT!
AND THAT'S NOT ALL!
THE MELTDOWN ARC WILL HAVE TO BE COMPLETELY REBUILT! RECYCLING OPERATIONS WILL BE AT A STANDSTILL UNTIL IT IS!
HARDSHIP IS PART OF WAR.
AT LEAST THE BATTLE WAS WON.
WAS IT? GRANDMOTHER CONTROLLED THE ENTIRE COUNTRY, COULD HAVE TURNED ANYTHING IN IT TO HER DEFENSE.
WHY WOULD SHE NEED A PERSONAL DEFLECTION FIELD?
GRANDMOTHER HELD MANY SECRETS, EVEN FROM YOU. COULD ANYONE HAVE SUSPECTED SHE'D "ELOPE" WITH 1-A?
ACCEPT THINGS. LIKE THE PEACE AND BENEFITS YOUR ALLIANCE WITH US BRINGS.
TAKASHI WILL ENJOY SEEING HIS FATHER MORE OFTEN.
ONLY TAKASHI?
ONE CONQUEST AT A TIME, TOHRU.

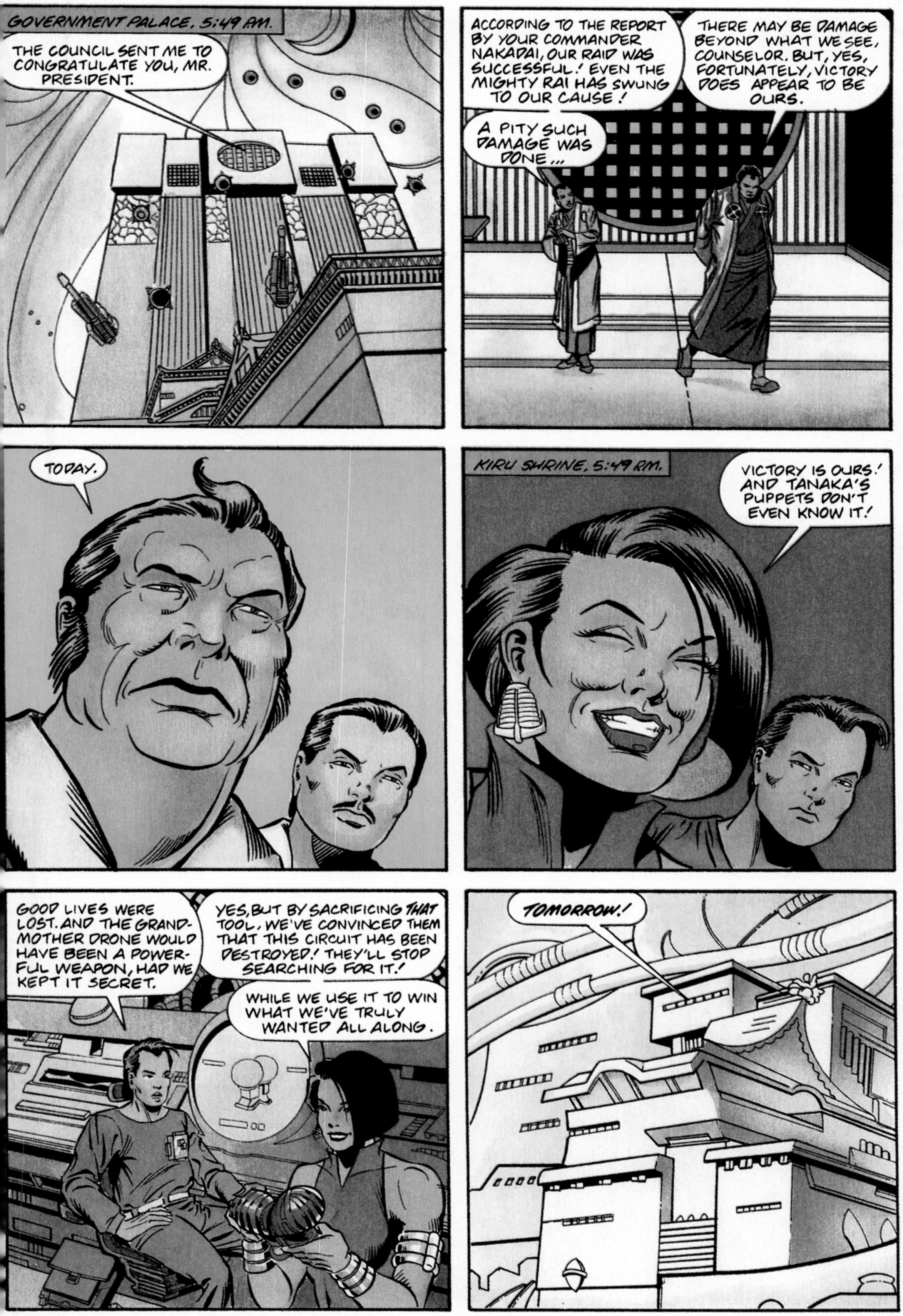
GOVERNMENT PALACE, 5:49 AM.
THE COUNCIL SENT ME TO CONGRATULATE YOU, MR. PRESIDENT.
ACCORDING TO THE REPORT BY YOUR COMMANDER NAKADAI, OUR RAID WAS SUCCESSFUL! EVEN THE MIGHTY RAI HAS SWUNG TO OUR CAUSE!
A PITY SUCH DAMAGE WAS DONE...
THERE MAY BE DAMAGE BEYOND WHAT WE SEE, COUNSELOR. BUT, YES, FORTUNATELY, VICTORY DOES APPEAR TO BE OURS.
TODAY.
KIRU SHRINE, 5:49 AM.
VICTORY IS OURS! AND TANAKA'S PUPPETS DON'T EVEN KNOW IT!
GOOD LIVES WERE LOST. AND THE GRAND-MOTHER DRONE WOULD HAVE BEEN A POWER-FUL WEAPON, HAD WE KEPT IT SECRET.
YES, BUT BY SACRIFICING THAT TOOL, WE'VE CONVINCED THEM THAT THIS CIRCUIT HAS BEEN DESTROYED! THEY'LL STOP SEARCHING FOR IT!
WHILE WE USE IT TO WIN WHAT WE'VE TRULY WANTED ALL ALONG.
TOMORROW!

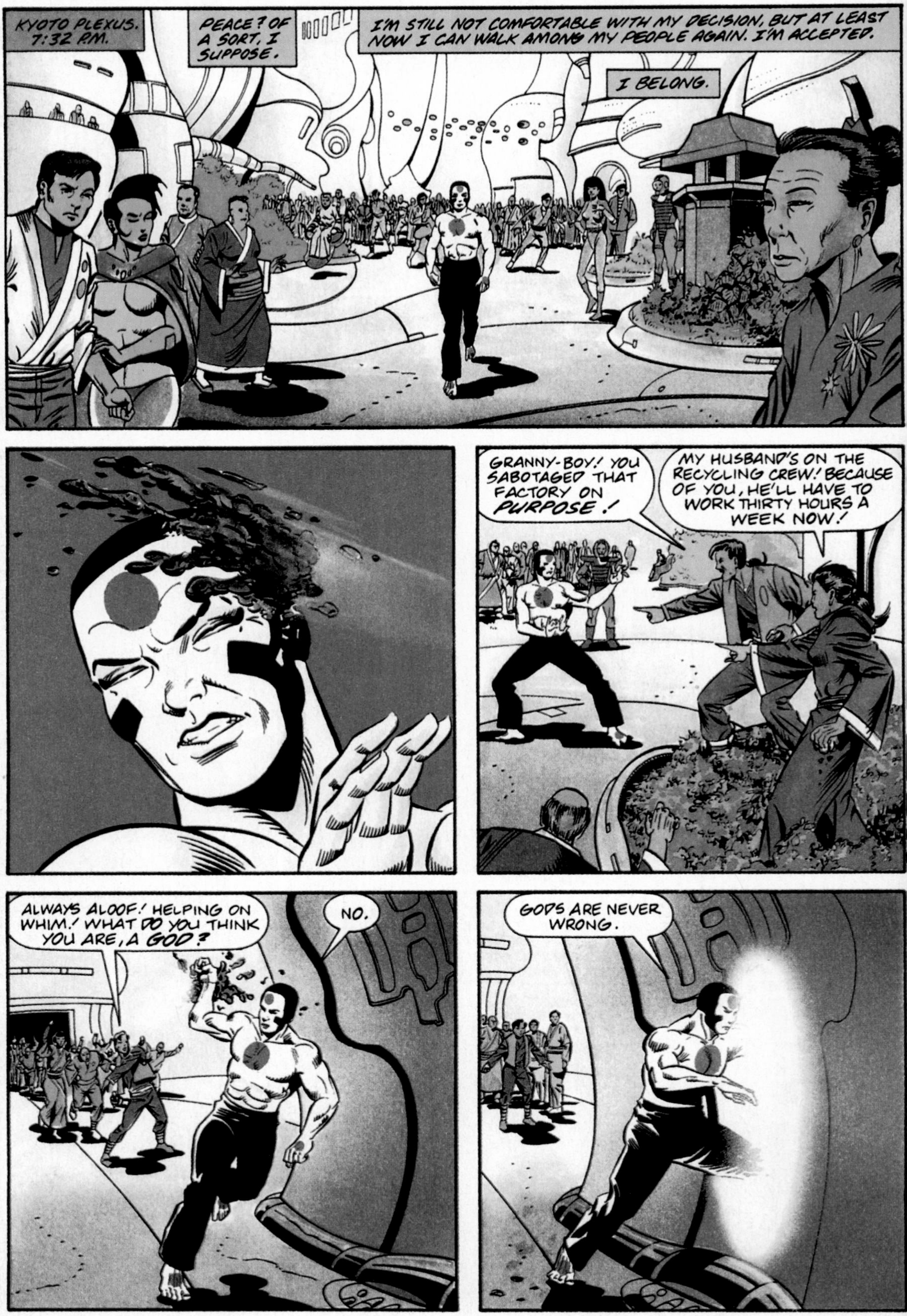
KYOTO PLEXUS. 7:32 P.M.
PEACE? OF A SORT, I SUPPOSE.
I'M STILL NOT COMFORTABLE WITH MY DECISION, BUT AT LEAST NOW I CAN WALK AMONG MY PEOPLE AGAIN. I'M ACCEPTED.
I BELONG.
GRANNY-BOY! YOU SABOTAGED THAT FACTORY ON PURPOSE!
MY HUSBAND'S ON THE RECYCLING CREW! BECAUSE OF YOU, HE'LL HAVE TO WORK THIRTY HOURS A WEEK NOW!
ALWAYS ALOOF! HELPING ON WHIM! WHAT DO YOU THINK YOU ARE, A GOD?
NO.
GODS ARE NEVER WRONG.

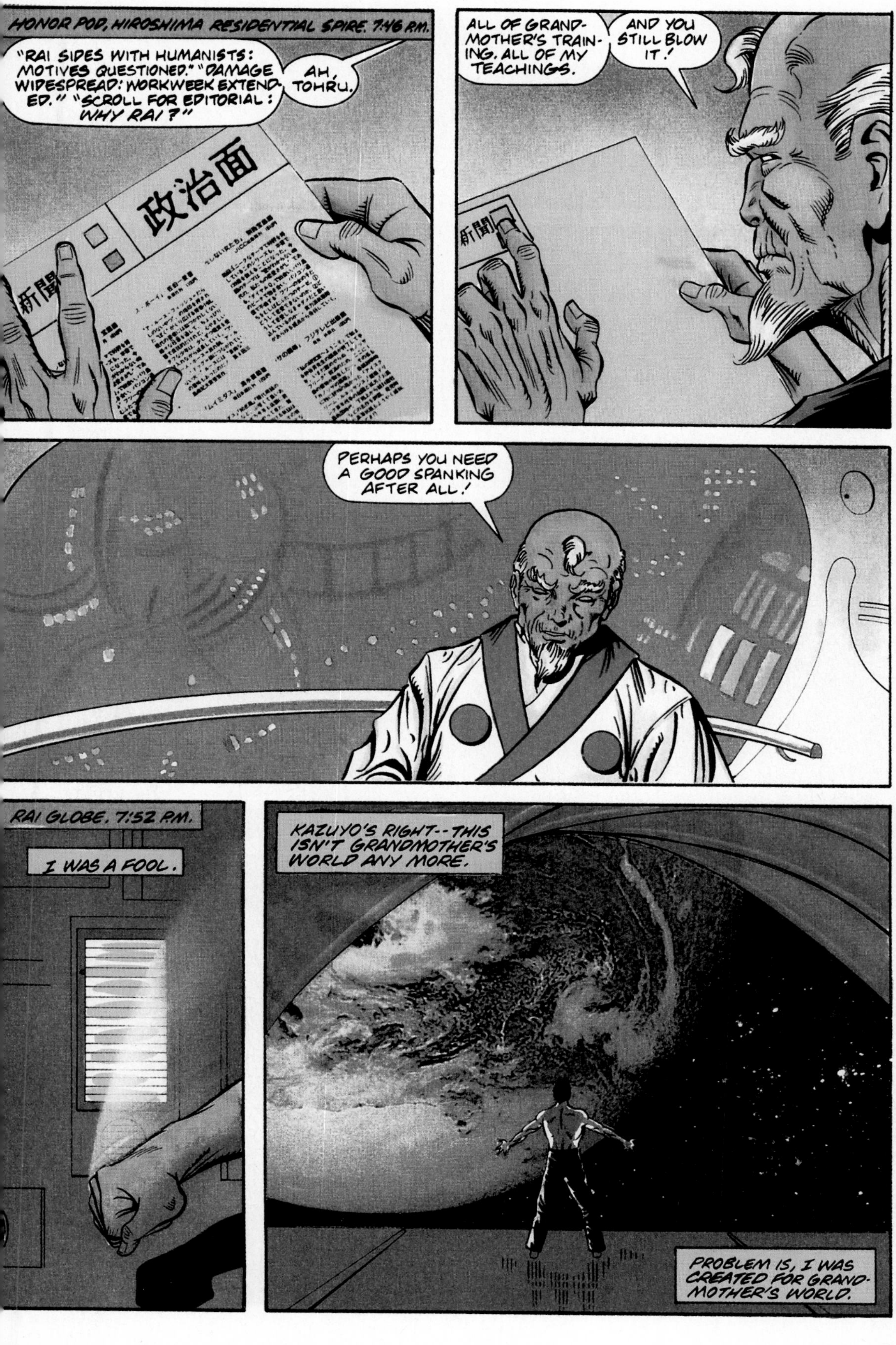
HONOR POD, HIROSHIMA RESIDENTIAL SPIRE. 7:46 P.M.
"RAI SIDES WITH HUMANISTS: MOTIVES QUESTIONED." "DAMAGE WIDESPREAD: WORKWEEK EXTENDED." "SCROLL FOR EDITORIAL: WHY RAI?"
AH, TOHRU.
政治面
新聞
ALL OF GRANDMOTHER'S TRAINING. ALL OF MY TEACHINGS.
AND YOU STILL BLOW IT!
新聞
PERHAPS YOU NEED A GOOD SPANKING AFTER ALL!
RAI GLOBE. 7:52 P.M.
I WAS A FOOL.
KAZUYO'S RIGHT--THIS ISN'T GRANDMOTHER'S WORLD ANY MORE.
PROBLEM IS, I WAS CREATED FOR GRANDMOTHER'S WORLD.

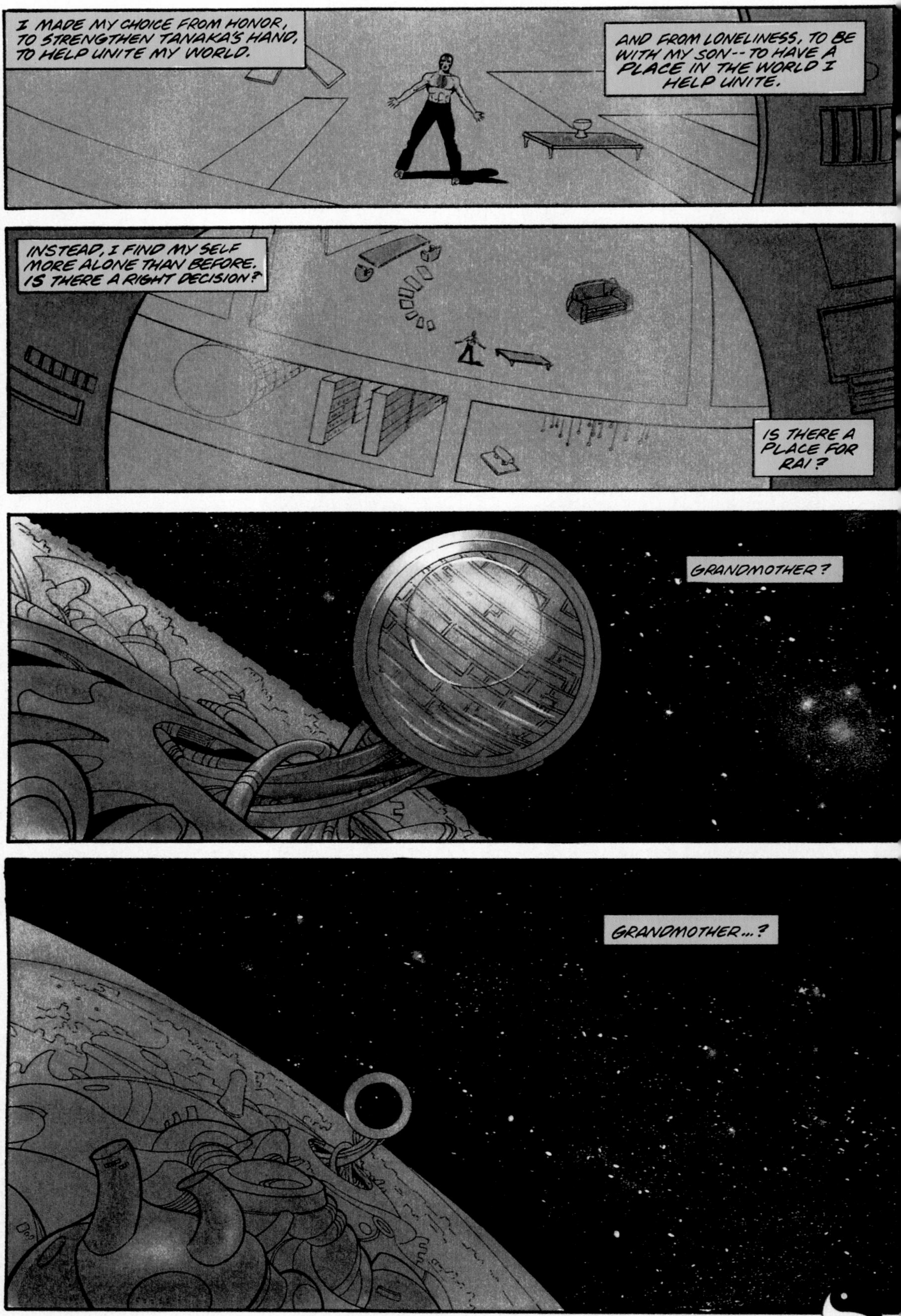
I MADE MY CHOICE FROM HONOR, TO STRENGTHEN TANAKA'S HAND, TO HELP UNITE MY WORLD.
AND FROM LONELINESS, TO BE WITH MY SON-- TO HAVE A PLACE IN THE WORLD I HELP UNITE.
INSTEAD, I FIND MY SELF MORE ALONE THAN BEFORE. IS THERE A RIGHT DECISION?
IS THERE A PLACE FOR RAI?
GRANDMOTHER?
GRANDMOTHER...?

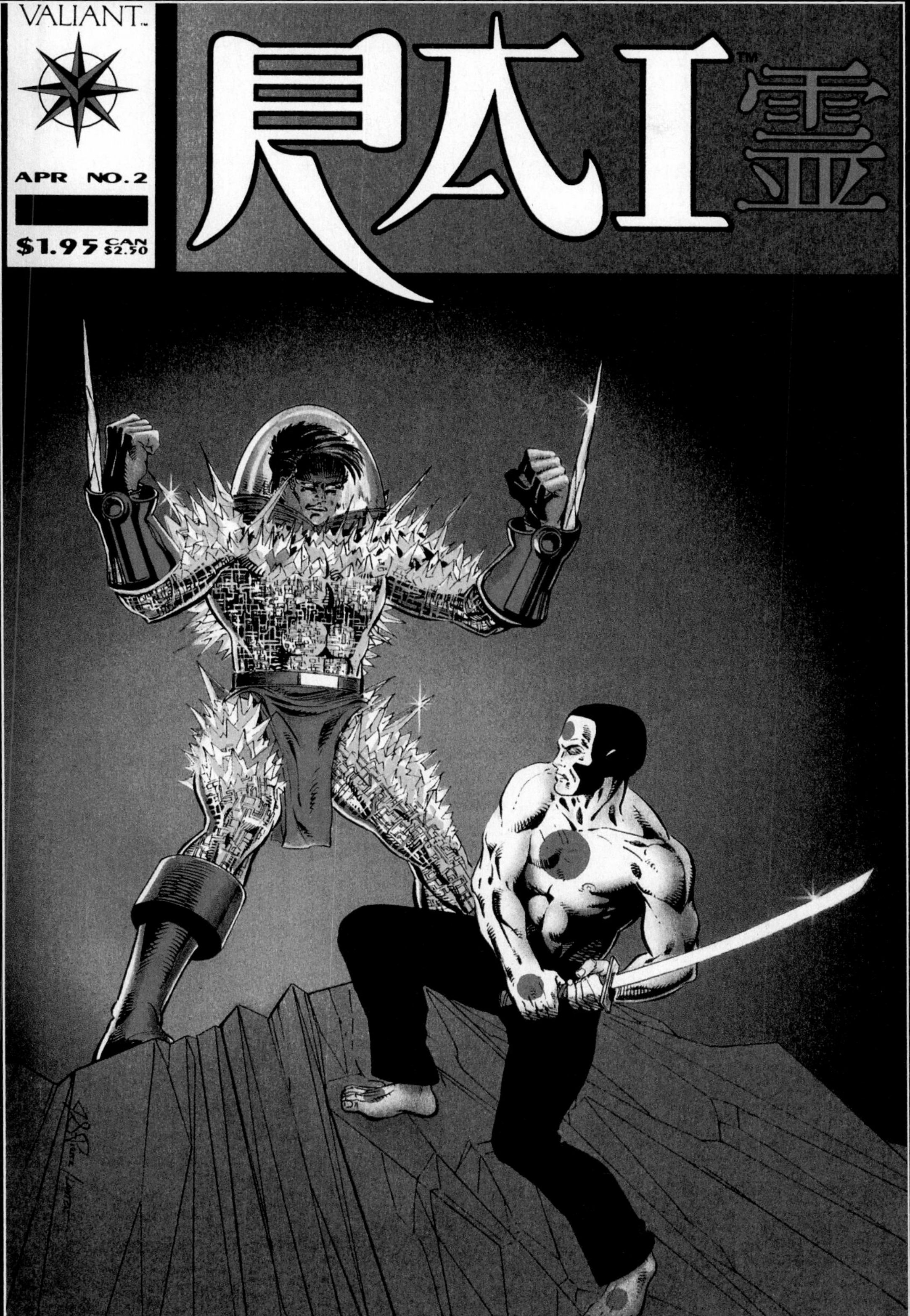

VALIANT™
APR NO.2
$1.95 CAN $2.50
RAI™
霊

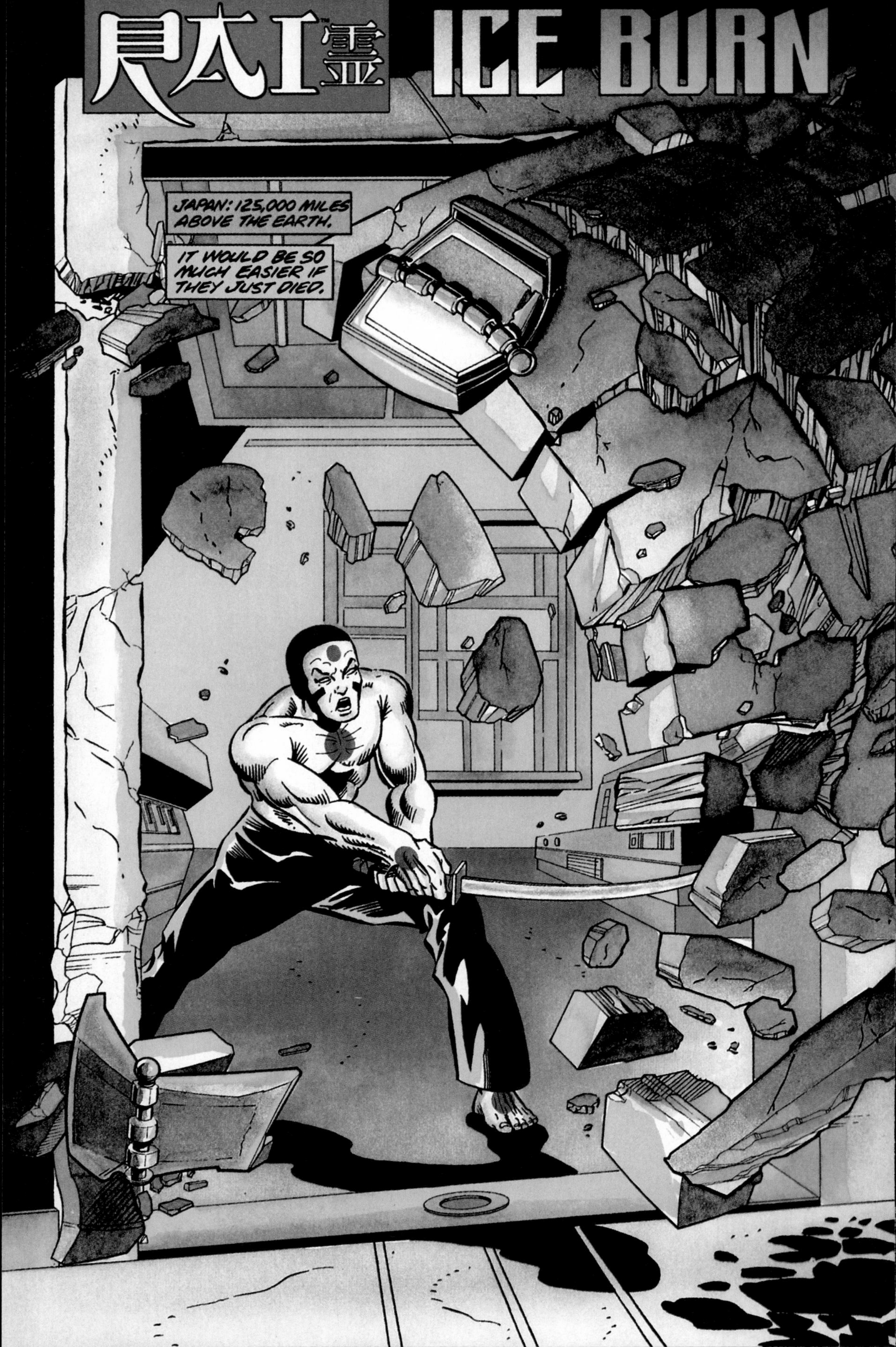
ICE BURN
JAPAN: 125,000 MILES ABOVE THE EARTH.
IT WOULD BE SO MUCH EASIER IF THEY JUST DIED.

IS THAT CRUEL? GRANDMOTHER WOULD NEVER APPROVE.

AFTER ALL, I'M RAI, HER "SPIRIT GUARDIAN". SHE CHARGED ME WITH PROTECTING OUR PEOPLE.

BUT HOW DO YOU PROTECT SOMEONE FROM A PLAGUE OF THIER OWN CHOOSING?

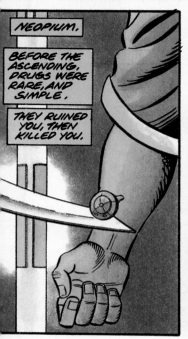

NEOPIUM.

BEFORE THE ASCENDING, DRUGS WERE RARE, AND SIMPLE.

THEY RUINED YOU, THEN KILLED YOU.

BUT NEOPIUM'S NASTY. IT DOESN'T BRING DEATH; IT BRINGS CONTENTMENT. AND WITH PROLONGED EXPOSURE, SOMETHING MUCH MORE INSIDIOUS:

CHANGE.

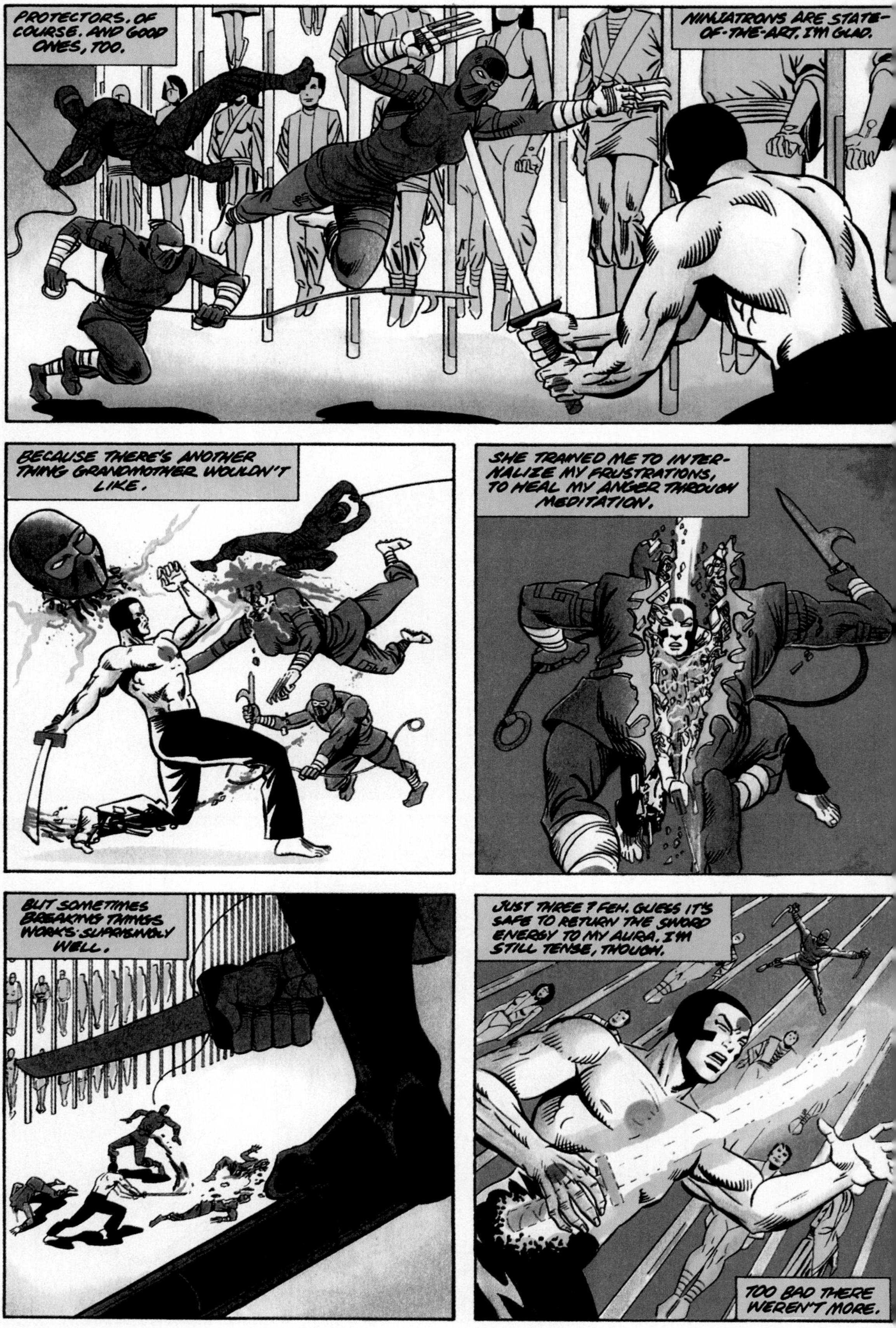
PROTECTORS, OF COURSE. AND GOOD ONES, TOO.
NINJATRONS ARE STATE-OF-THE-ART. I'M GLAD.
BECAUSE THERE'S ANOTHER THING GRANDMOTHER WOULDN'T LIKE.
SHE TRAINED ME TO INTER-NALIZE MY FRUSTRATIONS, TO HEAL MY ANGER THROUGH MEDITATION.
BUT SOMETIMES BREAKING THINGS WORKS SURPRISINGLY WELL.
JUST THREE? FEH. GUESS IT'S SAFE TO RETURN THE SWORD ENERGY TO MY AURA. I'M STILL TENSE, THOUGH.
TOO BAD THERE WEREN'T MORE.

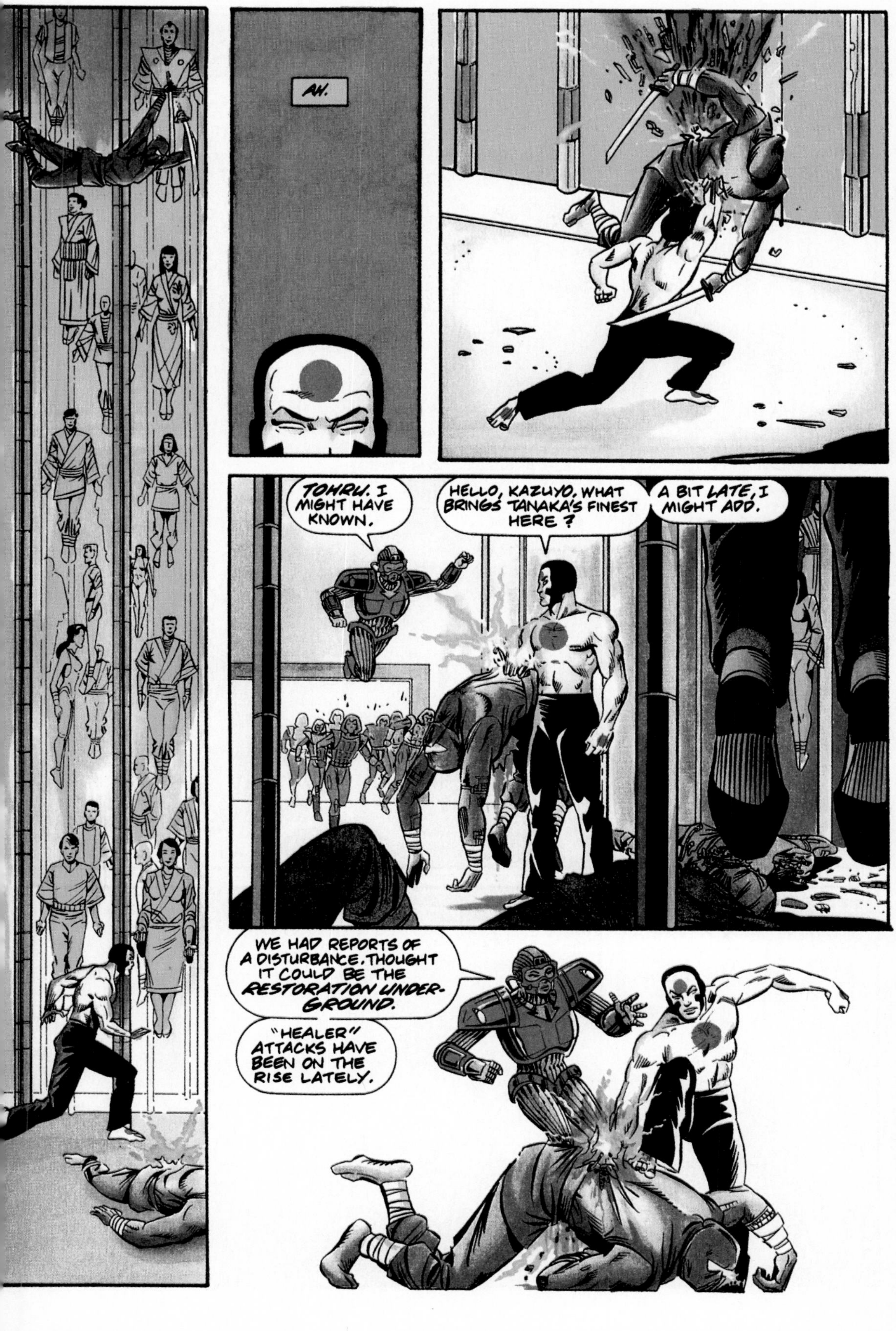
AH.
TOHRU. I MIGHT HAVE KNOWN.
HELLO, KAZUYO. WHAT BRINGS TANAKA'S FINEST HERE?
A BIT LATE, I MIGHT ADD.
WE HAD REPORTS OF A DISTURBANCE. THOUGHT IT COULD BE THE RESTORATION UNDER-GROUND.
"HEALER" ATTACKS HAVE BEEN ON THE RISE LATELY.

CAREFUL, WASABE! IF THOSE DISCS TOUCH SKIN--!

UNDERSTOOD, COMMANDER.

L-LET ME ALONE! WH-WHY DO YOU DO THIS...?

THIS RAID WASN'T SANCTIONED, TOHRU. YOU WERE TOLD THAT INDEPENDENT ACTION COULD WEAKEN PRESIDENT TANAKA'S POSITION.

AND DIDN'T YOU JOIN THE HUMANIST SIDE TO STRENGTHEN IT?

YES.

BUT THE GOVERNMENT TURNS IT'S BACK ON NEOPIUM, SMALL WONDER...

...WHEN THOSE WHO USE IT SWAY SUBTLY TO THE HUMANIST CAUSE, WHILE REMAINING SO CONVINCED THE DECISION IS THEIRS, THEY'D DIE DEFENDING IT.'

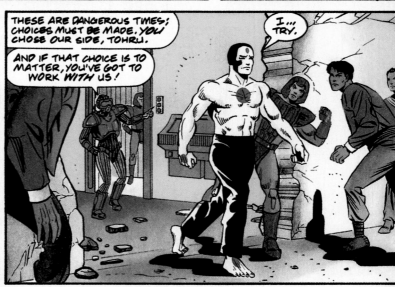

THESE ARE DANGEROUS TIMES; CHOICES MUST BE MADE. YOU CHOSE OUR SIDE, TOHRU.

AND IF THAT CHOICE IS TO MATTER, YOU'VE GOT TO WORK WITH US!

I .... TRY.

CITIZEN! MAY I USE YOUR VASCAR? I'LL PROGRAM IT TO RETURN WHEN I'M DONE.

YOU ARE RAI, WHAT IS MINE IS YOURS.

AM I THAT REBELLIOUS? DIDN'T I FOLLOW GRANDMOTHER'S EDICTS WHEN SHE WAS HERE? AND SHE WAS JUST A COMPUTER!

A COMPUTER THAT RAN ALL OF JAPAN, TRUE! BUT STILL...

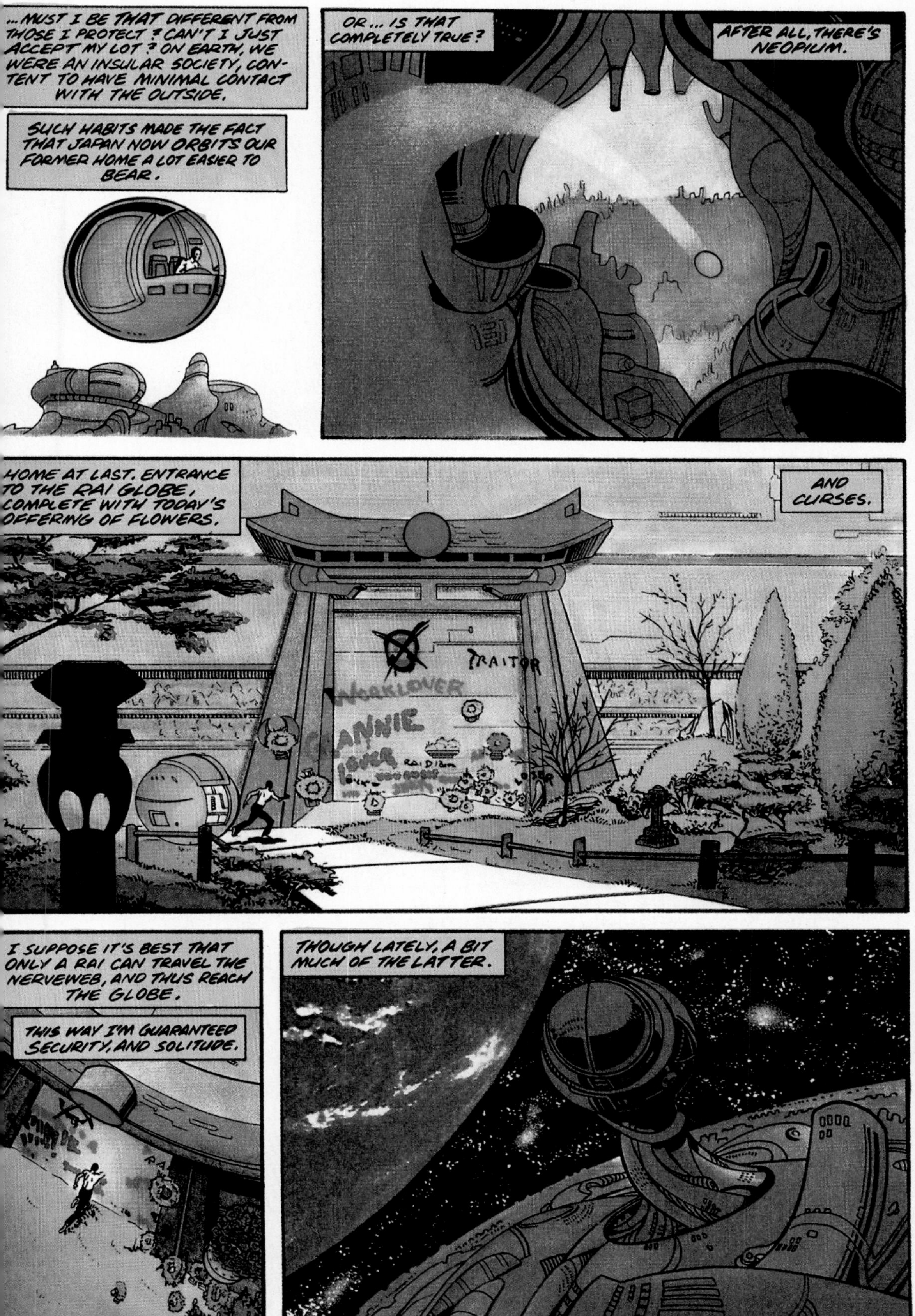
...MUST I BE THAT DIFFERENT FROM THOSE I PROTECT ? CAN'T I JUST ACCEPT MY LOT ? ON EARTH, WE WERE AN INSULAR SOCIETY, CONTENT TO HAVE MINIMAL CONTACT WITH THE OUTSIDE.
SUCH HABITS MADE THE FACT THAT JAPAN NOW ORBITS OUR FORMER HOME A LOT EASIER TO BEAR.
OR... IS THAT COMPLETELY TRUE ?
AFTER ALL, THERE'S NEOPIUM.
HOME AT LAST. ENTRANCE TO THE RAI GLOBE, COMPLETE WITH TODAY'S OFFERING OF FLOWERS.
AND CURSES.
TRAITOR
I SUPPOSE IT'S BEST THAT ONLY A RAI CAN TRAVEL THE NERVEWEB, AND THUS REACH THE GLOBE.
THIS WAY I'M GUARANTEED SECURITY, AND SOLITUDE.
THOUGH LATELY, A BIT MUCH OF THE LATTER.

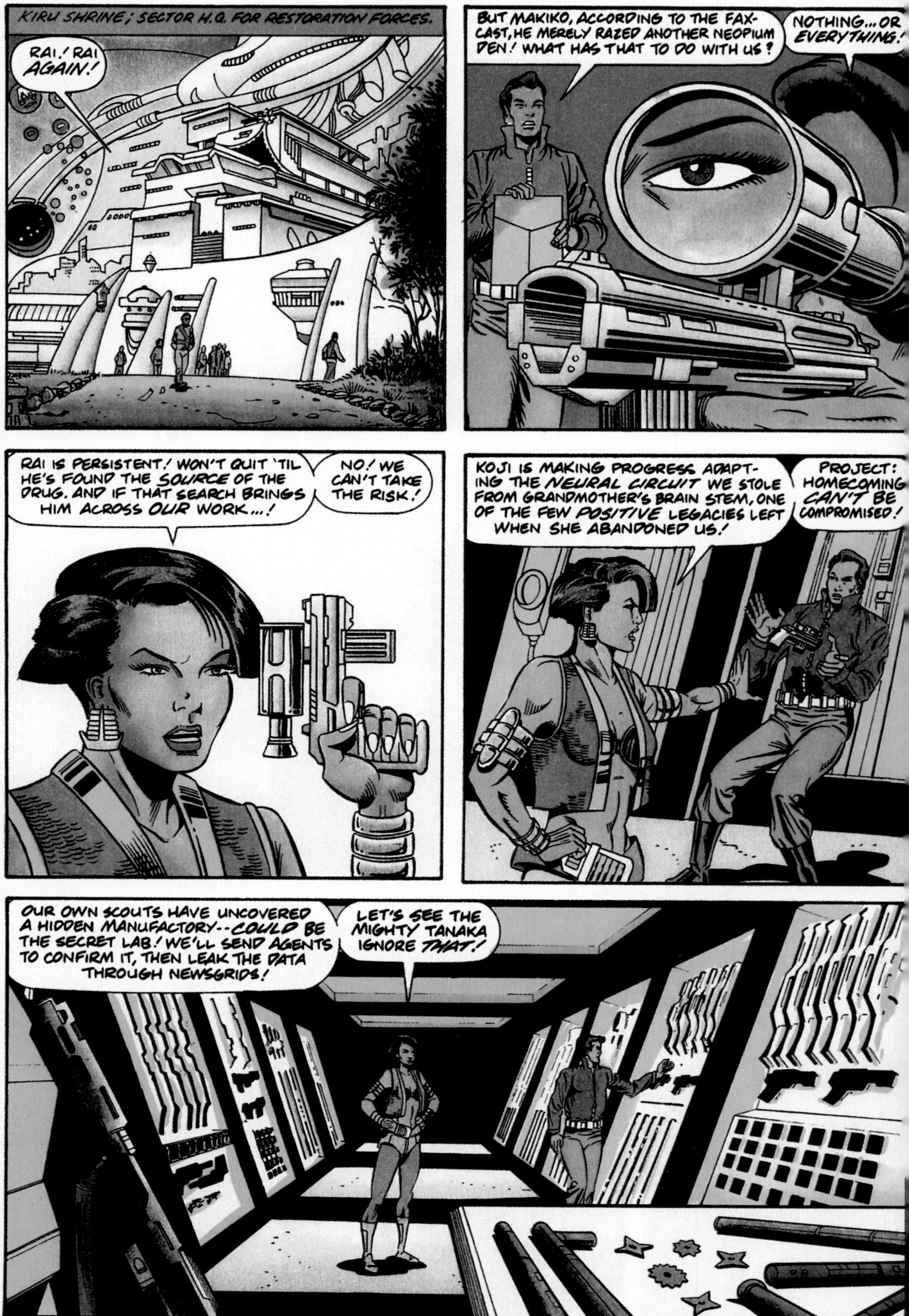
KIRU SHRINE; SECTOR H.Q. FOR RESTORATION FORCES.
RAI! RAI AGAIN!
BUT MAKIKO, ACCORDING TO THE FAX-CAST, HE MERELY RAZED ANOTHER NEOPIUM DEN! WHAT HAS THAT TO DO WITH US?
NOTHING...OR EVERYTHING!
RAI IS PERSISTENT! WON'T QUIT 'TIL HE'S FOUND THE SOURCE OF THE DRUG. AND IF THAT SEARCH BRINGS HIM ACROSS OUR WORK...!
NO! WE CAN'T TAKE THE RISK!
KOJI IS MAKING PROGRESS ADAPTING THE NEURAL CIRCUIT WE STOLE FROM GRANDMOTHER'S BRAIN STEM, ONE OF THE FEW POSITIVE LEGACIES LEFT WHEN SHE ABANDONED US!
PROJECT: HOMECOMING CAN'T BE COMPROMISED!
OUR OWN SCOUTS HAVE UNCOVERED A HIDDEN MANUFACTORY--COULD BE THE SECRET LAB! WE'LL SEND AGENTS TO CONFIRM IT, THEN LEAK THE DATA THROUGH NEWSGRIDS!
LET'S SEE THE MIGHTY TANAKA IGNORE THAT!

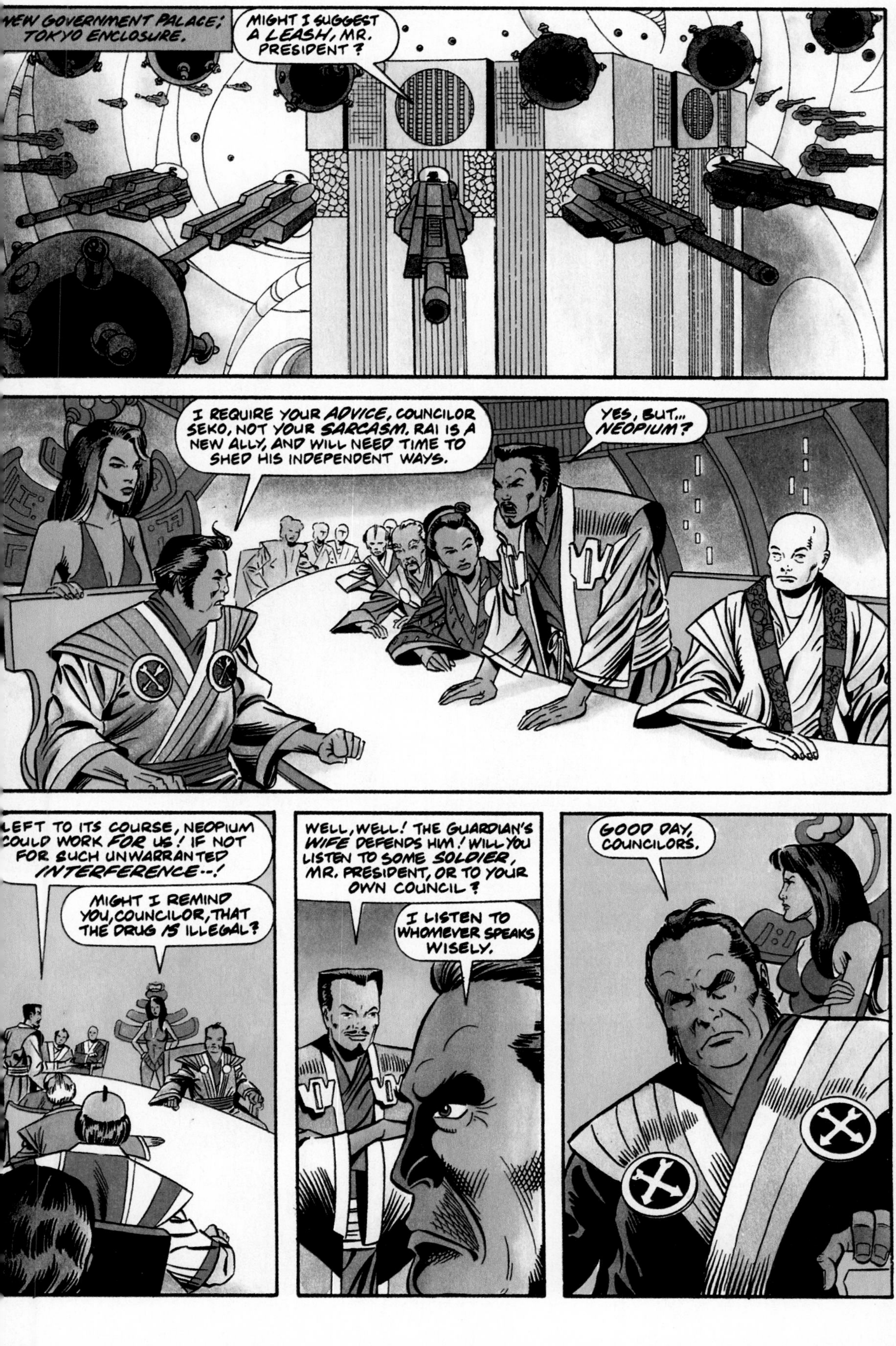
NEW GOVERNMENT PALACE; TOKYO ENCLOSURE.
MIGHT I SUGGEST A LEASH, MR. PRESIDENT?
I REQUIRE YOUR ADVICE, COUNCILOR SEKO, NOT YOUR SARCASM. RAI IS A NEW ALLY, AND WILL NEED TIME TO SHED HIS INDEPENDENT WAYS.
YES, BUT... NEOPIUM?
LEFT TO ITS COURSE, NEOPIUM COULD WORK FOR US! IF NOT FOR SUCH UNWARRANTED INTERFERENCE--!
MIGHT I REMIND YOU, COUNCILOR, THAT THE DRUG IS ILLEGAL?
WELL, WELL! THE GUARDIAN'S WIFE DEFENDS HIM! WILL YOU LISTEN TO SOME SOLDIER, MR. PRESIDENT, OR TO YOUR OWN COUNCIL?
I LISTEN TO WHOMEVER SPEAKS WISELY.
GOOD DAY, COUNCILORS.

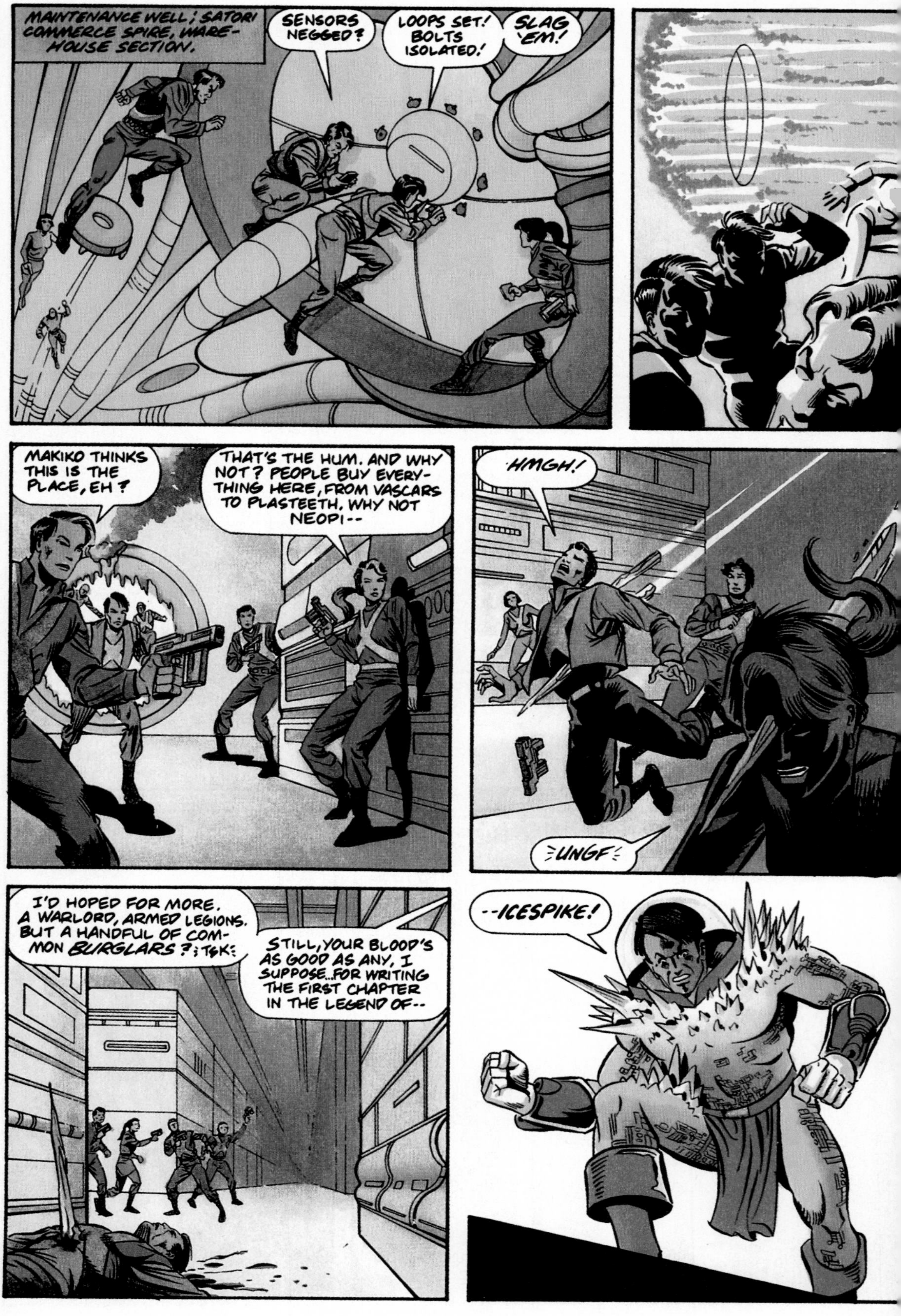
MAINTENANCE WELL; SATORI COMMERCE SPIRE, WAREHOUSE SECTION.
SENSORS NEGGED?
LOOPS SET! BOLTS ISOLATED!
SLAG 'EM!
MAKIKO THINKS THIS IS THE PLACE, EH?
THAT'S THE HUM. AND WHY NOT? PEOPLE BUY EVERYTHING HERE, FROM VASCARS TO PLASTEETH. WHY NOT NEOPI--
HMGH!
UNGF
I'D HOPED FOR MORE. A WARLORD, ARMED LEGIONS. BUT A HANDFUL OF COMMON BURGLARS? TSK.
STILL, YOUR BLOOD'S AS GOOD AS ANY, I SUPPOSE...FOR WRITING THE FIRST CHAPTER IN THE LEGEND OF--
--ICESPIKE!

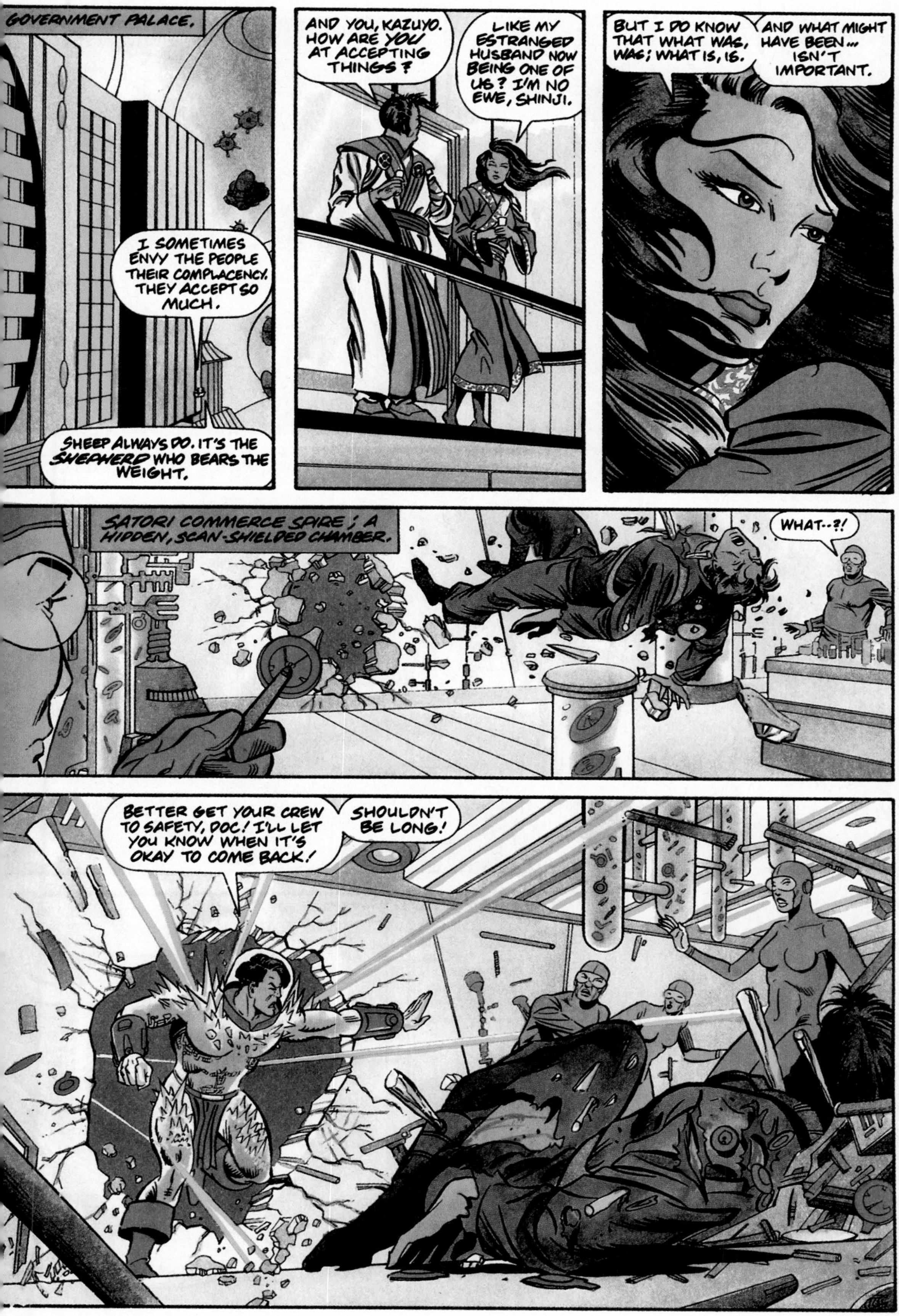
GOVERNMENT PALACE.
I SOMETIMES ENVY THE PEOPLE THEIR COMPLACENCY. THEY ACCEPT SO MUCH.
SHEEP ALWAYS DO. IT'S THE SHEPHERD WHO BEARS THE WEIGHT.
AND YOU, KAZUYO. HOW ARE YOU AT ACCEPTING THINGS?
LIKE MY ESTRANGED HUSBAND NOW BEING ONE OF US? I'M NO EWE, SHINJI.
BUT I DO KNOW THAT WHAT WAS, WAS; WHAT IS, IS.
AND WHAT MIGHT HAVE BEEN... ISN'T IMPORTANT.
SATORI COMMERCE SPIRE; A HIDDEN, SCAN-SHIELDED CHAMBER.
WHAT--?!
BETTER GET YOUR CREW TO SAFETY, DOC! I'LL LET YOU KNOW WHEN IT'S OKAY TO COME BACK!
SHOULDN'T BE LONG!

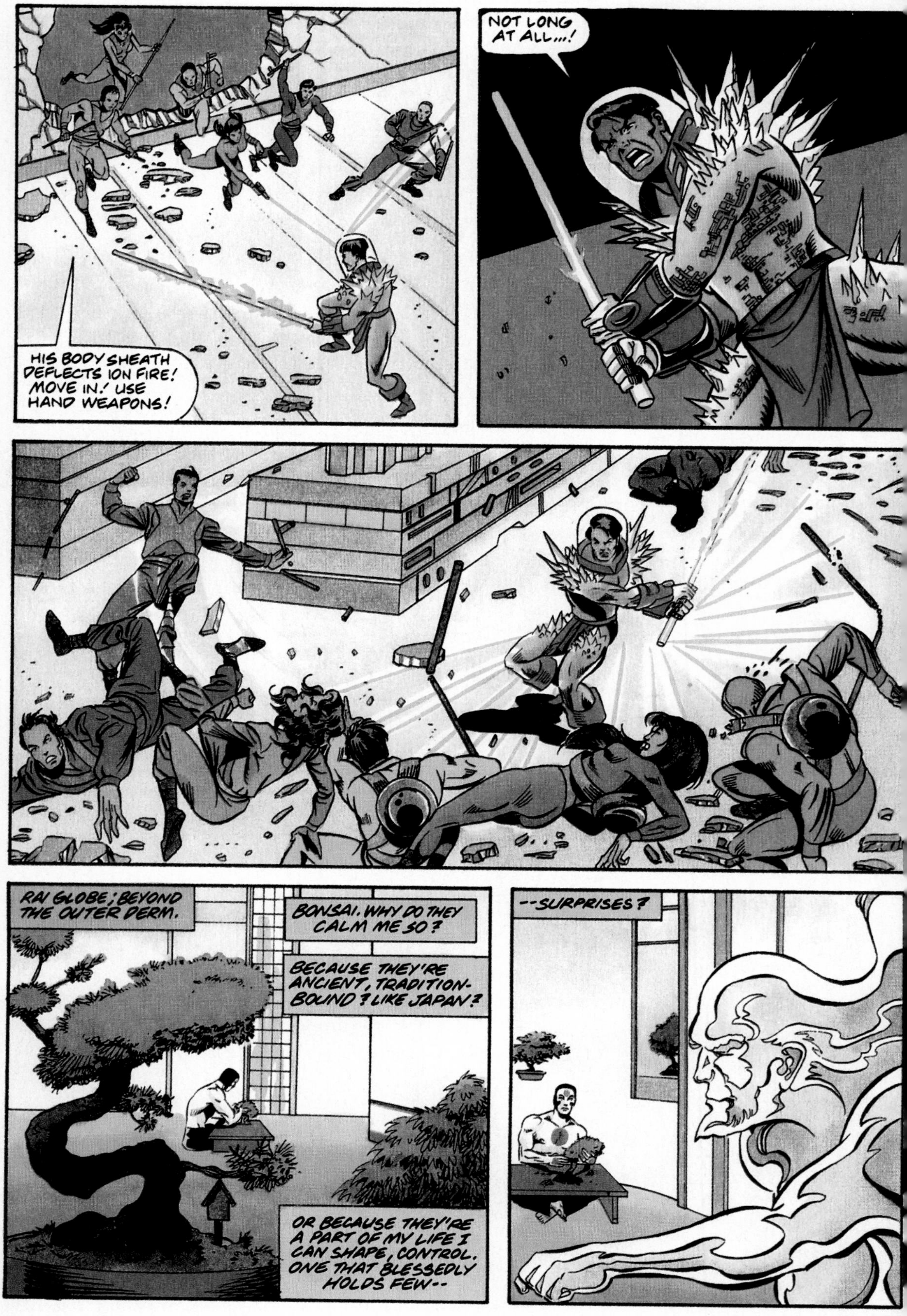
HIS BODY SHEATH DEFLECTS ION FIRE! MOVE IN! USE HAND WEAPONS!
NOT LONG AT ALL...!
RAI GLOBE; BEYOND THE OUTER DERM.
BONSAI. WHY DO THEY CALM ME SO?
BECAUSE THEY'RE ANCIENT, TRADITION-BOUND? LIKE JAPAN?
OR BECAUSE THEY'RE A PART OF MY LIFE I CAN SHAPE, CONTROL. ONE THAT BLESSEDLY HOLDS FEW--
--SURPRISES?

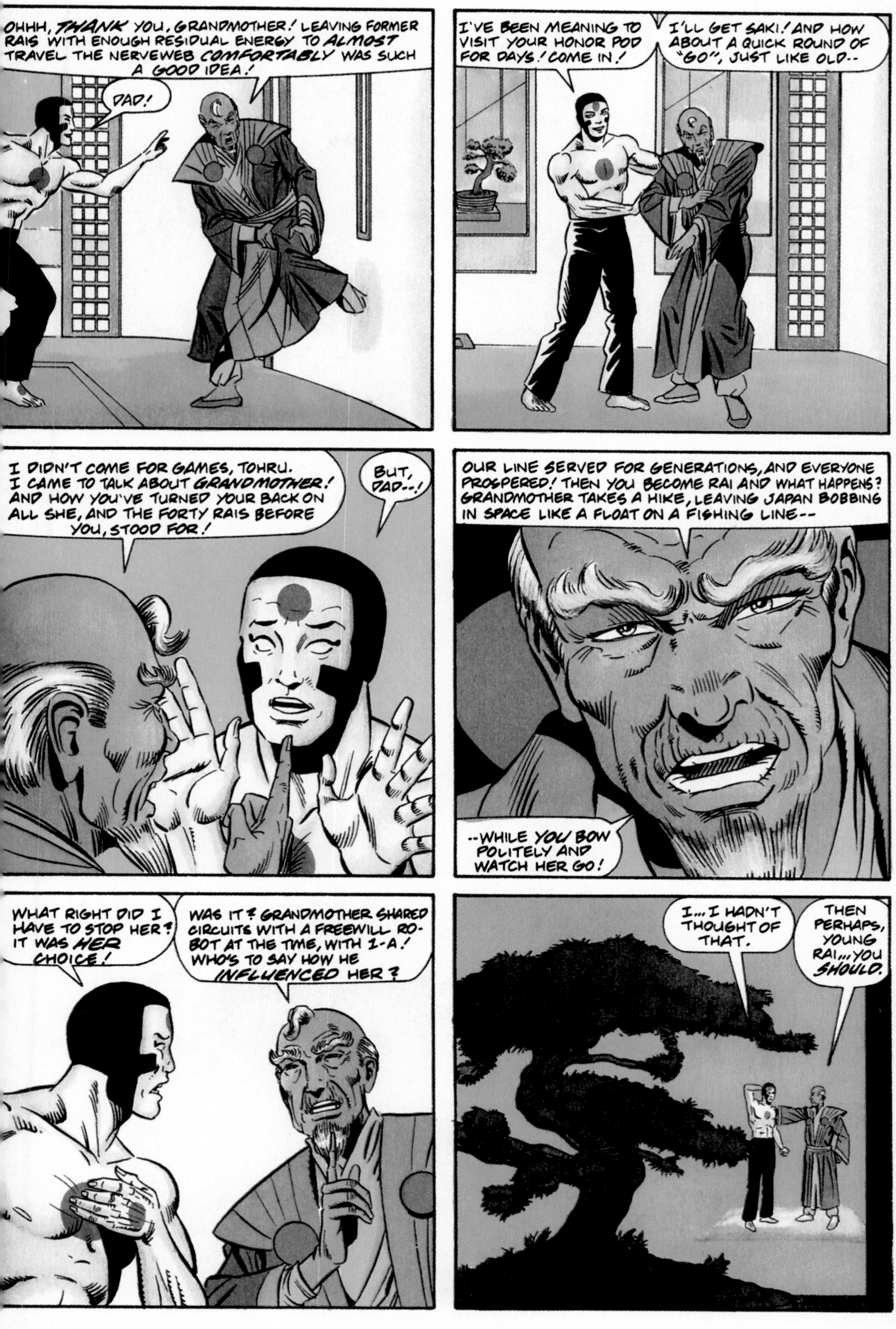

OHHH, THANK YOU, GRANDMOTHER! LEAVING FORMER RAIS WITH ENOUGH RESIDUAL ENERGY TO ALMOST TRAVEL THE NERVEWEB COMFORTABLY WAS SUCH A GOOD IDEA!
DAD!
I'VE BEEN MEANING TO VISIT YOUR HONOR POD FOR DAYS! COME IN!
I'LL GET SAKI! AND HOW ABOUT A QUICK ROUND OF "GO", JUST LIKE OLD--
I DIDN'T COME FOR GAMES, TOHRU. I CAME TO TALK ABOUT GRANDMOTHER! AND HOW YOU'VE TURNED YOUR BACK ON ALL SHE, AND THE FORTY RAIS BEFORE YOU, STOOD FOR!
BUT, DAD--!
OUR LINE SERVED FOR GENERATIONS, AND EVERYONE PROSPERED! THEN YOU BECOME RAI AND WHAT HAPPENS? GRANDMOTHER TAKES A HIKE, LEAVING JAPAN BOBBING IN SPACE LIKE A FLOAT ON A FISHING LINE--
--WHILE YOU BOW POLITELY AND WATCH HER GO!
WHAT RIGHT DID I HAVE TO STOP HER? IT WAS HER CHOICE!
WAS IT? GRANDMOTHER SHARED CIRCUITS WITH A FREEWILL ROBOT AT THE TIME, WITH 1-A! WHO'S TO SAY HOW HE INFLUENCED HER?
I... I HADN'T THOUGHT OF THAT.
THEN PERHAPS, YOUNG RAI... YOU SHOULD.

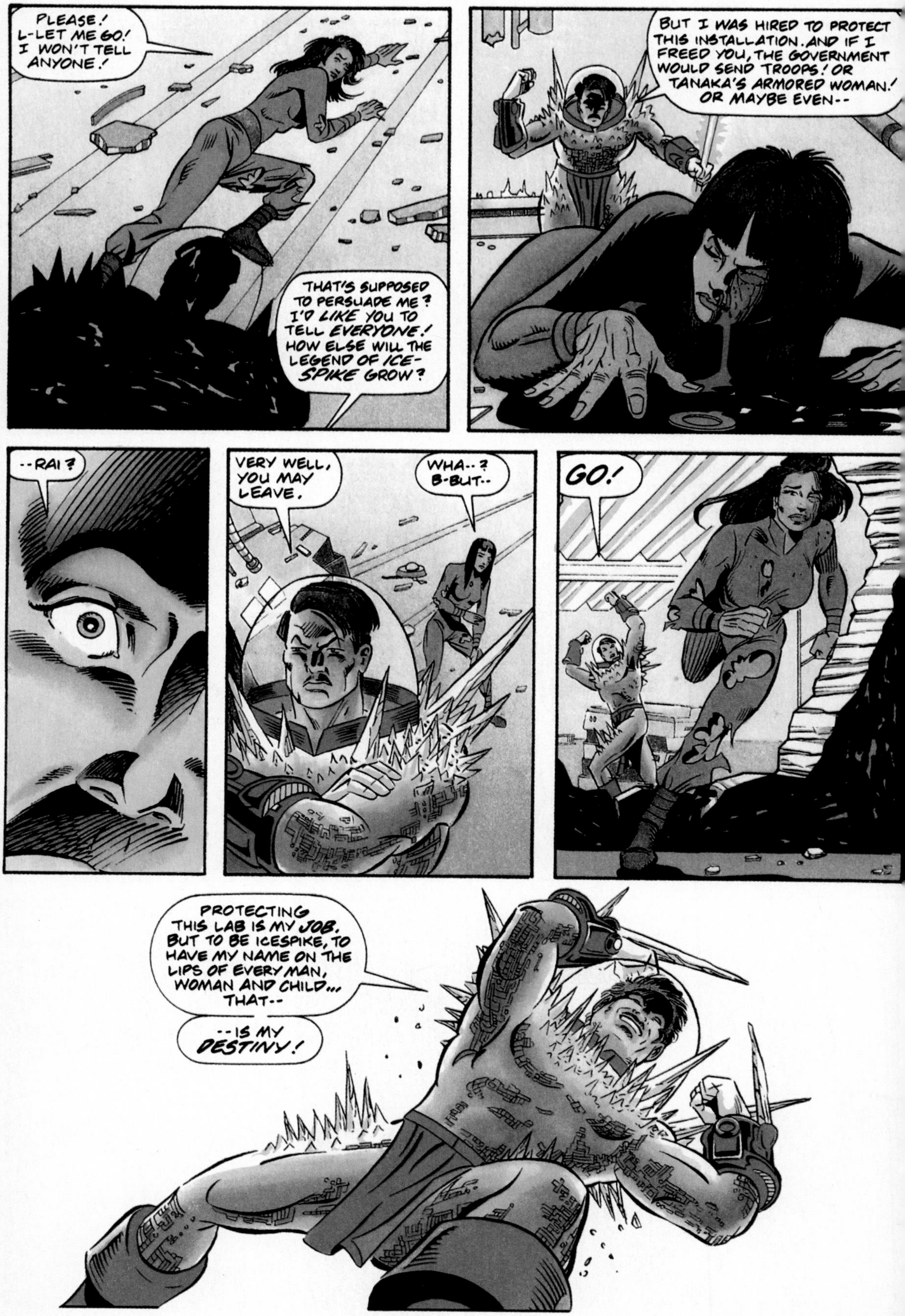
PLEASE! L-LET ME GO! I WON'T TELL ANYONE!
THAT'S SUPPOSED TO PERSUADE ME? I'D LIKE YOU TO TELL EVERYONE! HOW ELSE WILL THE LEGEND OF ICE-SPIKE GROW?
BUT I WAS HIRED TO PROTECT THIS INSTALLATION. AND IF I FREED YOU, THE GOVERNMENT WOULD SEND TROOPS! OR TANAKA'S ARMORED WOMAN! OR MAYBE EVEN--
--RAI?
VERY WELL, YOU MAY LEAVE.
WHA--? B-BUT--
GO!
PROTECTING THIS LAB IS MY JOB. BUT TO BE ICESPIKE, TO HAVE MY NAME ON THE LIPS OF EVERY MAN, WOMAN AND CHILD... THAT--
--IS MY DESTINY!

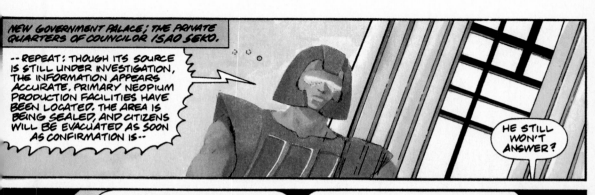

NEW GOVERNMENT PALACE; THE PRIVATE QUARTERS OF COUNCILOR ISAO SEKO.

--REPEAT: THOUGH ITS SOURCE IS STILL UNDER INVESTIGATION, THE INFORMATION APPEARS ACCURATE. PRIMARY NEOPIUM PRODUCTION FACILITIES HAVE BEEN LOCATED. THE AREA IS BEING SEALED, AND CITIZENS WILL BE EVACUATED AS SOON AS CONFIRMATION IS--

HE STILL WON'T ANSWER?

NO RESPONSE, ISAO. THOUGH DIAGNOSTICS SHOW OUR MESSAGES ARE BEING RECEIVED.

ICESPIKE! THAT EGOMANIAC! I KNEW WE COULDN'T TRUST HIM! IF HE TALKS TO THE PUBLIC--

--THEY'LL PROBABLY ERECT A *MONUMENT* TO HIM! THE PEOPLE ADORE NEOPIUM, THANKS TO OUR CELLULAR PROGRAMMING!

NO, IT'S *TANAKA* WHO'LL BE DANGEROUS IF HE DIS-COVERS IT'S HIS OWN *AD-VISORY COUNCIL* BEHIND THE DRUG!

FOR A SUCCESSFUL POLITICIAN, HE HAS AN AWKWARD SENSE OF *PRIORITIES.*

BUT... HMMM. SCRAMBLED INFO-CASTS ARE AUTOMATICALLY ROUTED TO THE RAI FACILITIES, AREN'T THEY?

OF COURSE.

THEN ALL ISN'T LOST. WE MAY YET KILL TWO BIRDS WITH ONE STONE. OR, EVEN BETTER--

--SEE THAT THE BIRDS KILL *EACH OTHER!*

RAI GLOBE.

I HAVE TO GO.

BUT WE HAVEN'T--!

OH, VERY WELL. I'LL FOLLOW ALONG AND WE CAN CON-TINUE OUR DISCUSSION IN THE NERVEWEB.

I'LL JUST... ξWFFξ...SQUEEZE RIGHT... ξHRNGξ... I-INTO... ξNNFξ

ξWHEWξ BETTER YET, WHY DON'T I HAVE ANOTHER SAKI ξPUFFξ AND WAIT FOR YOU HERE?

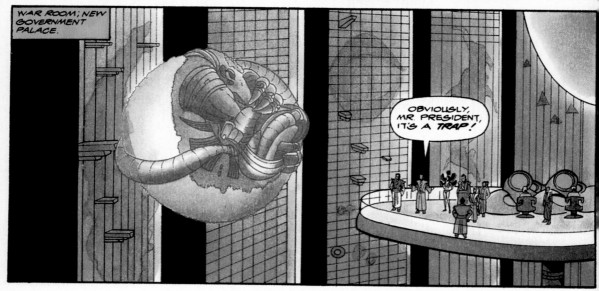

WAR ROOM; NEW GOVERNMENT PALACE.

OBVIOUSLY, MR. PRESIDENT, IT'S A TRAP!

THE INFORMATION WAS GAINED TOO EASILY, TOO CONVENIENTLY! THEY *WANT* US TO ATTACK!

MY ADVICE IS TO WAIT. SEND SPY VIDS TO ASSESS THE SITUATION. THEN, WHEN WE'VE AMASSED ENOUGH TROOPS--

IT COULD BE TOO LATE! I CONTACTED THE RAI GLOBE! TOHRU HAS ALREADY GONE!

HATRED FOR NEOPIUM OVERRIDES HIS CAUTION!

BUT IF I LEAVE NOW, I COULD WARN HIM BEFORE--

NO, COMMANDER. THIS TIME I HAVE TO AGREE WITH COUNCILOR SEKO.

YOU'RE TOO VALUABLE TO THE PARTY TO TAKE SUCH A RISK. I KNOW HOW DIFFICULT IT IS FOR YOU, BUT...

...WE WAIT.

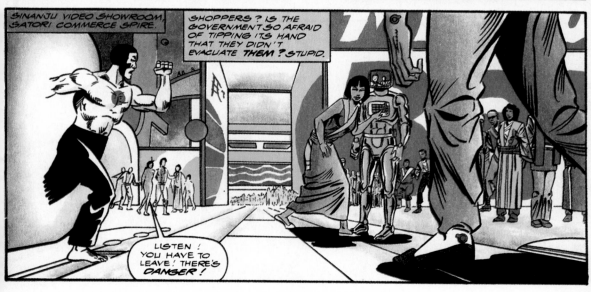

SINANJU VIDEO SHOWROOM, SATORI COMMERCE SPIRE.

SHOPPERS? IS THE GOVERNMENT SO AFRAID OF TIPPING ITS HAND THAT THEY DIDN'T EVACUATE *THEM*? STUPID.

LISTEN! YOU HAVE TO LEAVE! THERE'S *DANGER*!

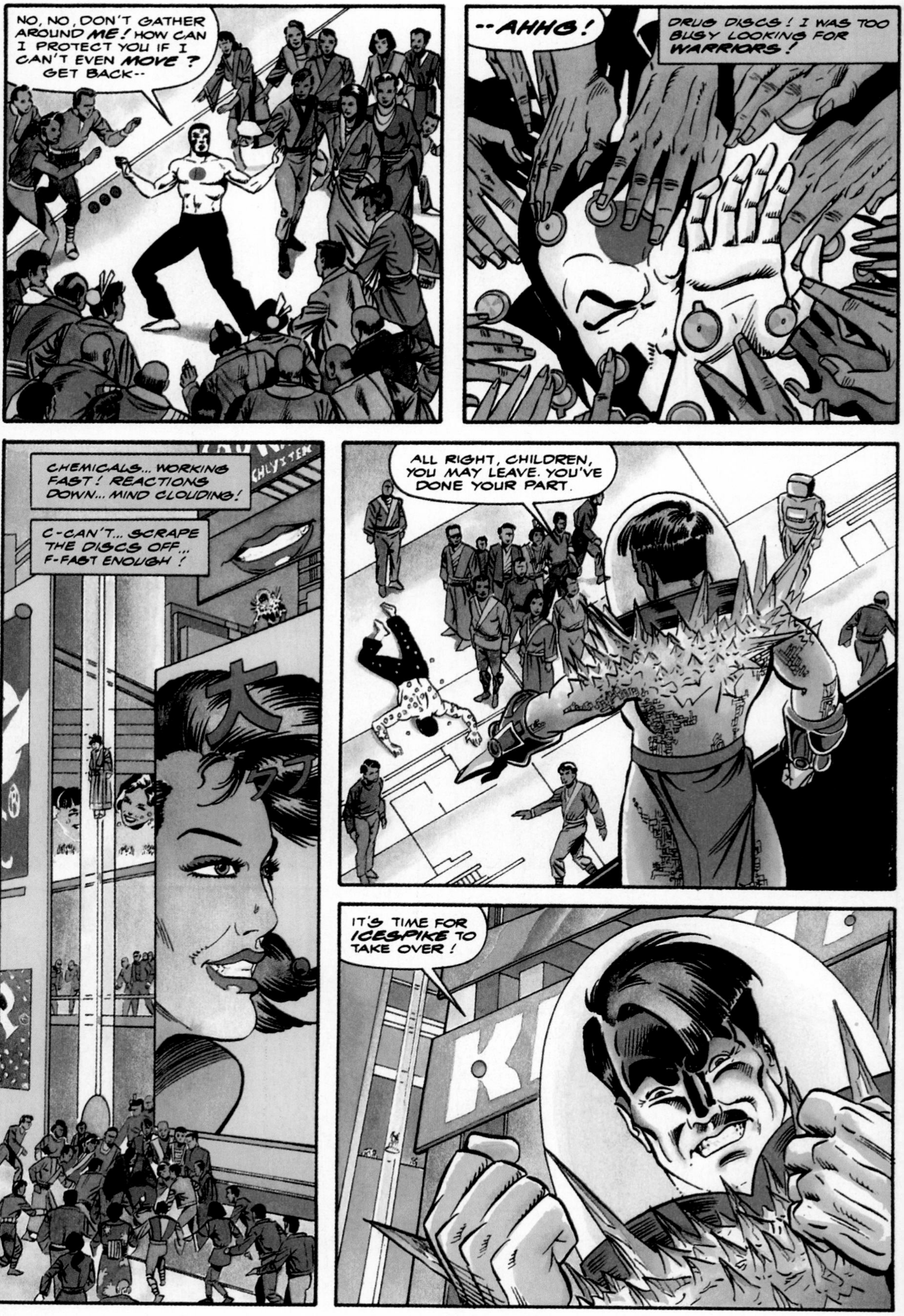
NO, NO, DON'T GATHER AROUND ME! HOW CAN I PROTECT YOU IF I CAN'T EVEN MOVE? GET BACK--
--AHHG!
DRUG DISCS! I WAS TOO BUSY LOOKING FOR WARRIORS!
CHEMICALS... WORKING FAST! REACTIONS DOWN... MIND CLOUDING!
C-CAN'T... SCRAPE THE DISCS OFF... F-FAST ENOUGH!
ALL RIGHT, CHILDREN, YOU MAY LEAVE. YOU'VE DONE YOUR PART.
IT'S TIME FOR ICESPIKE TO TAKE OVER!

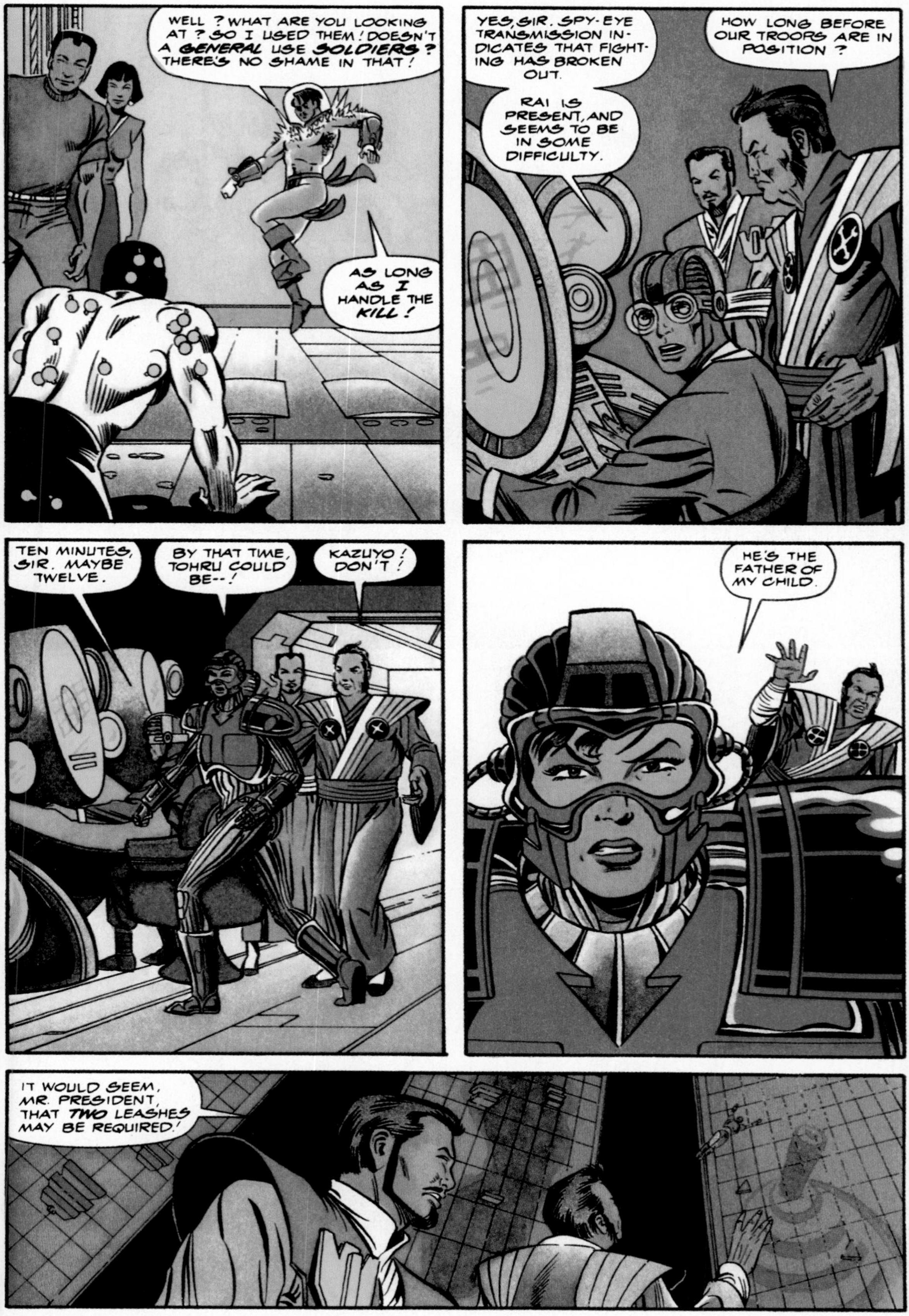
WELL ? WHAT ARE YOU LOOKING AT ? SO I USED THEM ! DOESN'T A **GENERAL** USE **SOLDIERS** ? THERE'S NO SHAME IN THAT !
AS LONG AS **I** HANDLE THE **KILL** !
YES, SIR. SPY-EYE TRANSMISSION INDICATES THAT FIGHTING HAS BROKEN OUT.
RAI IS PRESENT, AND SEEMS TO BE IN SOME DIFFICULTY.
HOW LONG BEFORE OUR TROOPS ARE IN POSITION ?
TEN MINUTES, SIR. MAYBE TWELVE.
BY THAT TIME, TOHRU COULD BE--!
KAZUYO ! DON'T !
HE'S THE FATHER OF MY CHILD.
IT WOULD SEEM, MR. PRESIDENT, THAT **TWO** LEASHES MAY BE REQUIRED!

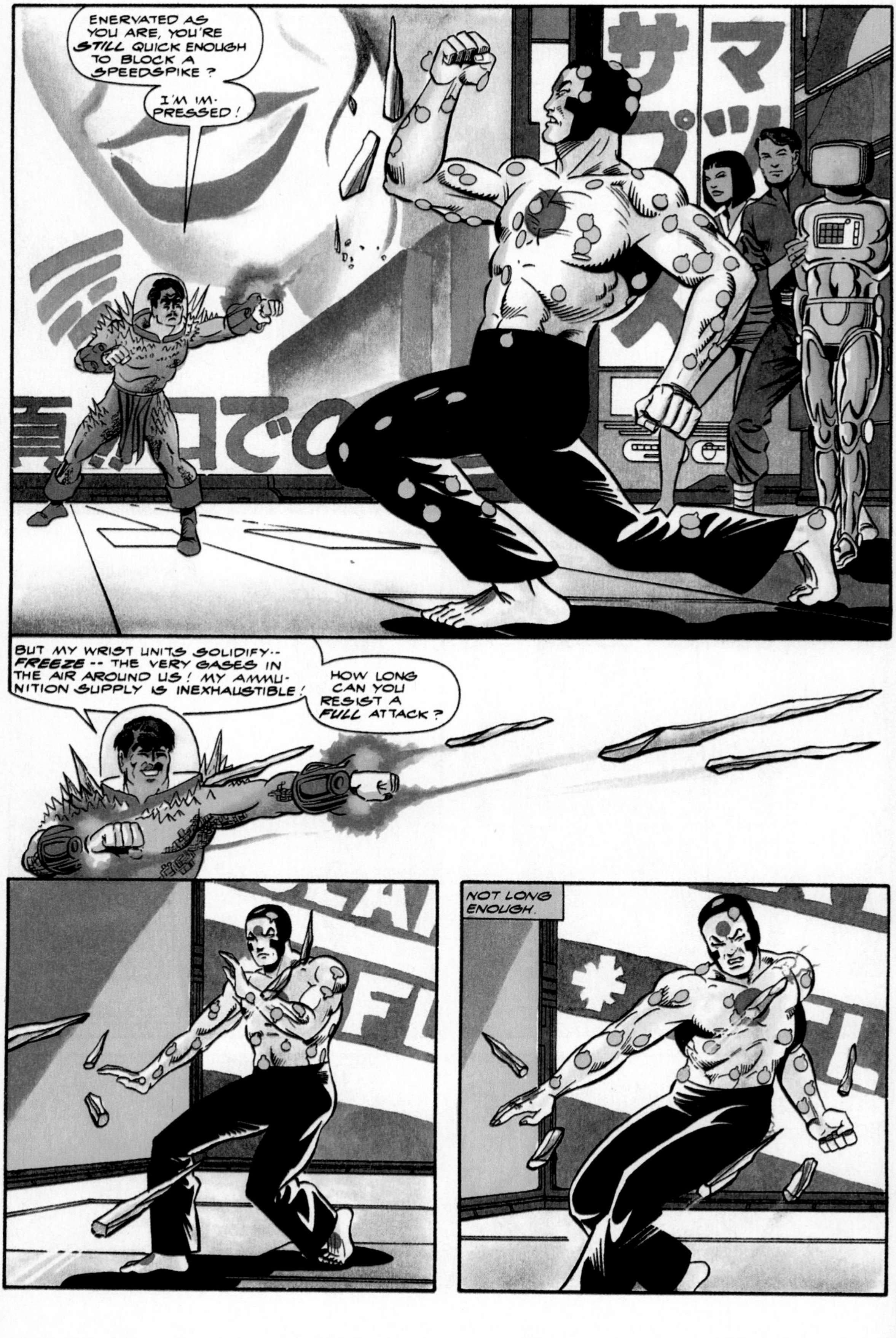
ENERVATED AS YOU ARE, YOU'RE STILL QUICK ENOUGH TO BLOCK A SPEEDSPIKE ?
I'M IM-PRESSED !
BUT MY WRIST UNITS SOLIDIFY-- FREEZE -- THE VERY GASES IN THE AIR AROUND US ! MY AMMU-NITION SUPPLY IS INEXHAUSTIBLE !
HOW LONG CAN YOU RESIST A FULL ATTACK ?
NOT LONG ENOUGH.

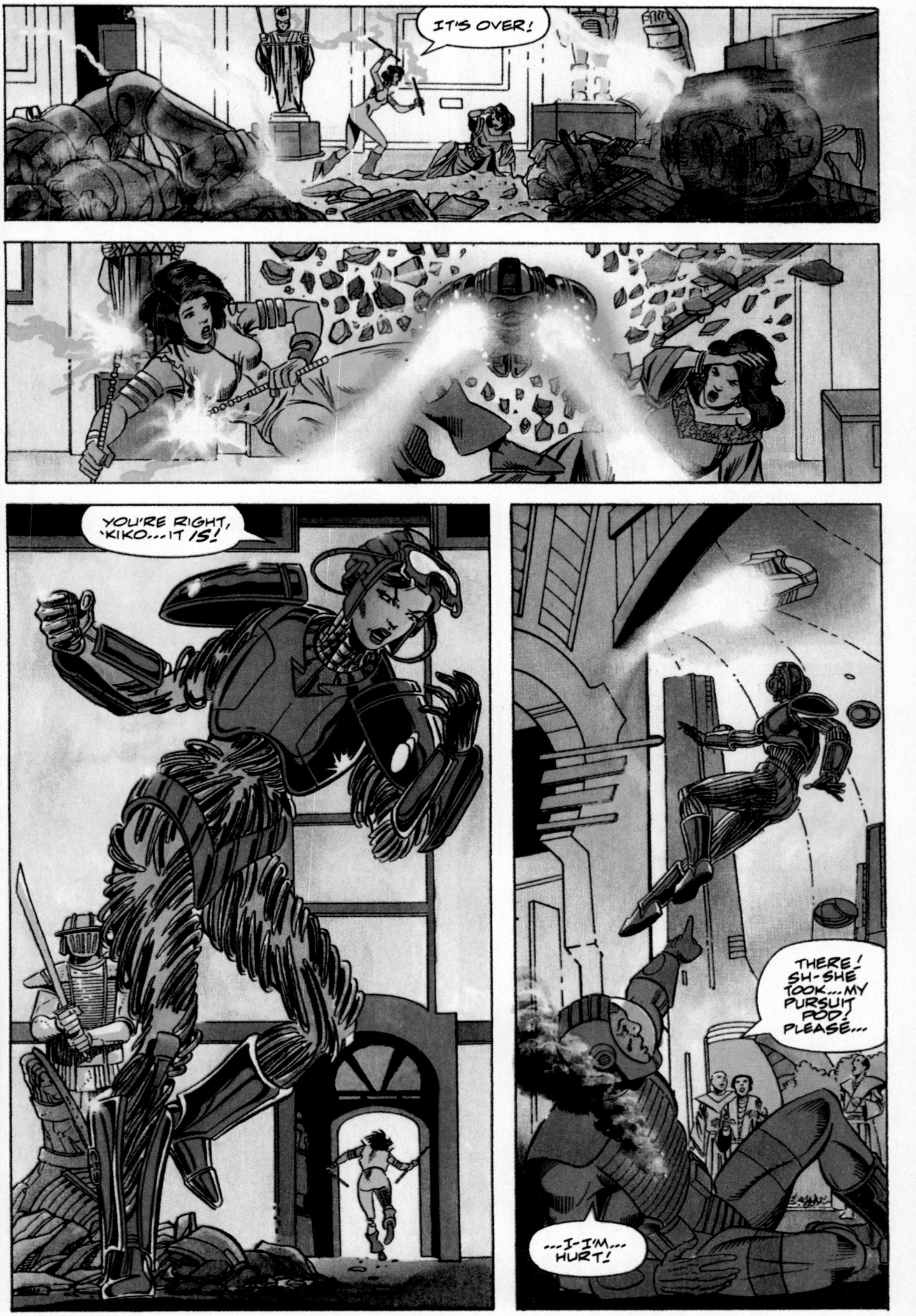
IT'S OVER!
YOU'RE RIGHT, 'KIKO...IT IS!
THERE! SH-SHE TOOK...MY PURSUIT POD! PLEASE...
...I-I'M... HURT!

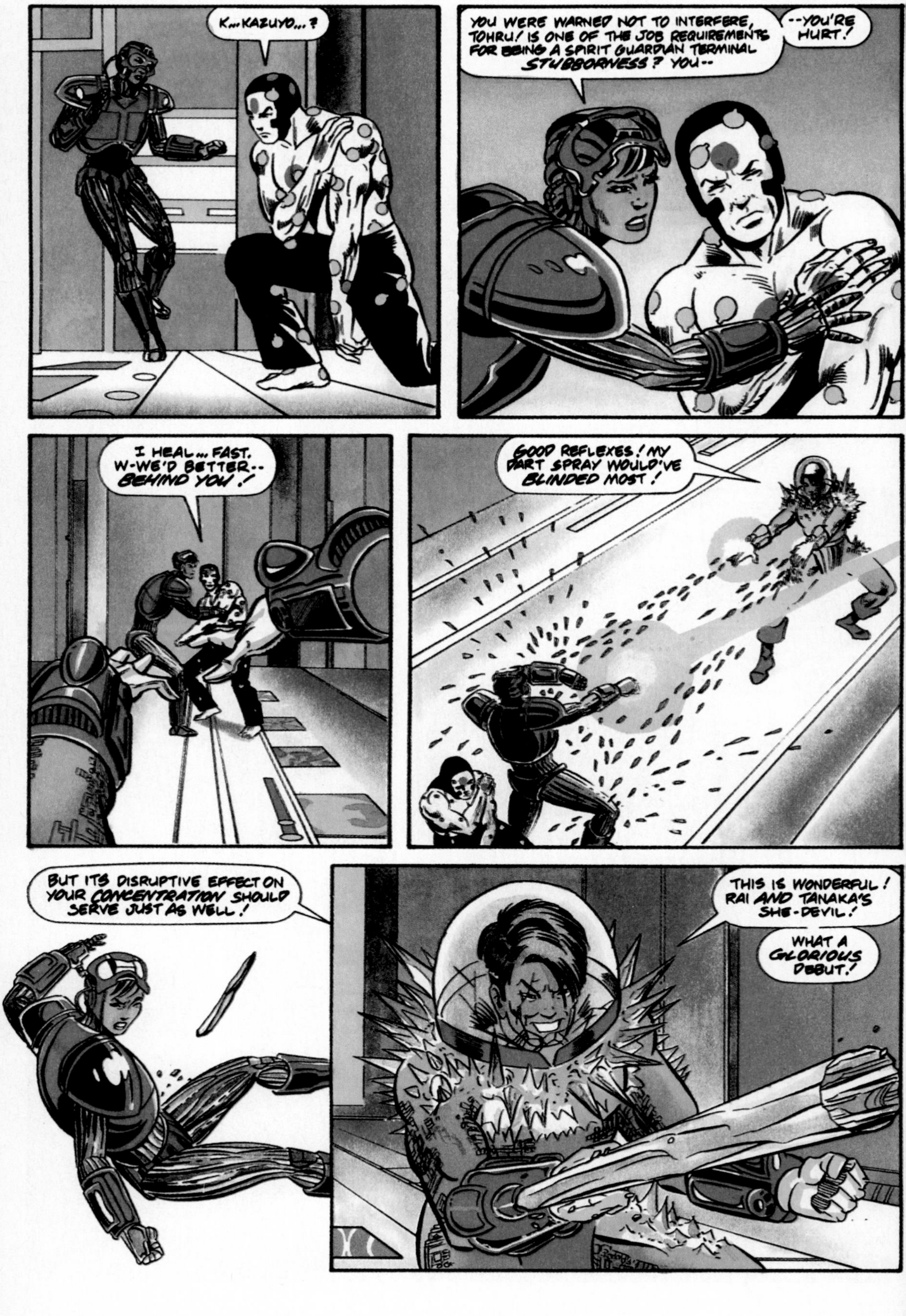
K...KAZUYO...?
YOU WERE WARNED NOT TO INTERFERE, TOHRU! IS ONE OF THE JOB REQUIREMENTS FOR BEING A SPIRIT GUARDIAN TERMINAL STUBBORNESS? YOU--
--YOU'RE HURT!
I HEAL... FAST. W-WE'D BETTER.. BEHIND YOU!
GOOD REFLEXES! MY DART SPRAY WOULD'VE BLINDED MOST!
BUT ITS DISRUPTIVE EFFECT ON YOUR CONCENTRATION SHOULD SERVE JUST AS WELL!
THIS IS WONDERFUL! RAI AND TANAKA'S SHE-DEVIL!
WHAT A GLORIOUS DEBUT!

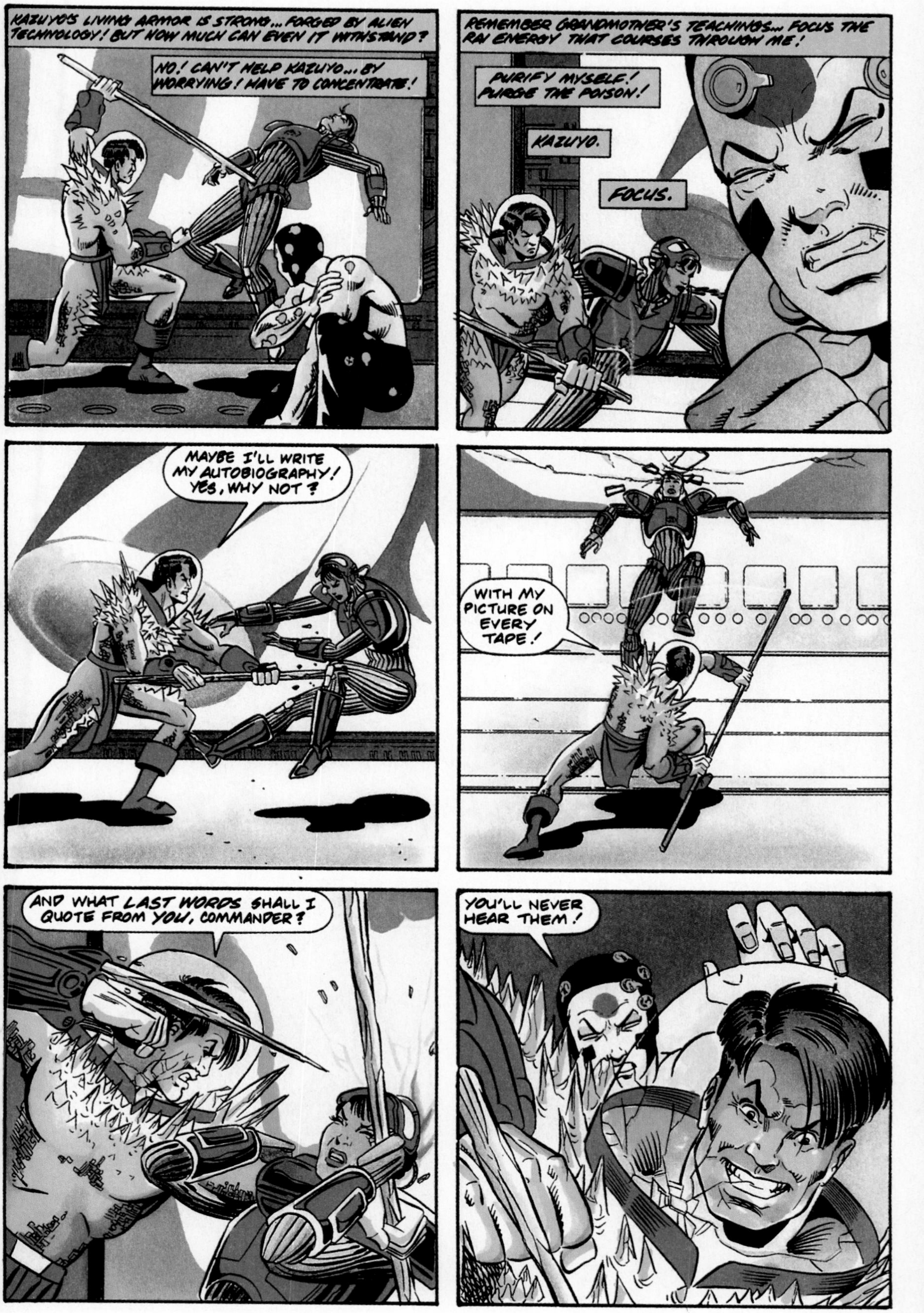
KAZUYO'S LIVING ARMOR IS STRONG... FORGED BY ALIEN TECHNOLOGY! BUT HOW MUCH CAN EVEN IT WITHSTAND?
NO! CAN'T HELP KAZUYO... BY WORRYING! HAVE TO CONCENTRATE!
REMEMBER GRANDMOTHER'S TEACHINGS... FOCUS THE RAI ENERGY THAT COURSES THROUGH ME!
PURIFY MYSELF! PURGE THE POISON!
KAZUYO.
FOCUS.
MAYBE I'LL WRITE MY AUTOBIOGRAPHY! YES, WHY NOT?
WITH MY PICTURE ON EVERY TAPE!
AND WHAT LAST WORDS SHALL I QUOTE FROM YOU, COMMANDER?
YOU'LL NEVER HEAR THEM!

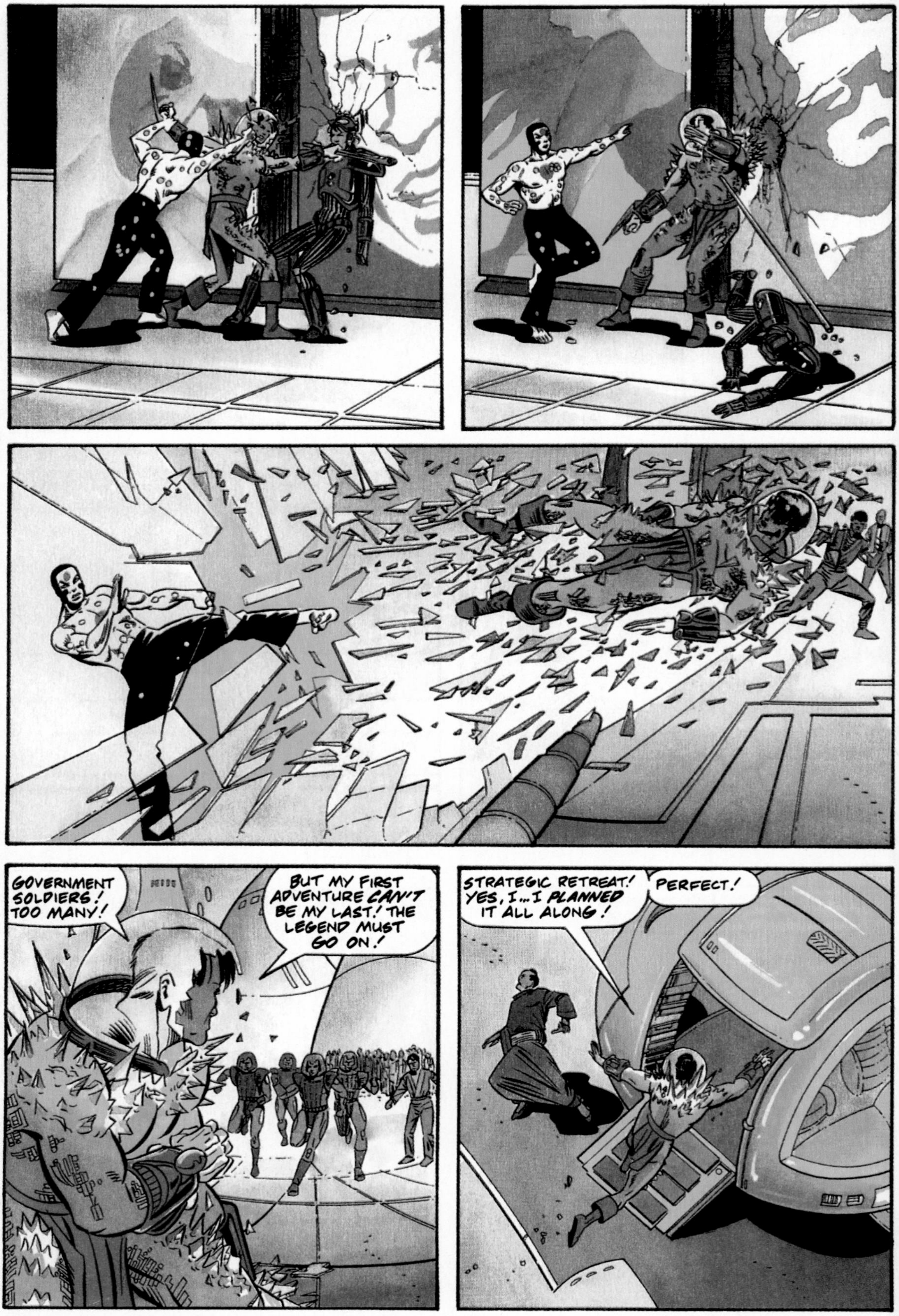
GOVERNMENT SOLDIERS! TOO MANY!
BUT MY FIRST ADVENTURE CAN'T BE MY LAST! THE LEGEND MUST GO ON!
STRATEGIC RETREAT! YES, I...I PLANNED IT ALL ALONG!
PERFECT!

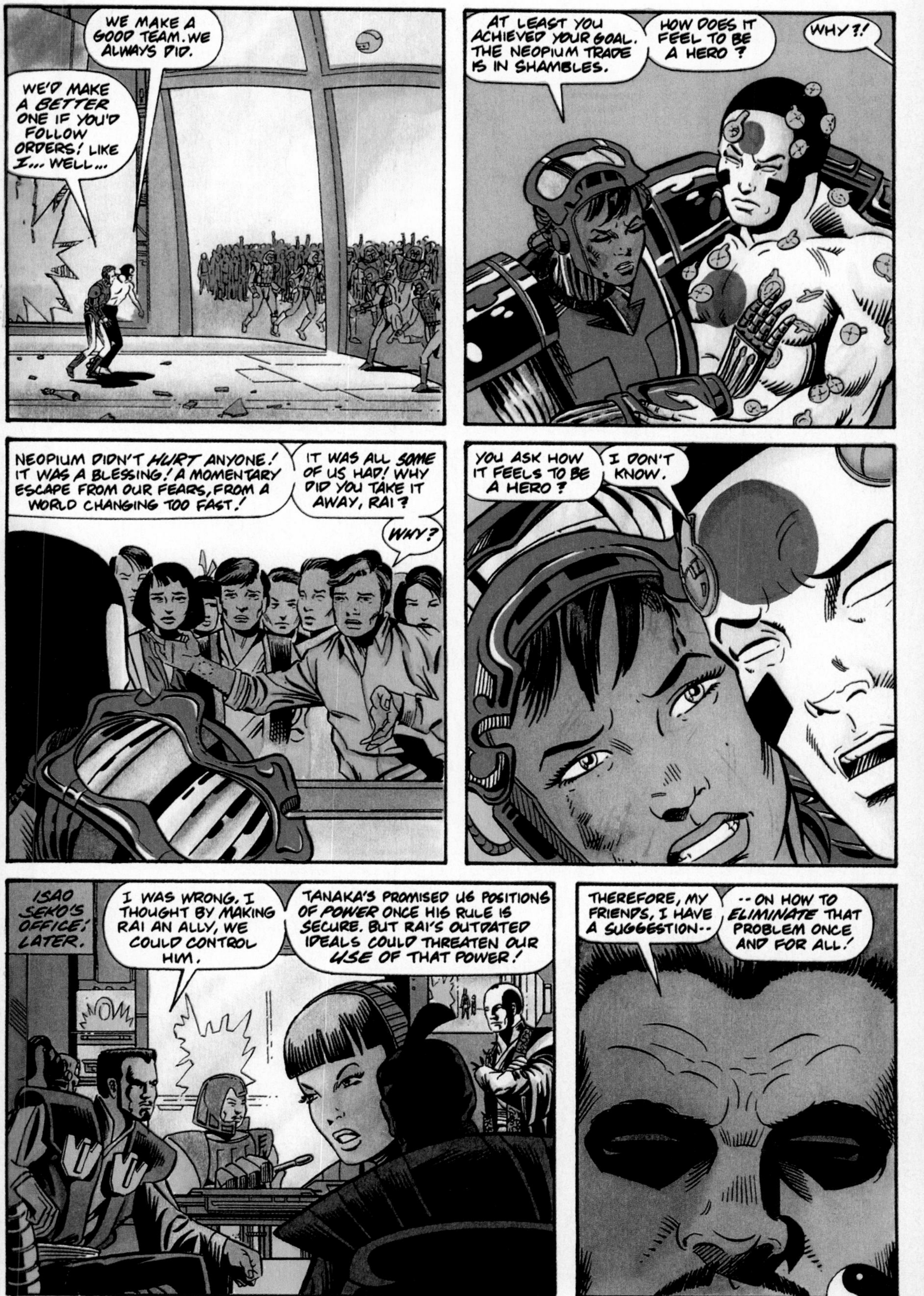
WE MAKE A GOOD TEAM. WE ALWAYS DID.
WE'D MAKE A *BETTER* ONE IF YOU'D FOLLOW ORDERS! LIKE I... WELL...
AT LEAST YOU ACHIEVED YOUR GOAL. THE NEOPIUM TRADE IS IN SHAMBLES.
HOW DOES IT FEEL TO BE A HERO?
WHY?!
NEOPIUM DIDN'T *HURT* ANYONE! IT WAS A BLESSING! A MOMENTARY ESCAPE FROM OUR FEARS, FROM A WORLD CHANGING TOO FAST!
IT WAS ALL *SOME* OF US HAD! WHY DID YOU TAKE IT AWAY, RAI?
WHY?
YOU ASK HOW IT FEELS TO BE A HERO?
I DON'T KNOW.
ISAO SEKO'S OFFICE; LATER.
I WAS WRONG. I THOUGHT BY MAKING RAI AN ALLY, WE COULD CONTROL HIM.
TANAKA'S PROMISED US POSITIONS OF *POWER* ONCE HIS RULE IS SECURE. BUT RAI'S OUTDATED IDEALS COULD THREATEN OUR *USE* OF THAT POWER!
THEREFORE, MY FRIENDS, I HAVE A SUGGESTION--
--ON HOW TO *ELIMINATE* THAT PROBLEM ONCE AND FOR ALL!

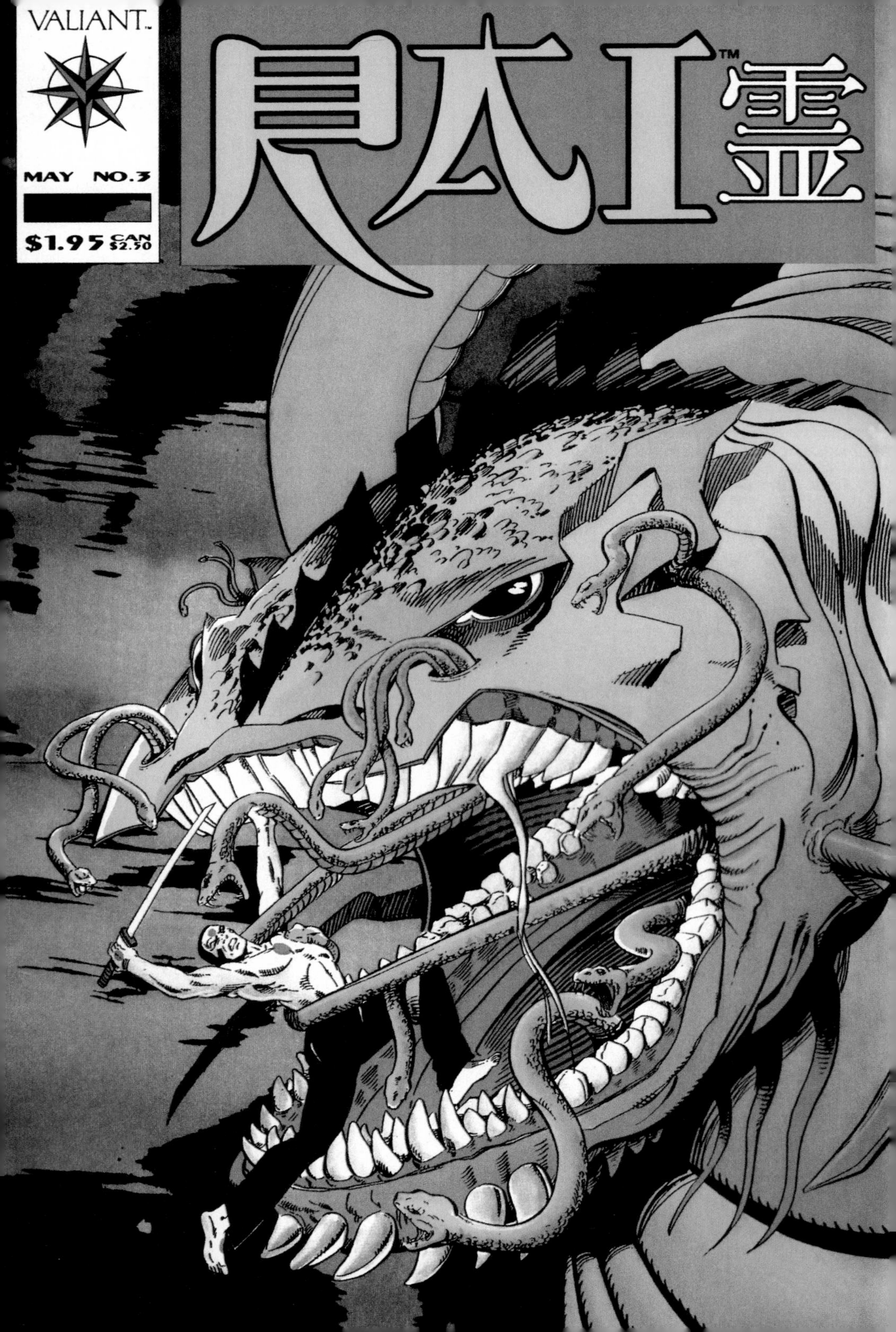
VALIANT™
MAY NO.3
$1.95 CAN $2.50
RAI™ 霊

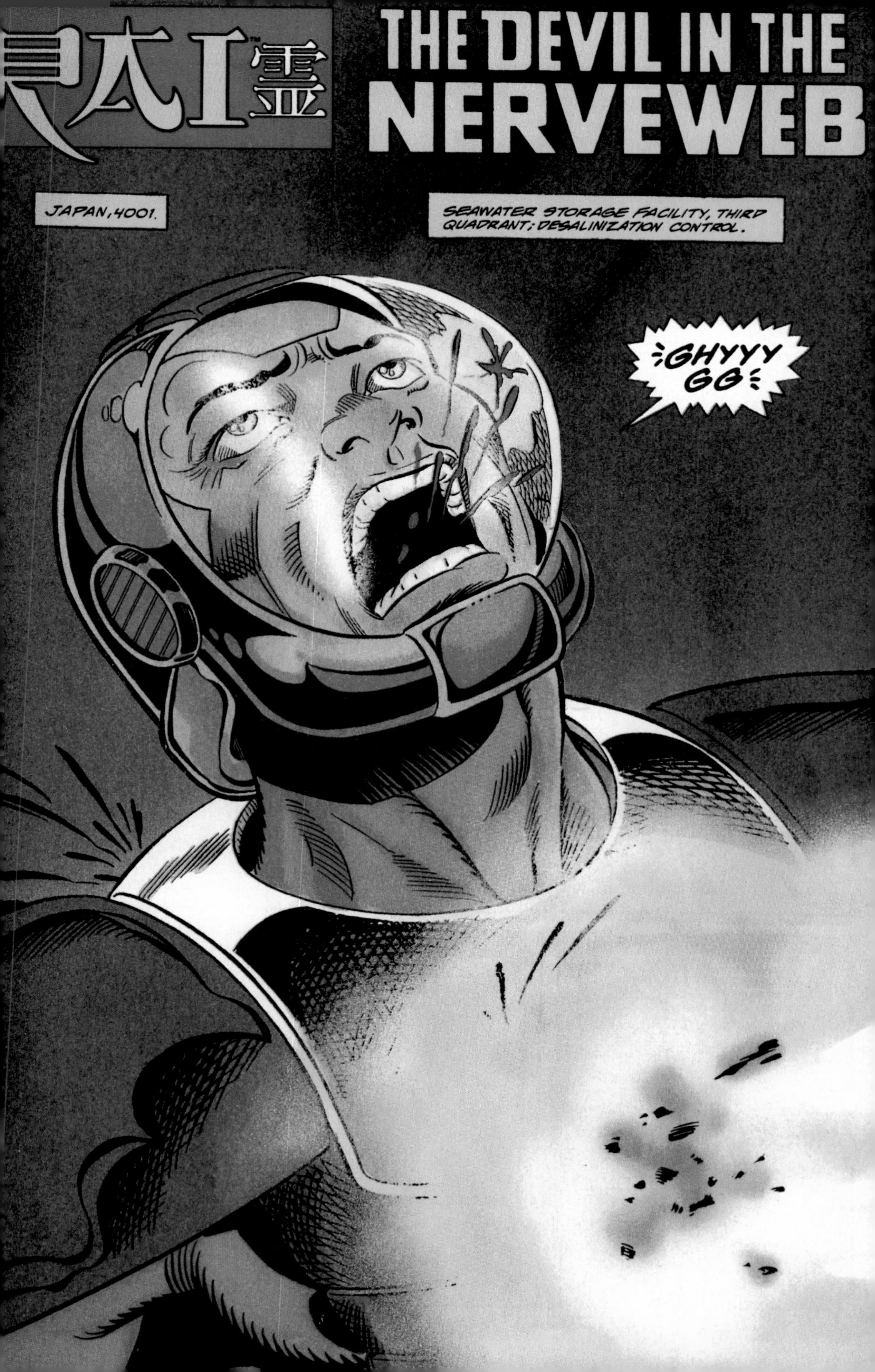
RAI™ 霊
THE DEVIL IN THE NERVEWEB
JAPAN, 4001.
SEAWATER STORAGE FACILITY, THIRD QUADRANT: DESALINIZATION CONTROL.
GHYYY GG

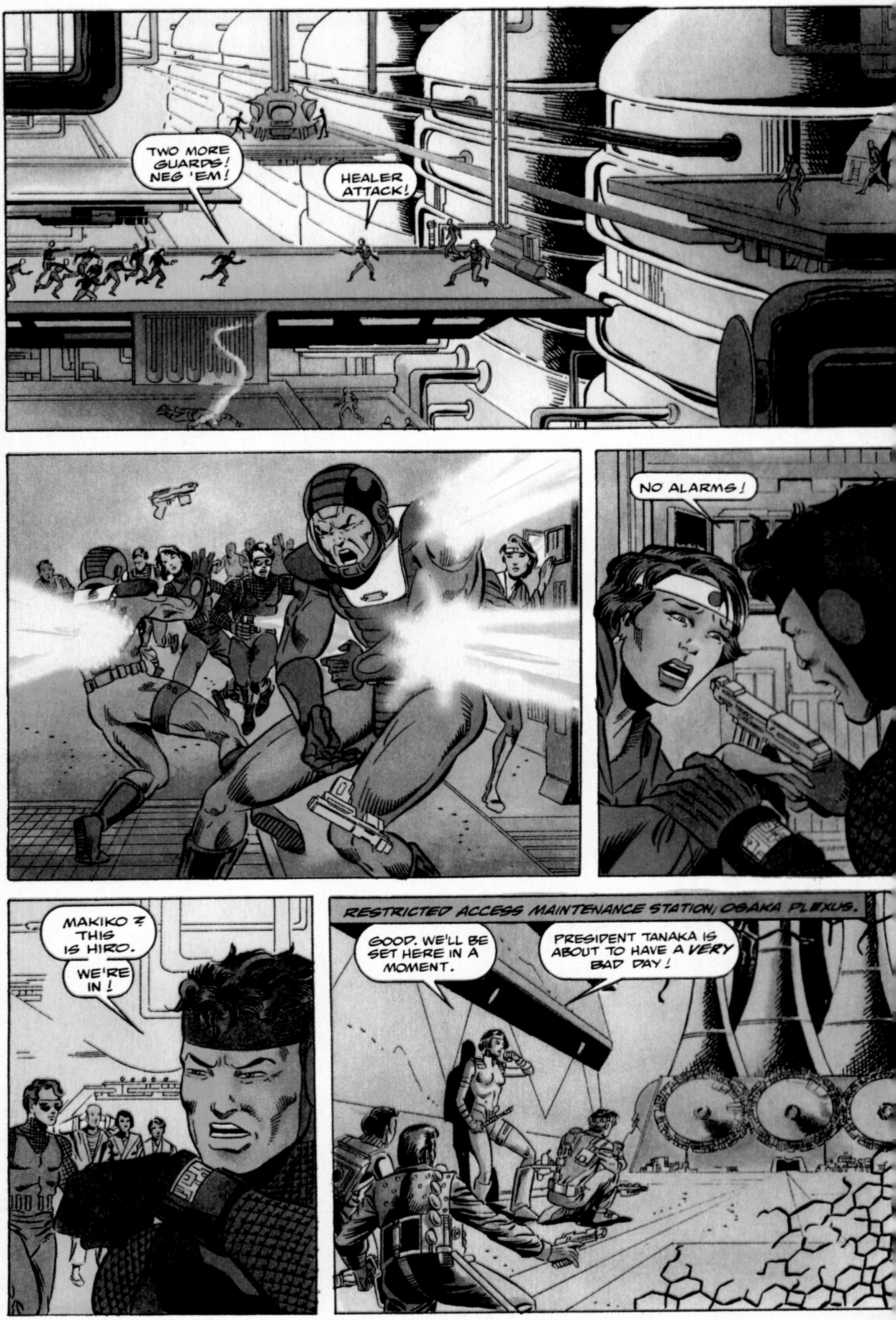
TWO MORE GUARDS! NEG 'EM!
HEALER ATTACK!
NO ALARMS!
MAKIKO? THIS IS HIRO.
WE'RE IN!
RESTRICTED ACCESS MAINTENANCE STATION, OSAKA PLEXUS.
GOOD. WE'LL BE SET HERE IN A MOMENT.
PRESIDENT TANAKA IS ABOUT TO HAVE A VERY BAD DAY!

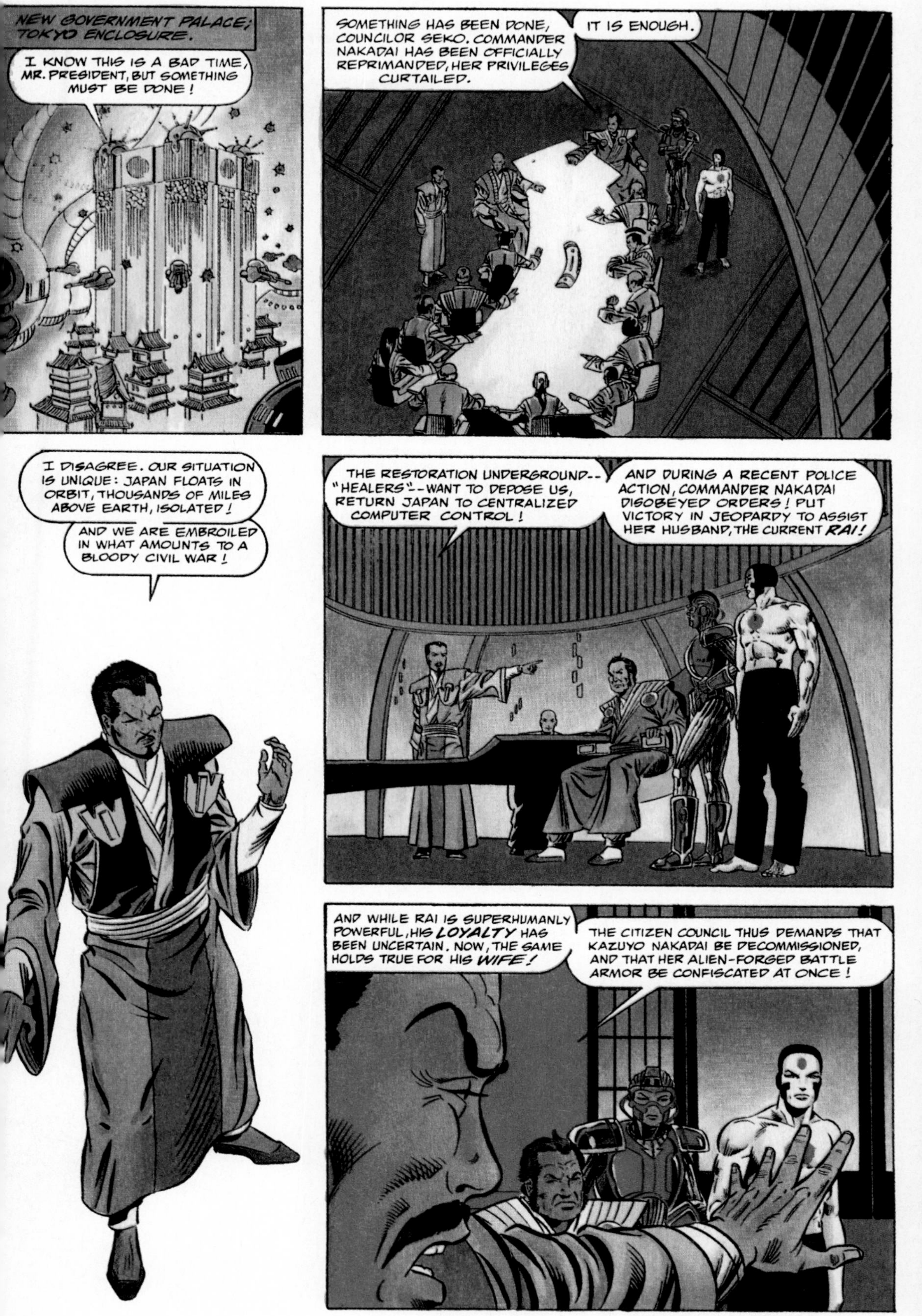
NEW GOVERNMENT PALACE; TOKYO ENCLOSURE.
I KNOW THIS IS A BAD TIME, MR. PRESIDENT, BUT SOMETHING MUST BE DONE!
SOMETHING HAS BEEN DONE, COUNCILOR SEKO. COMMANDER NAKADAI HAS BEEN OFFICIALLY REPRIMANDED, HER PRIVILEGES CURTAILED.
IT IS ENOUGH.
I DISAGREE. OUR SITUATION IS UNIQUE: JAPAN FLOATS IN ORBIT, THOUSANDS OF MILES ABOVE EARTH, ISOLATED!
AND WE ARE EMBROILED IN WHAT AMOUNTS TO A BLOODY CIVIL WAR!
THE RESTORATION UNDERGROUND-- "HEALERS"--WANT TO DEPOSE US, RETURN JAPAN TO CENTRALIZED COMPUTER CONTROL!
AND DURING A RECENT POLICE ACTION, COMMANDER NAKADAI DISOBEYED ORDERS! PUT VICTORY IN JEOPARDY TO ASSIST HER HUSBAND, THE CURRENT RAI!
AND WHILE RAI IS SUPERHUMANLY POWERFUL, HIS LOYALTY HAS BEEN UNCERTAIN. NOW, THE SAME HOLDS TRUE FOR HIS WIFE!
THE CITIZEN COUNCIL THUS DEMANDS THAT KAZUYO NAKADAI BE DECOMMISSIONED, AND THAT HER ALIEN-FORGED BATTLE ARMOR BE CONFISCATED AT ONCE!

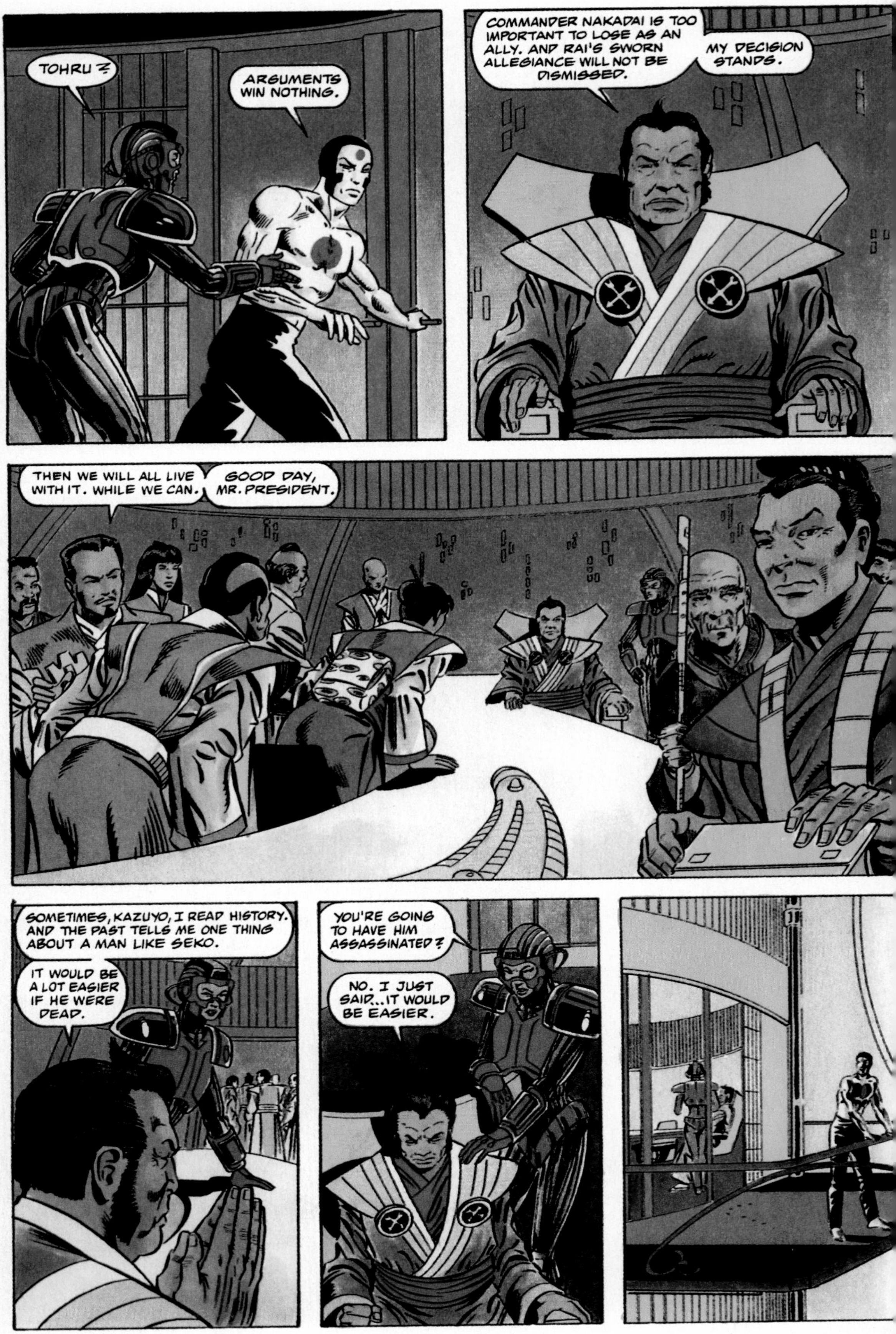
TOHRU ?
ARGUMENTS WIN NOTHING.
COMMANDER NAKADAI IS TOO IMPORTANT TO LOSE AS AN ALLY. AND RAI'S SWORN ALLEGIANCE WILL NOT BE DISMISSED.
MY DECISION STANDS.
THEN WE WILL ALL LIVE WITH IT. WHILE WE CAN.
GOOD DAY, MR. PRESIDENT.
SOMETIMES, KAZUYO, I READ HISTORY. AND THE PAST TELLS ME ONE THING ABOUT A MAN LIKE SEKO.
IT WOULD BE A LOT EASIER IF HE WERE DEAD.
YOU'RE GOING TO HAVE HIM ASSASSINATED ?
NO. I JUST SAID...IT WOULD BE EASIER.

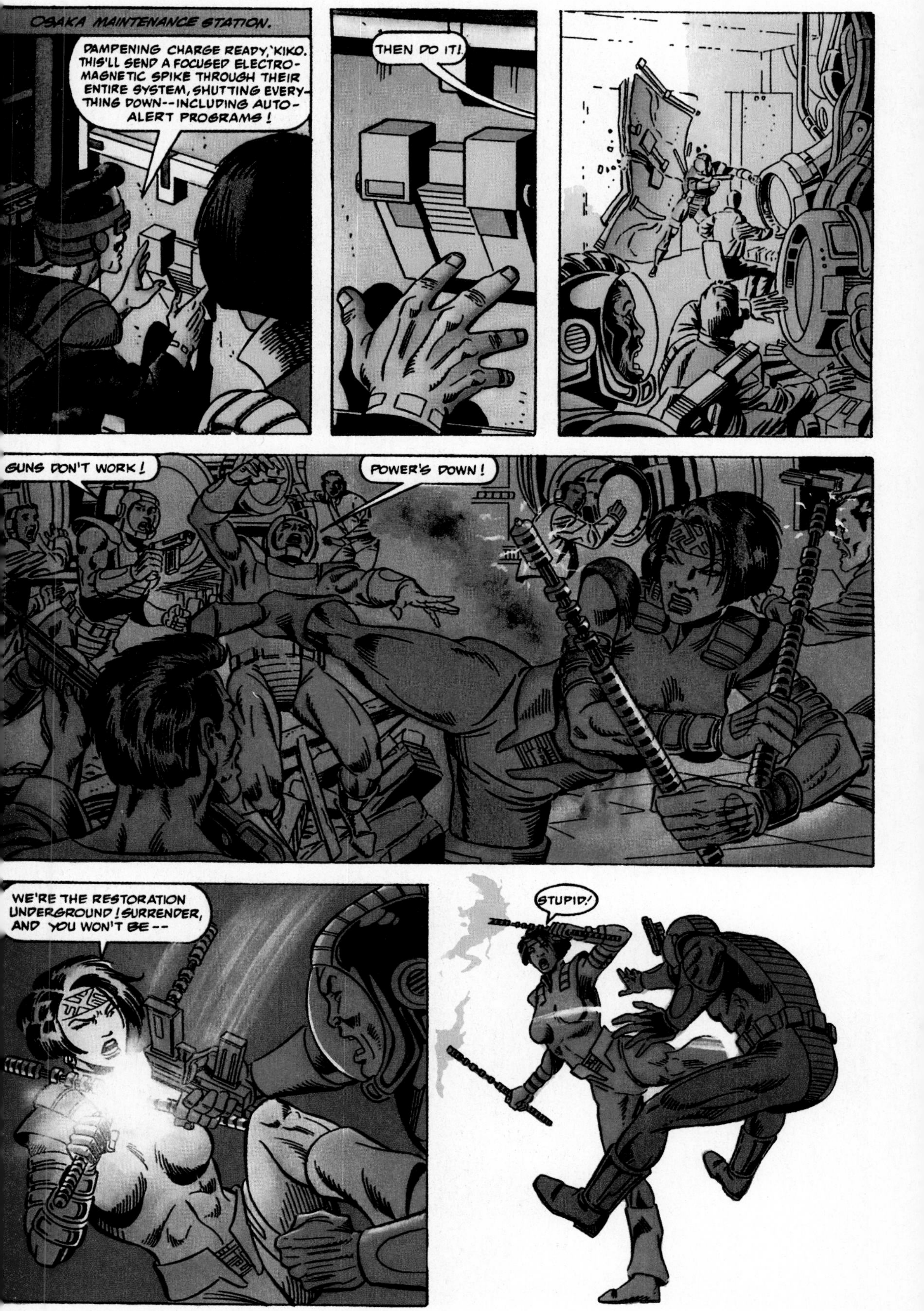
OSAKA MAINTENANCE STATION.
DAMPENING CHARGE READY, 'KIKO. THIS'LL SEND A FOCUSED ELECTRO-MAGNETIC SPIKE THROUGH THEIR ENTIRE SYSTEM, SHUTTING EVERY-THING DOWN--INCLUDING AUTO-ALERT PROGRAMS!
THEN DO IT!
GUNS DON'T WORK!
POWER'S DOWN!
WE'RE THE RESTORATION UNDERGROUND! SURRENDER, AND YOU WON'T BE--
STUPID!

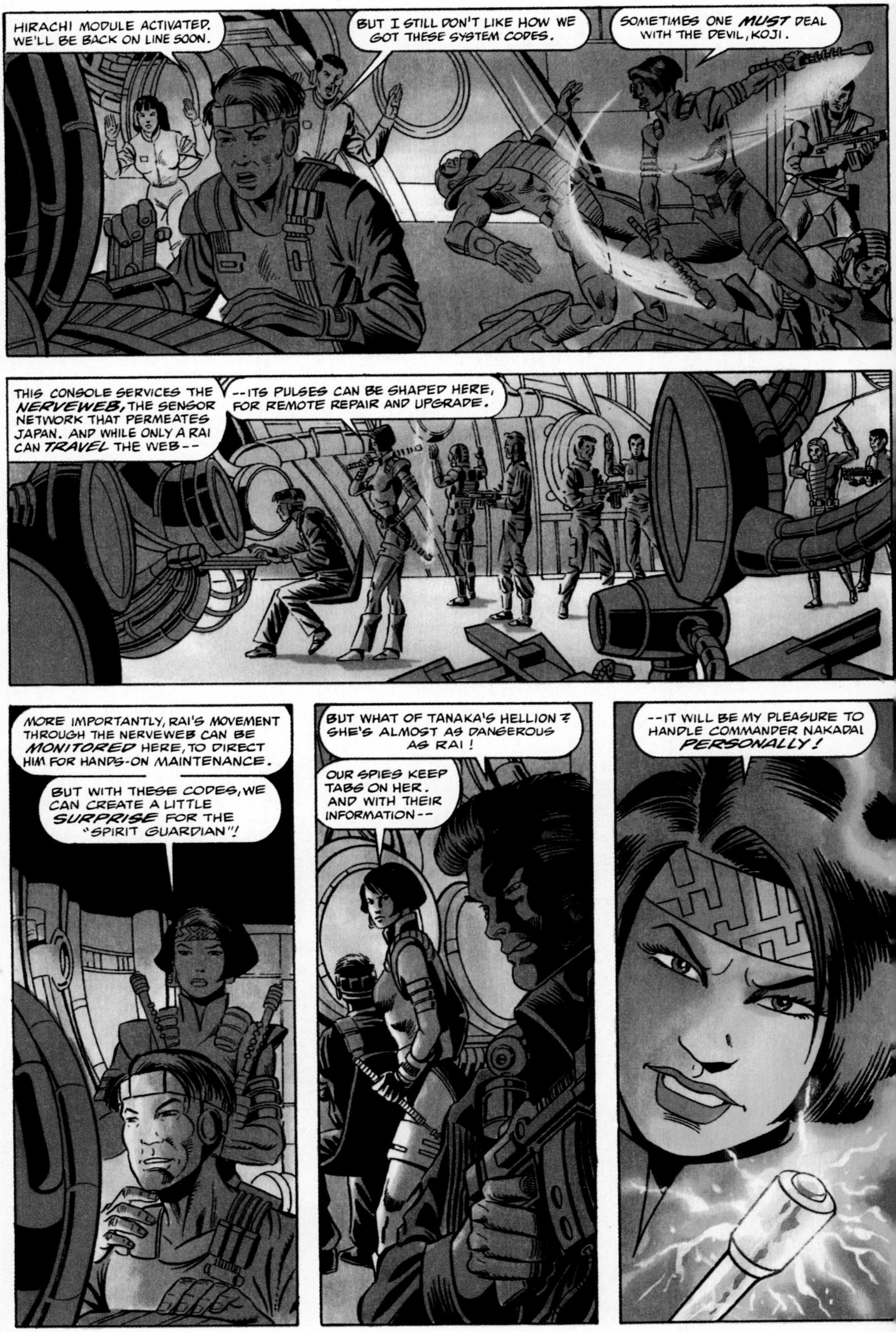
HIRACHI MODULE ACTIVATED. WE'LL BE BACK ON LINE SOON.
BUT I STILL DON'T LIKE HOW WE GOT THESE SYSTEM CODES.
SOMETIMES ONE MUST DEAL WITH THE DEVIL, KOJI.
THIS CONSOLE SERVICES THE NERVEWEB, THE SENSOR NETWORK THAT PERMEATES JAPAN. AND WHILE ONLY A RAI CAN TRAVEL THE WEB--
--ITS PULSES CAN BE SHAPED HERE, FOR REMOTE REPAIR AND UPGRADE.
MORE IMPORTANTLY, RAI'S MOVEMENT THROUGH THE NERVEWEB CAN BE MONITORED HERE, TO DIRECT HIM FOR HANDS-ON MAINTENANCE.
BUT WITH THESE CODES, WE CAN CREATE A LITTLE SURPRISE FOR THE "SPIRIT GUARDIAN"!
BUT WHAT OF TANAKA'S HELLION? SHE'S ALMOST AS DANGEROUS AS RAI!
OUR SPIES KEEP TABS ON HER. AND WITH THEIR INFORMATION--
--IT WILL BE MY PLEASURE TO HANDLE COMMANDER NAKADAI PERSONALLY!

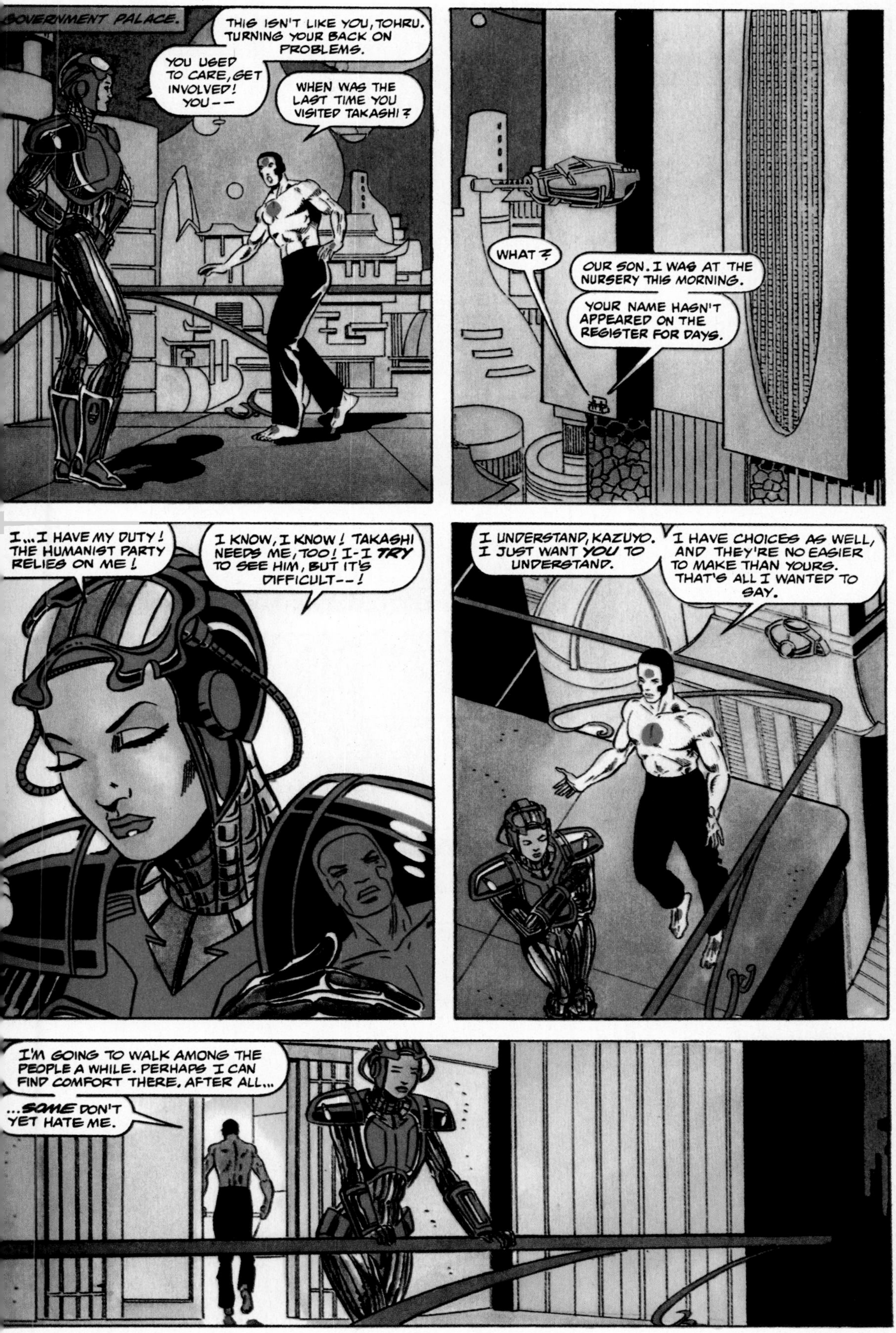
GOVERNMENT PALACE.
THIS ISN'T LIKE YOU, TOHRU. TURNING YOUR BACK ON PROBLEMS.
YOU USED TO CARE, GET INVOLVED! YOU--
WHEN WAS THE LAST TIME YOU VISITED TAKASHI?
WHAT?
OUR SON. I WAS AT THE NURSERY THIS MORNING.
YOUR NAME HASN'T APPEARED ON THE REGISTER FOR DAYS.
I...I HAVE MY DUTY! THE HUMANIST PARTY RELIES ON ME!
I KNOW, I KNOW! TAKASHI NEEDS ME, TOO! I-I TRY TO SEE HIM, BUT IT'S DIFFICULT--!
I UNDERSTAND, KAZUYO. I JUST WANT YOU TO UNDERSTAND.
I HAVE CHOICES AS WELL, AND THEY'RE NO EASIER TO MAKE THAN YOURS. THAT'S ALL I WANTED TO SAY.
I'M GOING TO WALK AMONG THE PEOPLE A WHILE. PERHAPS I CAN FIND COMFORT THERE. AFTER ALL...
...SOME DON'T YET HATE ME.

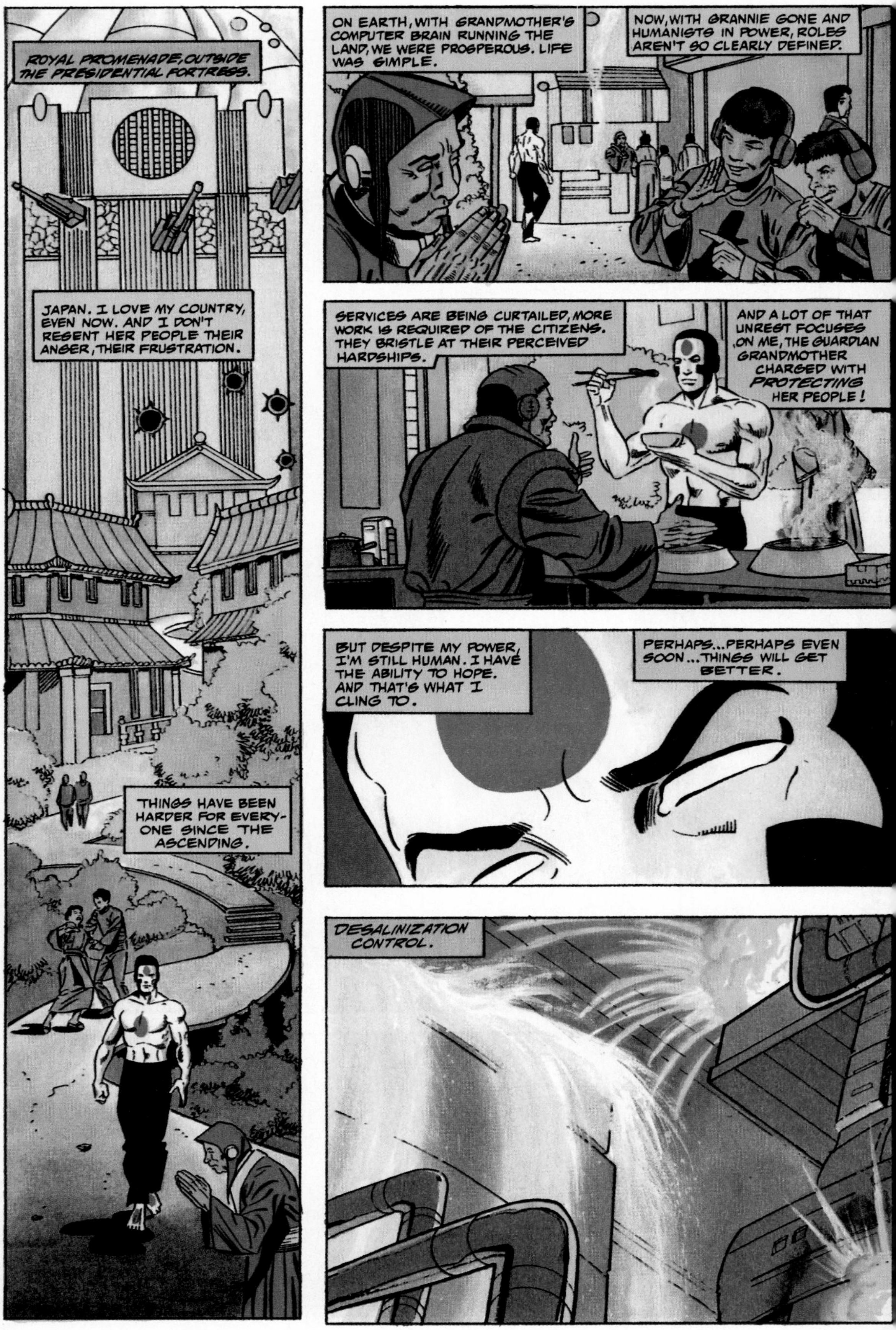

ROYAL PROMENADE, OUTSIDE THE PRESIDENTIAL FORTRESS.
JAPAN. I LOVE MY COUNTRY, EVEN NOW. AND I DON'T RESENT HER PEOPLE THEIR ANGER, THEIR FRUSTRATION.
THINGS HAVE BEEN HARDER FOR EVERY-ONE SINCE THE ASCENDING.
ON EARTH, WITH GRANDMOTHER'S COMPUTER BRAIN RUNNING THE LAND, WE WERE PROSPEROUS. LIFE WAS SIMPLE.
NOW, WITH GRANNIE GONE AND HUMANISTS IN POWER, ROLES AREN'T SO CLEARLY DEFINED.
SERVICES ARE BEING CURTAILED, MORE WORK IS REQUIRED OF THE CITIZENS. THEY BRISTLE AT THEIR PERCEIVED HARDSHIPS.
AND A LOT OF THAT UNREST FOCUSES ON ME, THE GUARDIAN GRANDMOTHER CHARGED WITH PROTECTING HER PEOPLE!
BUT DESPITE MY POWER, I'M STILL HUMAN. I HAVE THE ABILITY TO HOPE. AND THAT'S WHAT I CLING TO.
PERHAPS...PERHAPS EVEN SOON...THINGS WILL GET BETTER.
DESALINIZATION CONTROL.

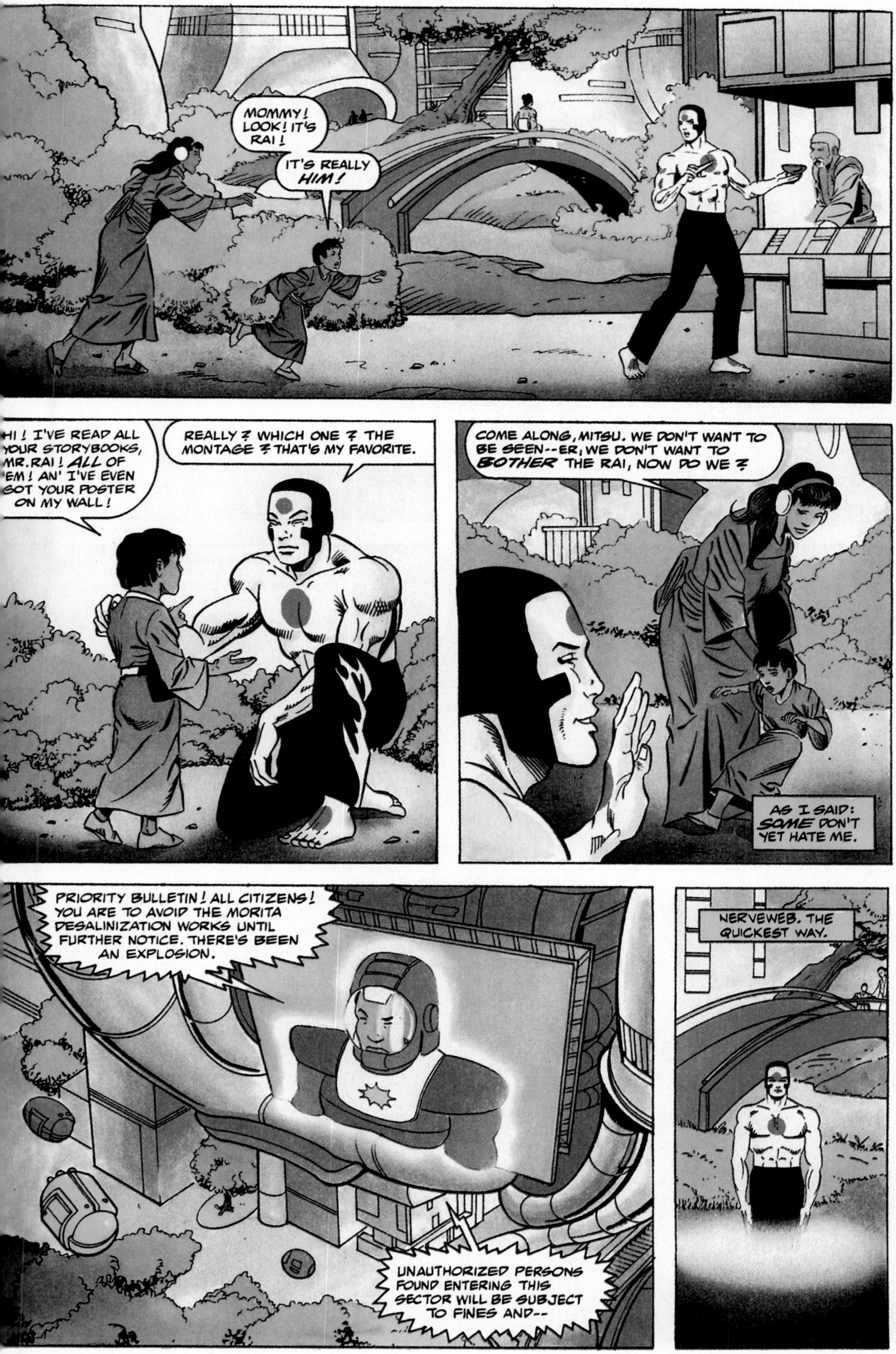
MOMMY! LOOK! IT'S RAI!
IT'S REALLY HIM!
HI! I'VE READ ALL YOUR STORYBOOKS, MR. RAI! ALL OF 'EM! AN' I'VE EVEN GOT YOUR POSTER ON MY WALL!
REALLY? WHICH ONE? THE MONTAGE? THAT'S MY FAVORITE.
COME ALONG, MITSU. WE DON'T WANT TO BE SEEN--ER, WE DON'T WANT TO BOTHER THE RAI, NOW DO WE?
AS I SAID: SOME DON'T YET HATE ME.
PRIORITY BULLETIN! ALL CITIZENS! YOU ARE TO AVOID THE MORITA DESALINIZATION WORKS UNTIL FURTHER NOTICE. THERE'S BEEN AN EXPLOSION.
UNAUTHORIZED PERSONS FOUND ENTERING THIS SECTOR WILL BE SUBJECT TO FINES AND--
NERVEWEB. THE QUICKEST WAY.

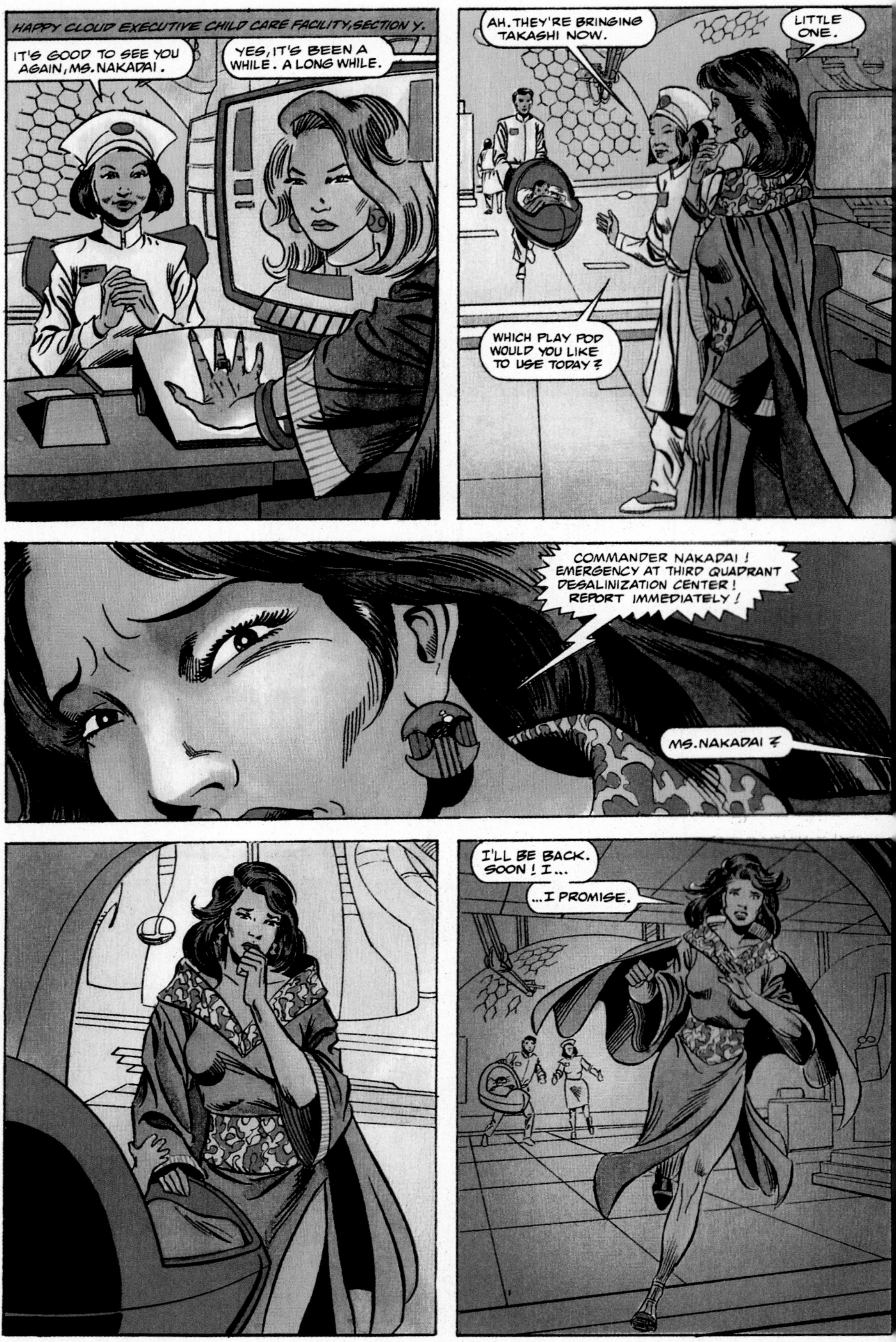
HAPPY CLOUD EXECUTIVE CHILD CARE FACILITY, SECTION Y.
IT'S GOOD TO SEE YOU AGAIN, MS. NAKADAI.
YES, IT'S BEEN A WHILE. A LONG WHILE.
AH. THEY'RE BRINGING TAKASHI NOW.
LITTLE ONE.
WHICH PLAY POD WOULD YOU LIKE TO USE TODAY?
COMMANDER NAKADAI! EMERGENCY AT THIRD QUADRANT DESALINIZATION CENTER! REPORT IMMEDIATELY!
MS. NAKADAI?
I'LL BE BACK. SOON! I...
...I PROMISE.

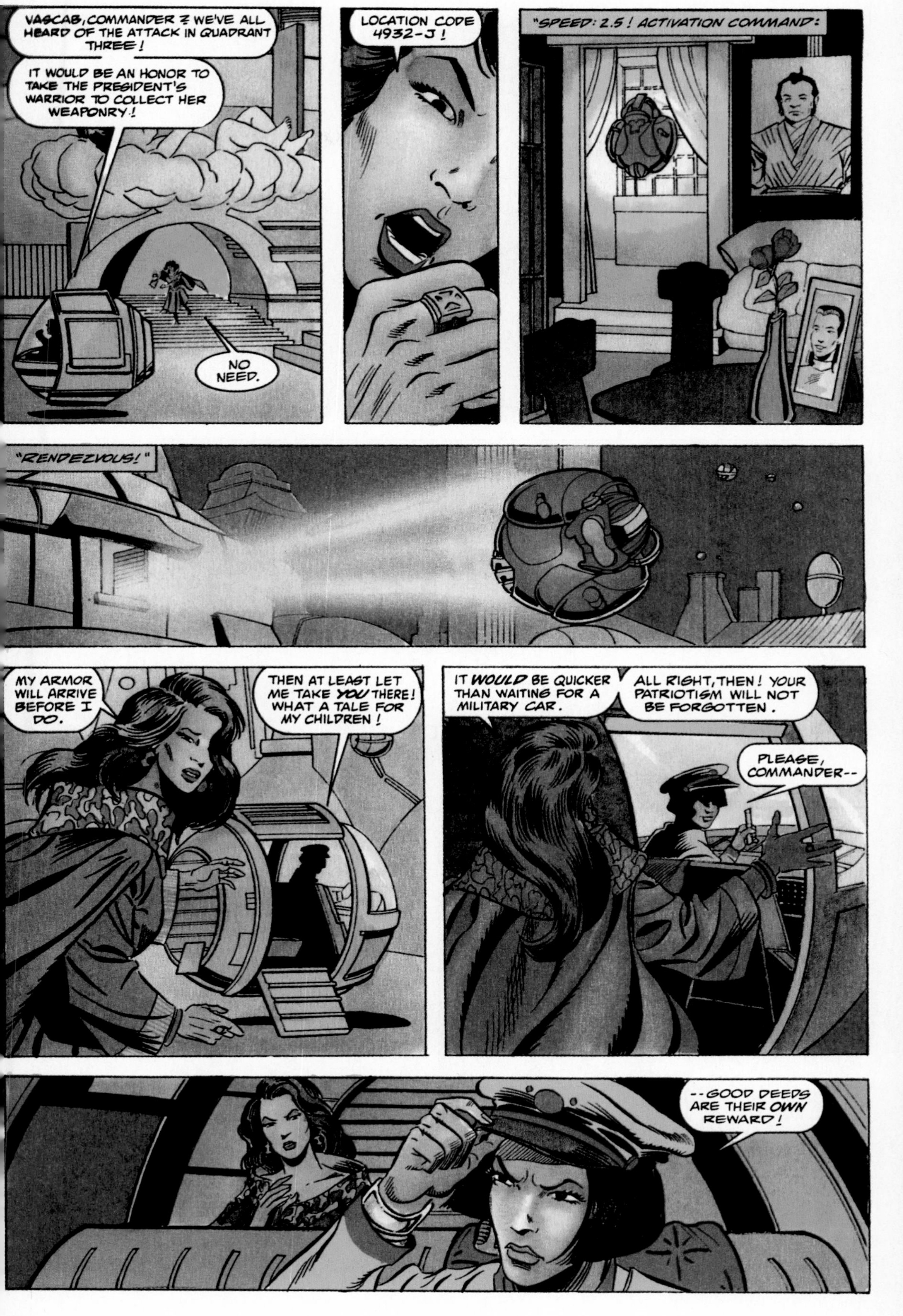
VASCAB, COMMANDER Z WE'VE ALL HEARD OF THE ATTACK IN QUADRANT THREE!
IT WOULD BE AN HONOR TO TAKE THE PRESIDENT'S WARRIOR TO COLLECT HER WEAPONRY!
NO NEED.
LOCATION CODE 4932-J!
"SPEED: 2.5! ACTIVATION COMMAND:
"RENDEZVOUS!"
MY ARMOR WILL ARRIVE BEFORE I DO.
THEN AT LEAST LET ME TAKE YOU THERE! WHAT A TALE FOR MY CHILDREN!
IT WOULD BE QUICKER THAN WAITING FOR A MILITARY CAR.
ALL RIGHT, THEN! YOUR PATRIOTISM WILL NOT BE FORGOTTEN.
PLEASE, COMMANDER--
--GOOD DEEDS ARE THEIR OWN REWARD!

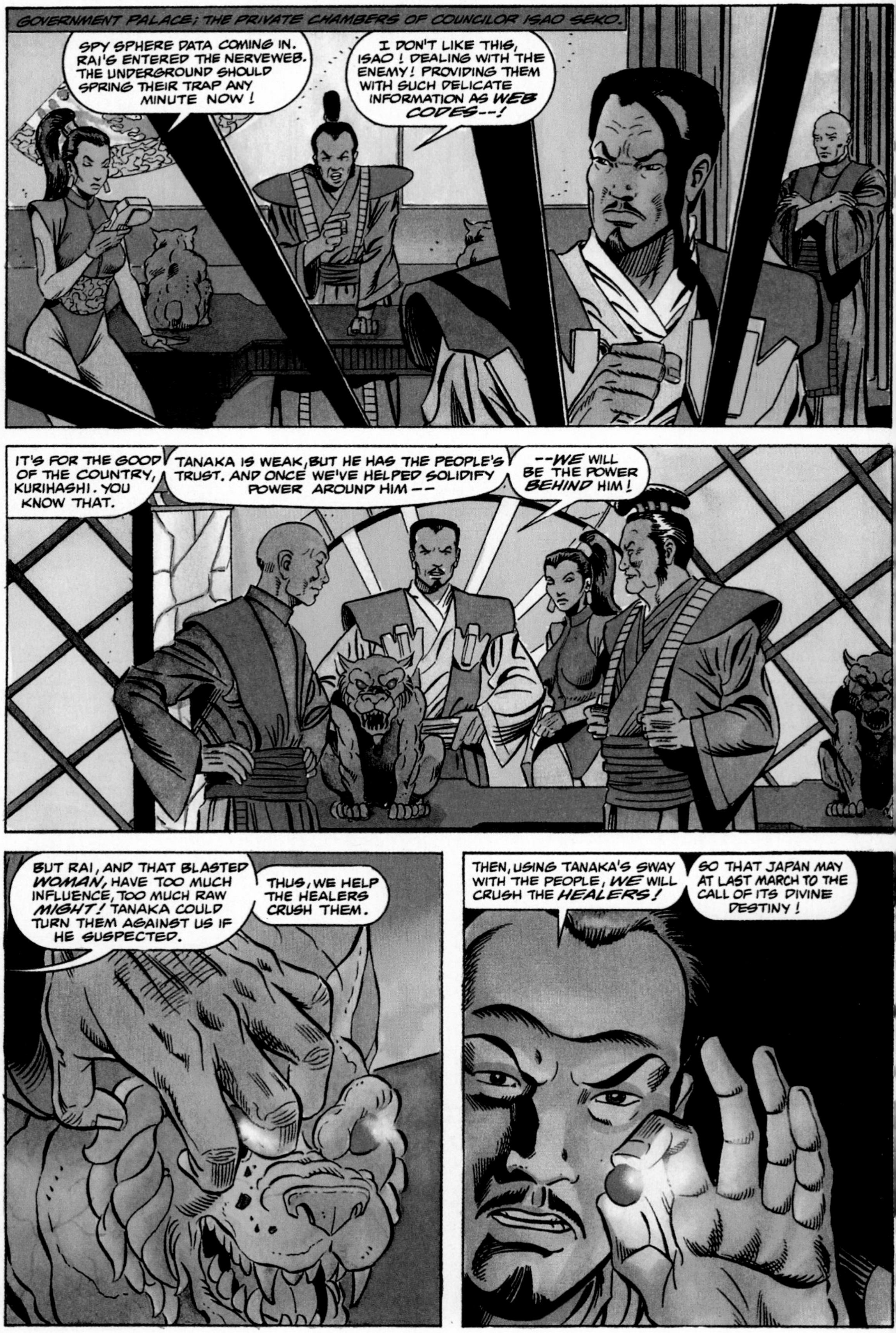
GOVERNMENT PALACE; THE PRIVATE CHAMBERS OF COUNCILOR ISAO SEKO.
SPY SPHERE DATA COMING IN. RAI'S ENTERED THE NERVEWEB. THE UNDERGROUND SHOULD SPRING THEIR TRAP ANY MINUTE NOW!
I DON'T LIKE THIS, ISAO! DEALING WITH THE ENEMY! PROVIDING THEM WITH SUCH DELICATE INFORMATION AS WEB CODES--!
IT'S FOR THE GOOD OF THE COUNTRY, KURIHASHI. YOU KNOW THAT.
TANAKA IS WEAK, BUT HE HAS THE PEOPLE'S TRUST. AND ONCE WE'VE HELPED SOLIDIFY POWER AROUND HIM --
--WE WILL BE THE POWER BEHIND HIM!
BUT RAI, AND THAT BLASTED WOMAN, HAVE TOO MUCH INFLUENCE, TOO MUCH RAW MIGHT! TANAKA COULD TURN THEM AGAINST US IF HE SUSPECTED.
THUS, WE HELP THE HEALERS CRUSH THEM.
THEN, USING TANAKA'S SWAY WITH THE PEOPLE, WE WILL CRUSH THE HEALERS!
SO THAT JAPAN MAY AT LAST MARCH TO THE CALL OF ITS DIVINE DESTINY!

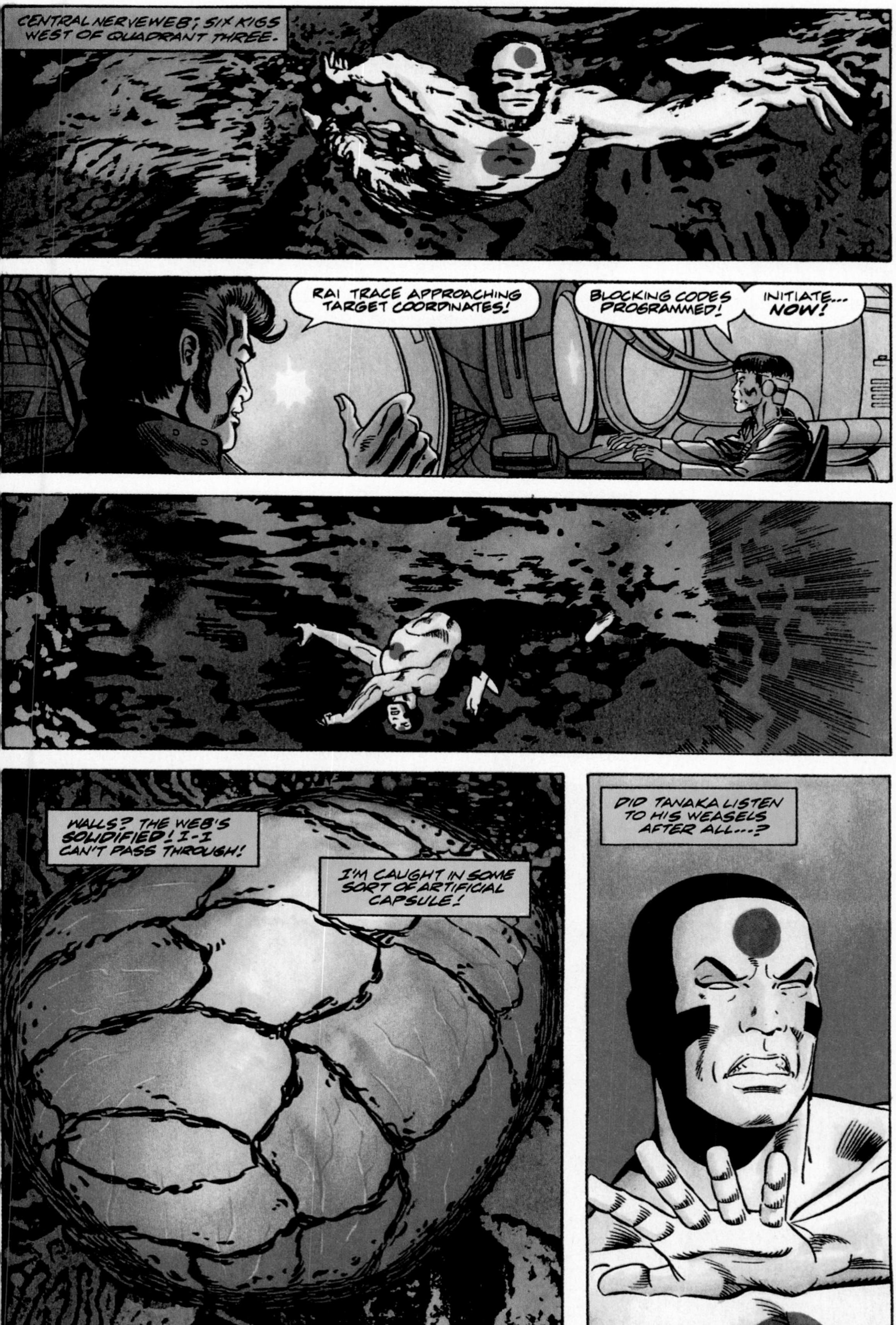
CENTRAL NERVEWEB; SIX KIGS WEST OF QUADRANT THREE.
RAI TRACE APPROACHING TARGET COORDINATES!
BLOCKING CODES PROGRAMMED!
INITIATE... NOW!
WALLS? THE WEB'S SOLIDIFIED! I-I CAN'T PASS THROUGH!
I'M CAUGHT IN SOME SORT OF ARTIFICIAL CAPSULE!
DID TANAKA LISTEN TO HIS WEASELS AFTER ALL...?

DON'T YOU FEEL VULNERABLE WITHOUT YOUR FAMOUS ARMOR, COMMANDER? I'VE HEARD YOU HAVE ENEMIES.

I CAN TAKE CARE OF MYSELF.

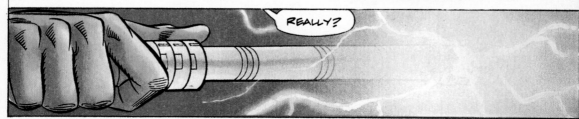

REALLY?

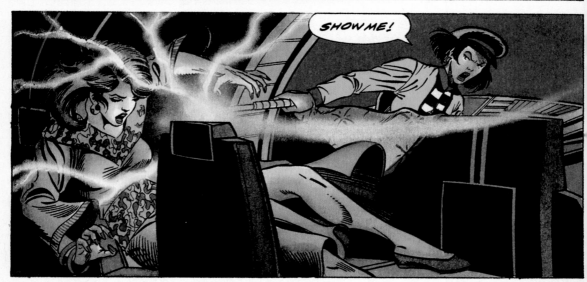

SHOW ME!

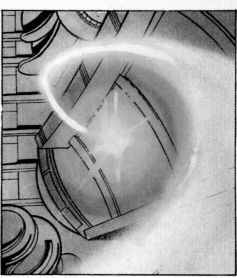

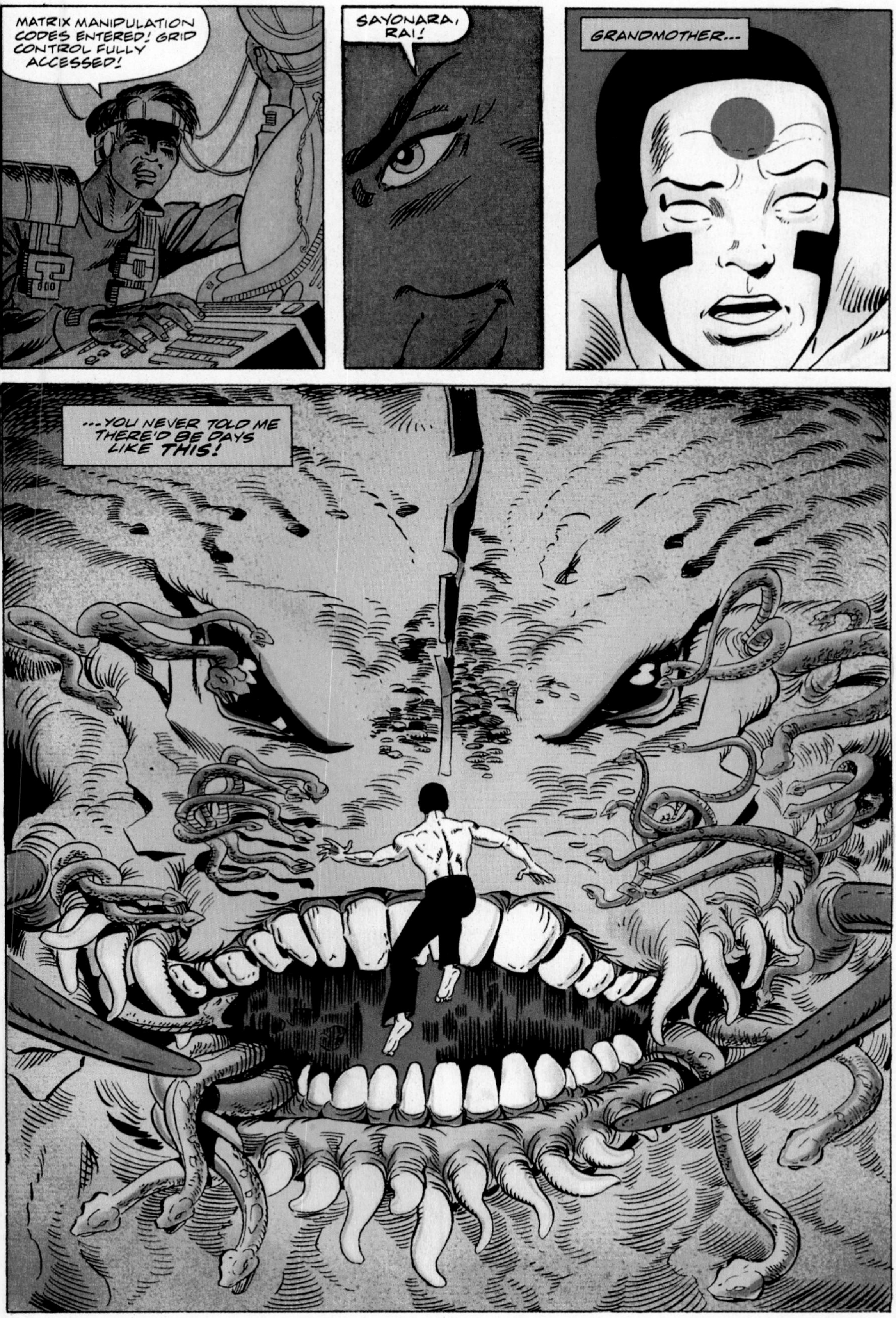
MATRIX MANIPULATION CODES ENTERED! GRID CONTROL FULLY ACCESSED!
SAYONARA, RAI!
GRANDMOTHER...
...YOU NEVER TOLD ME THERE'D BE DAYS LIKE THIS!

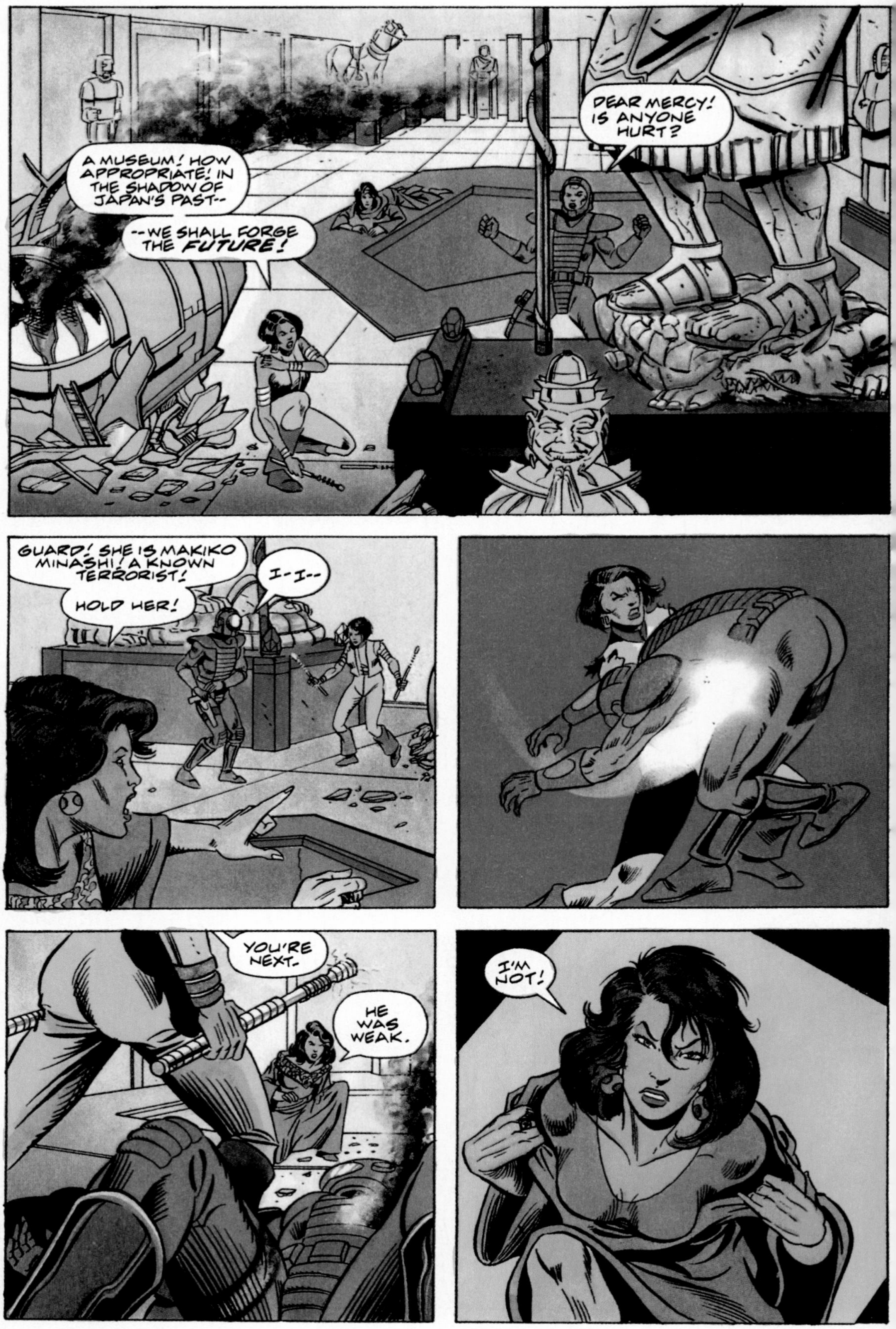
A MUSEUM! HOW APPROPRIATE! IN THE SHADOW OF JAPAN'S PAST--
--WE SHALL FORGE THE *FUTURE!*
DEAR MERCY! IS ANYONE HURT?
GUARD! SHE IS MAKIKO MINASHI! A KNOWN TERRORIST!
HOLD HER!
I--I--
YOU'RE NEXT.
HE WAS WEAK.
I'M NOT!

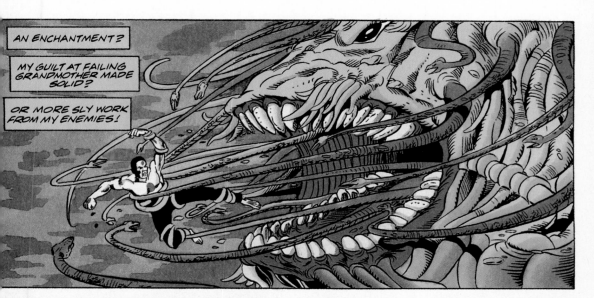

AN ENCHANTMENT?

MY GUILT AT FAILING GRANDMOTHER MADE SOLID?

OR MORE SLY WORK FROM MY ENEMIES!

WHATEVER THE CAUSE, I'M STILL RAI!

WITH ENERGY PASSED DOWN TO ME THROUGH FORTY GENERATIONS!

ENERGY TO HOLD!

TO FORM!

TO USE!

THE SERPENTS GROW BACK! MULTIPLY!

THE DRAGON HAS ITS OWN ENERGY SOURCE, ONE THAT MAY DWARF EVEN MINE!

THE NERVEWEB OF JAPAN!

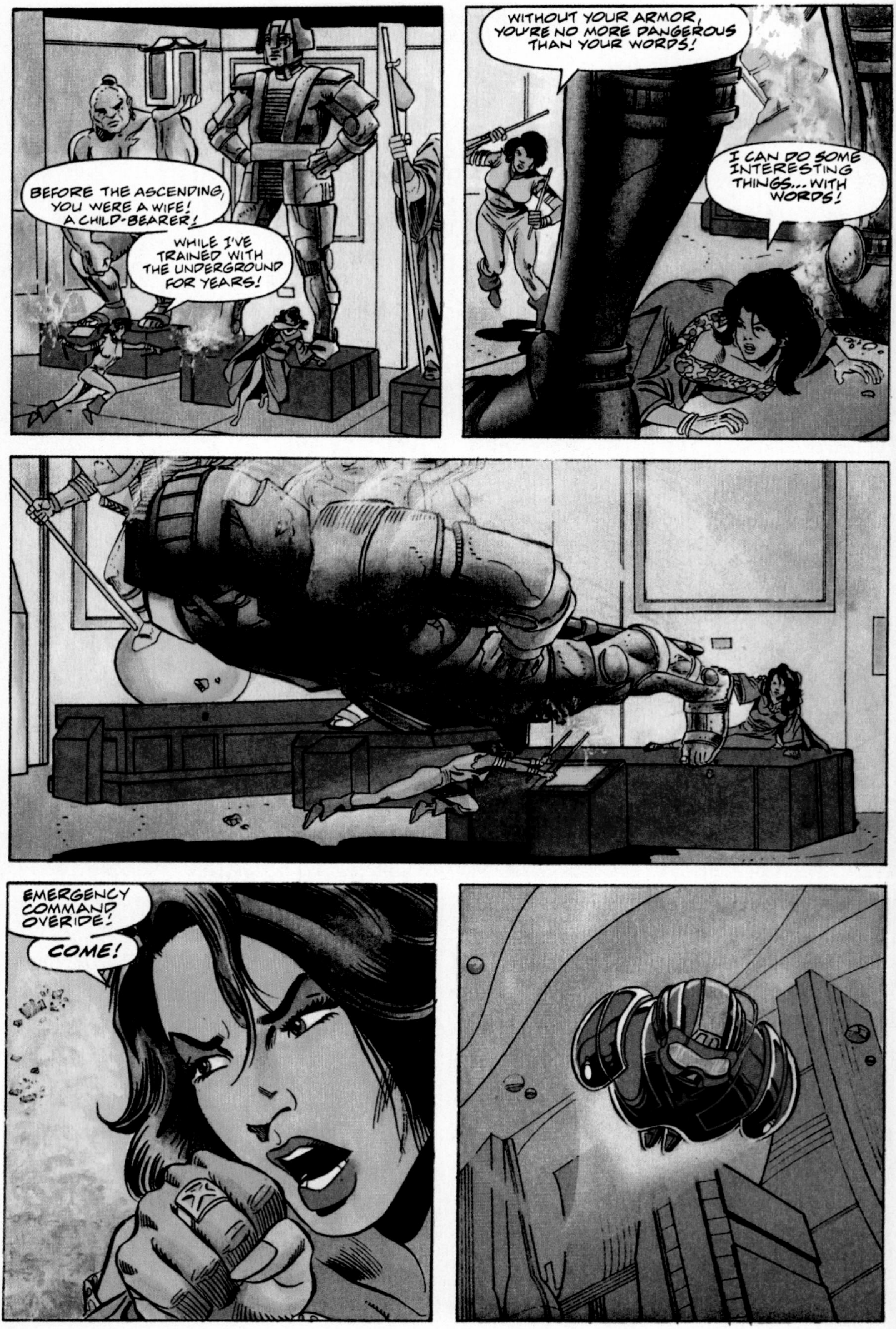
BEFORE THE ASCENDING, YOU WERE A WIFE! A CHILD-BEARER!
WHILE I'VE TRAINED WITH THE UNDERGROUND FOR YEARS!
WITHOUT YOUR ARMOR, YOU'RE NO MORE DANGEROUS THAN YOUR WORDS!
I CAN DO SOME INTERESTING THINGS... WITH WORDS!
EMERGENCY COMMAND OVERIDE!
COME!

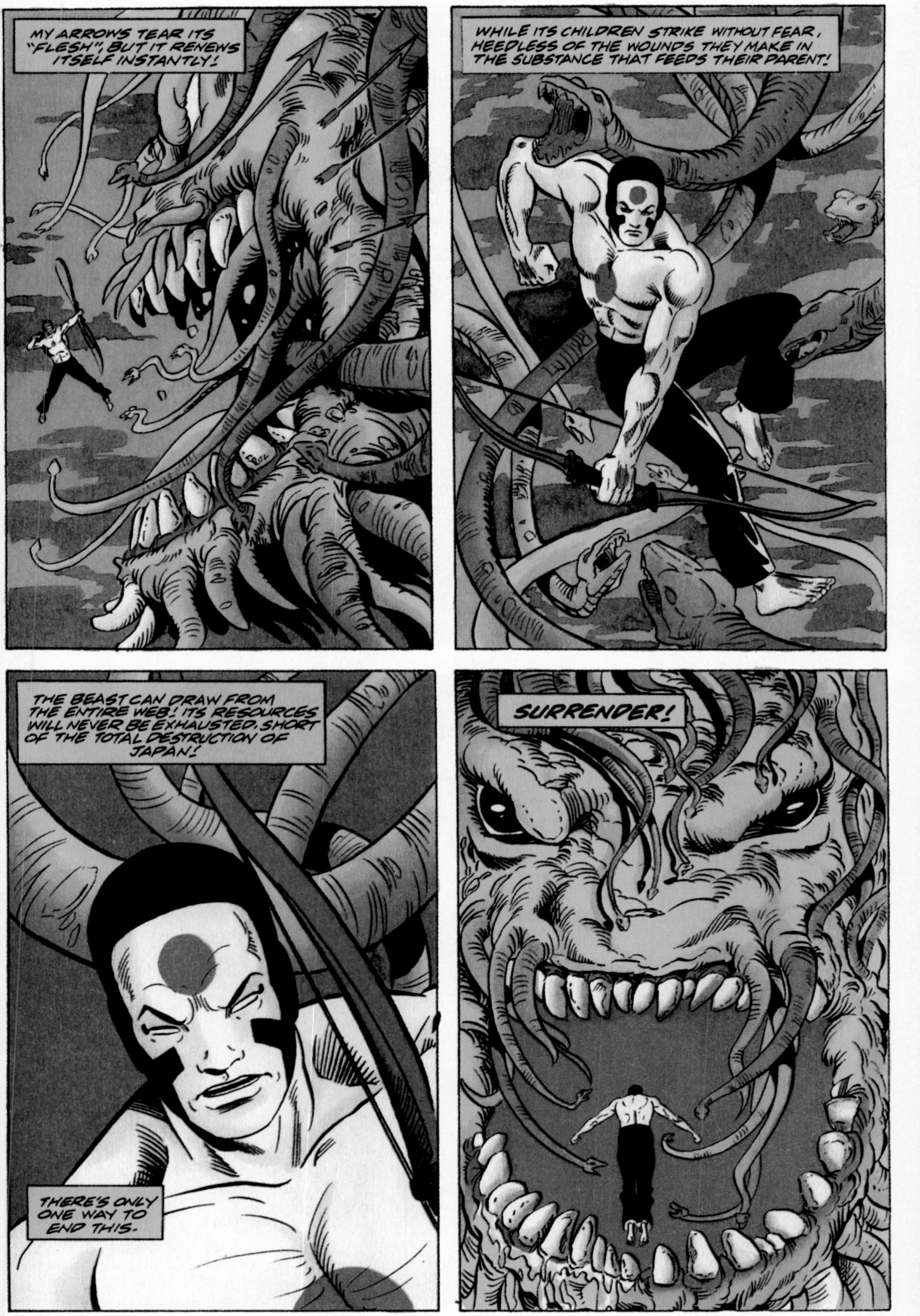
MY ARROWS TEAR ITS "FLESH", BUT IT RENEWS ITSELF INSTANTLY!
WHILE ITS CHILDREN STRIKE WITHOUT FEAR, HEEDLESS OF THE WOUNDS THEY MAKE IN THE SUBSTANCE THAT FEEDS THEIR PARENT!
THE BEAST CAN DRAW FROM THE ENTIRE WEB! ITS RESOURCES WILL NEVER BE EXHAUSTED, SHORT OF THE TOTAL DESTRUCTION OF JAPAN!
THERE'S ONLY ONE WAY TO END THIS.
SURRENDER!

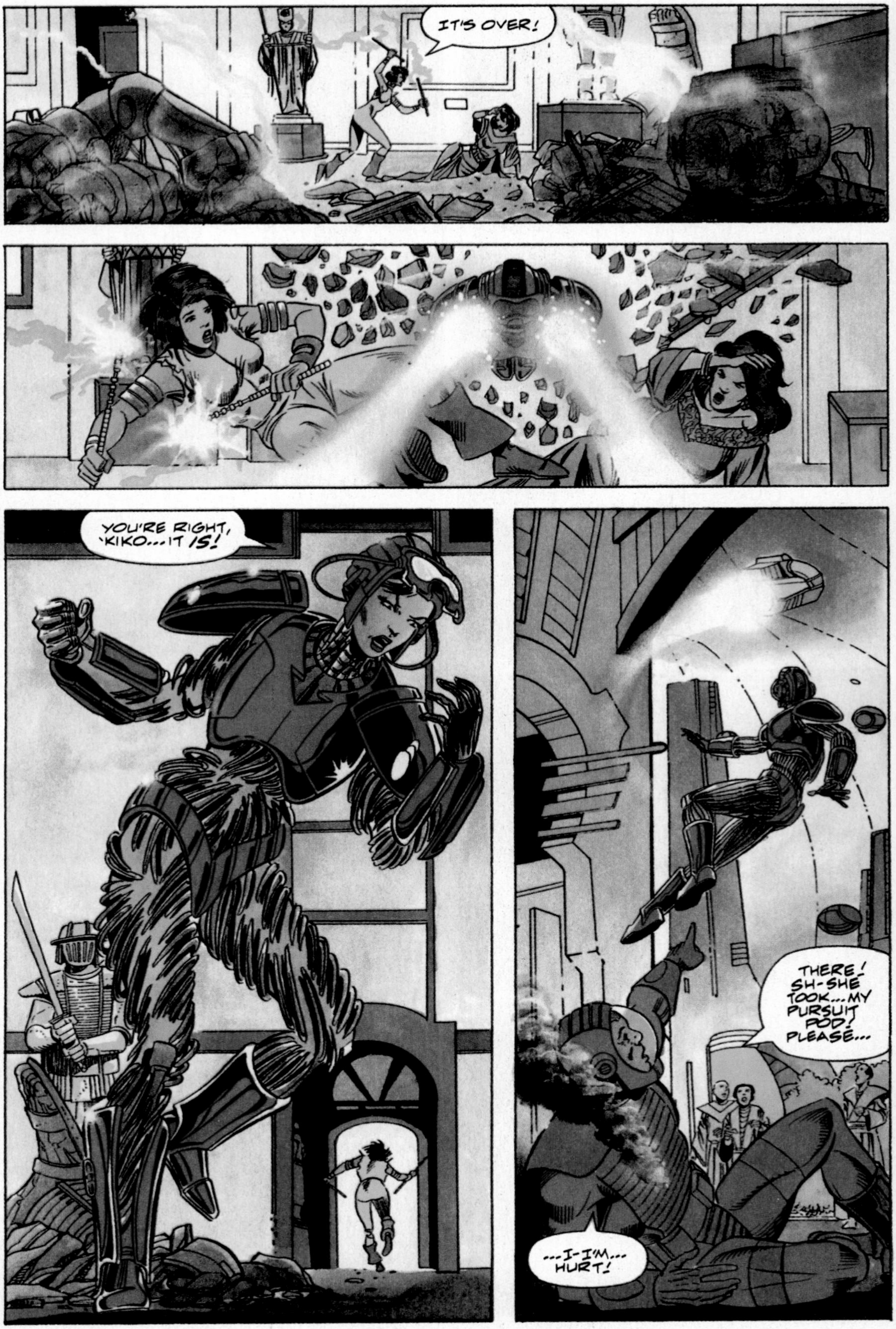
IT'S OVER!
YOU'RE RIGHT, 'KIKO...IT IS!
THERE! SH-SHE TOOK...MY PURSUIT POD! PLEASE...
...I-I'M... HURT!

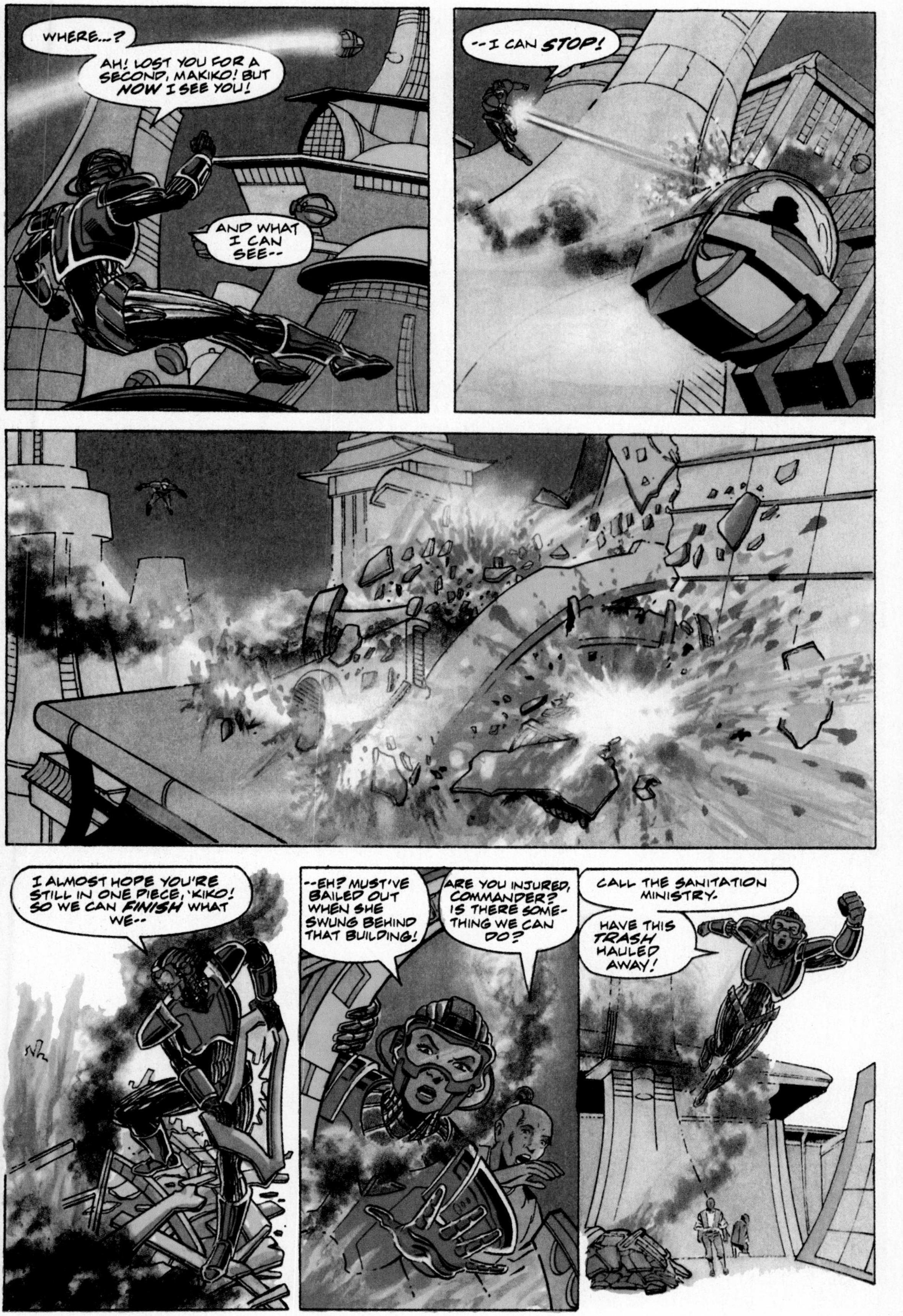
WHERE...?
AH! LOST YOU FOR A SECOND, MAKIKO! BUT NOW I SEE YOU!
AND WHAT I CAN SEE--
--I CAN STOP!
I ALMOST HOPE YOU'RE STILL IN ONE PIECE, 'KIKO! SO WE CAN FINISH WHAT WE--
--EH? MUST'VE BAILED OUT WHEN SHE SWUNG BEHIND THAT BUILDING!
ARE YOU INJURED, COMMANDER? IS THERE SOMETHING WE CAN DO?
CALL THE SANITATION MINISTRY.
HAVE THIS TRASH HAULED AWAY!

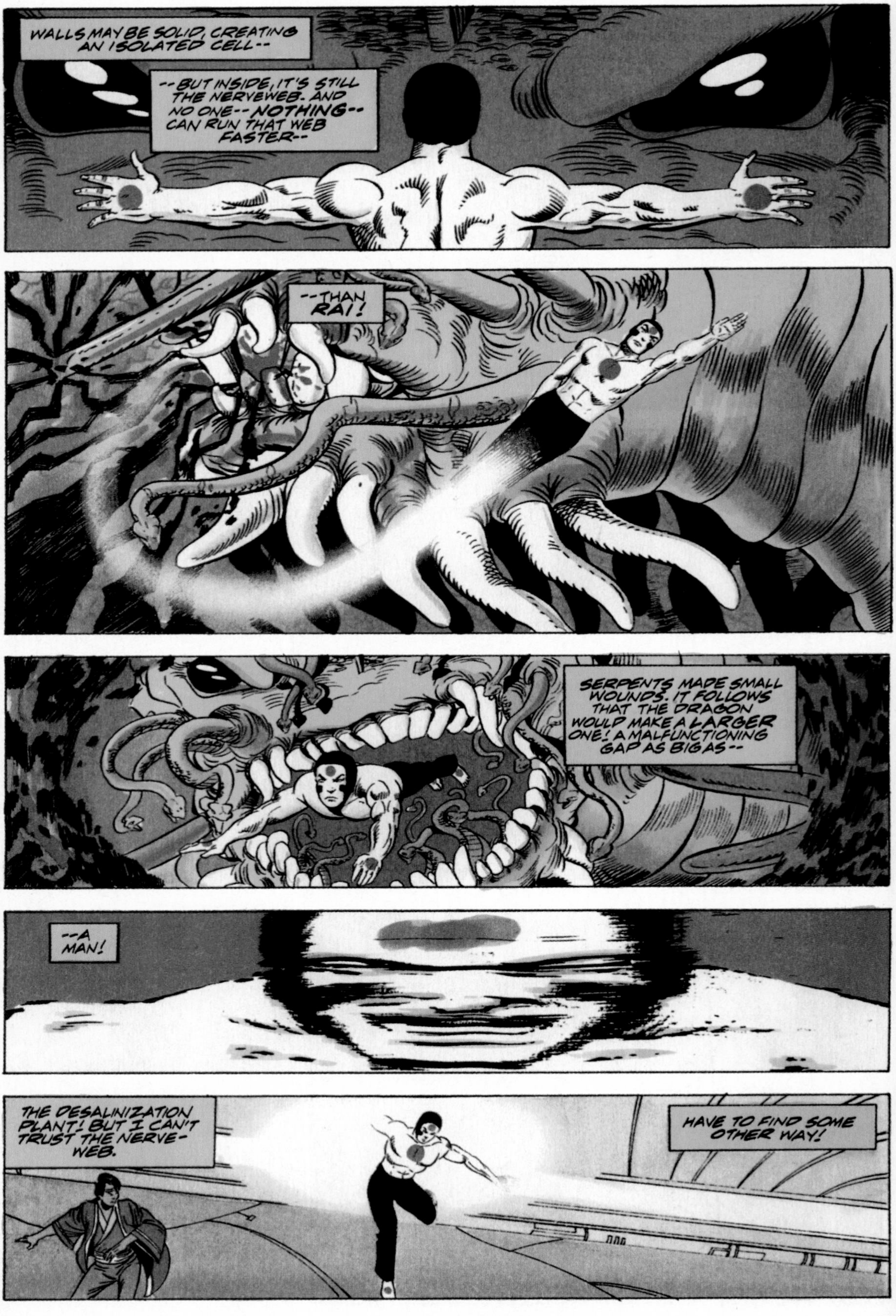
WALLS MAY BE SOLID, CREATING AN ISOLATED CELL--
--BUT INSIDE, IT'S STILL THE NERVEWEB. AND NO ONE--NOTHING--CAN RUN THAT WEB FASTER--
--THAN RAI!
SERPENTS MADE SMALL WOUNDS. IT FOLLOWS THAT THE DRAGON WOULD MAKE A LARGER ONE! A MALFUNCTIONING GAP AS BIG AS--
--A MAN!
THE DESALINIZATION PLANT! BUT I CAN'T TRUST THE NERVE-WEB.
HAVE TO FIND SOME OTHER WAY!

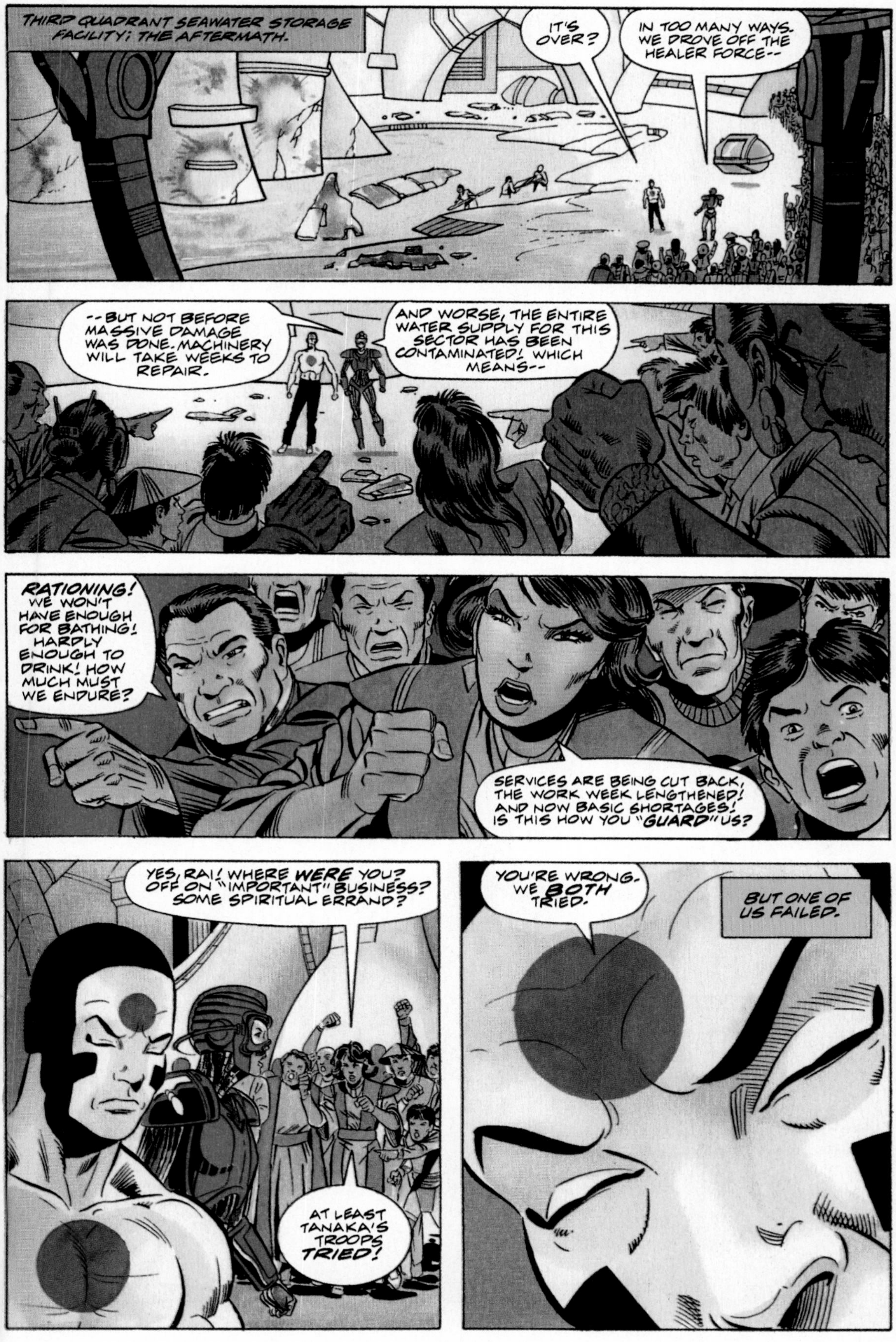
THIRD QUADRANT SEAWATER STORAGE FACILITY; THE AFTERMATH.
IT'S OVER?
IN TOO MANY WAYS. WE DROVE OFF THE HEALER FORCE--
--BUT NOT BEFORE MASSIVE DAMAGE WAS DONE. MACHINERY WILL TAKE WEEKS TO REPAIR.
AND WORSE, THE ENTIRE WATER SUPPLY FOR THIS SECTOR HAS BEEN CONTAMINATED! WHICH MEANS--
RATIONING! WE WON'T HAVE ENOUGH FOR BATHING! HARDLY ENOUGH TO DRINK! HOW MUCH MUST WE ENDURE?
SERVICES ARE BEING CUT BACK, THE WORK WEEK LENGTHENED! AND NOW BASIC SHORTAGES! IS THIS HOW YOU "GUARD" US?
YES, RAI! WHERE WERE YOU? OFF ON "IMPORTANT" BUSINESS? SOME SPIRITUAL ERRAND?
AT LEAST TANAKA'S TROOPS TRIED!
YOU'RE WRONG. WE BOTH TRIED.
BUT ONE OF US FAILED.

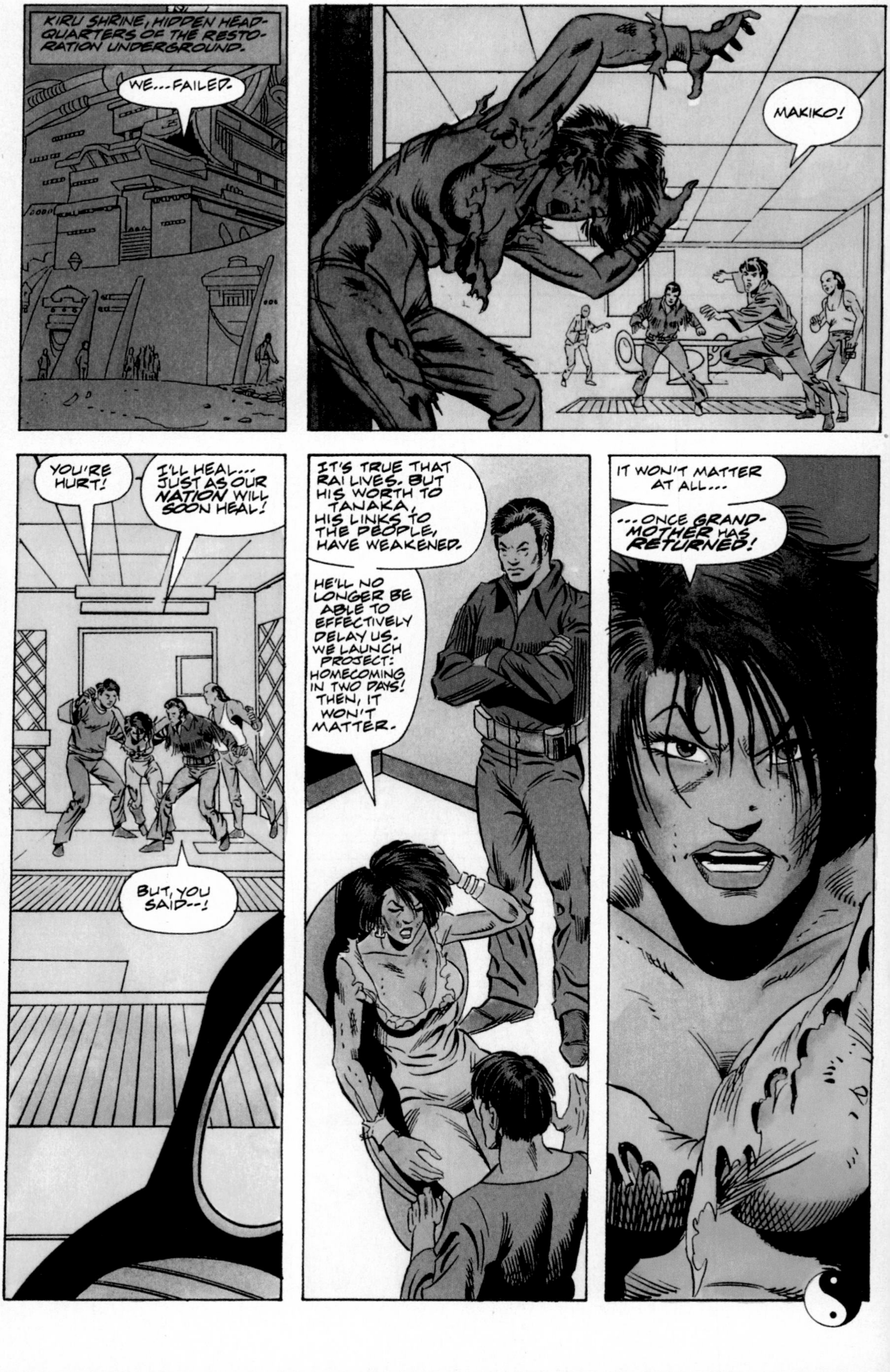
KIRU SHRINE, HIDDEN HEAD-QUARTERS OF THE RESTO-RATION UNDERGROUND.
WE...FAILED.
MAKIKO!
YOU'RE HURT!
I'LL HEAL... JUST AS OUR NATION WILL SOON HEAL!
BUT, YOU SAID--!
IT'S TRUE THAT RAI LIVES. BUT HIS WORTH TO TANAKA, HIS LINKS TO THE PEOPLE, HAVE WEAKENED.
HE'LL NO LONGER BE ABLE TO EFFECTIVELY DELAY US. WE LAUNCH PROJECT: HOMECOMING IN TWO DAYS! THEN, IT WON'T MATTER.
IT WON'T MATTER AT ALL...
...ONCE GRAND-MOTHER HAS RETURNED!

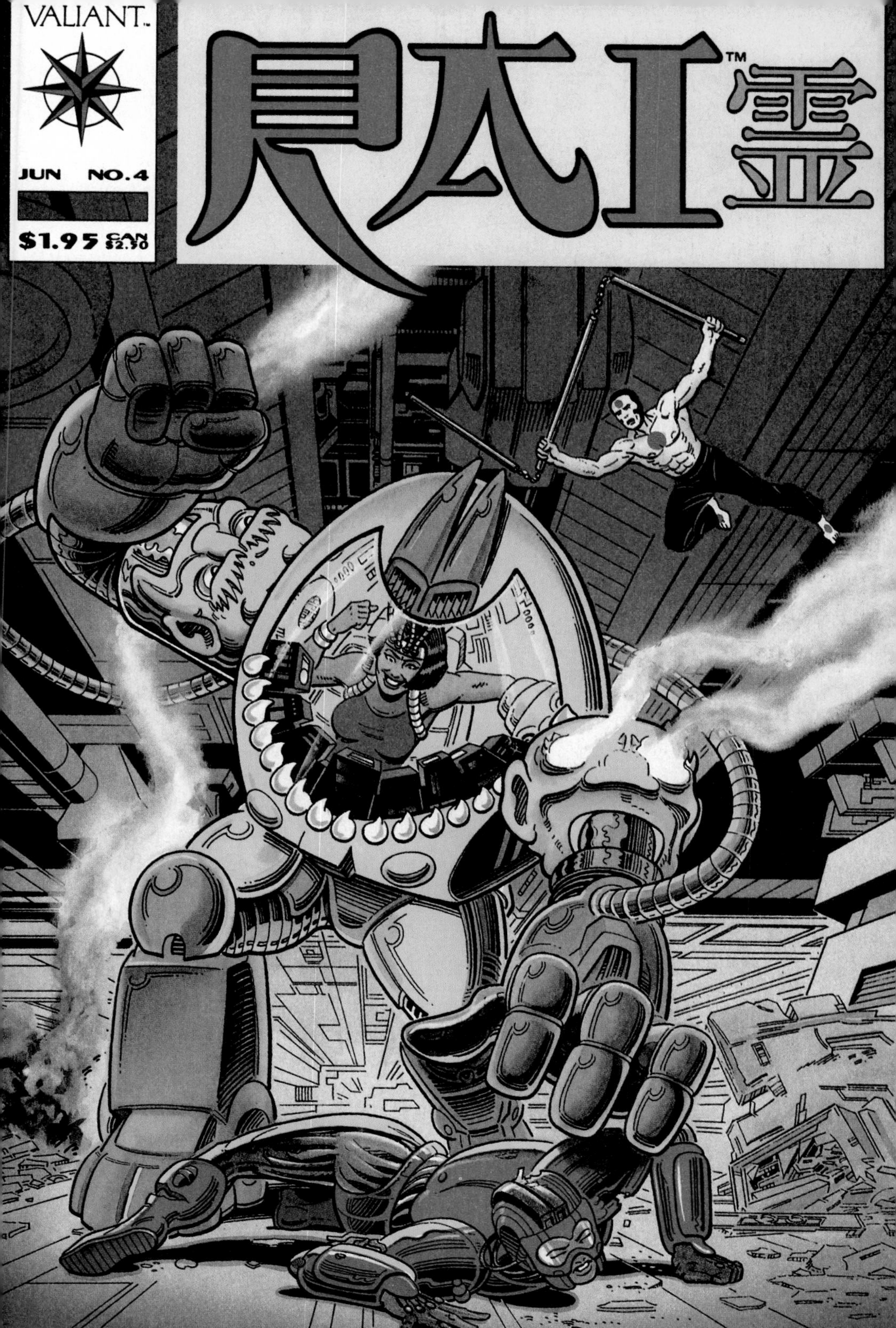
VALIANT™
RAI™ 霊
JUN NO.4
$1.95 CAN $2.50

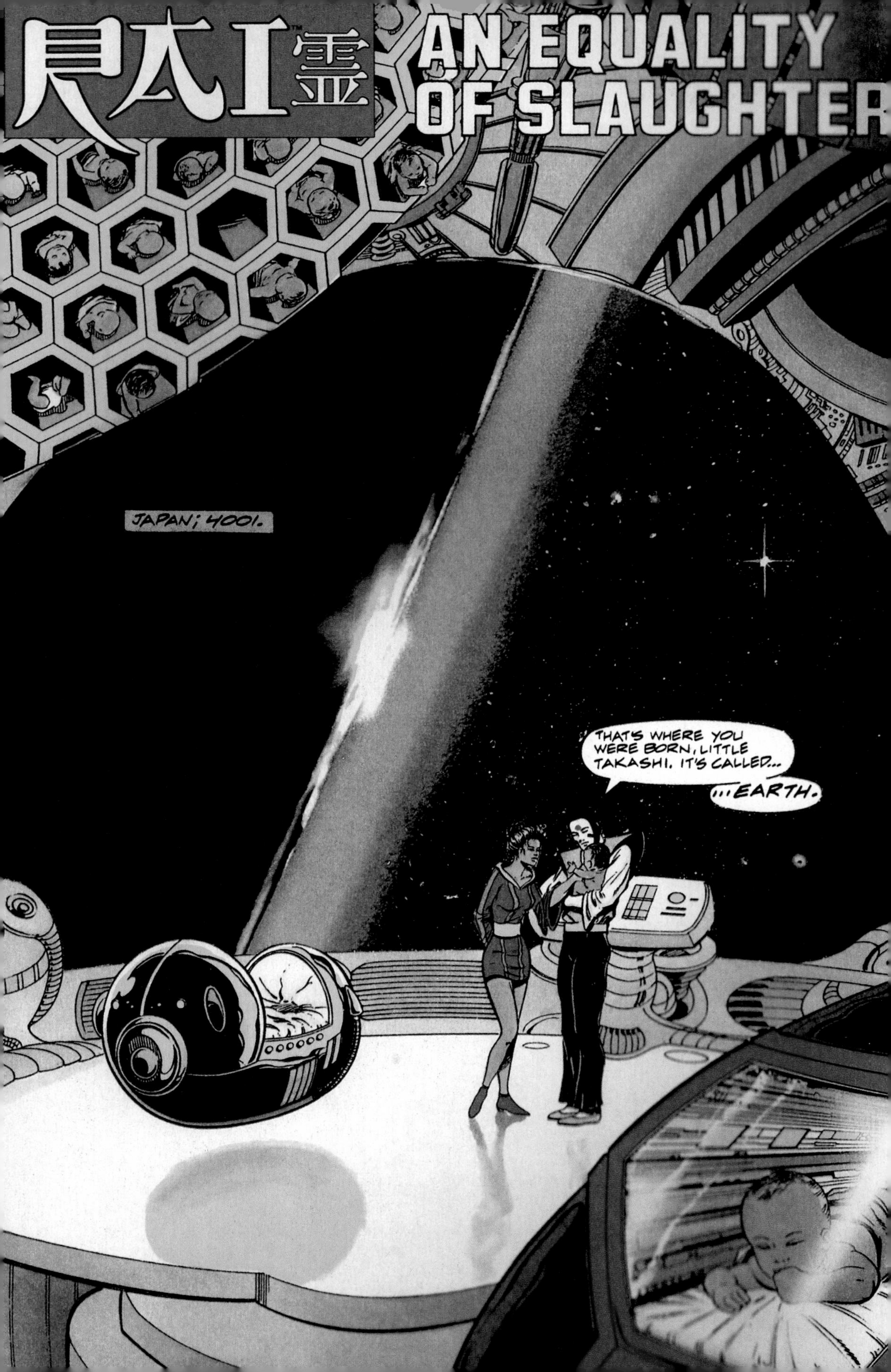

AN EQUALITY OF SLAUGHTER
JAPAN; 4001.
THAT'S WHERE YOU WERE BORN, LITTLE TAKASHI. IT'S CALLED...
...EARTH.

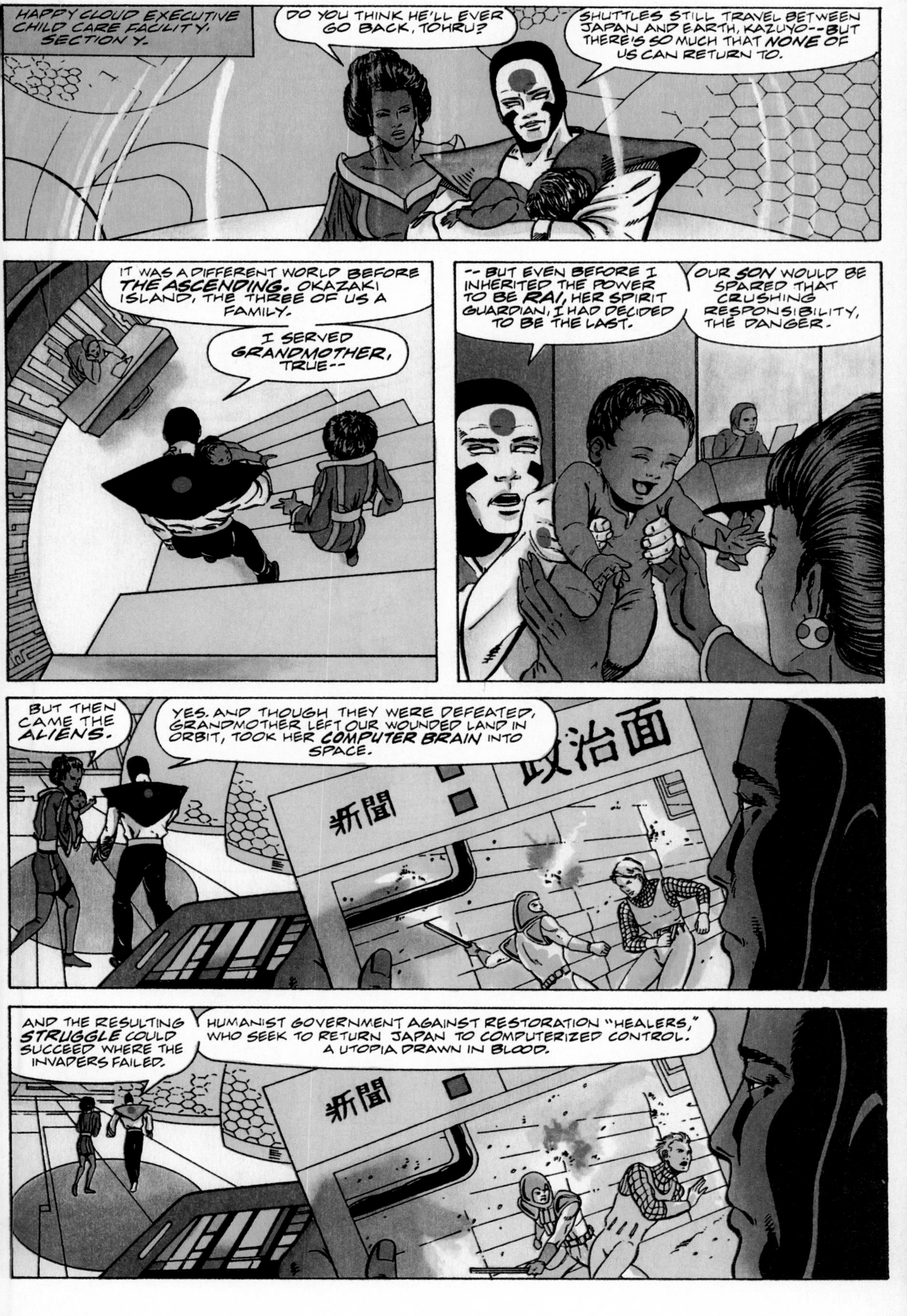
HAPPY CLOUD EXECUTIVE CHILD CARE FACILITY. SECTION Y.
DO YOU THINK HE'LL EVER GO BACK, TOHRU?
SHUTTLES STILL TRAVEL BETWEEN JAPAN AND EARTH, KAZUYO--BUT THERE'S SO MUCH THAT NONE OF US CAN RETURN TO.
IT WAS A DIFFERENT WORLD BEFORE THE ASCENDING. OKAZAKI ISLAND, THE THREE OF US A FAMILY.
I SERVED GRANDMOTHER, TRUE--
-- BUT EVEN BEFORE I INHERITED THE POWER TO BE RAI, HER SPIRIT GUARDIAN, I HAD DECIDED TO BE THE LAST.
OUR SON WOULD BE SPARED THAT CRUSHING RESPONSIBILITY, THE DANGER.
BUT THEN CAME THE ALIENS.
YES. AND THOUGH THEY WERE DEFEATED, GRANDMOTHER LEFT OUR WOUNDED LAND IN ORBIT, TOOK HER COMPUTER BRAIN INTO SPACE.
政治面
新聞
AND THE RESULTING STRUGGLE COULD SUCCEED WHERE THE INVADERS FAILED.
HUMANIST GOVERNMENT AGAINST RESTORATION "HEALERS," WHO SEEK TO RETURN JAPAN TO COMPUTERIZED CONTROL. A UTOPIA DRAWN IN BLOOD.
新聞

AT LEAST WE FIGHT ON THE SAME SIDE NOW. THE WAR HASN'T TORN APART OUR FAMILY.

NO? ON EARTH, YOU WORRIED THAT MY OBLIGATIONS COULD PREVENT ME BEING THERE FOR TAKASHI.

BUT HERE, AS PRESIDENT TANAKA'S RIGHT HAND, YOUR DUTIES KEEP YOU FROM THE NURSERY FOR DAYS. PERHAPS, KAZUYO...

...YOU SHOULD BE RAI.

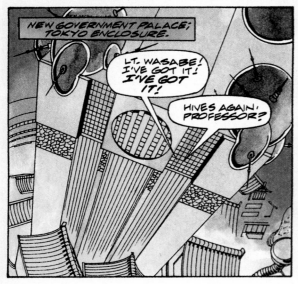

NEW GOVERNMENT PALACE; TOKYO ENCLOSURE.

LT. WASABE! I'VE GOT IT! I'VE GOT IT!

HIVES AGAIN, PROFESSOR?

NO, NO! THE KEY! I'VE BROKEN THE CYBER-CODE THAT HEALERS USE!

NOW WE CAN MAKE SENSE OF THE CIRCUIT-BABBLE WE'VE BEEN INTERCEPTING!

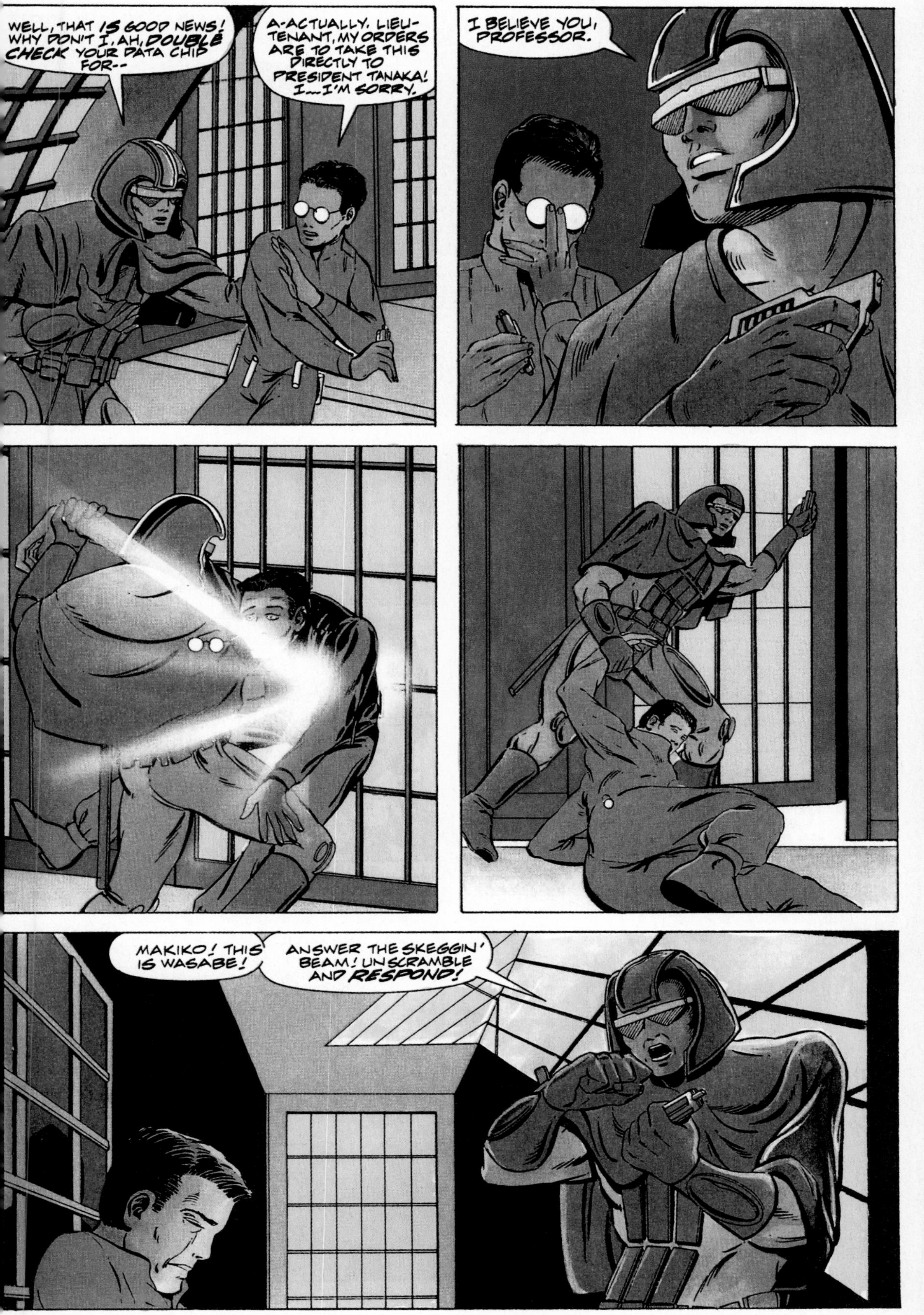
WELL, THAT IS GOOD NEWS! WHY DON'T I, AH, DOUBLE CHECK YOUR DATA CHIP FOR--
A-ACTUALLY, LIEUTENANT, MY ORDERS ARE TO TAKE THIS DIRECTLY TO PRESIDENT TANAKA! I... I'M SORRY.
I BELIEVE YOU, PROFESSOR.
MAKIKO! THIS IS WASABE!
ANSWER THE SKEGGIN' BEAM! UNSCRAMBLE AND RESPOND!

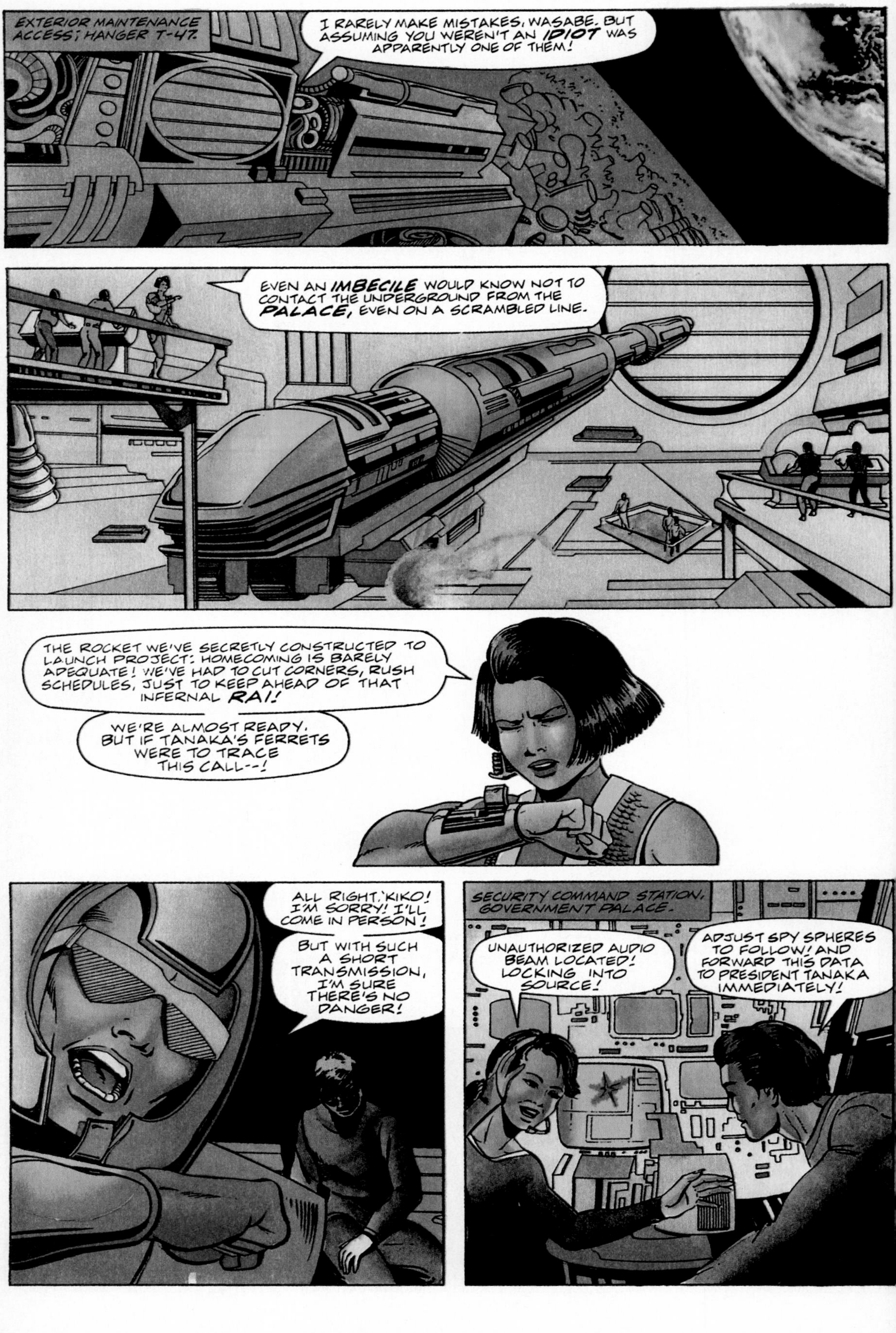
EXTERIOR MAINTENANCE ACCESS; HANGER T-47.
I RARELY MAKE MISTAKES, WASABE. BUT ASSUMING YOU WEREN'T AN IDIOT WAS APPARENTLY ONE OF THEM!
EVEN AN IMBECILE WOULD KNOW NOT TO CONTACT THE UNDERGROUND FROM THE PALACE, EVEN ON A SCRAMBLED LINE.
THE ROCKET WE'VE SECRETLY CONSTRUCTED TO LAUNCH PROJECT: HOMECOMING IS BARELY ADEQUATE! WE'VE HAD TO CUT CORNERS, RUSH SCHEDULES, JUST TO KEEP AHEAD OF THAT INFERNAL RAI!
WE'RE ALMOST READY. BUT IF TANAKA'S FERRETS WERE TO TRACE THIS CALL--!
ALL RIGHT, KIKO! I'M SORRY! I'LL COME IN PERSON!
BUT WITH SUCH A SHORT TRANSMISSION, I'M SURE THERE'S NO DANGER!
SECURITY COMMAND STATION, GOVERNMENT PALACE.
UNAUTHORIZED AUDIO BEAM LOCATED! LOCKING INTO SOURCE!
ADJUST SPY SPHERES TO FOLLOW! AND FORWARD THIS DATA TO PRESIDENT TANAKA IMMEDIATELY!

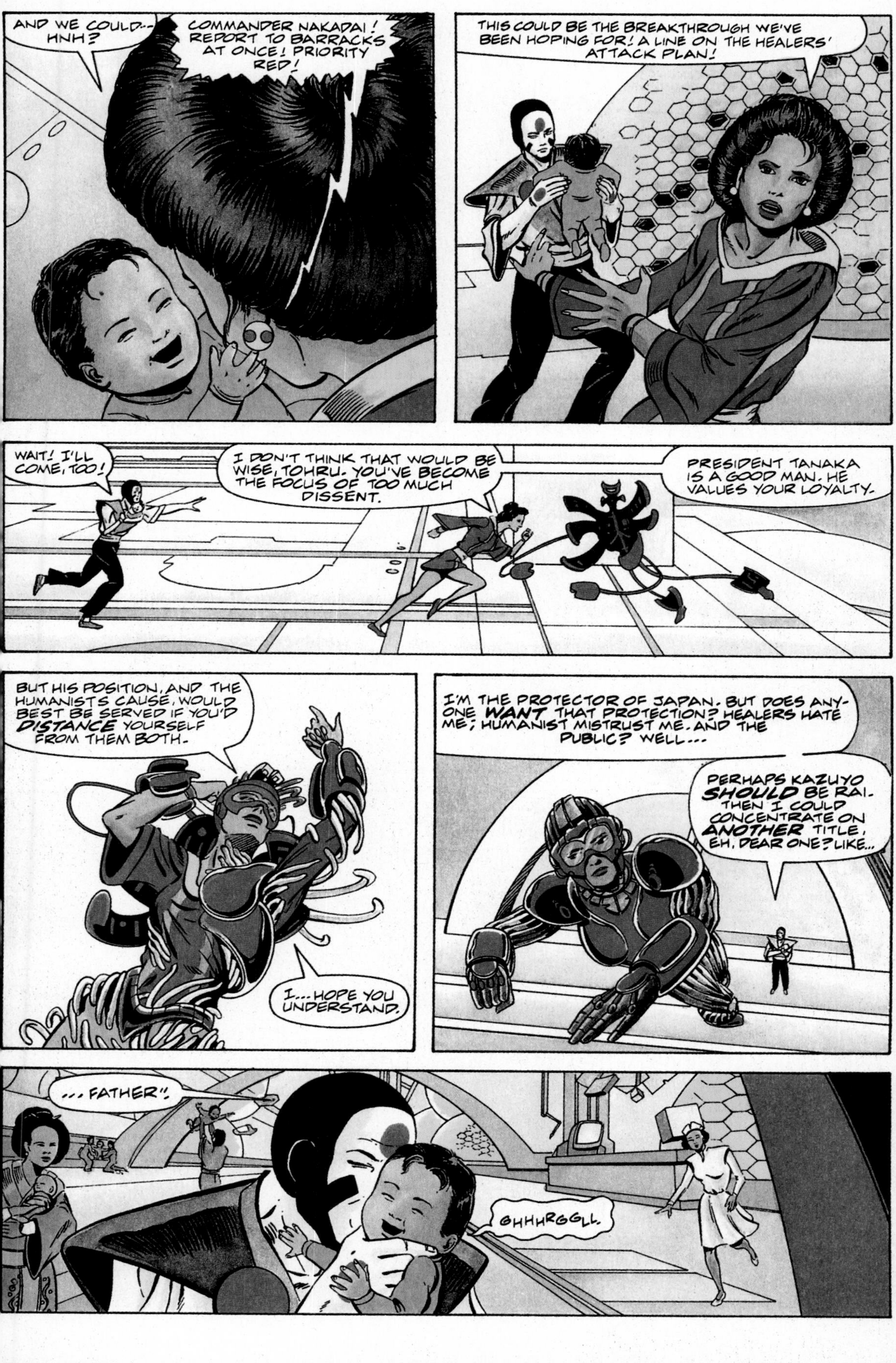
AND WE COULD-- HNH?
COMMANDER NAKADAI! REPORT TO BARRACKS AT ONCE! PRIORITY RED!
THIS COULD BE THE BREAKTHROUGH WE'VE BEEN HOPING FOR! A LINE ON THE HEALERS' ATTACK PLAN!
WAIT! I'LL COME, TOO!
I DON'T THINK THAT WOULD BE WISE, TOHRU. YOU'VE BECOME THE FOCUS OF TOO MUCH DISSENT.
PRESIDENT TANAKA IS A GOOD MAN. HE VALUES YOUR LOYALTY.
BUT HIS POSITION, AND THE HUMANISTS CAUSE, WOULD BEST BE SERVED IF YOU'D DISTANCE YOURSELF FROM THEM BOTH.
I... HOPE YOU UNDERSTAND.
I'M THE PROTECTOR OF JAPAN. BUT DOES ANYONE WANT THAT PROTECTION? HEALERS HATE ME; HUMANIST MISTRUST ME. AND THE PUBLIC? WELL...
PERHAPS KAZUYO SHOULD BE RAI. THEN I COULD CONCENTRATE ON ANOTHER TITLE, EH, DEAR ONE? LIKE...
... FATHER"!
GHHHRGGLL.

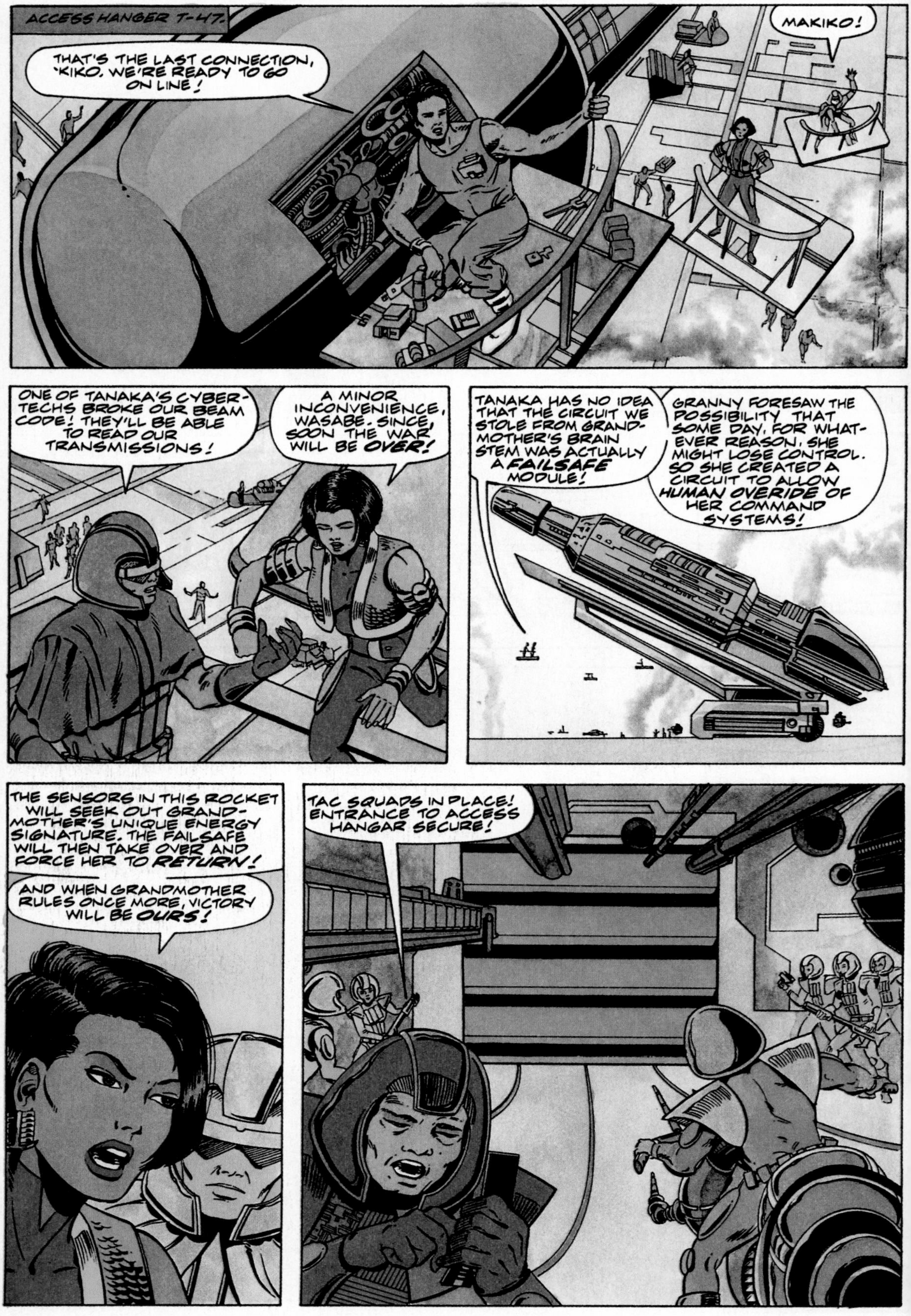
ACCESS HANGER T-47.
THAT'S THE LAST CONNECTION, 'KIKO. WE'RE READY TO GO ON LINE!
MAKIKO!
ONE OF TANAKA'S CYBER-TECHS BROKE OUR BEAM CODE! THEY'LL BE ABLE TO READ OUR TRANSMISSIONS!
A MINOR INCONVENIENCE, WASABE. SINCE, SOON THE WAR WILL BE OVER!
TANAKA HAS NO IDEA THAT THE CIRCUIT WE STOLE FROM GRAND-MOTHER'S BRAIN STEM WAS ACTUALLY A FAILSAFE MODULE!
GRANNY FORESAW THE POSSIBILITY THAT SOME DAY, FOR WHAT-EVER REASON, SHE MIGHT LOSE CONTROL. SO SHE CREATED A CIRCUIT TO ALLOW HUMAN OVERIDE OF HER COMMAND SYSTEMS!
THE SENSORS IN THIS ROCKET WILL SEEK OUT GRAND-MOTHER'S UNIQUE ENERGY SIGNATURE. THE FAILSAFE WILL THEN TAKE OVER AND FORCE HER TO RETURN!
AND WHEN GRANDMOTHER RULES ONCE MORE, VICTORY WILL BE OURS!
TAC SQUADS IN PLACE! ENTRANCE TO ACCESS HANGAR SECURE!

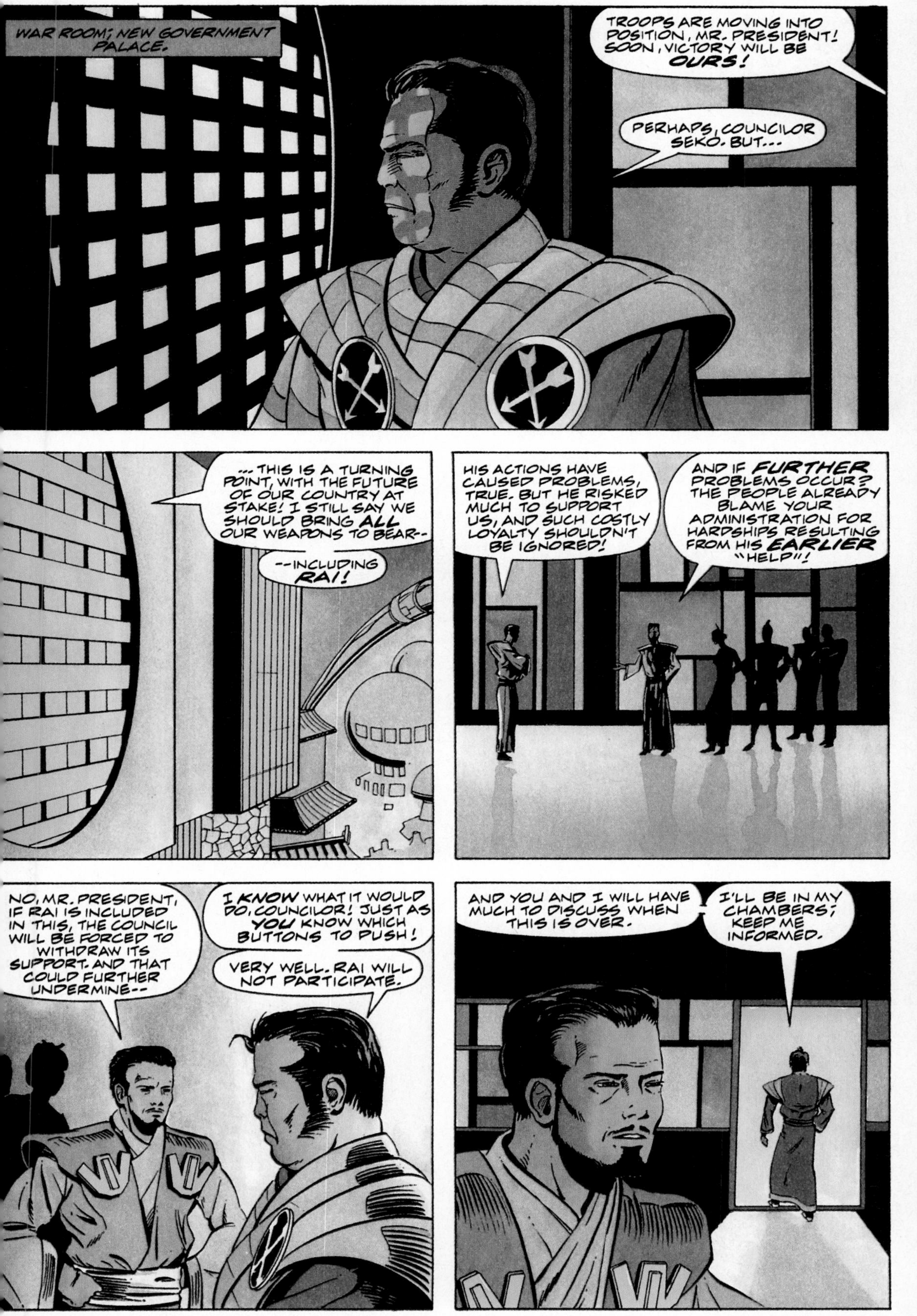
WAR ROOM; NEW GOVERNMENT PALACE.
TROOPS ARE MOVING INTO POSITION, MR. PRESIDENT! SOON, VICTORY WILL BE OURS!
PERHAPS, COUNCILOR SEKO. BUT...
...THIS IS A TURNING POINT, WITH THE FUTURE OF OUR COUNTRY AT STAKE! I STILL SAY WE SHOULD BRING ALL OUR WEAPONS TO BEAR--
--INCLUDING RAI!
HIS ACTIONS HAVE CAUSED PROBLEMS, TRUE. BUT HE RISKED MUCH TO SUPPORT US, AND SUCH COSTLY LOYALTY SHOULDN'T BE IGNORED!
AND IF FURTHER PROBLEMS OCCUR? THE PEOPLE ALREADY BLAME YOUR ADMINISTRATION FOR HARDSHIPS RESULTING FROM HIS EARLIER "HELP"!
NO, MR. PRESIDENT, IF RAI IS INCLUDED IN THIS, THE COUNCIL WILL BE FORCED TO WITHDRAW ITS SUPPORT. AND THAT COULD FURTHER UNDERMINE--
I KNOW WHAT IT WOULD DO, COUNCILOR! JUST AS YOU KNOW WHICH BUTTONS TO PUSH!
VERY WELL. RAI WILL NOT PARTICIPATE.
AND YOU AND I WILL HAVE MUCH TO DISCUSS WHEN THIS IS OVER.
I'LL BE IN MY CHAMBERS; KEEP ME INFORMED.

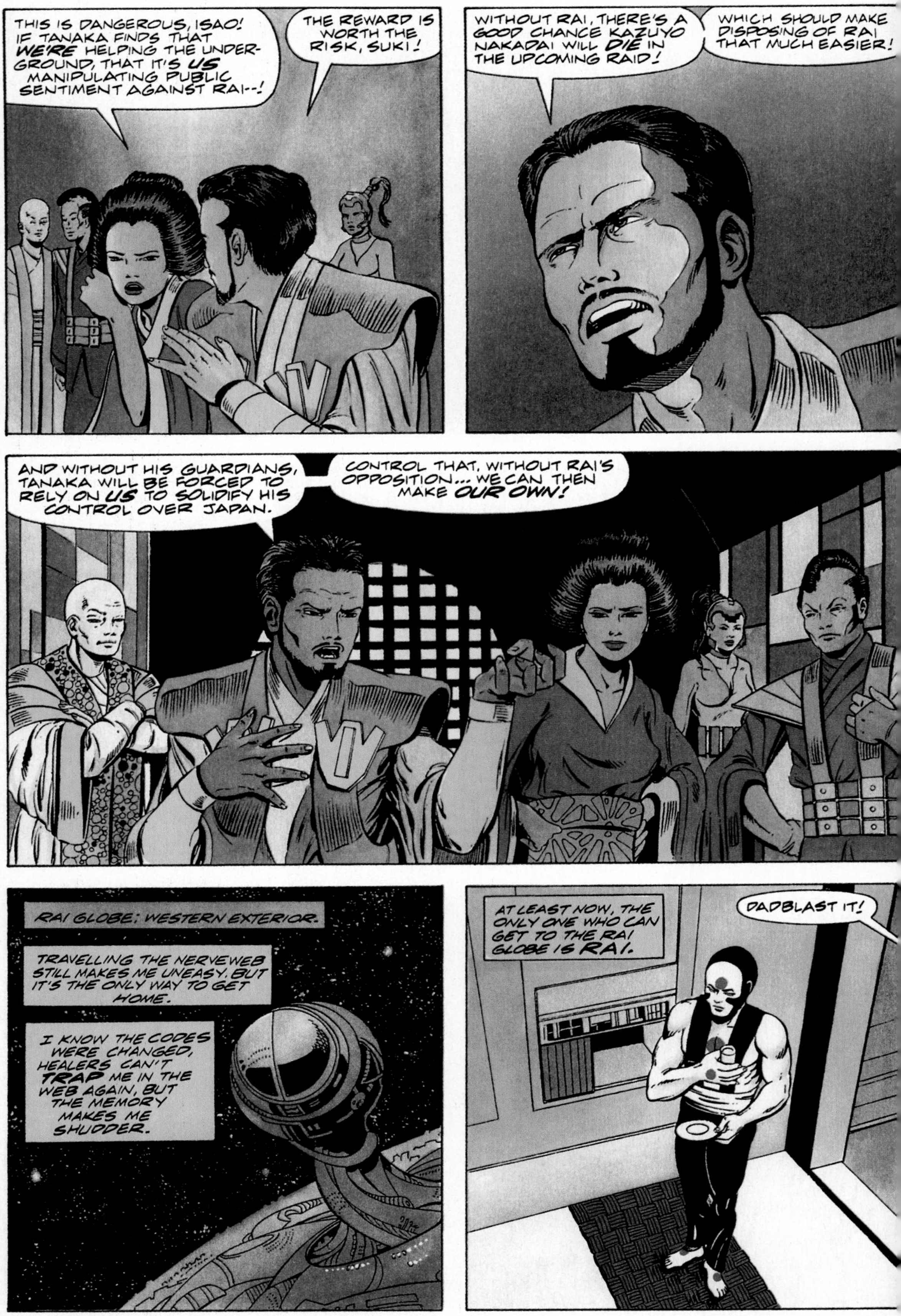
THIS IS DANGEROUS, ISAO! IF TANAKA FINDS THAT WE'RE HELPING THE UNDERGROUND, THAT IT'S US MANIPULATING PUBLIC SENTIMENT AGAINST RAI--!
THE REWARD IS WORTH THE RISK, SUKI!
WITHOUT RAI, THERE'S A GOOD CHANCE KAZUYO NAKADAI WILL DIE IN THE UPCOMING RAID!
WHICH SHOULD MAKE DISPOSING OF RAI THAT MUCH EASIER!
AND WITHOUT HIS GUARDIANS, TANAKA WILL BE FORCED TO RELY ON US TO SOLIDIFY HIS CONTROL OVER JAPAN.
CONTROL THAT, WITHOUT RAI'S OPPOSITION... WE CAN THEN MAKE OUR OWN!
RAI GLOBE: WESTERN EXTERIOR.
TRAVELLING THE NERVEWEB STILL MAKES ME UNEASY. BUT IT'S THE ONLY WAY TO GET HOME.
I KNOW THE CODES WERE CHANGED, HEALERS CAN'T TRAP ME IN THE WEB AGAIN, BUT THE MEMORY MAKES ME SHUDDER.
AT LEAST NOW, THE ONLY ONE WHO CAN GET TO THE RAI GLOBE IS RAI.
DADBLAST IT!

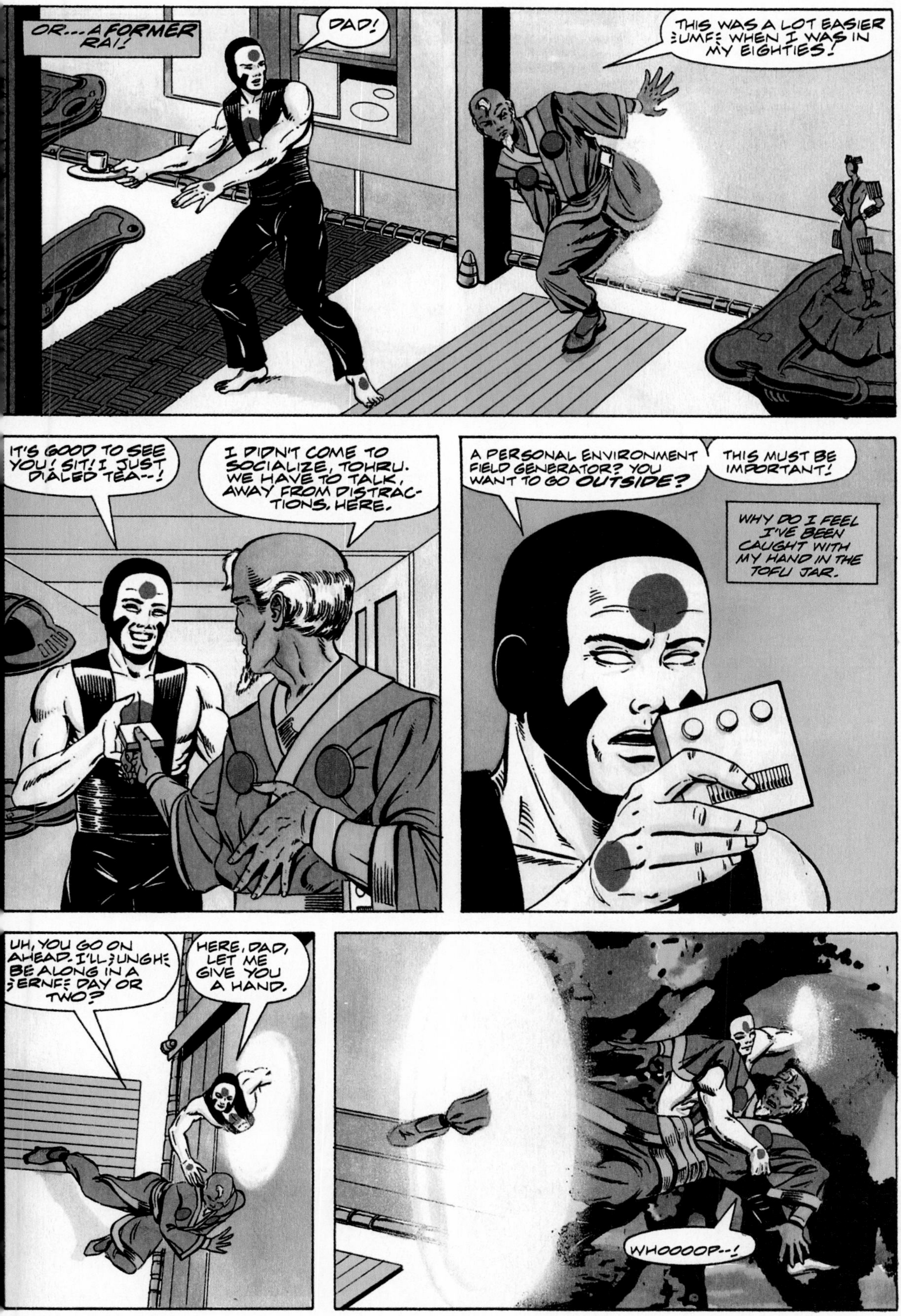
OR...A FORMER RAI!
DAD!
THIS WAS A LOT EASIER :UMF: WHEN I WAS IN MY EIGHTIES!
IT'S GOOD TO SEE YOU! SIT! I JUST DIALED TEA--!
I DIDN'T COME TO SOCIALIZE, TOHRU. WE HAVE TO TALK, AWAY FROM DISTRACTIONS. HERE.
A PERSONAL ENVIRONMENT FIELD GENERATOR? YOU WANT TO GO OUTSIDE?
THIS MUST BE IMPORTANT!
WHY DO I FEEL I'VE BEEN CAUGHT WITH MY HAND IN THE TOFU JAR.
UH, YOU GO ON AHEAD. I'LL :UNGH: BE ALONG IN A :ERNF: DAY OR TWO?
HERE, DAD, LET ME GIVE YOU A HAND.
WHOOOOP--!

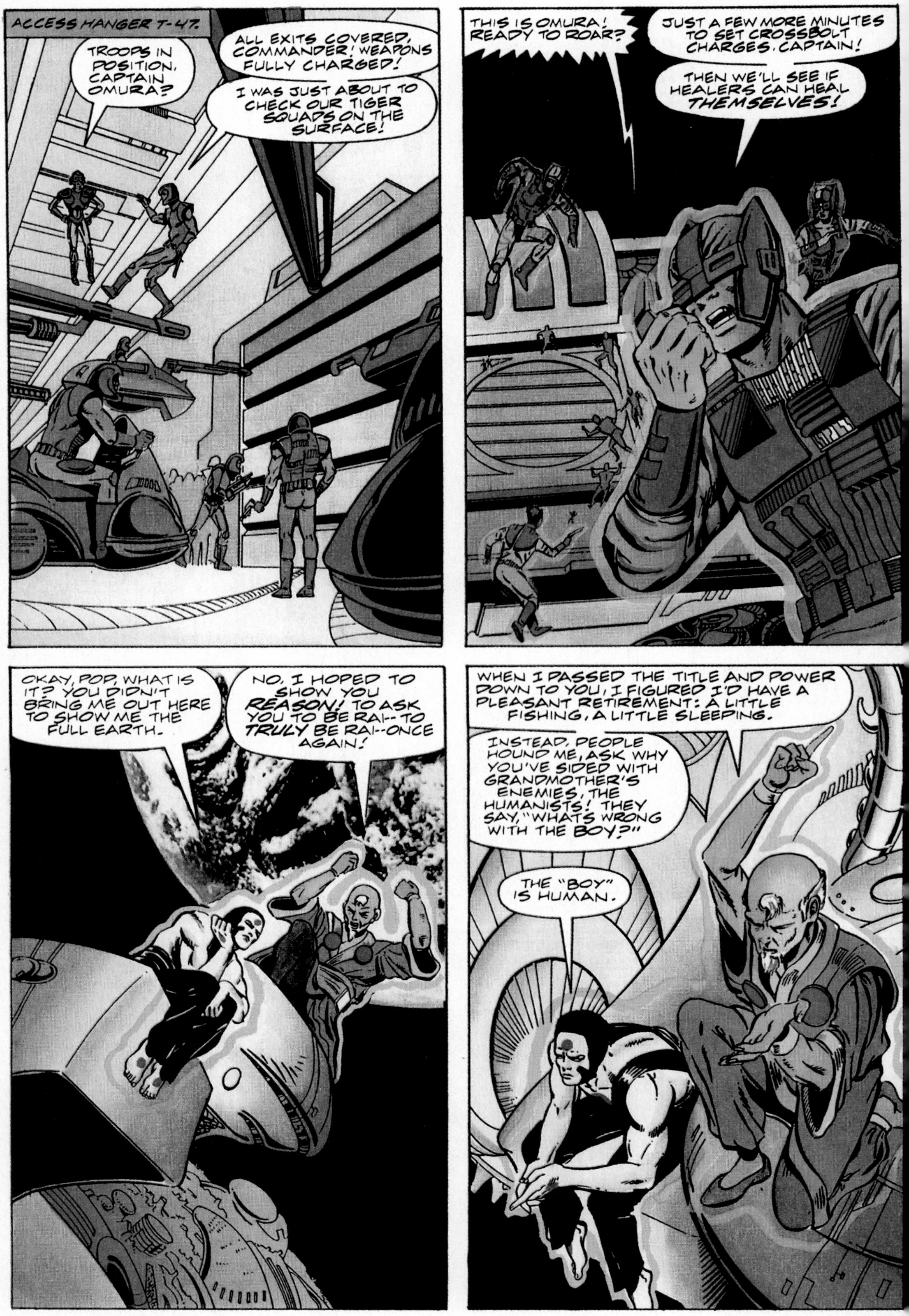

ACCESS HANGER T-47.
TROOPS IN POSITION, CAPTAIN OMURA?
ALL EXITS COVERED, COMMANDER! WEAPONS FULLY CHARGED!
I WAS JUST ABOUT TO CHECK OUR TIGER SQUADS ON THE SURFACE!
THIS IS OMURA! READY TO ROAR?
JUST A FEW MORE MINUTES TO SET CROSSBOLT CHARGES, CAPTAIN!
THEN WE'LL SEE IF HEALERS CAN HEAL THEMSELVES!
OKAY, POP, WHAT IS IT? YOU DIDN'T BRING ME OUT HERE TO SHOW ME THE FULL EARTH.
NO, I HOPED TO SHOW YOU REASON! TO ASK YOU TO BE RAI-- TO TRULY BE RAI--ONCE AGAIN!
WHEN I PASSED THE TITLE AND POWER DOWN TO YOU, I FIGURED I'D HAVE A PLEASANT RETIREMENT: A LITTLE FISHING, A LITTLE SLEEPING.
INSTEAD, PEOPLE HOUND ME, ASK WHY YOU'VE SIDED WITH GRANDMOTHER'S ENEMIES, THE HUMANISTS! THEY SAY, "WHAT'S WRONG WITH THE BOY?"
THE "BOY" IS HUMAN.

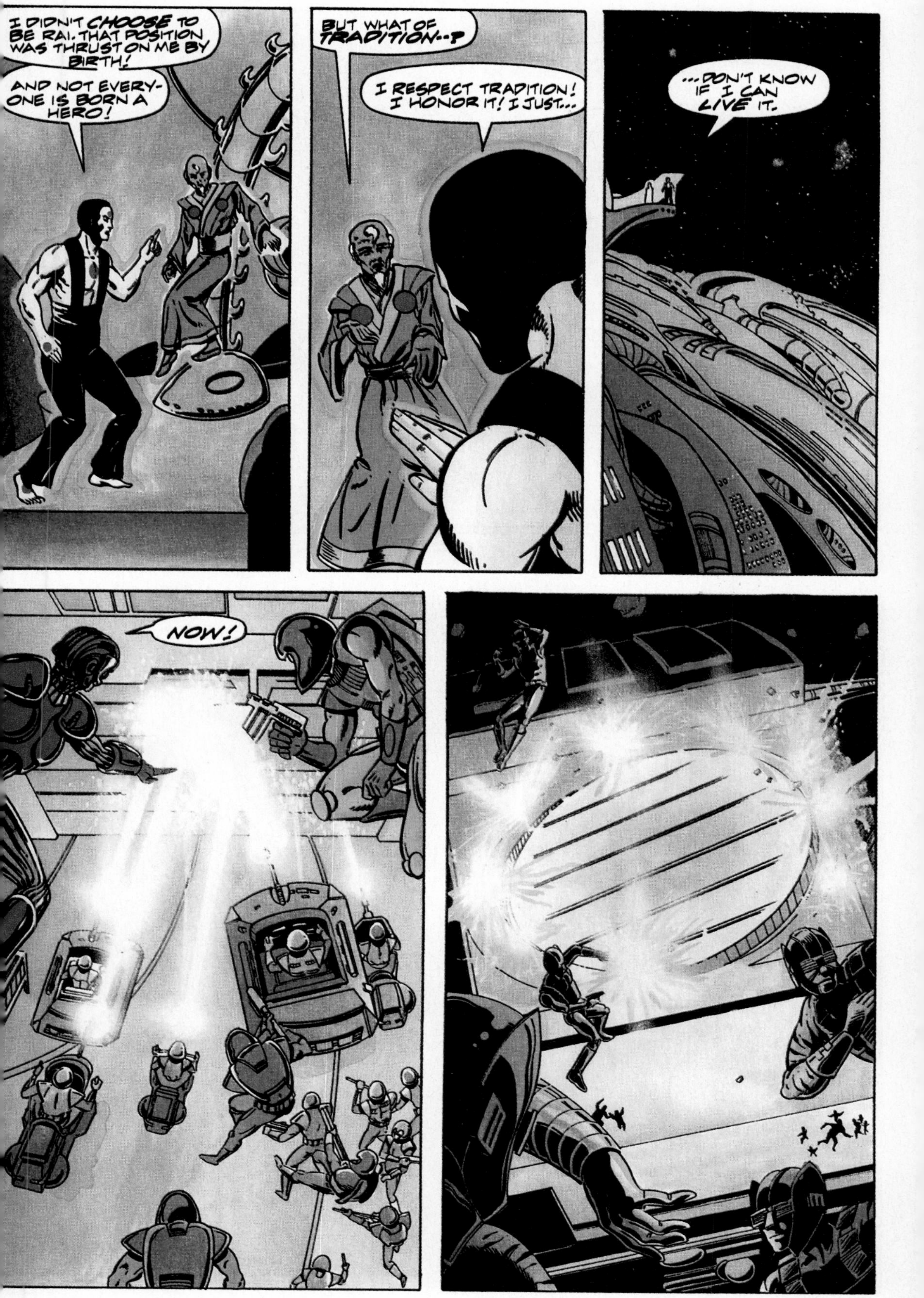
I DIDN'T CHOOSE TO BE RAI. THAT POSITION WAS THRUST ON ME BY BIRTH!
AND NOT EVERY-ONE IS BORN A HERO!
BUT WHAT OF TRADITION..?
I RESPECT TRADITION! I HONOR IT! I JUST...
...DON'T KNOW IF I CAN LIVE IT.
NOW!

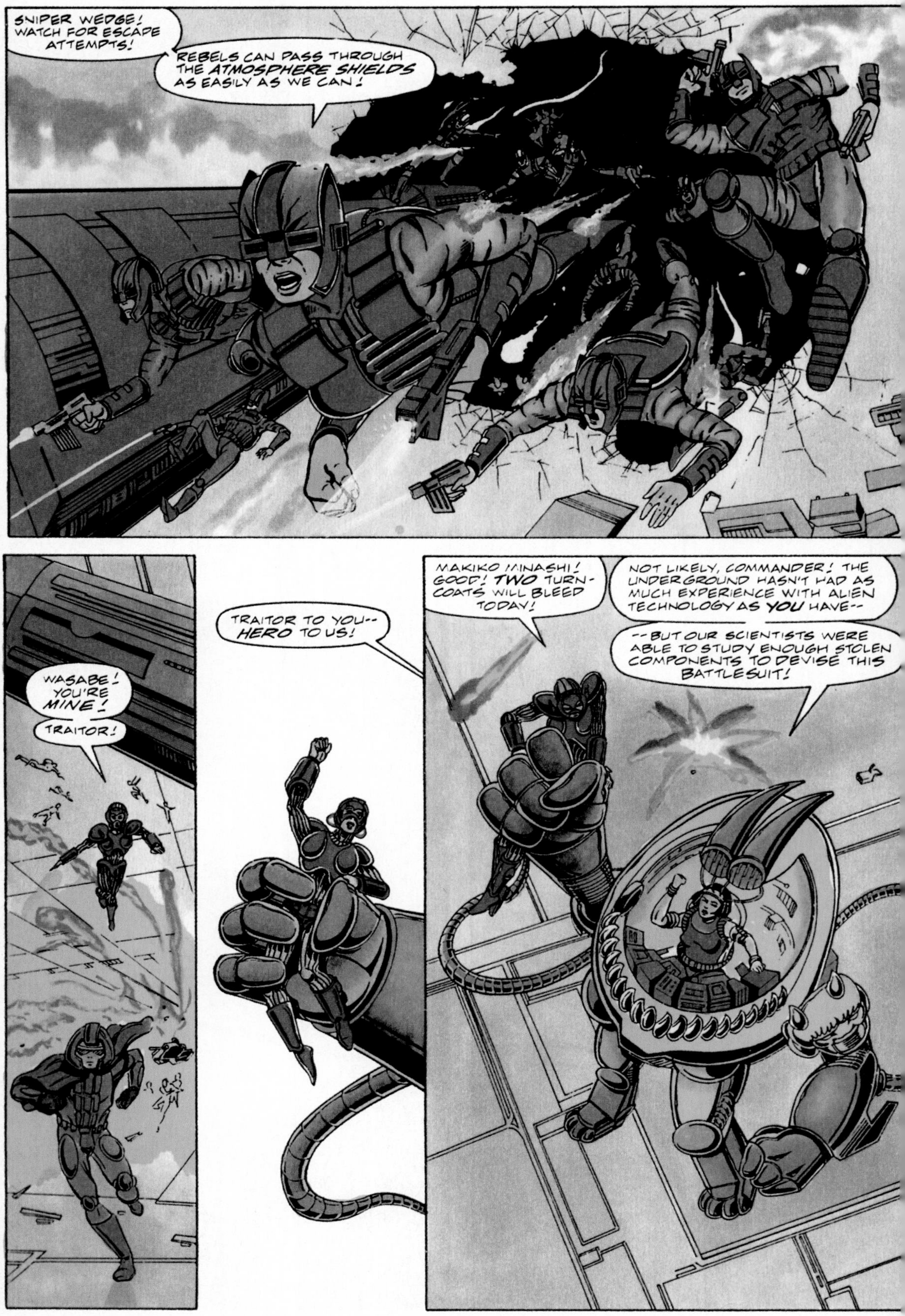
SNIPER WEDGE! WATCH FOR ESCAPE ATTEMPTS!
REBELS CAN PASS THROUGH THE ATMOSPHERE SHIELDS AS EASILY AS WE CAN!
WASABE! YOU'RE MINE!
TRAITOR!
TRAITOR TO YOU-- HERO TO US!
MAKIKO MINASHI! GOOD! TWO TURN-COATS WILL BLEED TODAY!
NOT LIKELY, COMMANDER! THE UNDERGROUND HASN'T HAD AS MUCH EXPERIENCE WITH ALIEN TECHNOLOGY AS YOU HAVE--
--BUT OUR SCIENTISTS WERE ABLE TO STUDY ENOUGH STOLEN COMPONENTS TO DEVISE THIS BATTLESUIT!

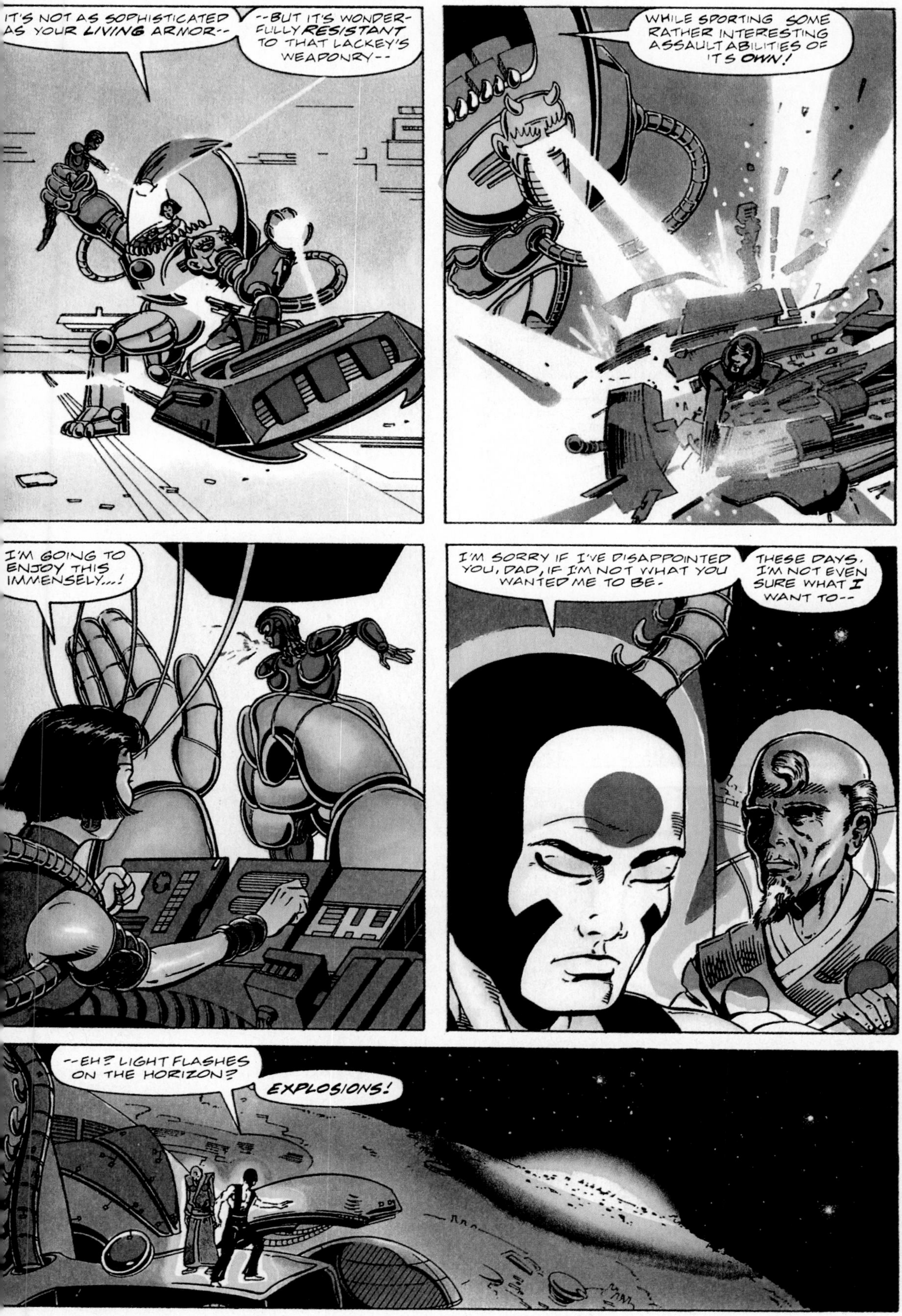
IT'S NOT AS SOPHISTICATED AS YOUR LIVING ARMOR--
--BUT IT'S WONDERFULLY RESISTANT TO THAT LACKEY'S WEAPONRY--
WHILE SPORTING SOME RATHER INTERESTING ASSAULT ABILITIES OF ITS OWN!
I'M GOING TO ENJOY THIS IMMENSELY...!
I'M SORRY IF I'VE DISAPPOINTED YOU, DAD, IF I'M NOT WHAT YOU WANTED ME TO BE.
THESE DAYS, I'M NOT EVEN SURE WHAT I WANT TO--
--EH? LIGHT FLASHES ON THE HORIZON?
EXPLOSIONS!

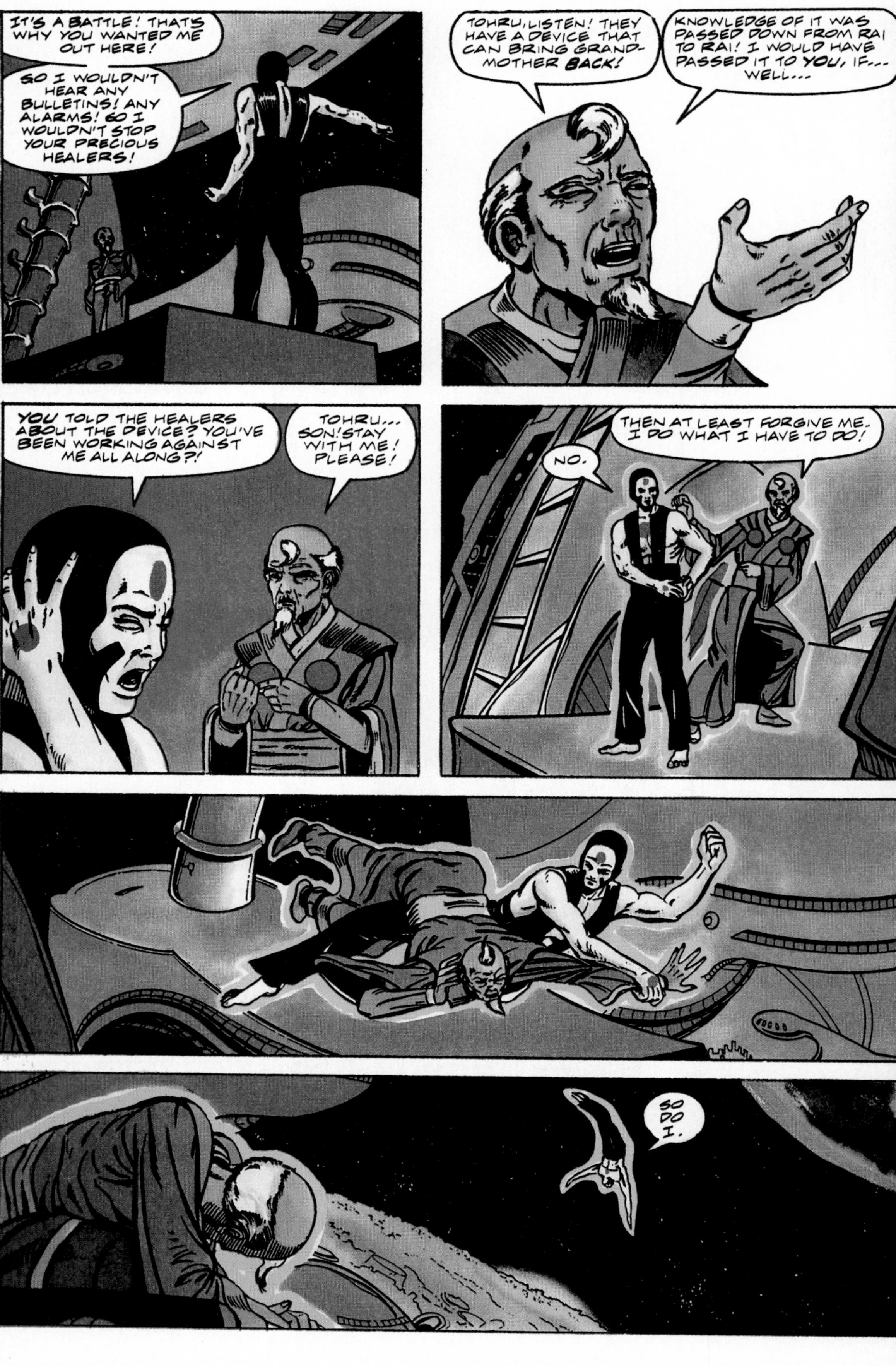
IT'S A BATTLE! THAT'S WHY YOU WANTED ME OUT HERE!
SO I WOULDN'T HEAR ANY BULLETINS! ANY ALARMS! SO I WOULDN'T STOP YOUR PRECIOUS HEALERS!
TOHRU, LISTEN! THEY HAVE A DEVICE THAT CAN BRING GRAND-MOTHER BACK!
KNOWLEDGE OF IT WAS PASSED DOWN FROM RAI TO RAI! I WOULD HAVE PASSED IT TO YOU, IF... WELL...
YOU TOLD THE HEALERS ABOUT THE DEVICE? YOU'VE BEEN WORKING AGAINST ME ALL ALONG?!
TOHRU... SON! STAY WITH ME! PLEASE!
THEN AT LEAST FORGIVE ME. I DO WHAT I HAVE TO DO!
NO.
SO DO I.

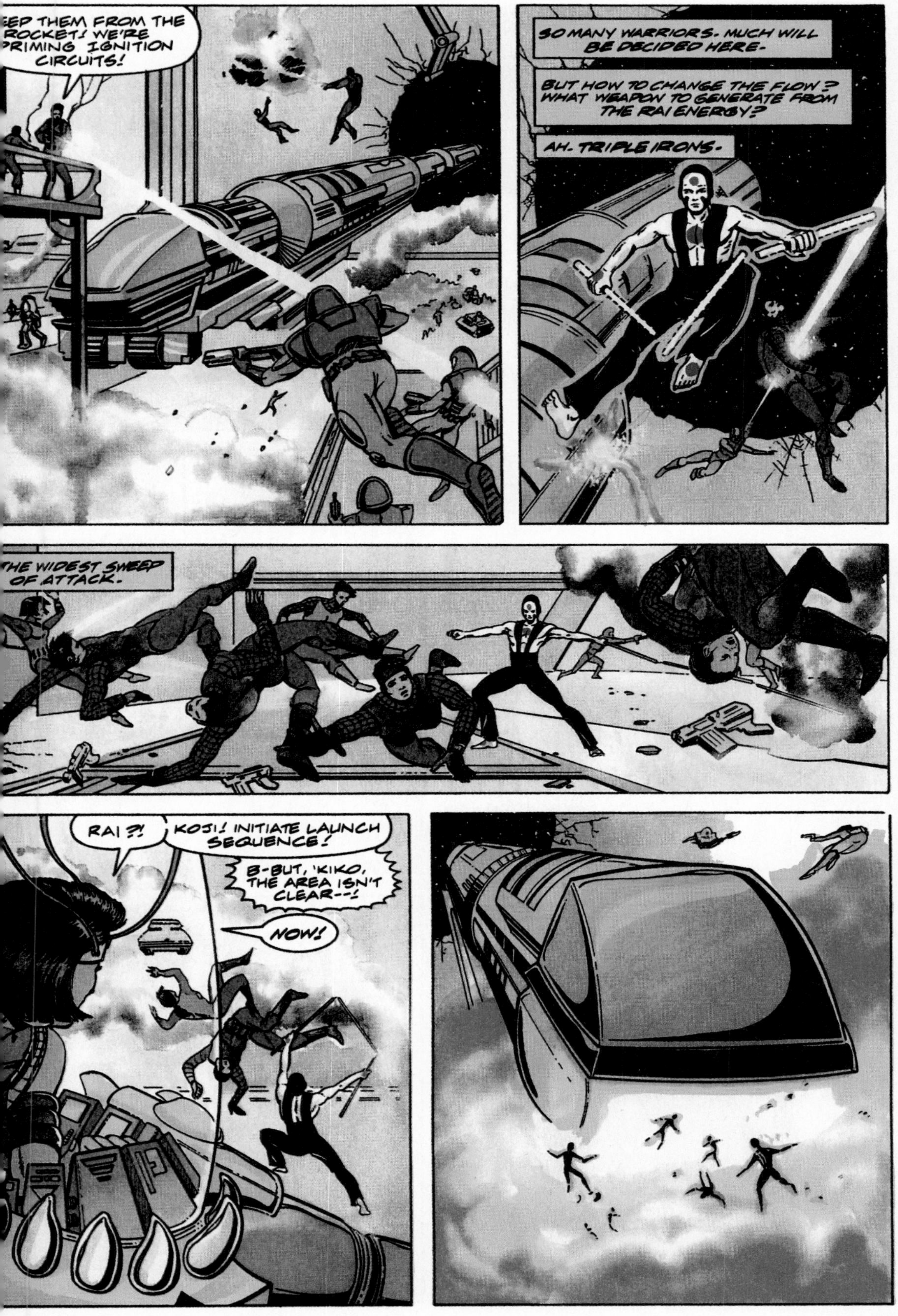

EEP THEM FROM THE ROCKET! WE'RE PRIMING IGNITION CIRCUITS!
SO MANY WARRIORS. MUCH WILL BE DECIDED HERE.
BUT HOW TO CHANGE THE FLOW? WHAT WEAPON TO GENERATE FROM THE RAI ENERGY?
AH. TRIPLE IRONS.
THE WIDEST SWEEP OF ATTACK.
RAI?!
KOJI! INITIATE LAUNCH SEQUENCE!
B-BUT, 'KIKO, THE AREA ISN'T CLEAR--!
NOW!

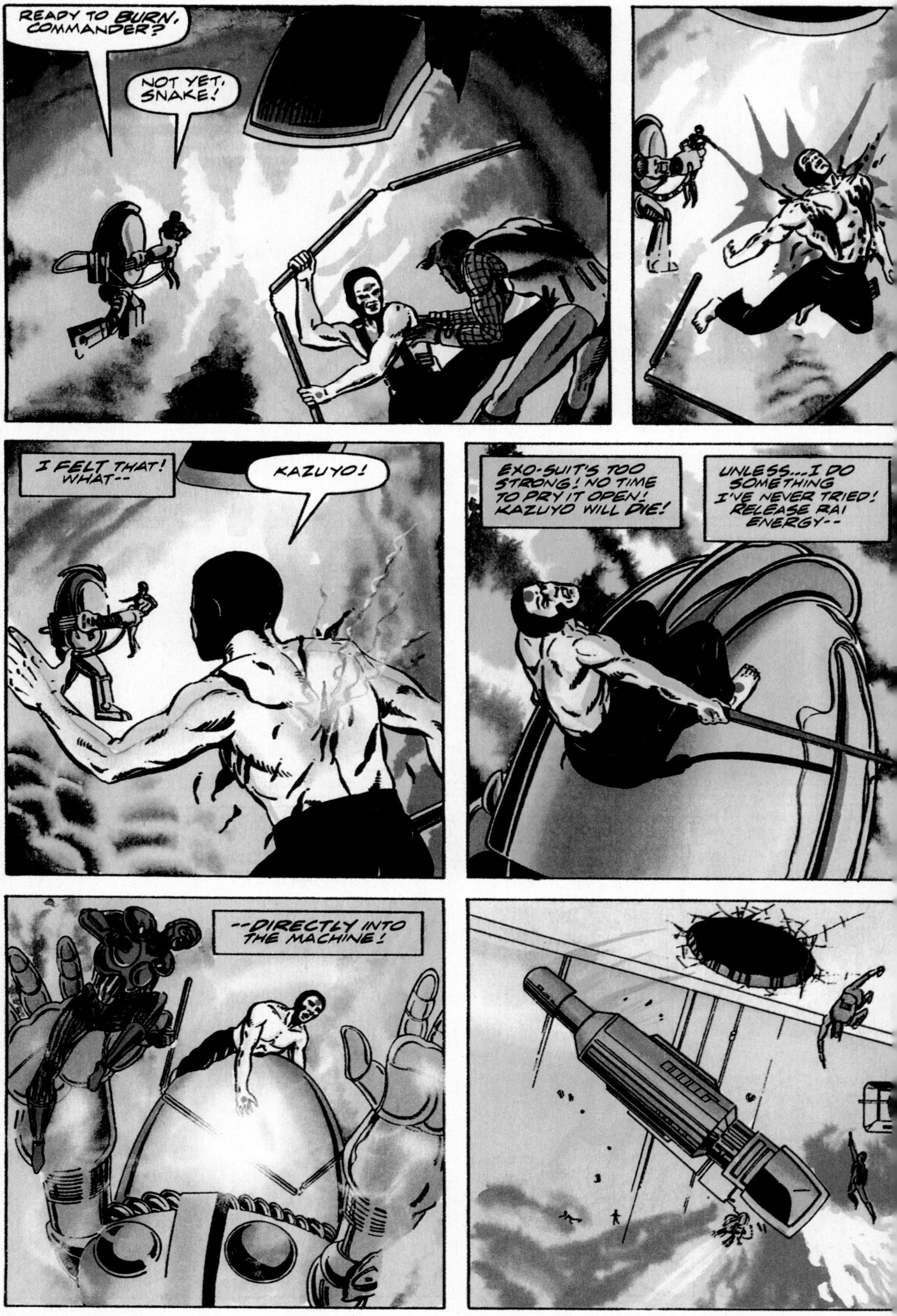
READY TO BURN, COMMANDER?
NOT YET, SNAKE!
I FELT THAT! WHAT--
KAZUYO!
EXO-SUIT'S TOO STRONG! NO TIME TO PRY IT OPEN! KAZUYO WILL DIE!
UNLESS...I DO SOMETHING I'VE NEVER TRIED! RELEASE RAI ENERGY--
--DIRECTLY INTO THE MACHINE!

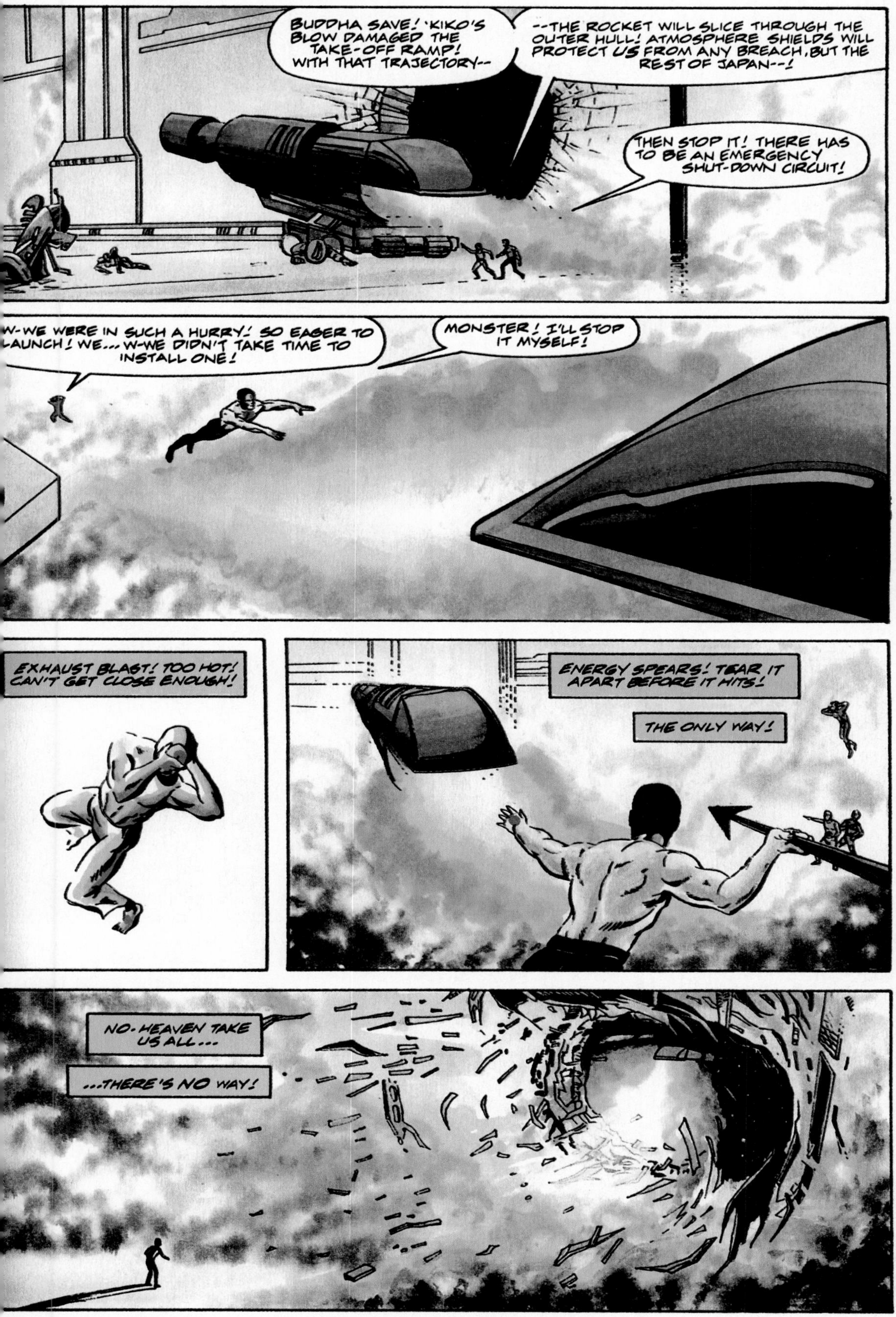
BUDDHA SAVE! 'KIKO'S BLOW DAMAGED THE TAKE-OFF RAMP! WITH THAT TRAJECTORY--
--THE ROCKET WILL SLICE THROUGH THE OUTER HULL! ATMOSPHERE SHIELDS WILL PROTECT US FROM ANY BREACH, BUT THE REST OF JAPAN--!
THEN STOP IT! THERE HAS TO BE AN EMERGENCY SHUT-DOWN CIRCUIT!
W-WE WERE IN SUCH A HURRY! SO EAGER TO LAUNCH! WE... W-WE DIDN'T TAKE TIME TO INSTALL ONE!
MONSTER! I'LL STOP IT MYSELF!
EXHAUST BLAST! TOO HOT! CAN'T GET CLOSE ENOUGH!
ENERGY SPEARS! TEAR IT APART BEFORE IT HITS!
THE ONLY WAY!
NO. HEAVEN TAKE US ALL...
...THERE'S NO WAY!

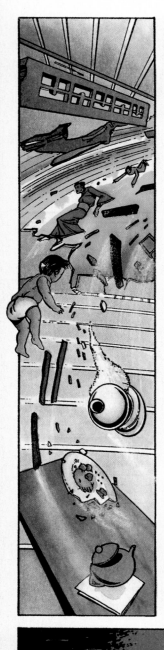

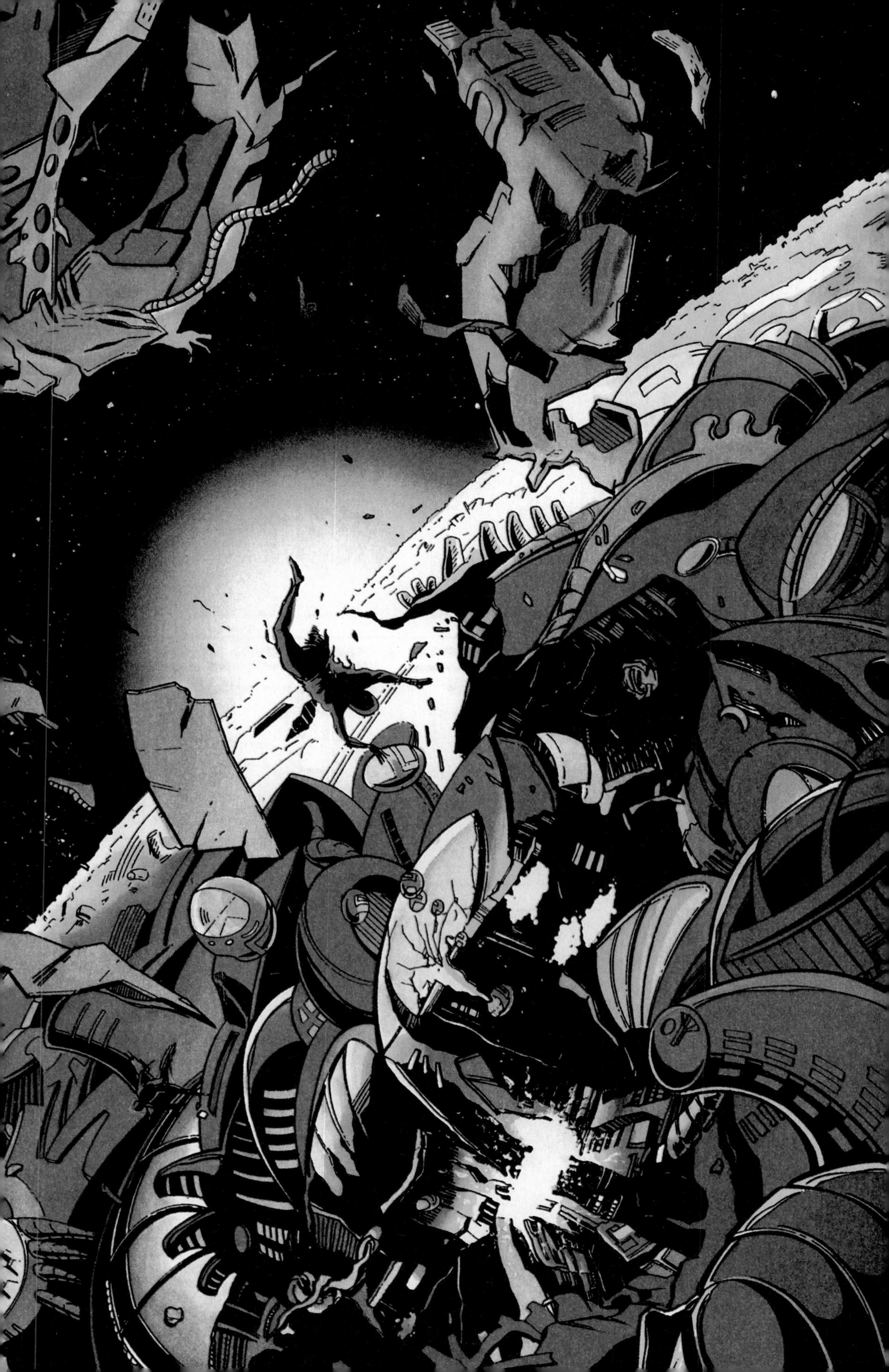

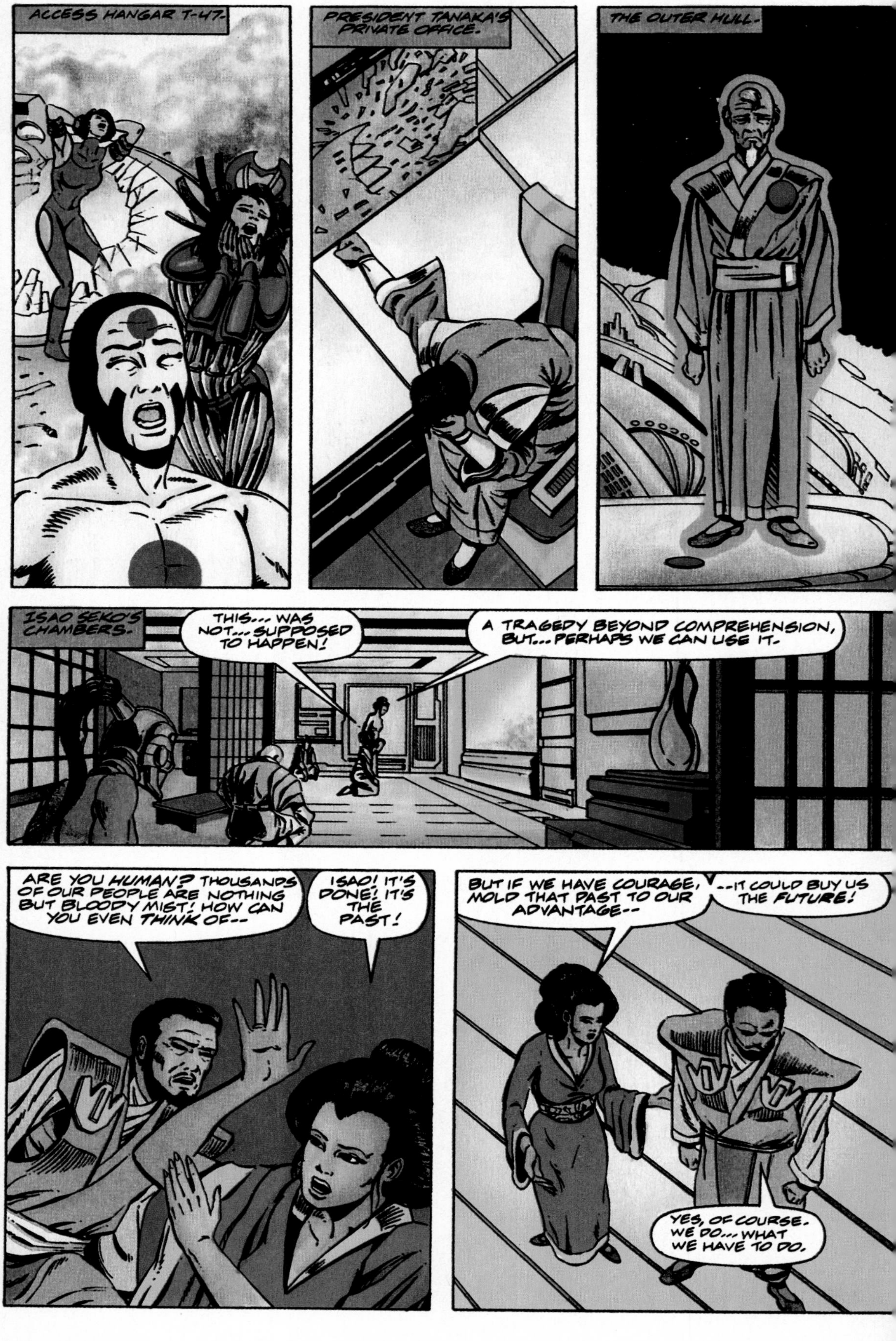
ACCESS HANGAR T-47.
PRESIDENT TANAKA'S PRIVATE OFFICE.
THE OUTER HULL.
ISAO SEKO'S CHAMBERS.
THIS... WAS NOT... SUPPOSED TO HAPPEN!
A TRAGEDY BEYOND COMPREHENSION, BUT... PERHAPS WE CAN USE IT.
ARE YOU HUMAN? THOUSANDS OF OUR PEOPLE ARE NOTHING BUT BLOODY MIST! HOW CAN YOU EVEN THINK OF--
ISAO! IT'S DONE! IT'S THE PAST!
BUT IF WE HAVE COURAGE, MOLD THAT PAST TO OUR ADVANTAGE--
--IT COULD BUY US THE FUTURE!
YES, OF COURSE. WE DO... WHAT WE HAVE TO DO.

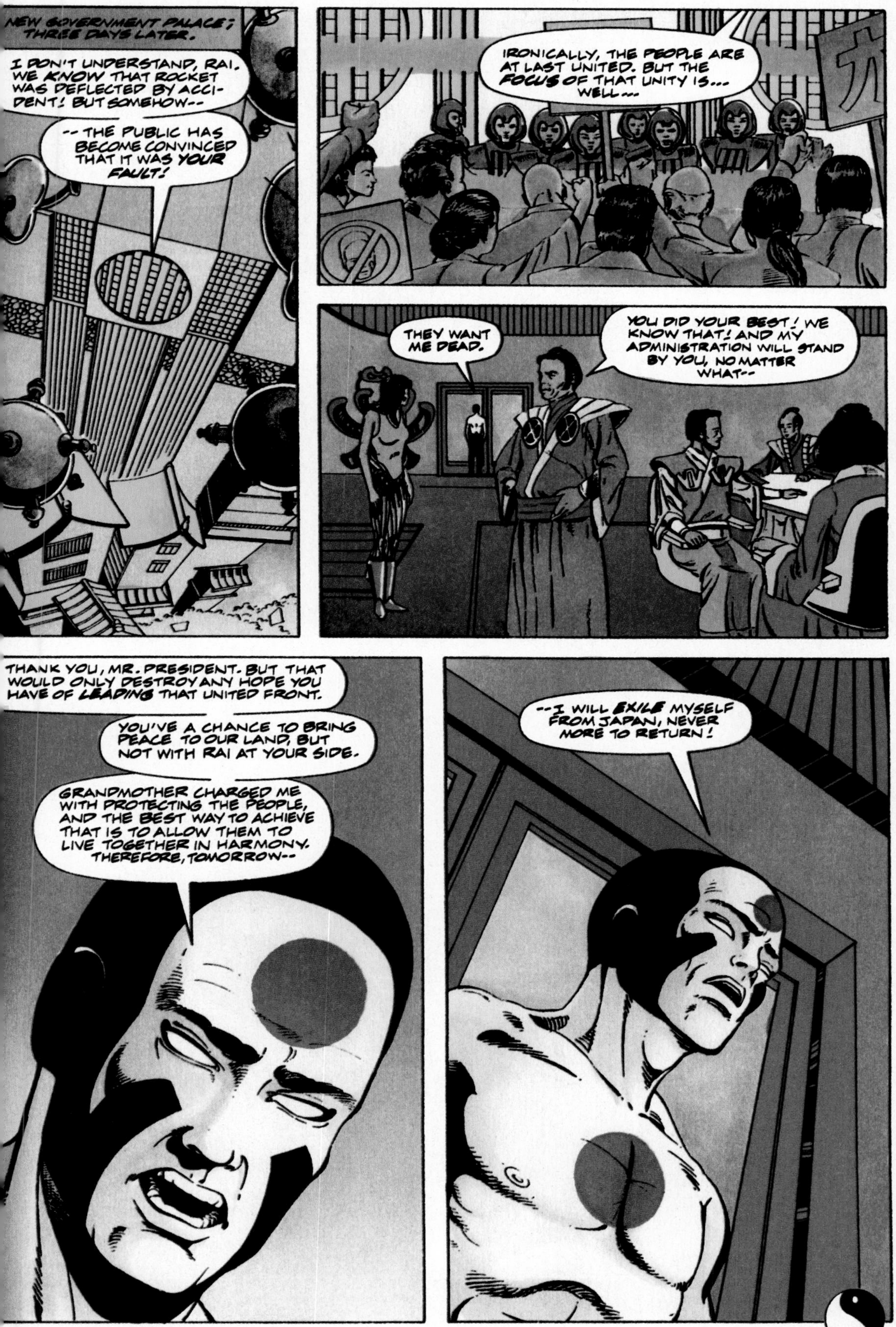
NEW GOVERNMENT PALACE; THREE DAYS LATER.
I DON'T UNDERSTAND, RAI. WE KNOW THAT ROCKET WAS DEFLECTED BY ACCIDENT! BUT SOMEHOW--
-- THE PUBLIC HAS BECOME CONVINCED THAT IT WAS YOUR FAULT!
IRONICALLY, THE PEOPLE ARE AT LAST UNITED. BUT THE FOCUS OF THAT UNITY IS... WELL...
THEY WANT ME DEAD.
YOU DID YOUR BEST! WE KNOW THAT! AND MY ADMINISTRATION WILL STAND BY YOU, NO MATTER WHAT--
THANK YOU, MR. PRESIDENT. BUT THAT WOULD ONLY DESTROY ANY HOPE YOU HAVE OF LEADING THAT UNITED FRONT.
YOU'VE A CHANCE TO BRING PEACE TO OUR LAND, BUT NOT WITH RAI AT YOUR SIDE.
GRANDMOTHER CHARGED ME WITH PROTECTING THE PEOPLE, AND THE BEST WAY TO ACHIEVE THAT IS TO ALLOW THEM TO LIVE TOGETHER IN HARMONY. THEREFORE, TOMORROW--
--I WILL EXILE MYSELF FROM JAPAN, NEVER MORE TO RETURN!

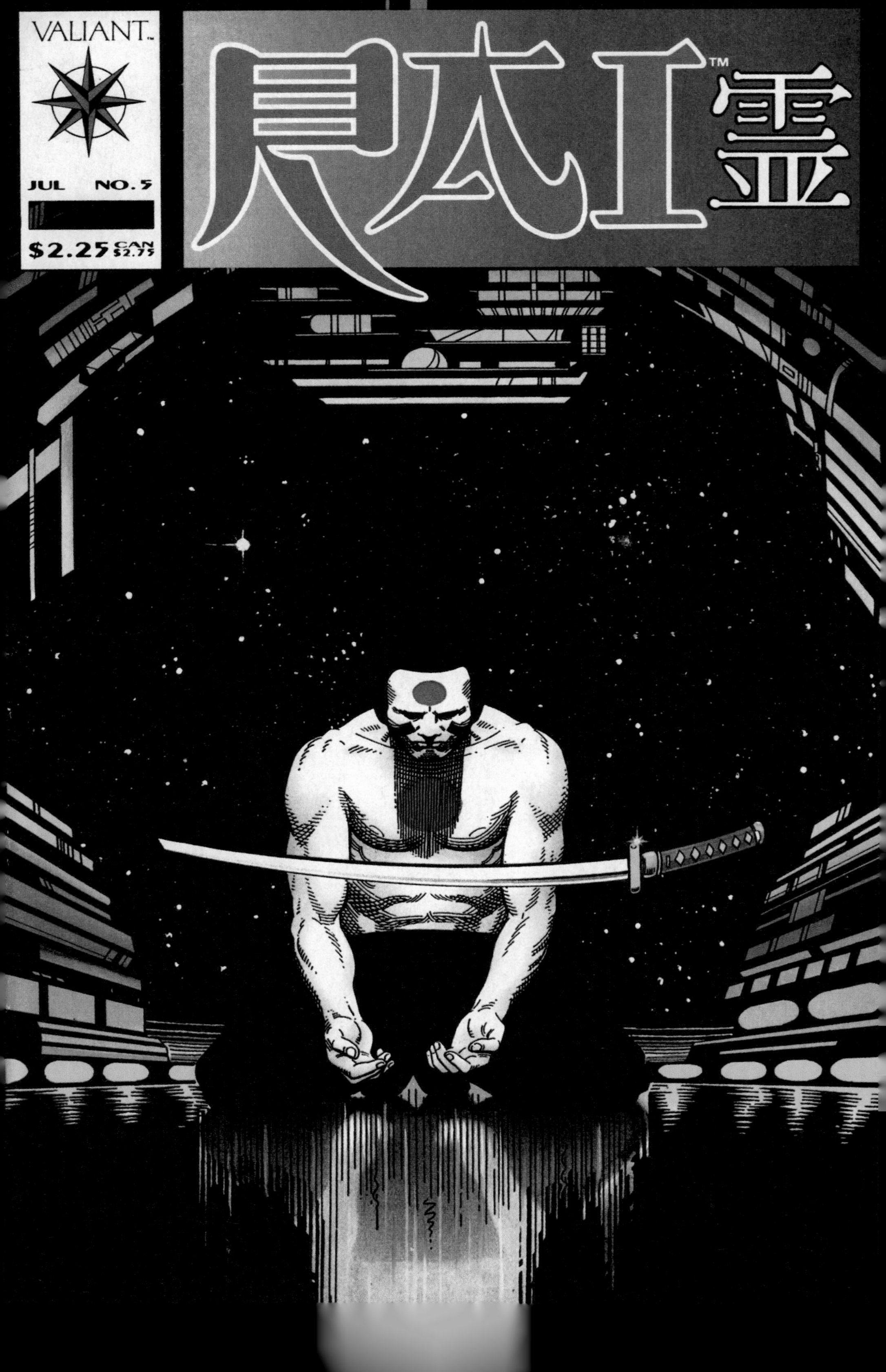
VALIANT™
JUL NO. 5
$2.25 CAN $2.75
RAI™
霊

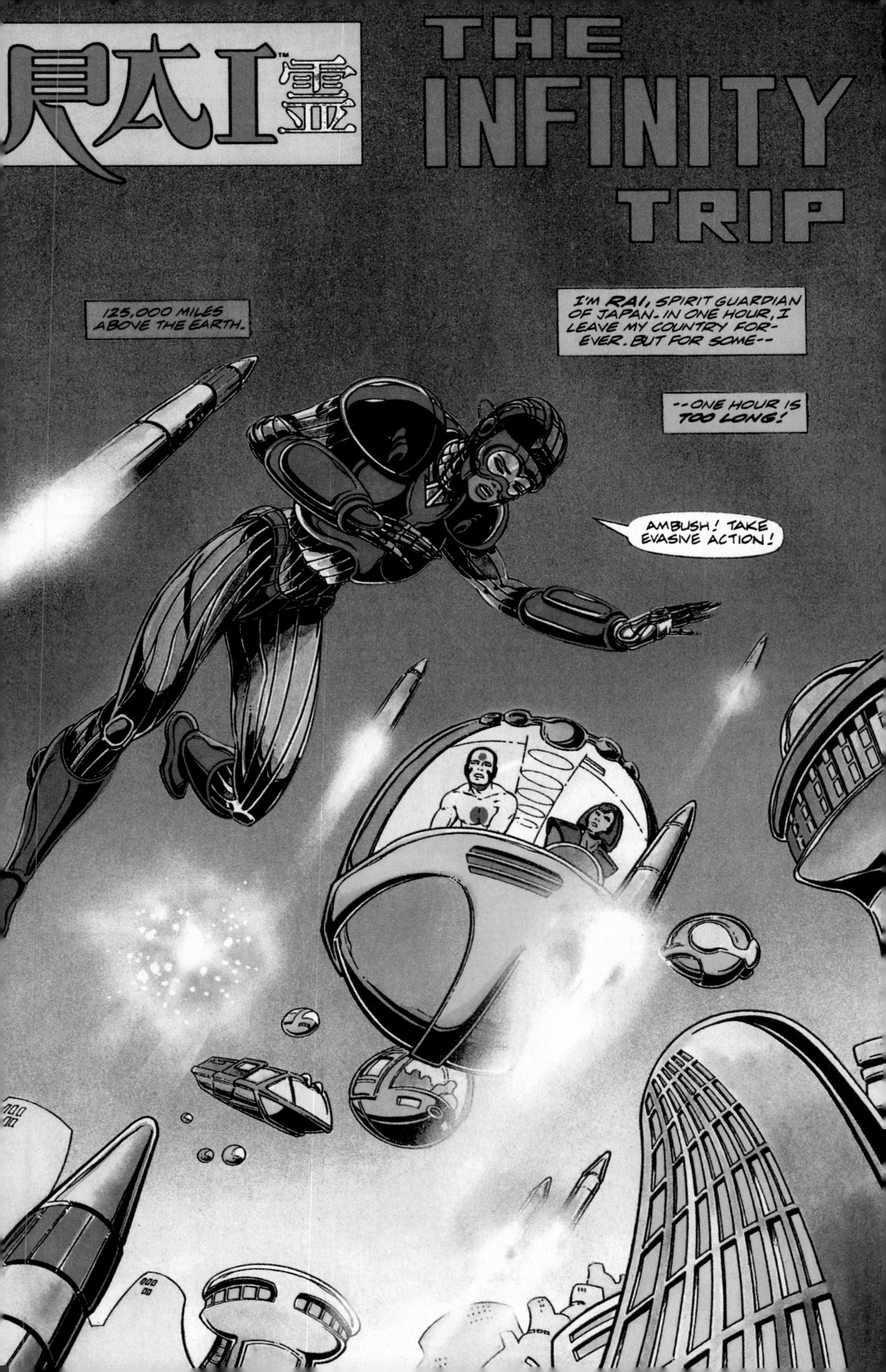
RAI™
THE INFINITY TRIP
125,000 MILES ABOVE THE EARTH.
I'M RAI, SPIRIT GUARDIAN OF JAPAN. IN ONE HOUR, I LEAVE MY COUNTRY FOREVER. BUT FOR SOME--
--ONE HOUR IS TOO LONG!
AMBUSH! TAKE EVASIVE ACTION!

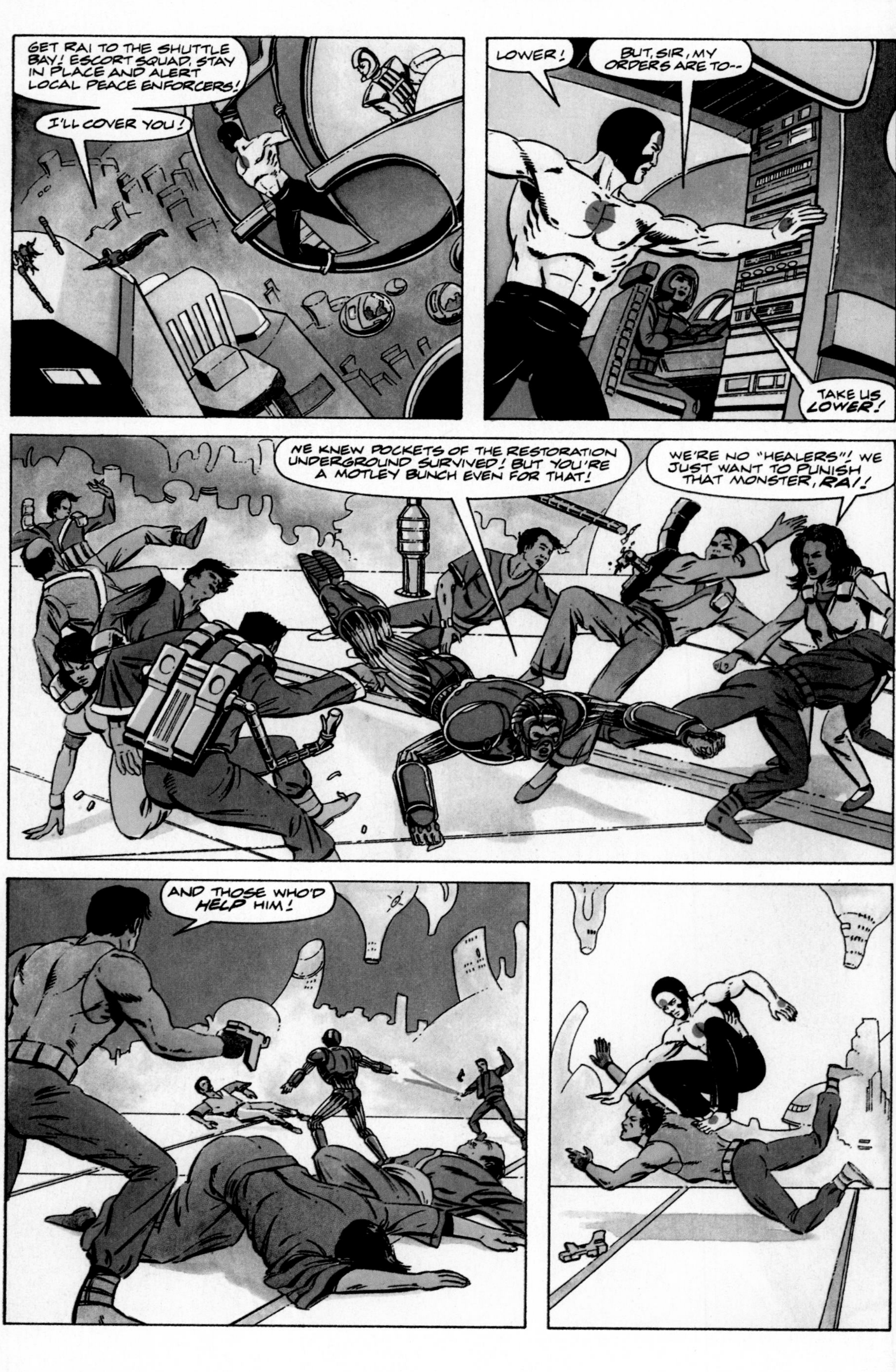

GET RAI TO THE SHUTTLE BAY! ESCORT SQUAD, STAY IN PLACE AND ALERT LOCAL PEACE ENFORCERS!
I'LL COVER YOU!
LOWER!
BUT, SIR, MY ORDERS ARE TO--
TAKE US LOWER!
WE KNEW POCKETS OF THE RESTORATION UNDERGROUND SURVIVED! BUT YOU'RE A MOTLEY BUNCH EVEN FOR THAT!
WE'RE NO "HEALERS"! WE JUST WANT TO PUNISH THAT MONSTER, RAI!
AND THOSE WHO'D HELP HIM!

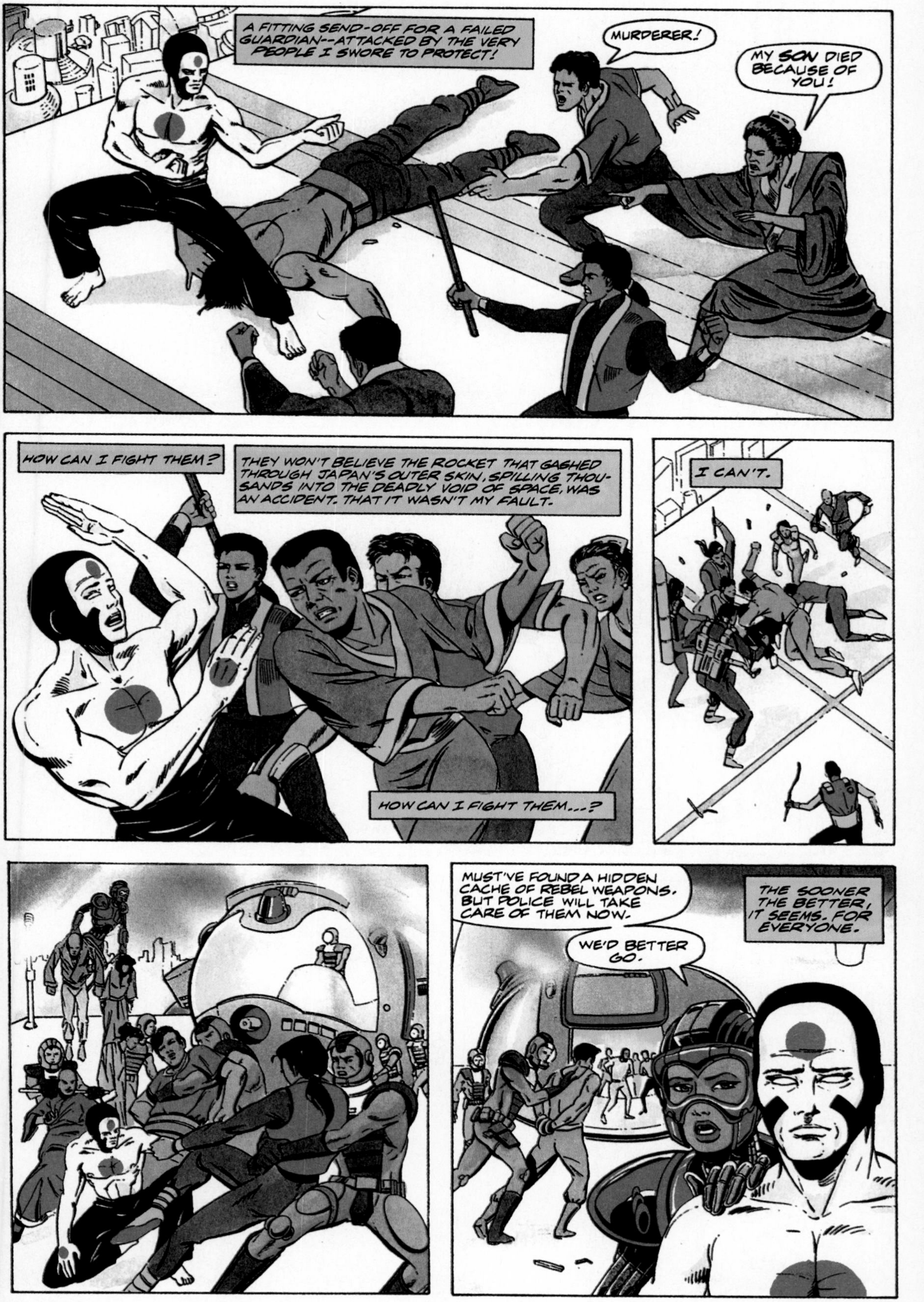
A FITTING SEND-OFF FOR A FAILED GUARDIAN--ATTACKED BY THE VERY PEOPLE I SWORE TO PROTECT!
MURDERER!
MY SON DIED BECAUSE OF YOU!
HOW CAN I FIGHT THEM?
THEY WON'T BELIEVE THE ROCKET THAT GASHED THROUGH JAPAN'S OUTER SKIN, SPILLING THOUSANDS INTO THE DEADLY VOID OF SPACE, WAS AN ACCIDENT. THAT IT WASN'T MY FAULT.
HOW CAN I FIGHT THEM...?
I CAN'T.
MUST'VE FOUND A HIDDEN CACHE OF REBEL WEAPONS. BUT POLICE WILL TAKE CARE OF THEM NOW.
WE'D BETTER GO.
THE SOONER THE BETTER, IT SEEMS. FOR EVERYONE.

MITSUTOMOE SHORT-RANGE TRANSPORT BAY.

THE AREA IS SECURE, LIEUTENANT? YOU'RE *CERTAIN*?

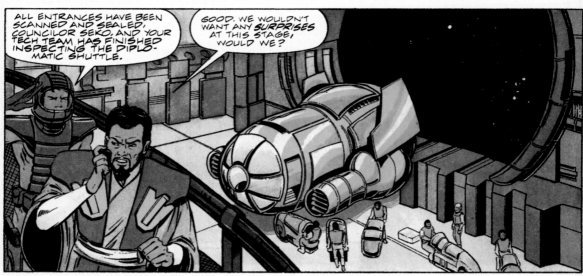

ALL ENTRANCES HAVE BEEN SCANNED AND SEALED, COUNCILOR SEKO, AND YOUR TECH TEAM HAS FINISHED INSPECTING THE DIPLOMATIC SHUTTLE.

GOOD. WE WOULDN'T WANT ANY *SURPRISES* AT THIS STAGE, WOULD WE?

YOUR SON, COMMANDER NAKADAI. AS YOU REQUESTED.

POOR TAKASHI. HE CAN'T POSSIBLY UNDERSTAND.

BUT HE'S RESILIENT. HE ACCEPTS. HE HASN'T HAD BOTH MOTHER AND FATHER SINCE THE ASCENDING, SINCE...OUR ESTRANGEMENT.

AND NOW HE'LL BE SEPARATED FROM ONE BY THOUSANDS OF COLD, HEARTLESS MILES.

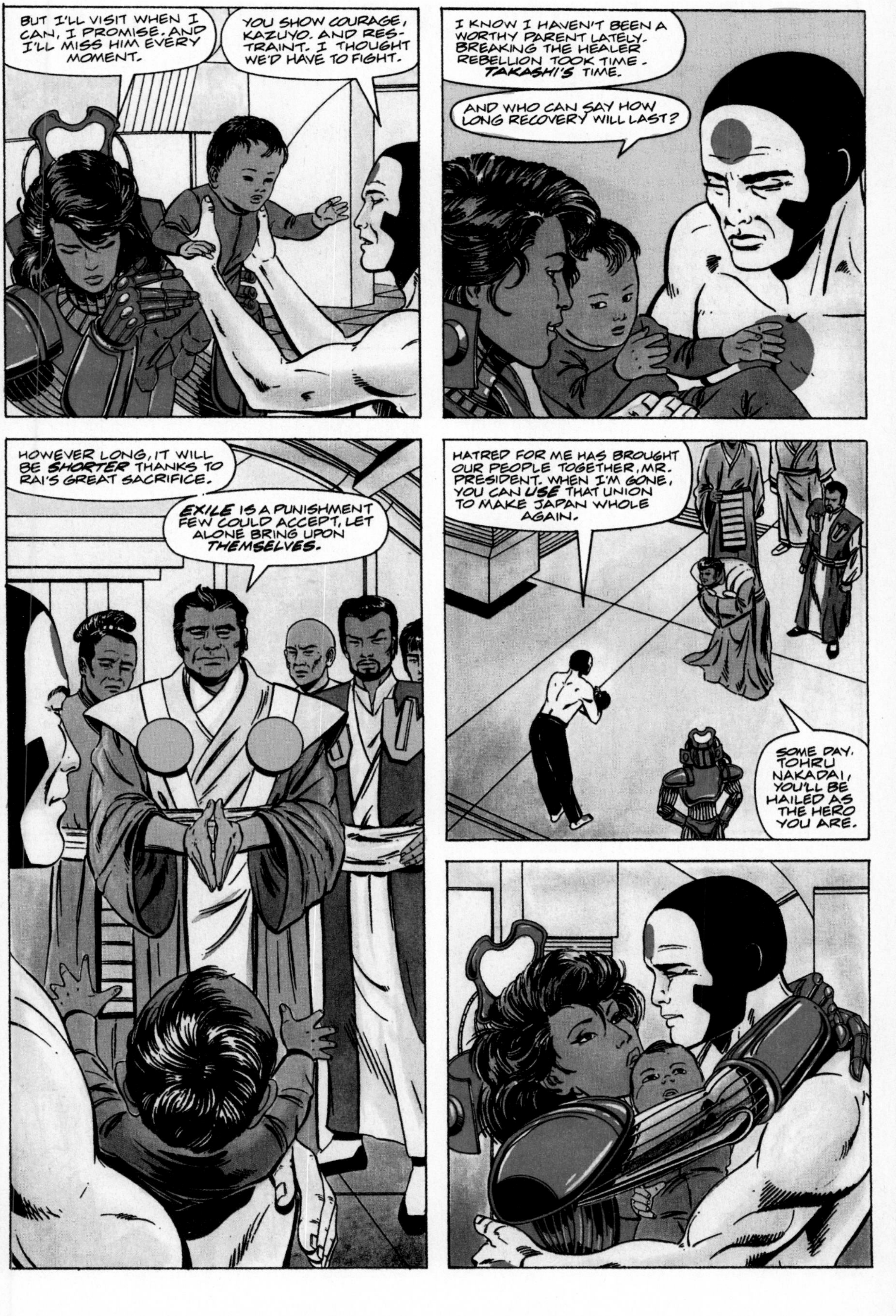
BUT I'LL VISIT WHEN I CAN, I PROMISE. AND I'LL MISS HIM EVERY MOMENT.
YOU SHOW COURAGE, KAZUYO. AND RESTRAINT. I THOUGHT WE'D HAVE TO FIGHT.
I KNOW I HAVEN'T BEEN A WORTHY PARENT LATELY. BREAKING THE HEALER REBELLION TOOK TIME. TAKASHI'S TIME.
AND WHO CAN SAY HOW LONG RECOVERY WILL LAST?
HOWEVER LONG, IT WILL BE SHORTER THANKS TO RAI'S GREAT SACRIFICE.
EXILE IS A PUNISHMENT FEW COULD ACCEPT, LET ALONE BRING UPON THEMSELVES.
HATRED FOR ME HAS BROUGHT OUR PEOPLE TOGETHER, MR. PRESIDENT. WHEN I'M GONE, YOU CAN USE THAT UNION TO MAKE JAPAN WHOLE AGAIN.
SOME DAY, TOHRU NAKADAI, YOU'LL BE HAILED AS THE HERO YOU ARE.

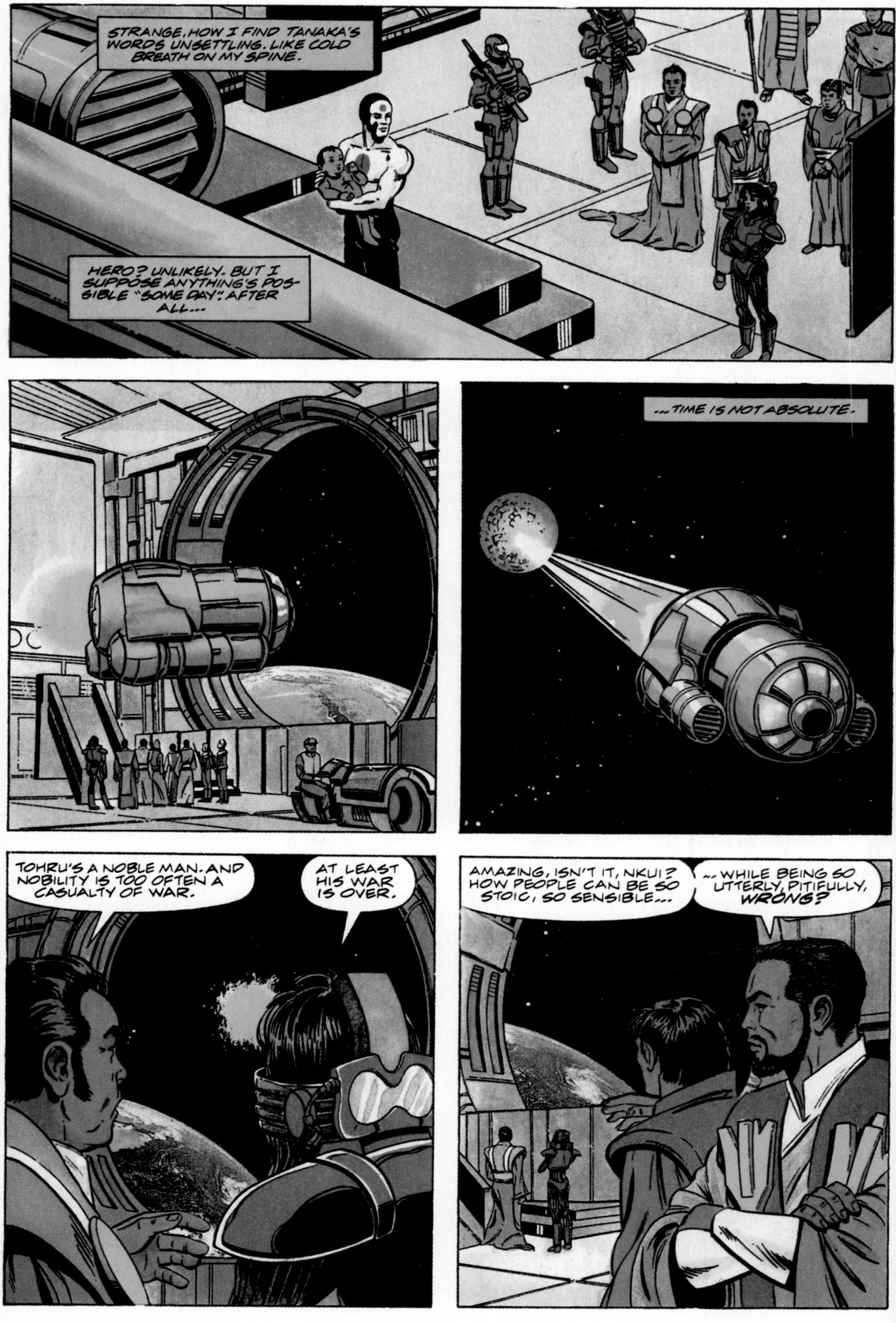

STRANGE, HOW I FIND TANAKA'S WORDS UNSETTLING. LIKE COLD BREATH ON MY SPINE.
HERO? UNLIKELY. BUT I SUPPOSE ANYTHING'S POSSIBLE "SOME DAY". AFTER ALL...
...TIME IS NOT ABSOLUTE.
TOHRU'S A NOBLE MAN. AND NOBILITY IS TOO OFTEN A CASUALTY OF WAR.
AT LEAST HIS WAR IS OVER.
AMAZING, ISN'T IT, NKUI? HOW PEOPLE CAN BE SO STOIC, SO SENSIBLE...
...WHILE BEING SO UTTERLY, PITIFULLY, WRONG?

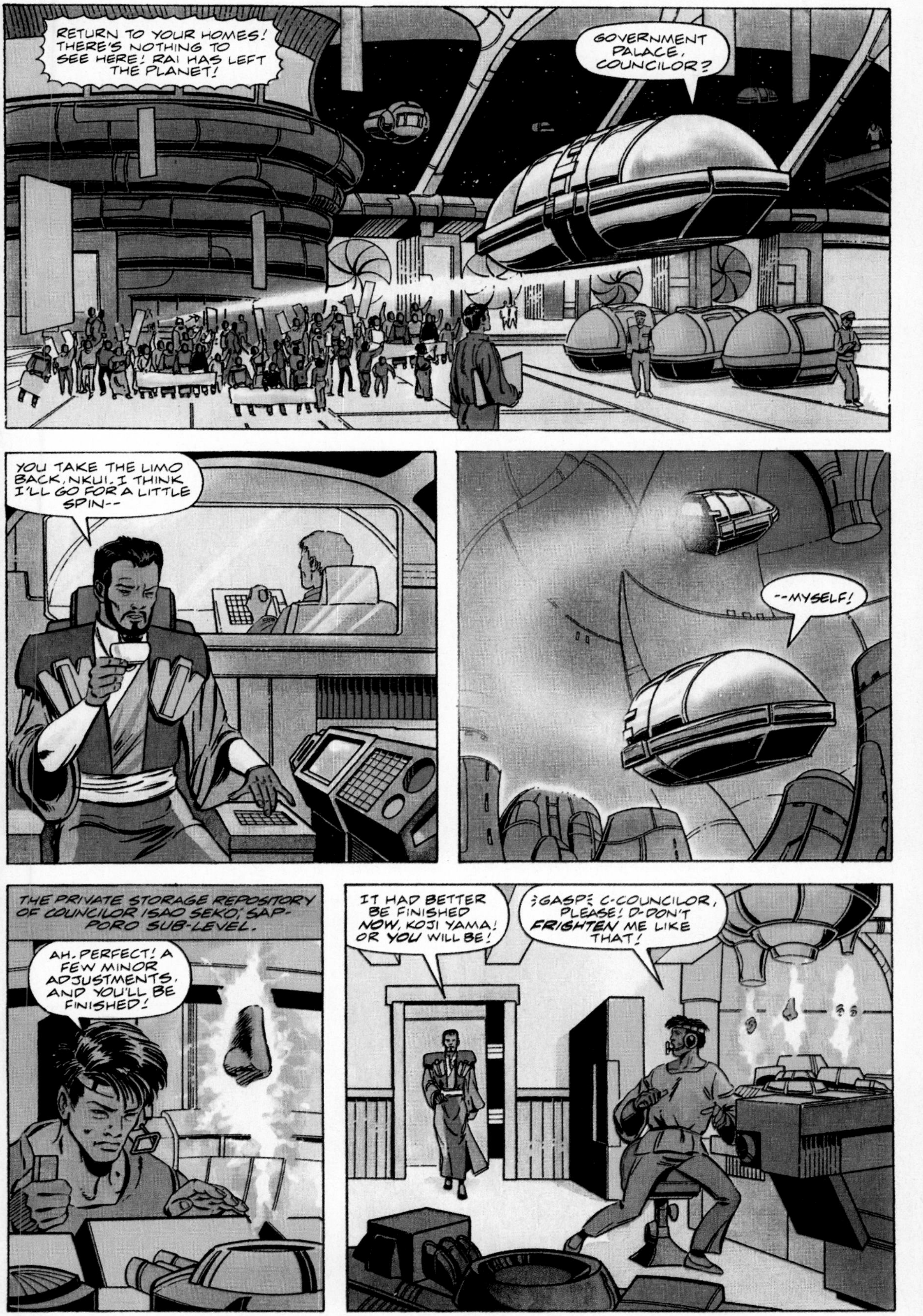

RETURN TO YOUR HOMES! THERE'S NOTHING TO SEE HERE! RAI HAS LEFT THE PLANET!
GOVERNMENT PALACE, COUNCILOR?
YOU TAKE THE LIMO BACK, NKUI. I THINK I'LL GO FOR A LITTLE SPIN--
--MYSELF!
THE PRIVATE STORAGE REPOSITORY OF COUNCILOR ISAO SEKO; SAPPORO SUB-LEVEL.
AH. PERFECT! A FEW MINOR ADJUSTMENTS, AND YOU'LL BE FINISHED!
IT HAD BETTER BE FINISHED NOW, KOJI YAMA! OR YOU WILL BE!
GASP C-COUNCILOR, PLEASE! D-DON'T FRIGHTEN ME LIKE THAT!

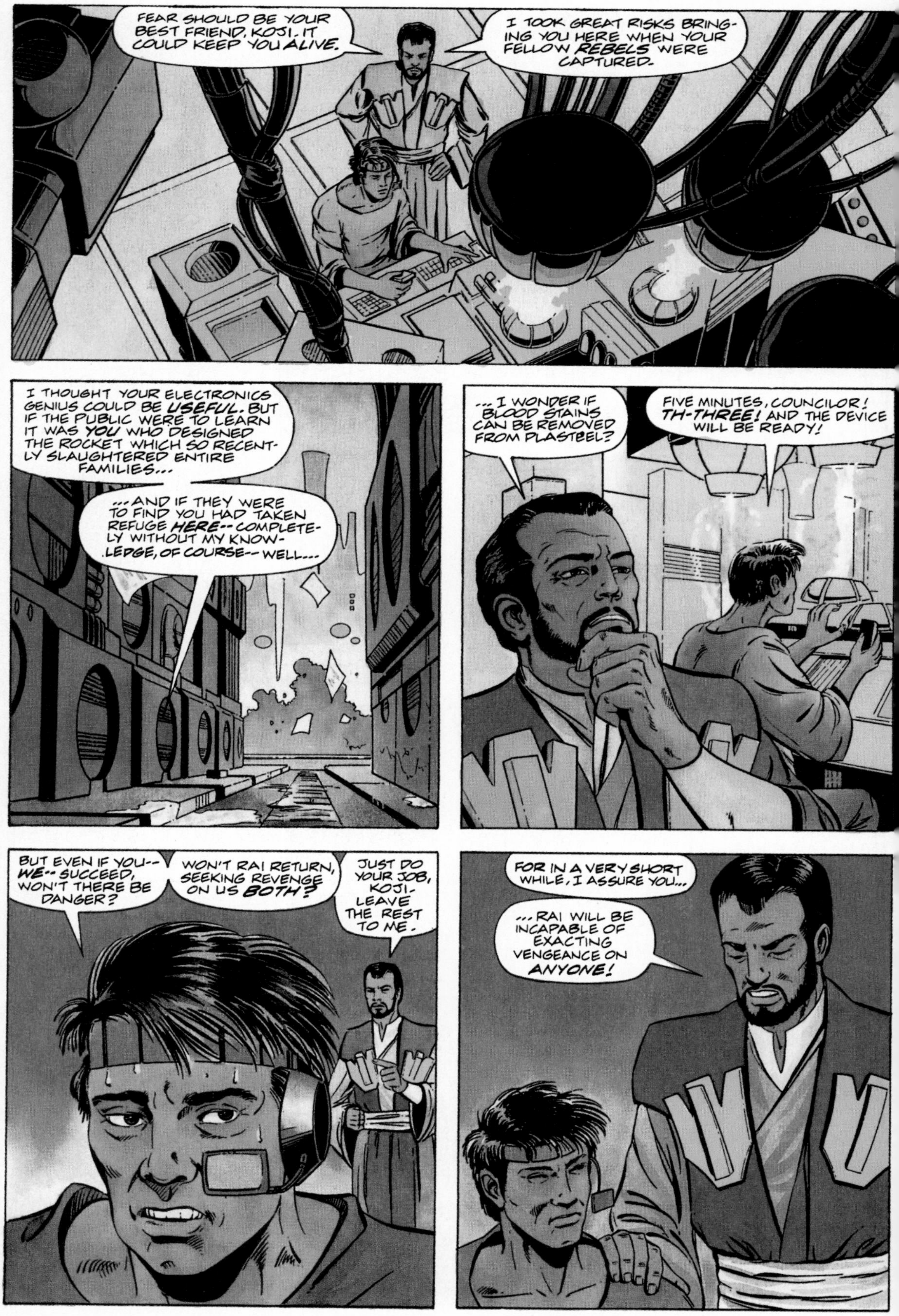
FEAR SHOULD BE YOUR BEST FRIEND, KOJI. IT COULD KEEP YOU ALIVE.
I TOOK GREAT RISKS BRINGING YOU HERE WHEN YOUR FELLOW REBELS WERE CAPTURED.
I THOUGHT YOUR ELECTRONICS GENIUS COULD BE USEFUL. BUT IF THE PUBLIC WERE TO LEARN IT WAS YOU WHO DESIGNED THE ROCKET WHICH SO RECENTLY SLAUGHTERED ENTIRE FAMILIES...
...AND IF THEY WERE TO FIND YOU HAD TAKEN REFUGE HERE--COMPLETELY WITHOUT MY KNOWLEDGE, OF COURSE--WELL...
...I WONDER IF BLOOD STAINS CAN BE REMOVED FROM PLASTEEL?
FIVE MINUTES, COUNCILOR! TH-THREE! AND THE DEVICE WILL BE READY!
BUT EVEN IF YOU--WE--SUCCEED, WON'T THERE BE DANGER?
WON'T RAI RETURN, SEEKING REVENGE ON US BOTH?
JUST DO YOUR JOB, KOJI. LEAVE THE REST TO ME.
FOR IN A VERY SHORT WHILE, I ASSURE YOU...
...RAI WILL BE INCAPABLE OF EXACTING VENGEANCE ON ANYONE!

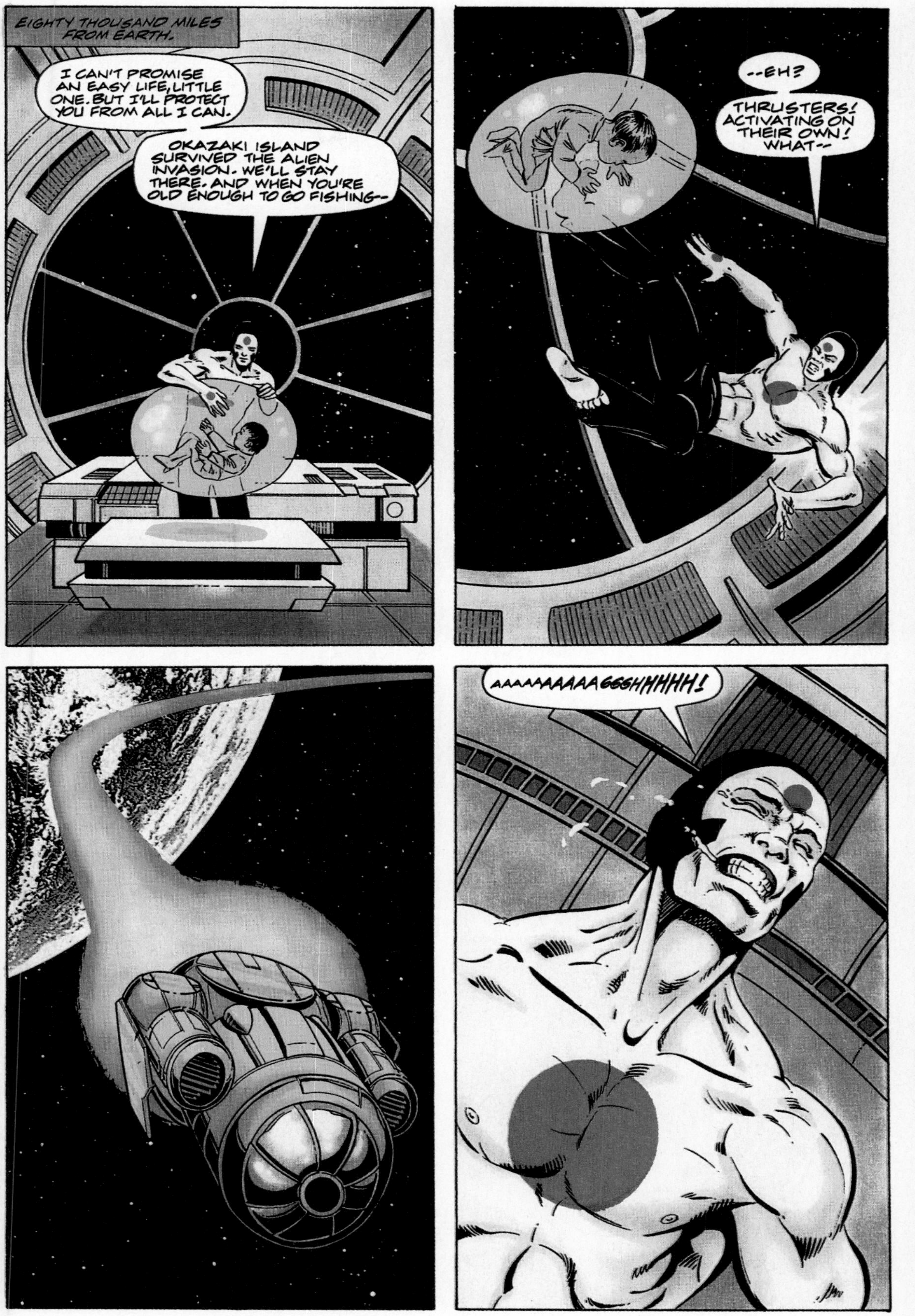
EIGHTY THOUSAND MILES FROM EARTH.
I CAN'T PROMISE AN EASY LIFE, LITTLE ONE. BUT I'LL PROTECT YOU FROM ALL I CAN.
OKAZAKI ISLAND SURVIVED THE ALIEN INVASION. WE'LL STAY THERE. AND WHEN YOU'RE OLD ENOUGH TO GO FISHING--
--EH?
THRUSTERS! ACTIVATING ON THEIR OWN! WHAT--
AAAAAAAAAAGGGHHHHH!

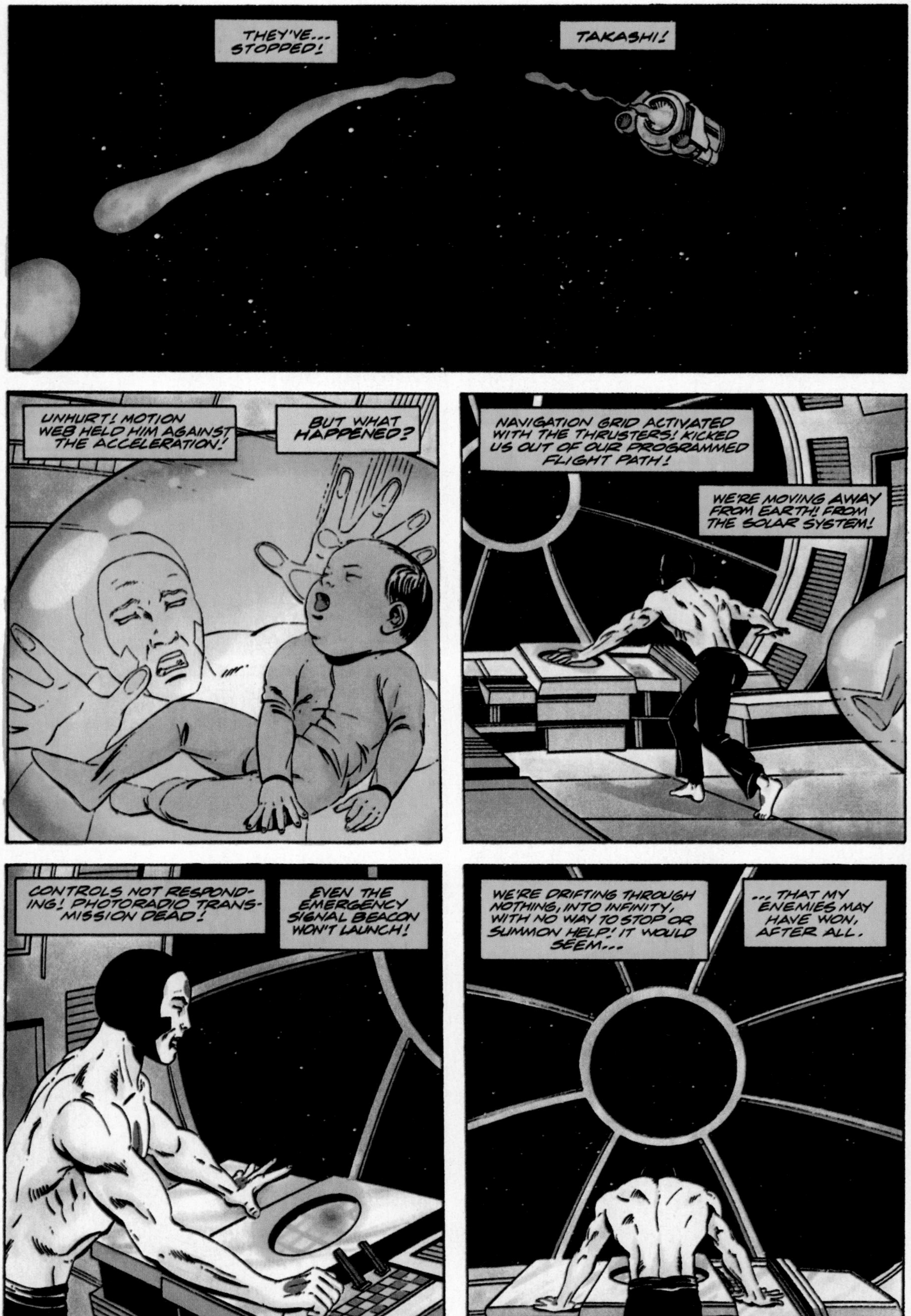
THEY'VE... STOPPED!
TAKASHI!
UNHURT! MOTION WEB HELD HIM AGAINST THE ACCELERATION!
BUT WHAT HAPPENED?
NAVIGATION GRID ACTIVATED WITH THE THRUSTERS! KICKED US OUT OF OUR PROGRAMMED FLIGHT PATH!
WE'RE MOVING AWAY FROM EARTH! FROM THE SOLAR SYSTEM!
CONTROLS NOT RESPONDING! PHOTORADIO TRANSMISSION DEAD!
EVEN THE EMERGENCY SIGNAL BEACON WON'T LAUNCH!
WE'RE DRIFTING THROUGH NOTHING, INTO INFINITY, WITH NO WAY TO STOP OR SUMMON HELP! IT WOULD SEEM...
...THAT MY ENEMIES MAY HAVE WON, AFTER ALL.

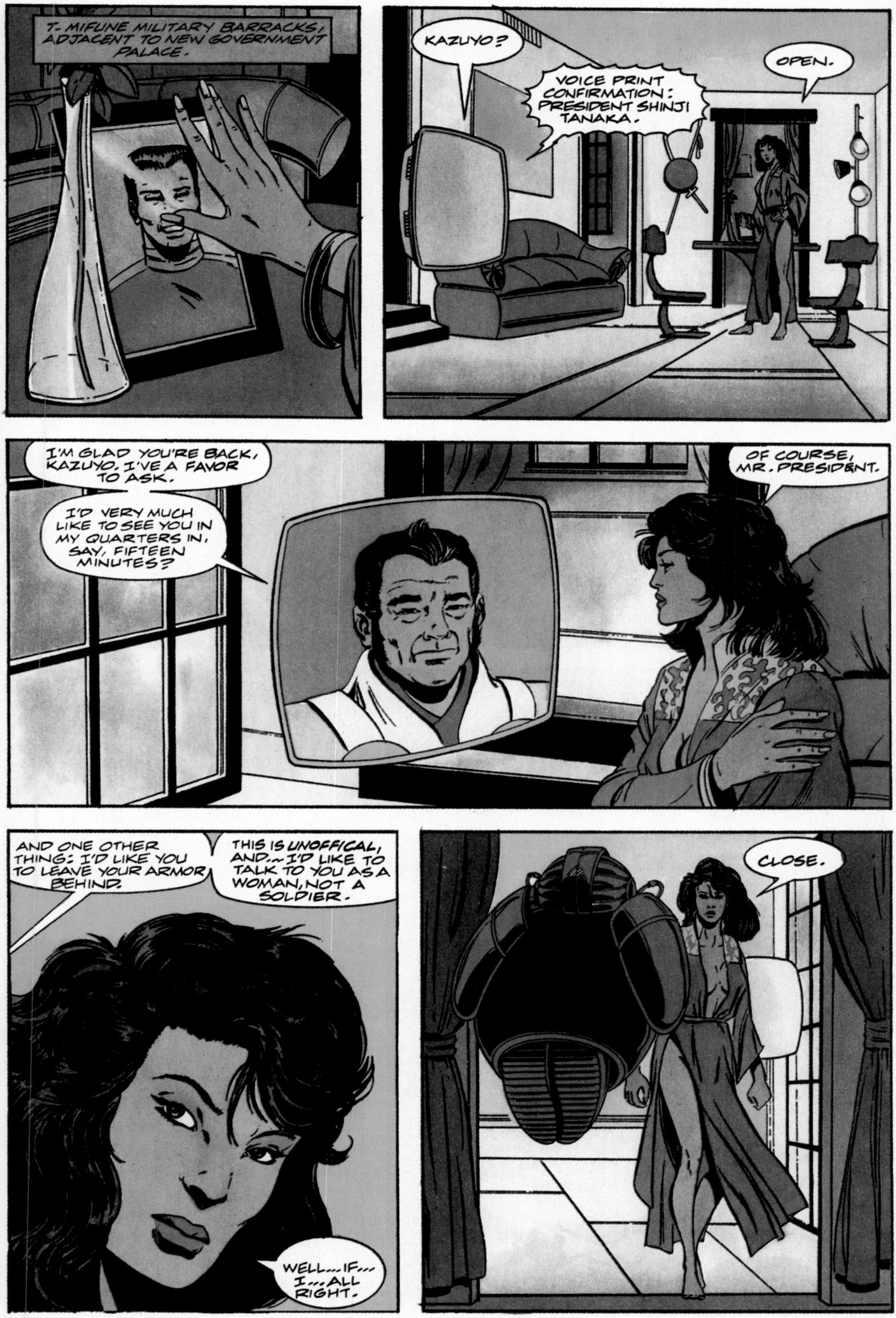
T. MIFUNE MILITARY BARRACKS, ADJACENT TO NEW GOVERNMENT PALACE.
KAZUYO?
VOICE PRINT CONFIRMATION: PRESIDENT SHINJI TANAKA.
OPEN.
I'M GLAD YOU'RE BACK, KAZUYO. I'VE A FAVOR TO ASK.
I'D VERY MUCH LIKE TO SEE YOU IN MY QUARTERS IN, SAY, FIFTEEN MINUTES?
OF COURSE, MR. PRESIDENT.
AND ONE OTHER THING: I'D LIKE YOU TO LEAVE YOUR ARMOR BEHIND.
THIS IS UNOFFICAL, AND...I'D LIKE TO TALK TO YOU AS A WOMAN, NOT A SOLDIER.
WELL...IF... I...ALL RIGHT.
CLOSE.

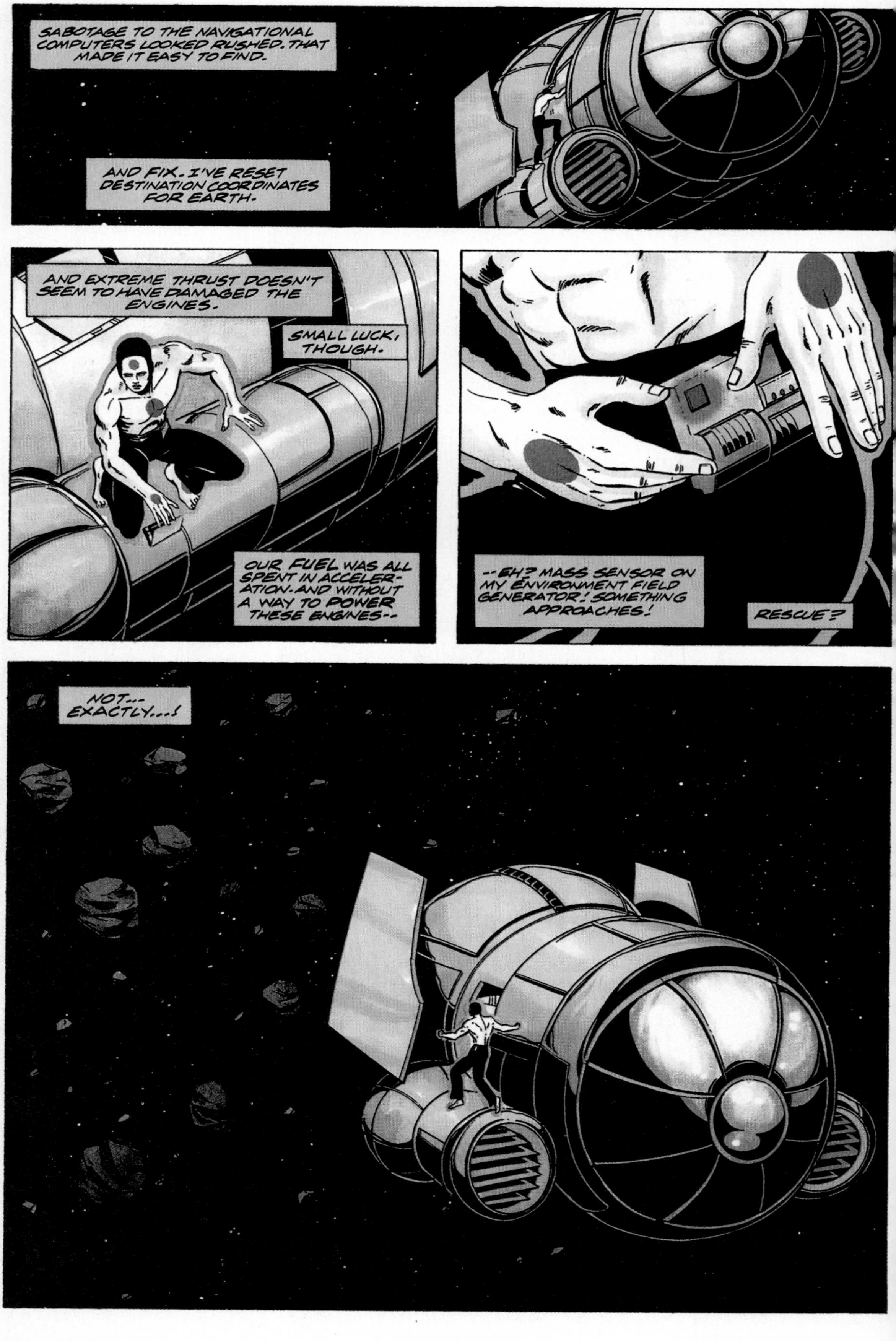
SABOTAGE TO THE NAVIGATIONAL COMPUTERS LOOKED RUSHED. THAT MADE IT EASY TO FIND.
AND FIX. I'VE RESET DESTINATION COORDINATES FOR EARTH.
AND EXTREME THRUST DOESN'T SEEM TO HAVE DAMAGED THE ENGINES.
SMALL LUCK, THOUGH.
OUR FUEL WAS ALL SPENT IN ACCELERATION. AND WITHOUT A WAY TO POWER THESE ENGINES--
--EH? MASS SENSOR ON MY ENVIRONMENT FIELD GENERATOR! SOMETHING APPROACHES!
RESCUE?
NOT... EXACTLY...!

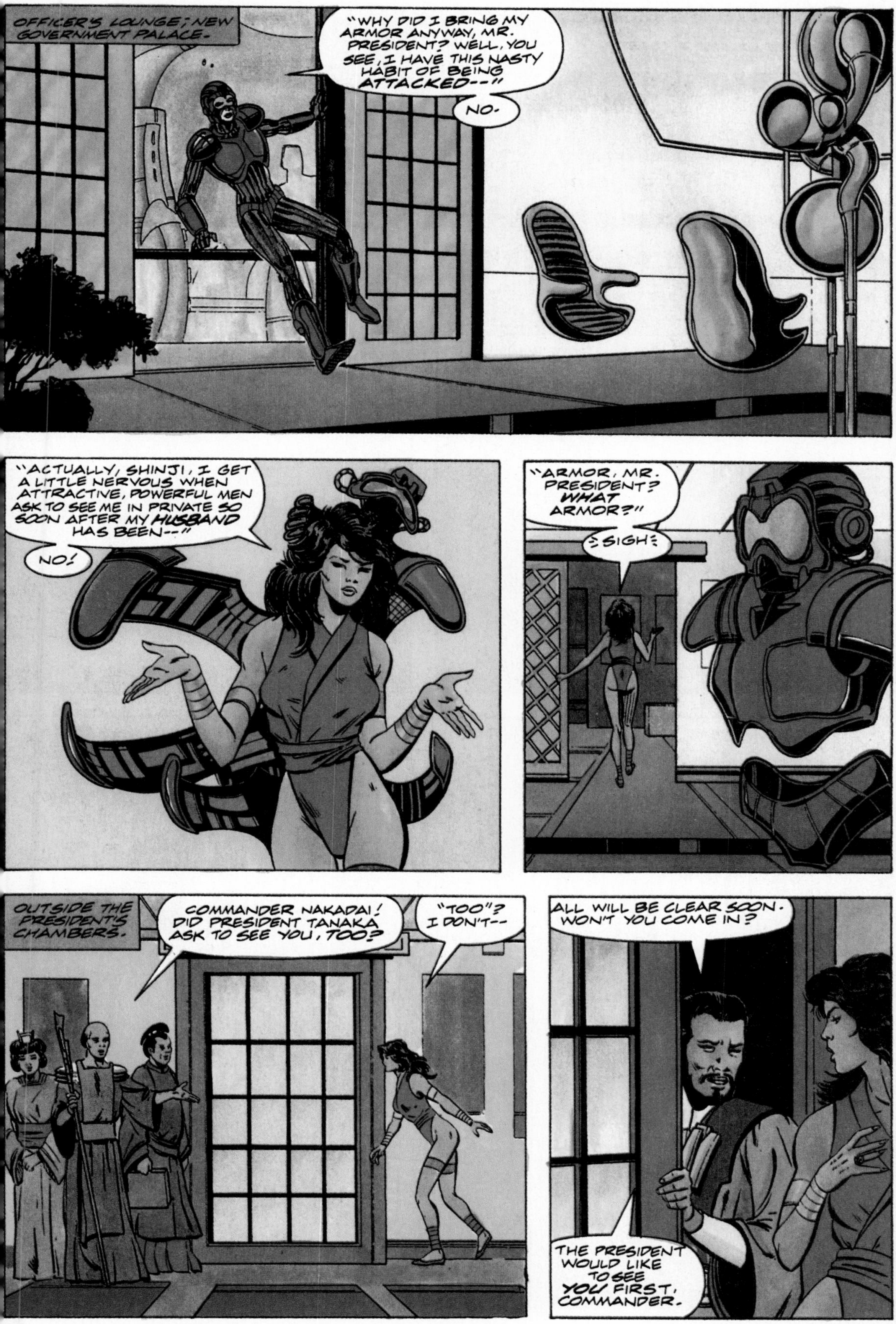
OFFICER'S LOUNGE; NEW GOVERNMENT PALACE.
"WHY DID I BRING MY ARMOR ANYWAY, MR. PRESIDENT? WELL, YOU SEE, I HAVE THIS NASTY HABIT OF BEING ATTACKED--"
NO.
"ACTUALLY, SHINJI, I GET A LITTLE NERVOUS WHEN ATTRACTIVE, POWERFUL MEN ASK TO SEE ME IN PRIVATE SO SOON AFTER MY HUSBAND HAS BEEN--"
NO!
"ARMOR, MR. PRESIDENT? WHAT ARMOR?"
SIGH
OUTSIDE THE PRESIDENT'S CHAMBERS.
COMMANDER NAKADAI! DID PRESIDENT TANAKA ASK TO SEE YOU, TOO?
"TOO"? I DON'T--
ALL WILL BE CLEAR SOON. WON'T YOU COME IN?
THE PRESIDENT WOULD LIKE TO SEE YOU FIRST, COMMANDER.

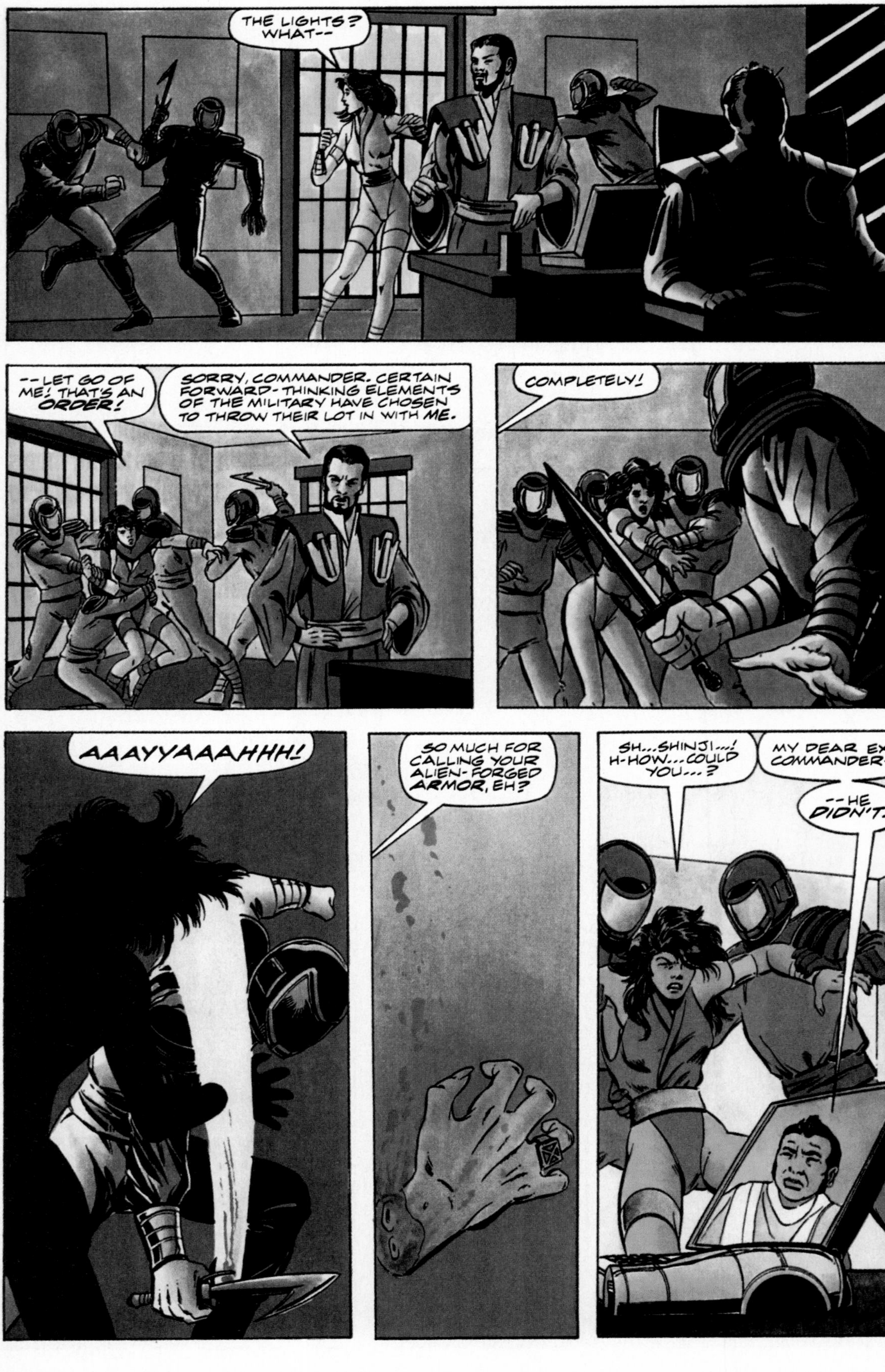
THE LIGHTS? WHAT--
--LET GO OF ME! THAT'S AN ORDER!
SORRY, COMMANDER. CERTAIN FORWARD-THINKING ELEMENTS OF THE MILITARY HAVE CHOSEN TO THROW THEIR LOT IN WITH ME.
COMPLETELY!
AAAYYAAAHHH!
SO MUCH FOR CALLING YOUR ALIEN-FORGED ARMOR, EH?
SH...SHINJI...! H-HOW...COULD YOU...?
MY DEAR EX-COMMANDER--
--HE DIDN'T!

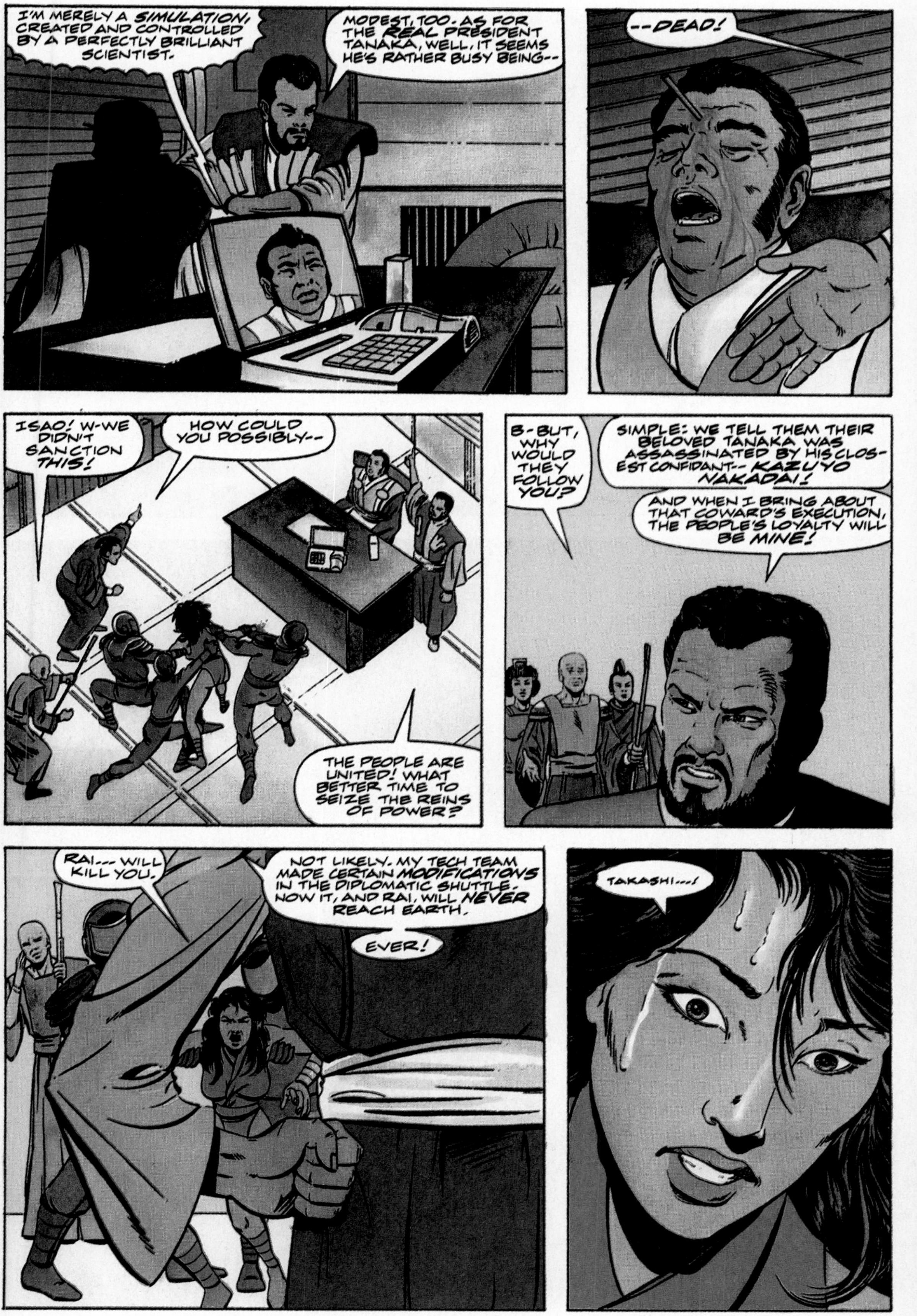
I'M MERELY A SIMULATION, CREATED AND CONTROLLED BY A PERFECTLY BRILLIANT SCIENTIST.
MODEST, TOO. AS FOR THE REAL PRESIDENT TANAKA, WELL, IT SEEMS HE'S RATHER BUSY BEING--
--DEAD!
ISAO! W-WE DIDN'T SANCTION THIS!
HOW COULD YOU POSSIBLY--
THE PEOPLE ARE UNITED! WHAT BETTER TIME TO SEIZE THE REINS OF POWER?
B-BUT, WHY WOULD THEY FOLLOW YOU?
SIMPLE: WE TELL THEM THEIR BELOVED TANAKA WAS ASSASSINATED BY HIS CLOSEST CONFIDANT-- KAZUYO NAKADAI!
AND WHEN I BRING ABOUT THAT COWARD'S EXECUTION, THE PEOPLE'S LOYALTY WILL BE MINE!
RAI... WILL KILL YOU.
NOT LIKELY. MY TECH TEAM MADE CERTAIN MODIFICATIONS IN THE DIPLOMATIC SHUTTLE. NOW IT, AND RAI, WILL NEVER REACH EARTH.
EVER!
TAKASHI...!

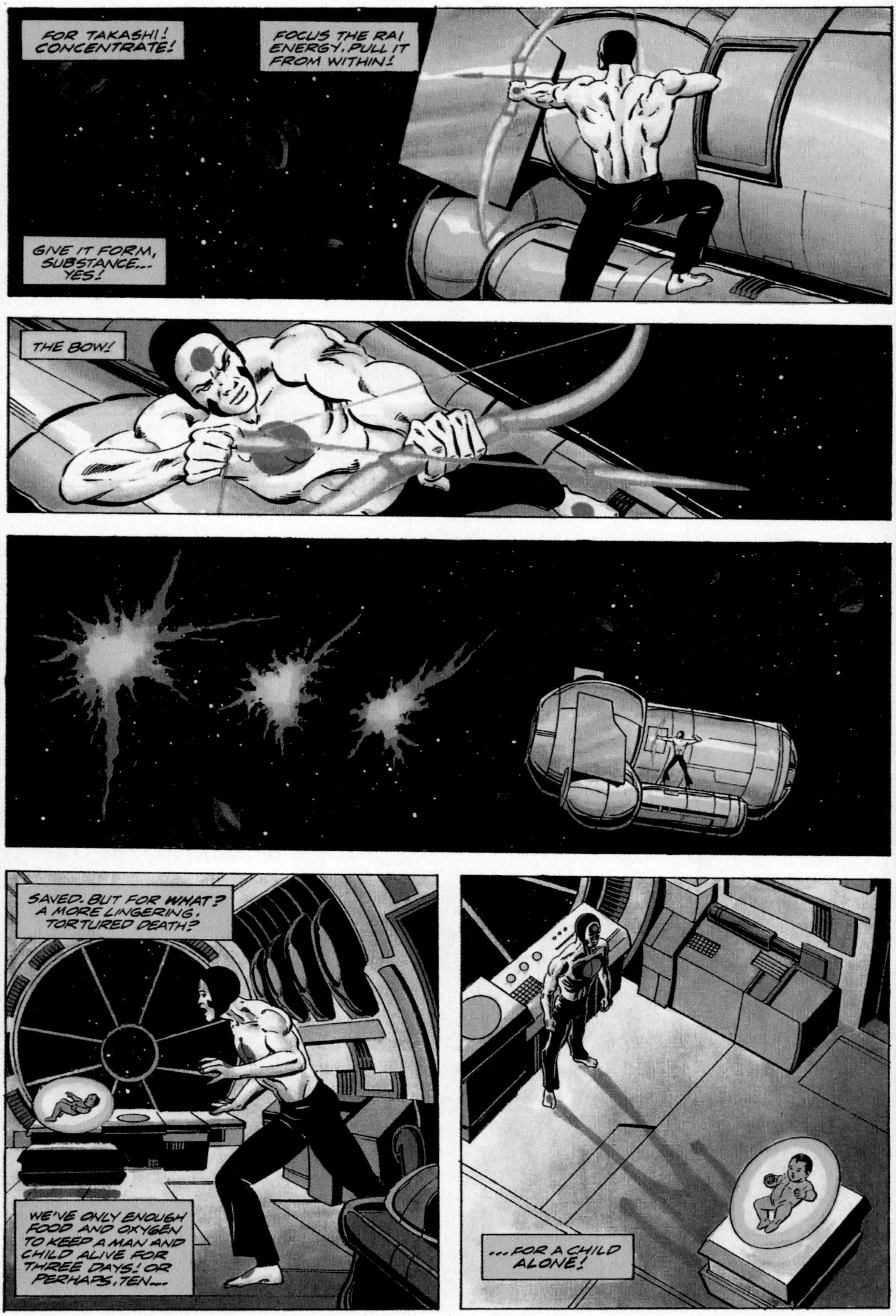
FOR TAKASHI! CONCENTRATE!
FOCUS THE RAI ENERGY. PULL IT FROM WITHIN!
GIVE IT FORM, SUBSTANCE... YES!
THE BOW!
SAVED. BUT FOR WHAT? A MORE LINGERING, TORTURED DEATH?
WE'VE ONLY ENOUGH FOOD AND OXYGEN TO KEEP A MAN AND CHILD ALIVE FOR THREE DAYS! OR PERHAPS, TEN...
...FOR A CHILD ALONE!

OBSERVATION WALL, DIPLOMATIC SHUTTLE; ONE HOUR LATER.

THERE'S TRAVEL BETWEEN THE PLANETS, THE MOONS. CHANCE OF OUR DRIFTING INTO A TRADE ROUTE IS SLIM, BUT IT'S THE ONLY CHANCE.

AND THE MORE TIME SPENT DRIFTING, THE *BETTER* THAT POSSIBILITY!

CONNECTING OUR ENTIRE SUPPLY OF NUTRIENTS TO AN INTRAVENOUS FEED FOR TAKASHI WAS TEDIOUS. AT LEAST SETTING ATMOSPHERE CONTROLS TO SIPHON OXYGEN FROM THE CABIN DIRECTLY INTO THE CRIB POD WAS SIMPLER.

I'M... SORRY.

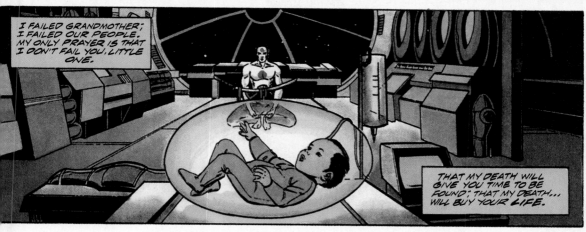

I FAILED GRANDMOTHER; I FAILED OUR PEOPLE. MY ONLY PRAYER IS THAT I DON'T FAIL YOU, LITTLE ONE.

THAT MY DEATH WILL GIVE YOU TIME TO BE FOUND; THAT MY DEATH... WILL BUY YOUR *LIFE*.

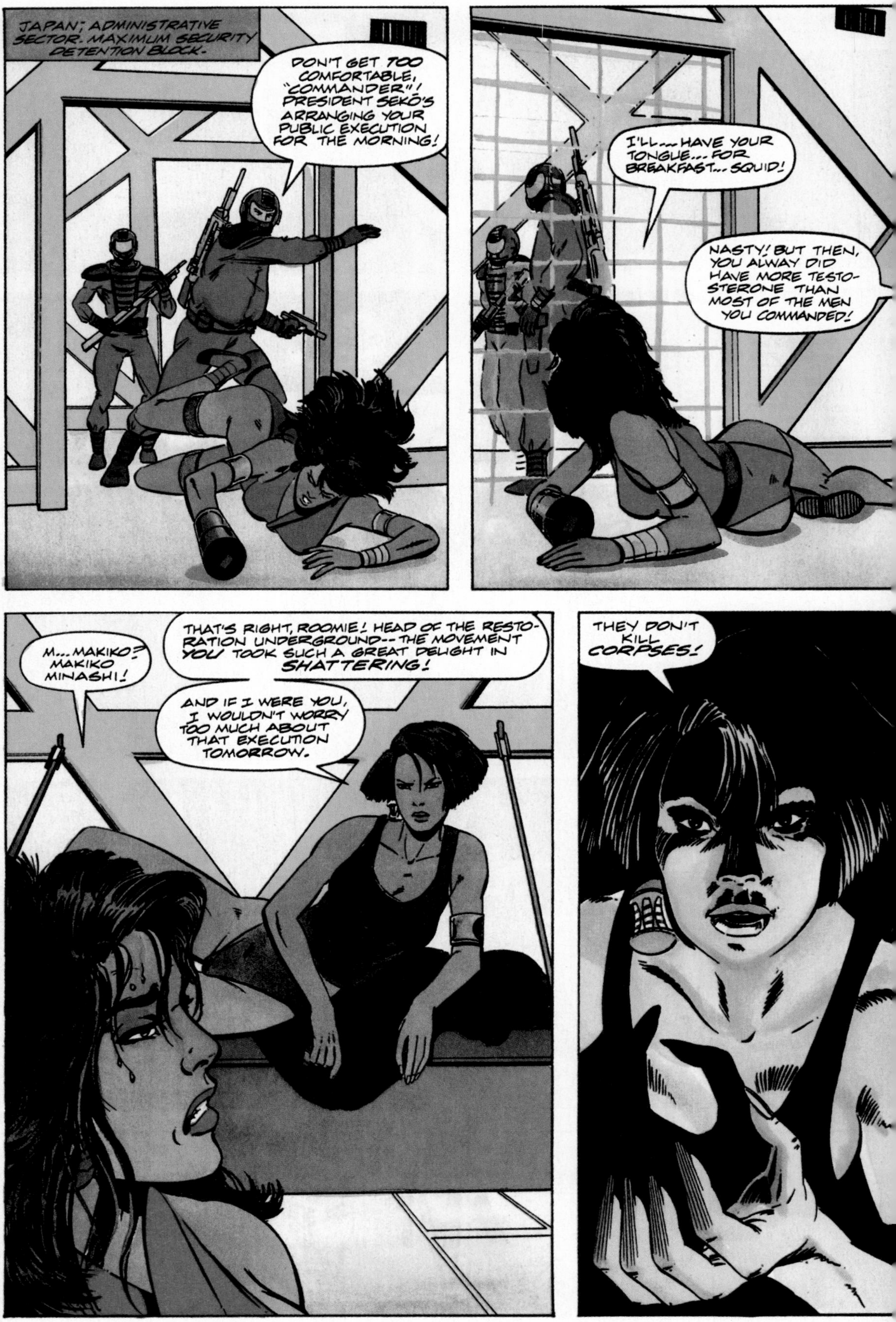
JAPAN; ADMINISTRATIVE SECTOR. MAXIMUM SECURITY DETENTION BLOCK.
DON'T GET TOO COMFORTABLE, "COMMANDER"! PRESIDENT SEKŌ'S ARRANGING YOUR PUBLIC EXECUTION FOR THE MORNING!
I'LL... HAVE YOUR TONGUE... FOR BREAKFAST... SQUID!
NASTY! BUT THEN, YOU ALWAY DID HAVE MORE TESTO-STERONE THAN MOST OF THE MEN YOU COMMANDED!
M... MAKIKO? MAKIKO MINASHI!
THAT'S RIGHT, ROOMIE! HEAD OF THE RESTO-RATION UNDERGROUND-- THE MOVEMENT YOU TOOK SUCH A GREAT DELIGHT IN SHATTERING!
AND IF I WERE YOU, I WOULDN'T WORRY TOO MUCH ABOUT THAT EXECUTION TOMORROW.
THEY DON'T KILL CORPSES!

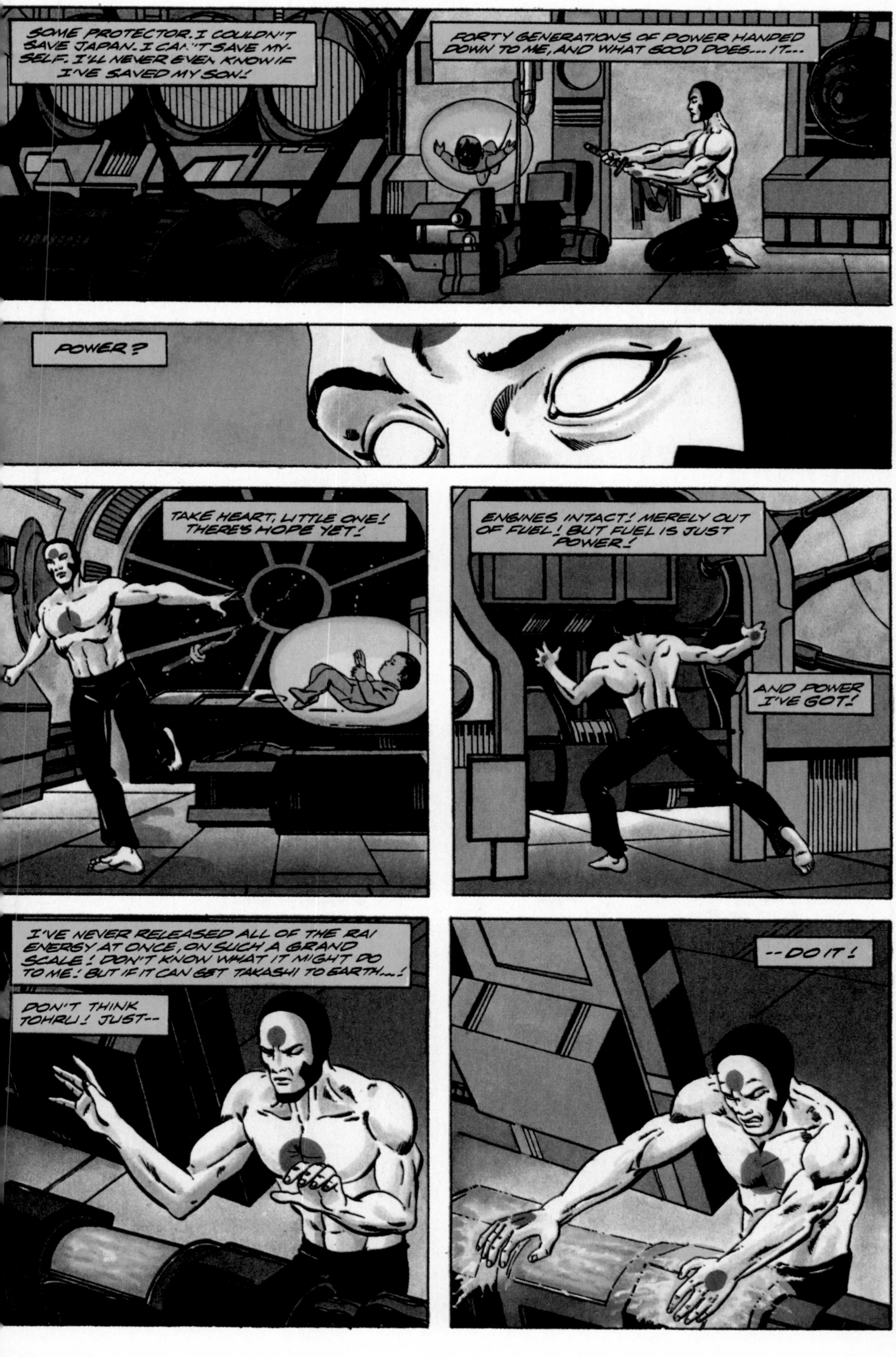
SOME PROTECTOR. I COULDN'T SAVE JAPAN. I CAN'T SAVE MY-SELF. I'LL NEVER EVEN KNOW IF I'VE SAVED MY SON!
FORTY GENERATIONS OF POWER HANDED DOWN TO ME, AND WHAT GOOD DOES... IT...
POWER?
TAKE HEART, LITTLE ONE! THERE'S HOPE YET!
ENGINES INTACT! MERELY OUT OF FUEL! BUT FUEL IS JUST POWER!
AND POWER I'VE GOT!
I'VE NEVER RELEASED ALL OF THE RAI ENERGY AT ONCE, ON SUCH A GRAND SCALE! DON'T KNOW WHAT IT MIGHT DO TO ME! BUT IF IT CAN GET TAKASHI TO EARTH...!
DON'T THINK TOHRU! JUST--
--DO IT!

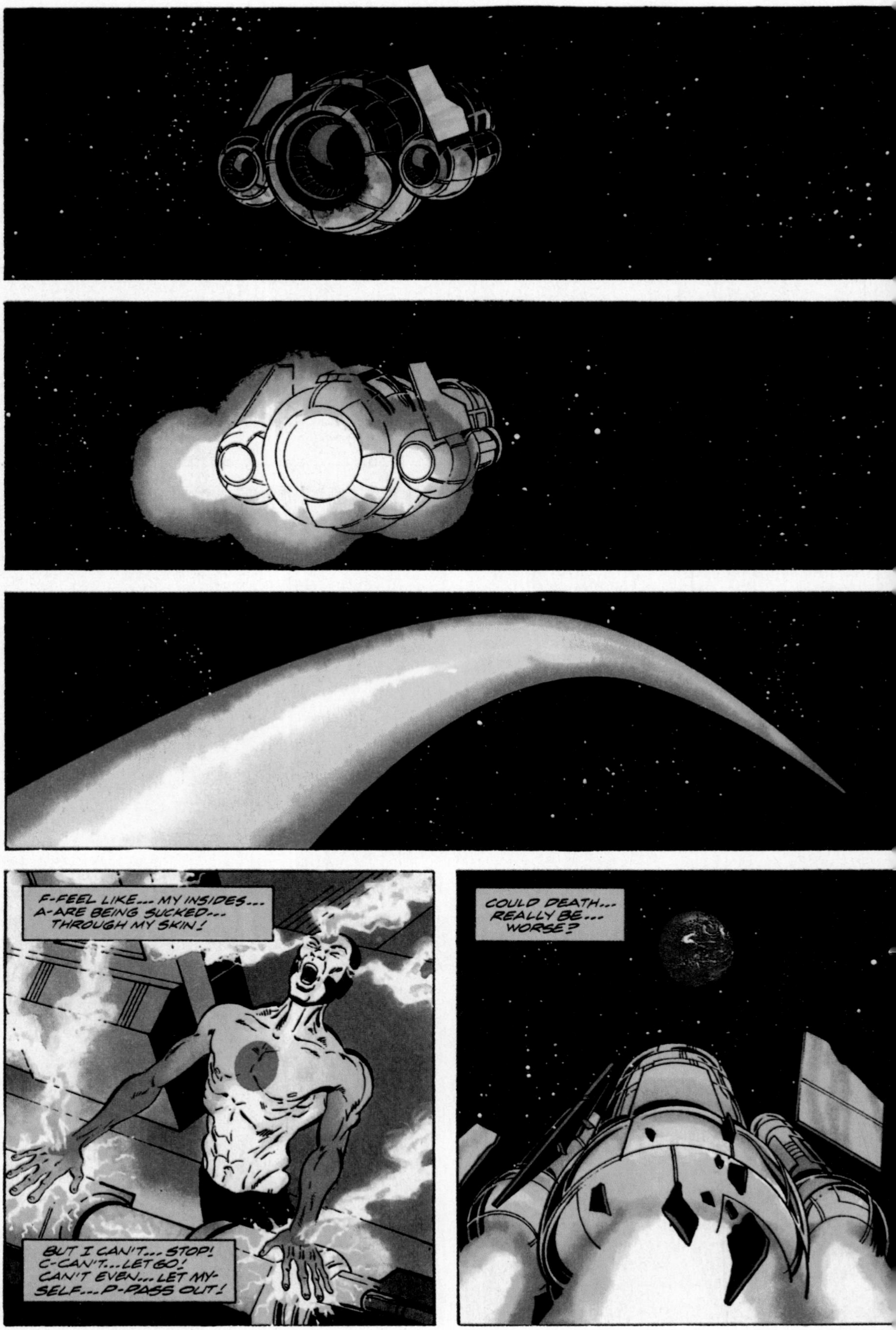
F-FEEL LIKE... MY INSIDES... A-ARE BEING SUCKED... THROUGH MY SKIN!
BUT I CAN'T... STOP! C-CAN'T... LET GO! CAN'T EVEN... LET MY-SELF... P-PASS OUT!
COULD DEATH... REALLY BE... WORSE?

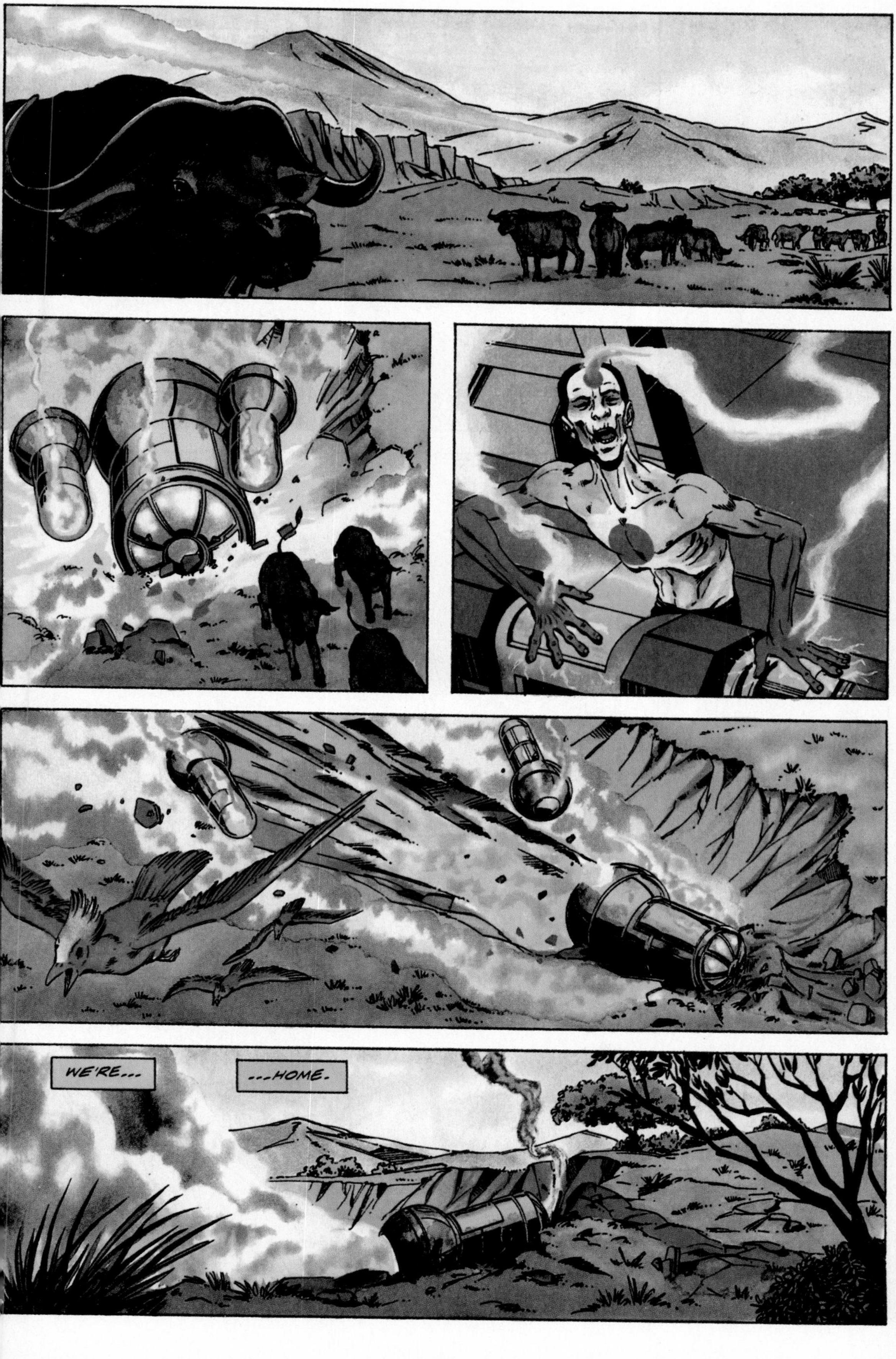
WE'RE...
...HOME.

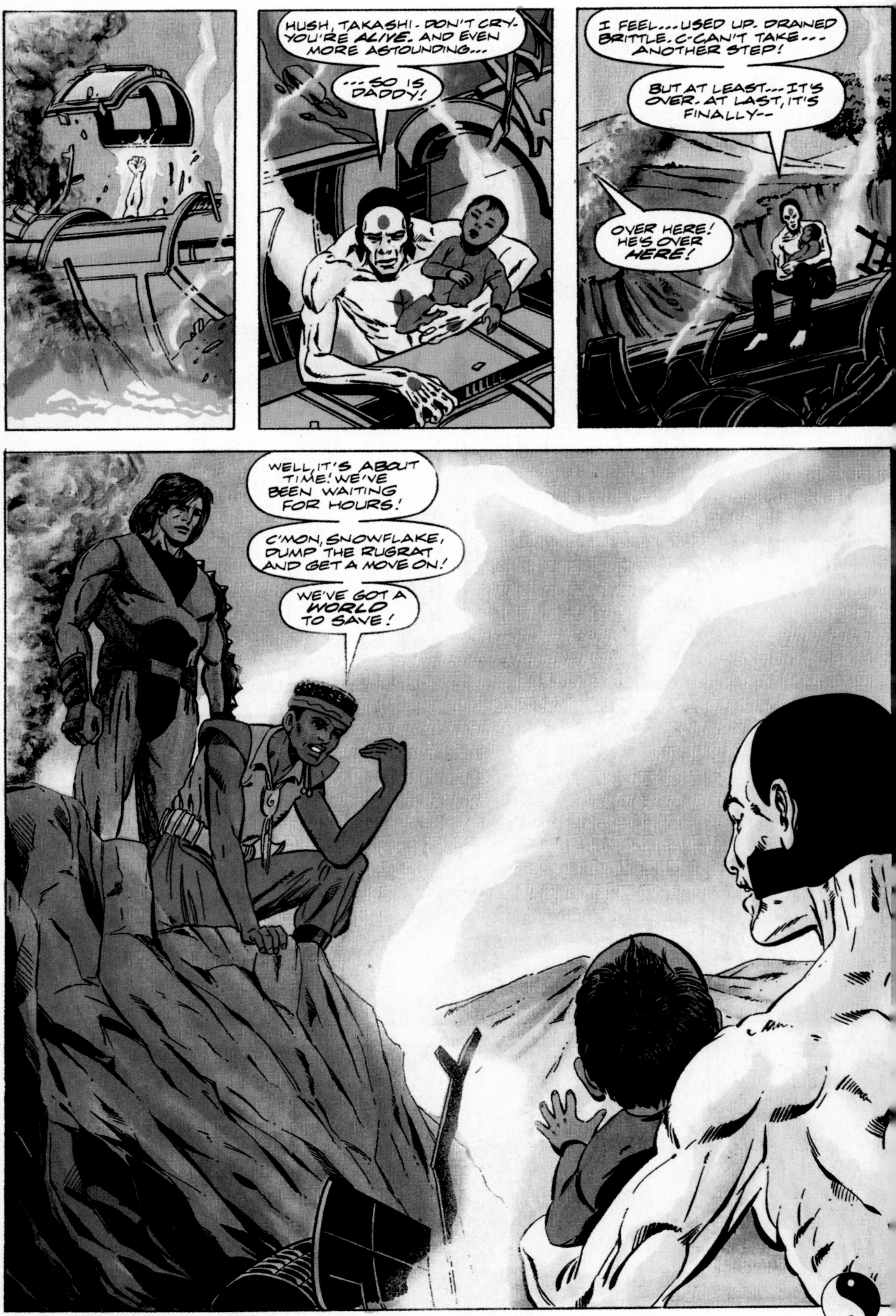
HUSH, TAKASHI - DON'T CRY. YOU'RE ALIVE. AND EVEN MORE ASTOUNDING...
...SO IS DADDY!
I FEEL... USED UP. DRAINED BRITTLE. C-CAN'T TAKE... ANOTHER STEP!
BUT AT LEAST... IT'S OVER. AT LAST, IT'S FINALLY--
OVER HERE! HE'S OVER HERE!
WELL, IT'S ABOUT TIME! WE'VE BEEN WAITING FOR HOURS!
C'MON, SNOWFLAKE, DUMP THE RUGRAT AND GET A MOVE ON!
WE'VE GOT A WORLD TO SAVE!

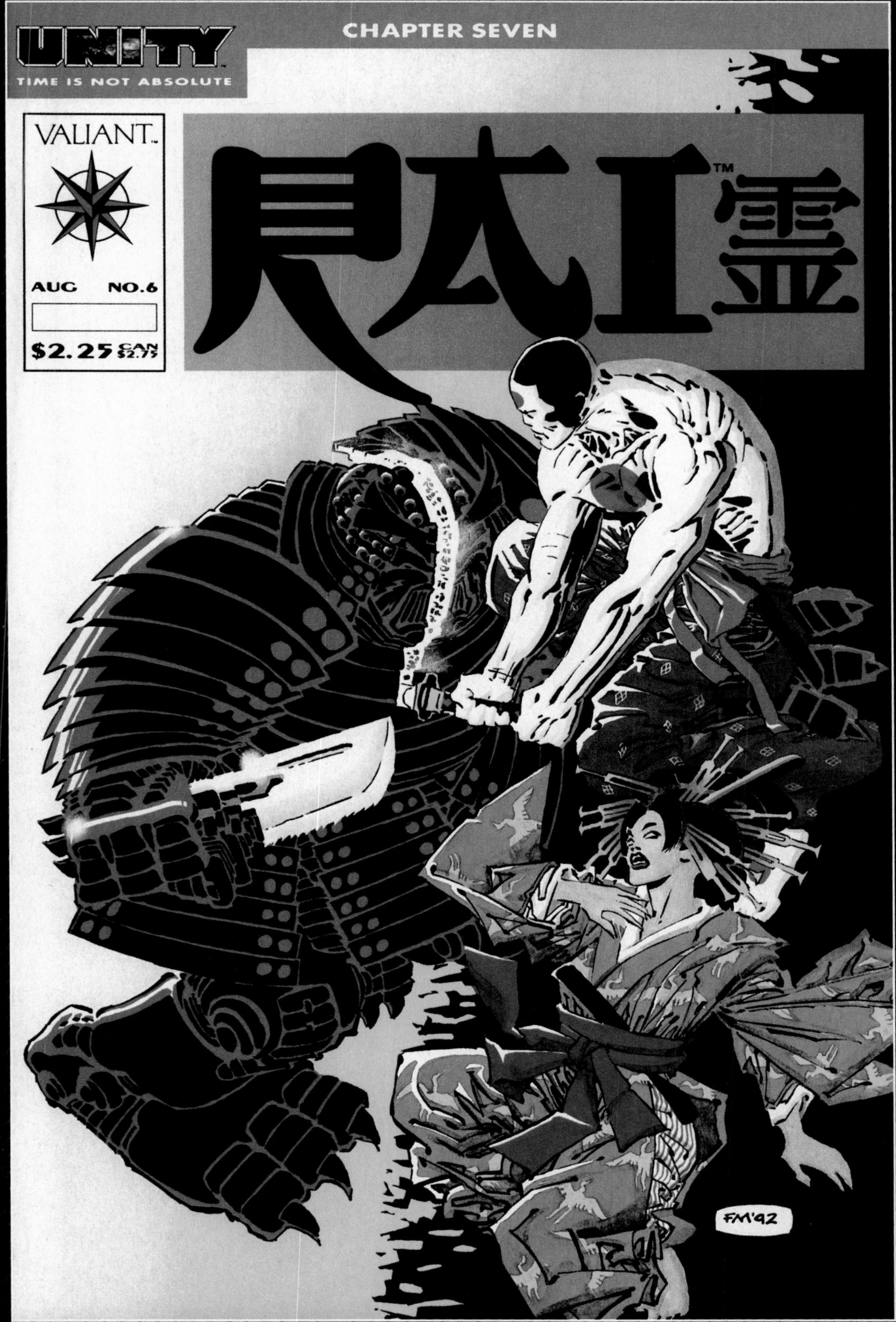

UNITY
TIME IS NOT ABSOLUTE
CHAPTER SEVEN
VALIANT™
AUG NO.6
$2.25 CAN $2.75
RAI™ 霊
FM'92

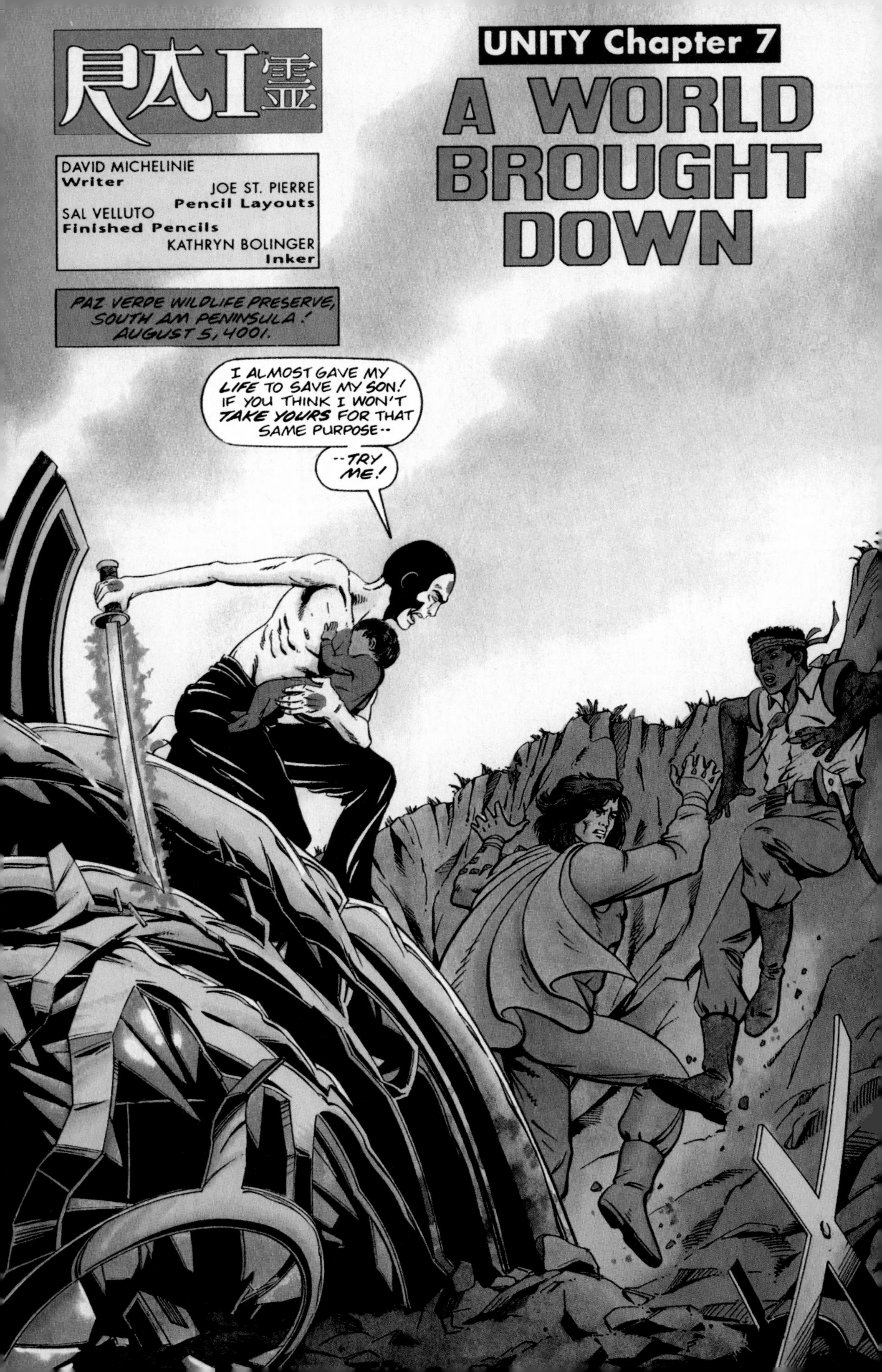

UNITY Chapter 7
A WORLD BROUGHT DOWN
DAVID MICHELINIE
Writer
JOE ST. PIERRE
Pencil Layouts
SAL VELLUTO
Finished Pencils
KATHRYN BOLINGER
Inker
PAZ VERDE WILDLIFE PRESERVE, SOUTH AM PENINSULA! AUGUST 5, 4001.
I ALMOST GAVE MY LIFE TO SAVE MY SON! IF YOU THINK I WON'T TAKE YOURS FOR THAT SAME PURPOSE--
--TRY ME!

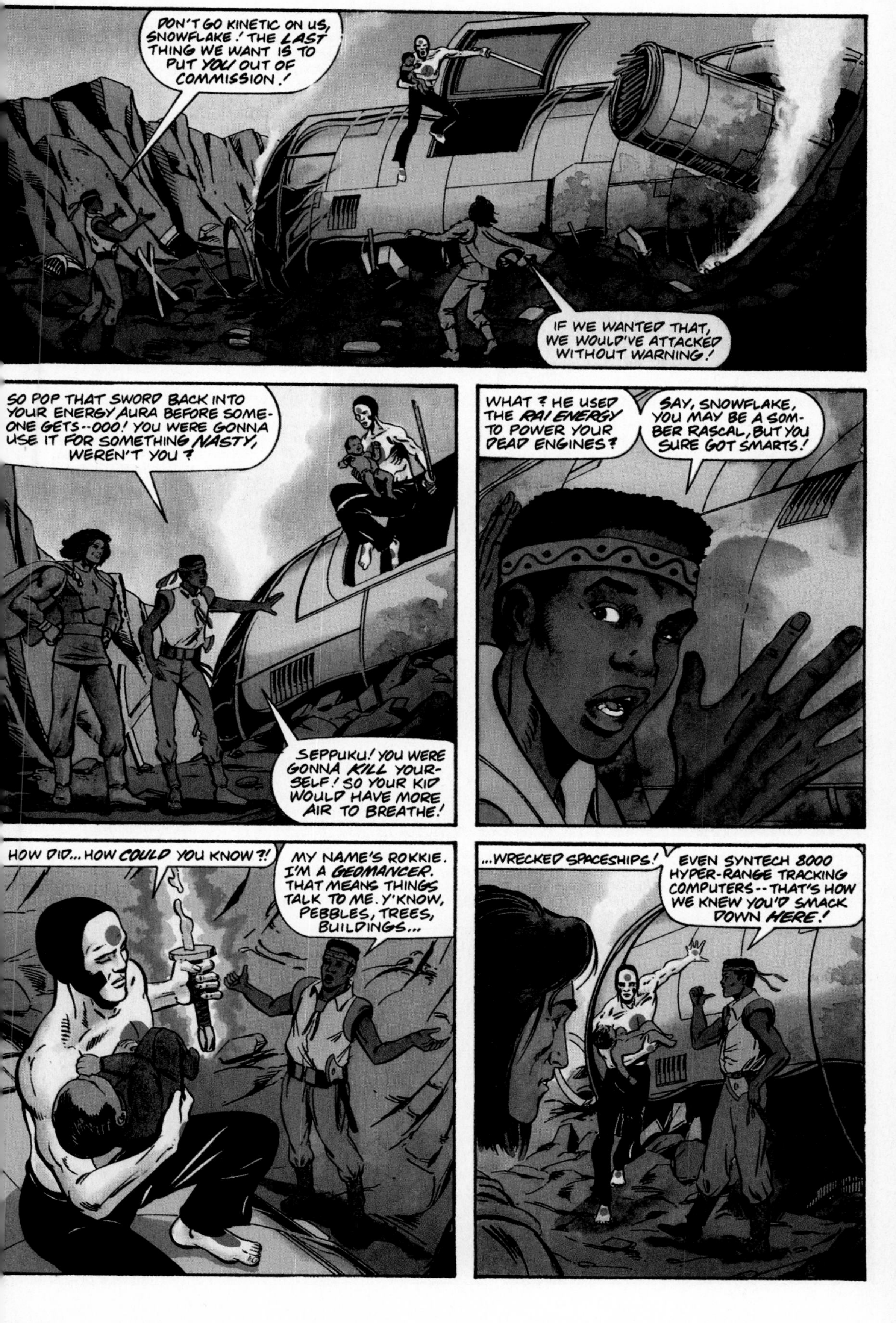
DON'T GO KINETIC ON US, SNOWFLAKE! THE LAST THING WE WANT IS TO PUT YOU OUT OF COMMISSION!
IF WE WANTED THAT, WE WOULD'VE ATTACKED WITHOUT WARNING!
SO POP THAT SWORD BACK INTO YOUR ENERGY AURA BEFORE SOMEONE GETS--OOO! YOU WERE GONNA USE IT FOR SOMETHING NASTY, WEREN'T YOU?
SEPPUKU! YOU WERE GONNA KILL YOURSELF! SO YOUR KID WOULD HAVE MORE AIR TO BREATHE!
WHAT? HE USED THE RAI ENERGY TO POWER YOUR DEAD ENGINES?
SAY, SNOWFLAKE, YOU MAY BE A SOMBER RASCAL, BUT YOU SURE GOT SMARTS!
HOW DID... HOW COULD YOU KNOW?!
MY NAME'S ROKKIE. I'M A GEOMANCER. THAT MEANS THINGS TALK TO ME. Y'KNOW, PEBBLES, TREES, BUILDINGS...
...WRECKED SPACESHIPS!
EVEN SYNTECH 8000 HYPER-RANGE TRACKING COMPUTERS--THAT'S HOW WE KNEW YOU'D SMACK DOWN HERE!

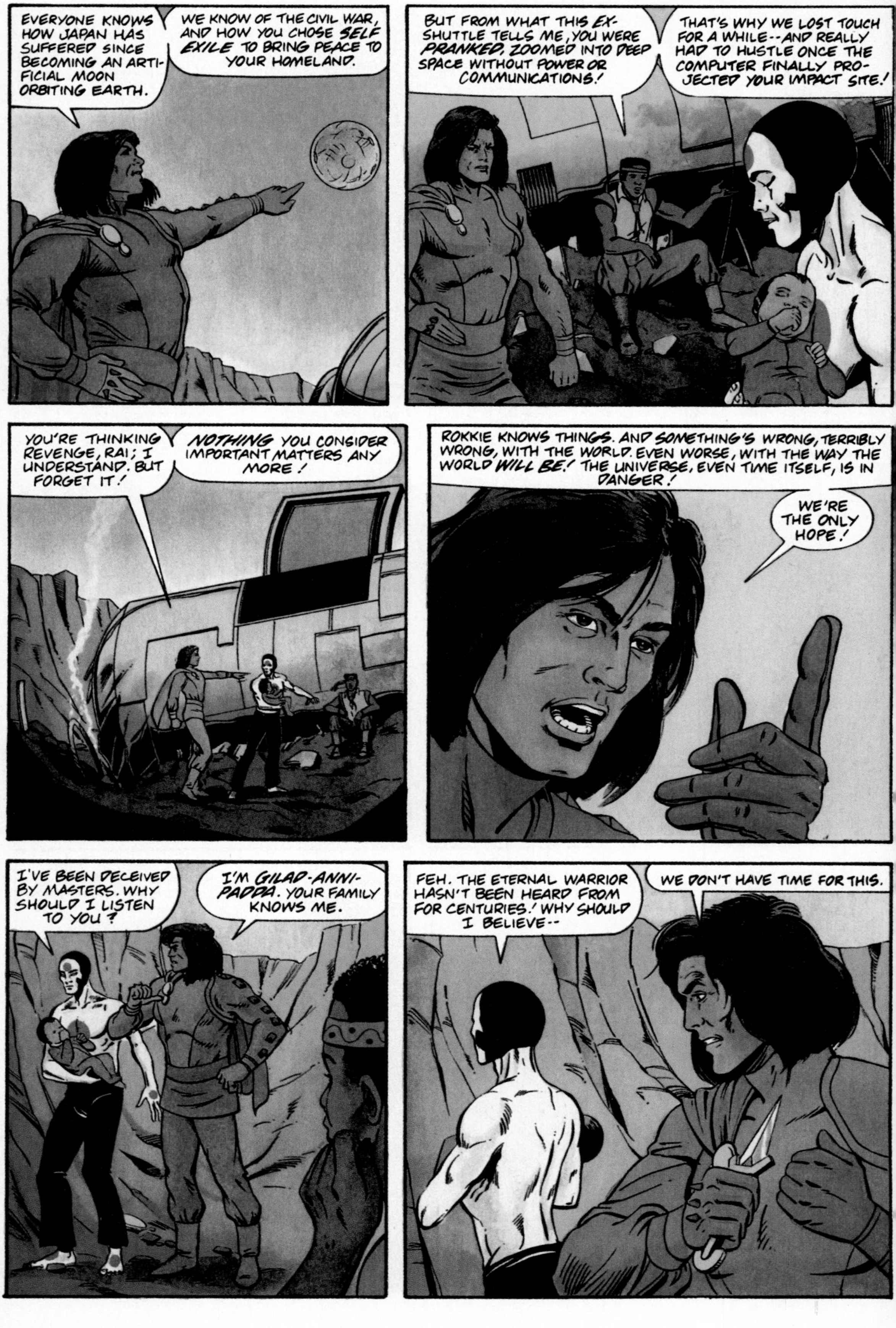
EVERYONE KNOWS HOW JAPAN HAS SUFFERED SINCE BECOMING AN ARTIFICIAL MOON ORBITING EARTH.
WE KNOW OF THE CIVIL WAR, AND HOW YOU CHOSE SELF EXILE TO BRING PEACE TO YOUR HOMELAND.
BUT FROM WHAT THIS EX-SHUTTLE TELLS ME, YOU WERE PRANKED, ZOOMED INTO DEEP SPACE WITHOUT POWER OR COMMUNICATIONS!
THAT'S WHY WE LOST TOUCH FOR A WHILE--AND REALLY HAD TO HUSTLE ONCE THE COMPUTER FINALLY PROJECTED YOUR IMPACT SITE!
YOU'RE THINKING REVENGE, RAI; I UNDERSTAND. BUT FORGET IT!
NOTHING YOU CONSIDER IMPORTANT MATTERS ANY MORE!
ROKKIE KNOWS THINGS. AND SOMETHING'S WRONG, TERRIBLY WRONG, WITH THE WORLD. EVEN WORSE, WITH THE WAY THE WORLD WILL BE! THE UNIVERSE, EVEN TIME ITSELF, IS IN DANGER!
WE'RE THE ONLY HOPE!
I'VE BEEN DECEIVED BY MASTERS. WHY SHOULD I LISTEN TO YOU?
I'M GILAD-ANNI-PADDA. YOUR FAMILY KNOWS ME.
FEH. THE ETERNAL WARRIOR HASN'T BEEN HEARD FROM FOR CENTURIES! WHY SHOULD I BELIEVE--
WE DON'T HAVE TIME FOR THIS.

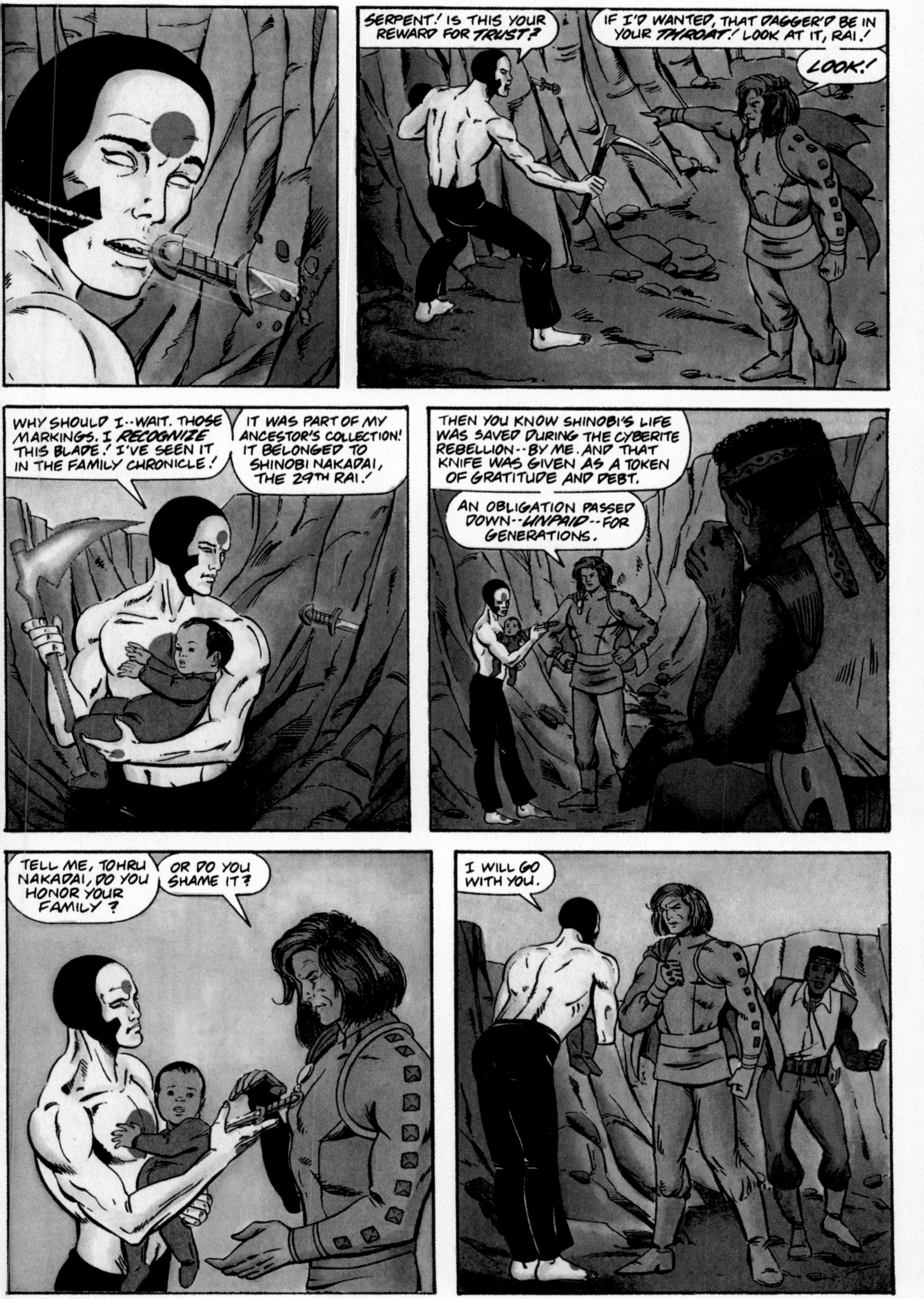
SERPENT! IS THIS YOUR REWARD FOR TRUST?
IF I'D WANTED, THAT DAGGER'D BE IN YOUR THROAT! LOOK AT IT, RAI!
LOOK!
WHY SHOULD I--WAIT. THOSE MARKINGS. I RECOGNIZE THIS BLADE! I'VE SEEN IT IN THE FAMILY CHRONICLE!
IT WAS PART OF MY ANCESTOR'S COLLECTION! IT BELONGED TO SHINOBI NAKADAI, THE 29TH RAI!
THEN YOU KNOW SHINOBI'S LIFE WAS SAVED DURING THE CYBERITE REBELLION--BY ME. AND THAT KNIFE WAS GIVEN AS A TOKEN OF GRATITUDE AND DEBT.
AN OBLIGATION PASSED DOWN--UNPAID--FOR GENERATIONS.
TELL ME, TOHRU NAKADAI, DO YOU HONOR YOUR FAMILY?
OR DO YOU SHAME IT?
I WILL GO WITH YOU.

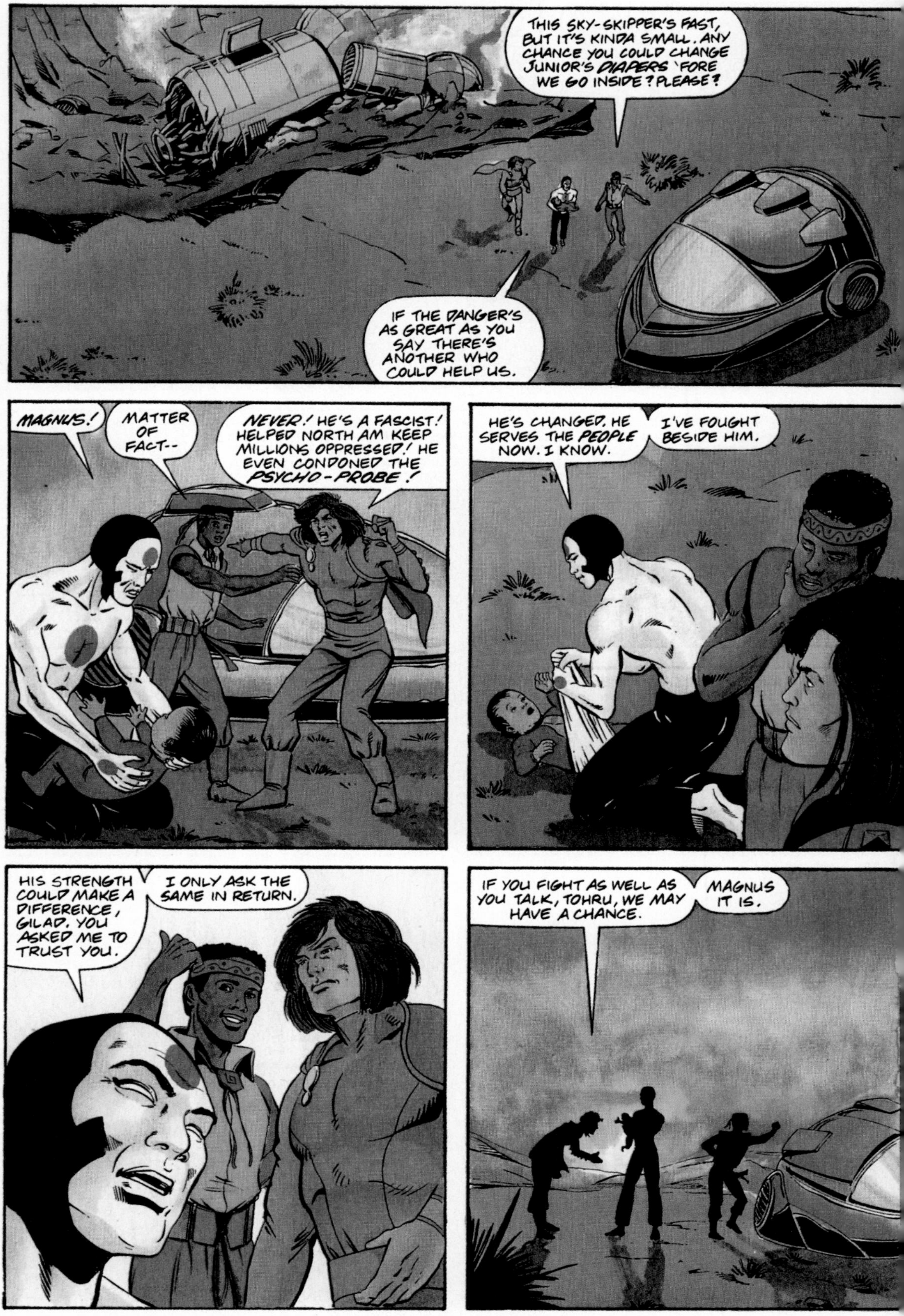
THIS SKY-SKIPPER'S FAST, BUT IT'S KINDA SMALL. ANY CHANCE YOU COULD CHANGE JUNIOR'S DIAPERS 'FORE WE GO INSIDE? PLEASE?
IF THE DANGER'S AS GREAT AS YOU SAY THERE'S ANOTHER WHO COULD HELP US.
MAGNUS!
MATTER OF FACT--
NEVER! HE'S A FASCIST! HELPED NORTH AM KEEP MILLIONS OPPRESSED! HE EVEN CONDONED THE PSYCHO-PROBE!
HE'S CHANGED. HE SERVES THE PEOPLE NOW. I KNOW.
I'VE FOUGHT BESIDE HIM.
HIS STRENGTH COULD MAKE A DIFFERENCE, GILAD. YOU ASKED ME TO TRUST YOU.
I ONLY ASK THE SAME IN RETURN.
IF YOU FIGHT AS WELL AS YOU TALK, TOHRU, WE MAY HAVE A CHANCE.
MAGNUS IT IS.

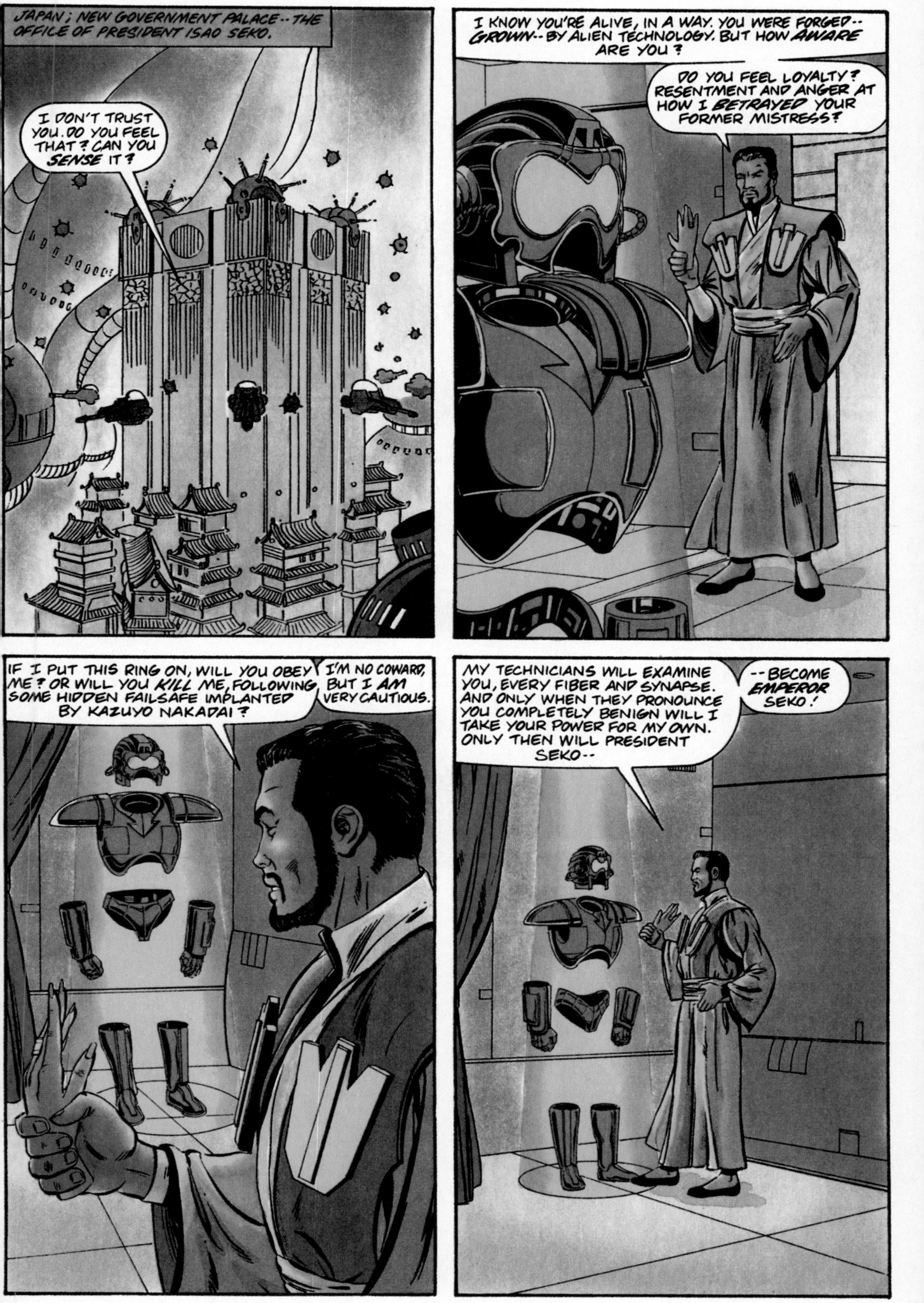

JAPAN; NEW GOVERNMENT PALACE -- THE OFFICE OF PRESIDENT ISAO SEKO.
I DON'T TRUST YOU. DO YOU FEEL THAT? CAN YOU SENSE IT?
I KNOW YOU'RE ALIVE, IN A WAY. YOU WERE FORGED -- GROWN -- BY ALIEN TECHNOLOGY. BUT HOW AWARE ARE YOU?
DO YOU FEEL LOYALTY? RESENTMENT AND ANGER AT HOW I BETRAYED YOUR FORMER MISTRESS?
IF I PUT THIS RING ON, WILL YOU OBEY ME? OR WILL YOU KILL ME, FOLLOWING SOME HIDDEN FAILSAFE IMPLANTED BY KAZUYO NAKADAI?
I'M NO COWARD, BUT I AM VERY CAUTIOUS.
MY TECHNICIANS WILL EXAMINE YOU, EVERY FIBER AND SYNAPSE. AND ONLY WHEN THEY PRONOUNCE YOU COMPLETELY BENIGN WILL I TAKE YOUR POWER FOR MY OWN. ONLY THEN WILL PRESIDENT SEKO --
-- BECOME EMPEROR SEKO!

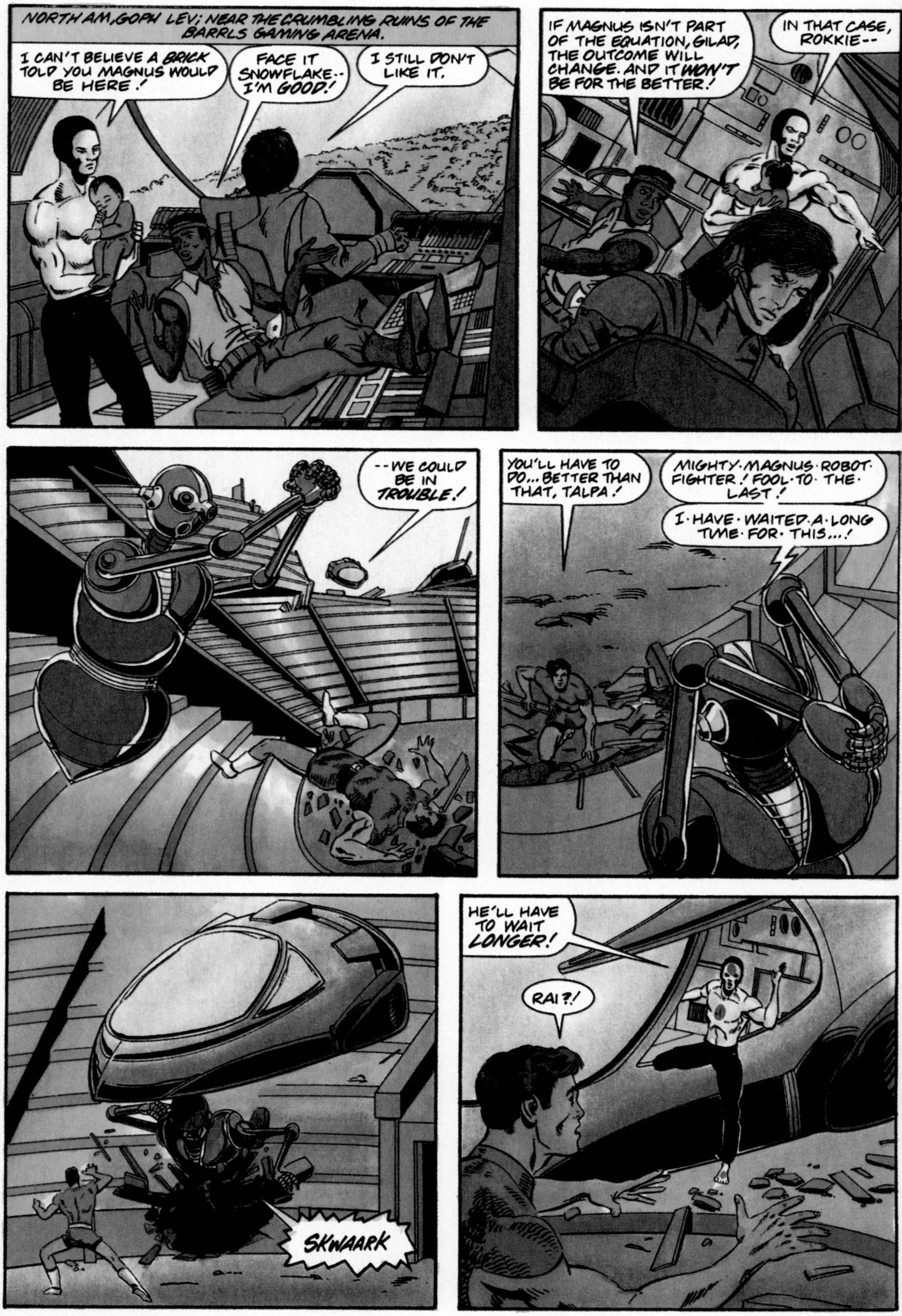
NORTH AM, GOPH LEV; NEAR THE CRUMBLING RUINS OF THE BARRLS GAMING ARENA.
I CAN'T BELIEVE A BRICK TOLD YOU MAGNUS WOULD BE HERE!
FACE IT SNOWFLAKE-- I'M GOOD!
I STILL DON'T LIKE IT.
IF MAGNUS ISN'T PART OF THE EQUATION, GILAD, THE OUTCOME WILL CHANGE. AND IT WON'T BE FOR THE BETTER!
IN THAT CASE, ROKKIE--
--WE COULD BE IN TROUBLE!
YOU'LL HAVE TO DO... BETTER THAN THAT, TALPA!
MIGHTY·MAGNUS·ROBOT·FIGHTER! FOOL·TO·THE·LAST!
I·HAVE·WAITED·A·LONG TIME·FOR·THIS...!
SKWAARK
HE'LL HAVE TO WAIT LONGER!
RAI?!

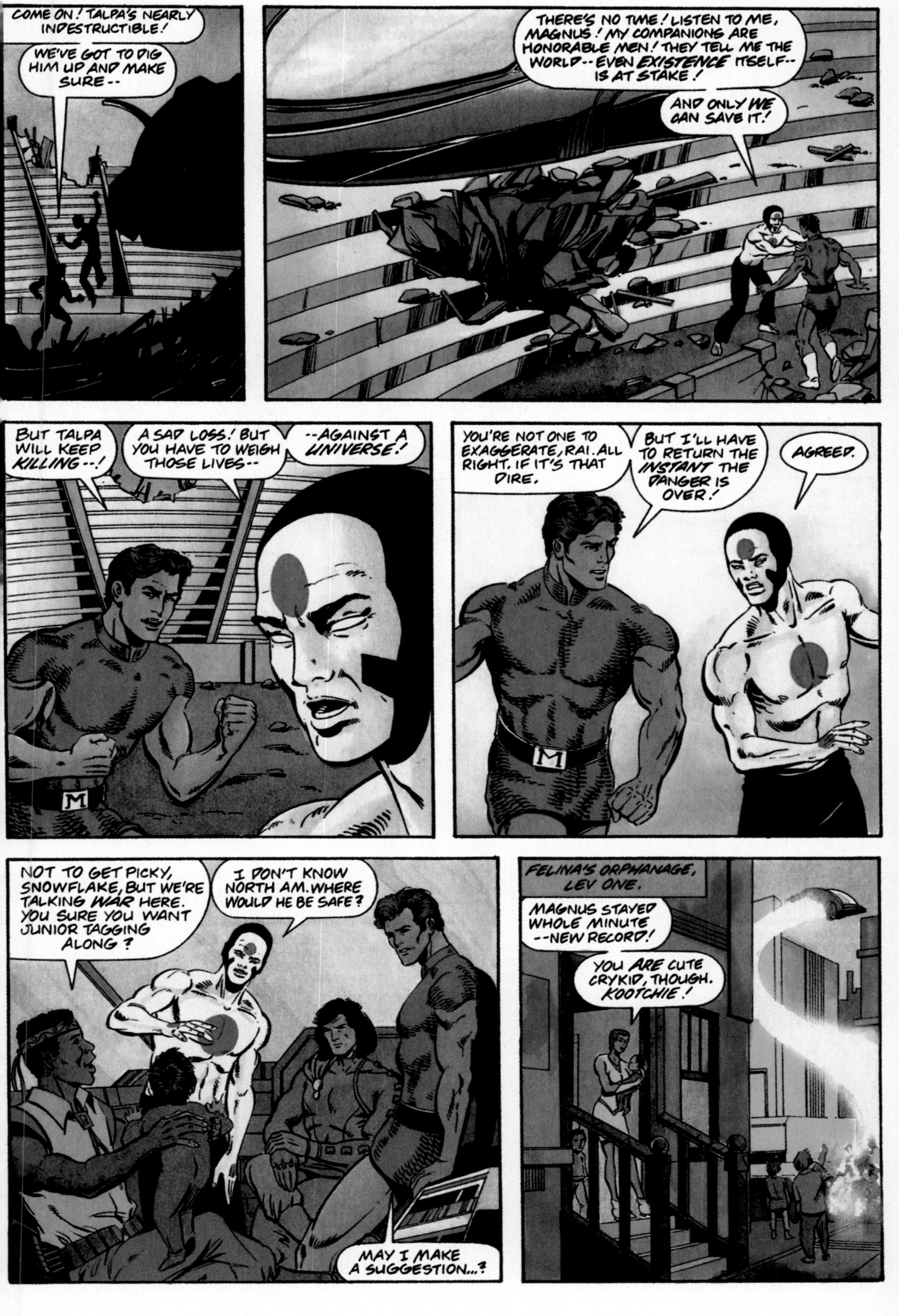
COME ON! TALPA'S NEARLY INDESTRUCTIBLE!
WE'VE GOT TO DIG HIM UP AND MAKE SURE--
THERE'S NO TIME! LISTEN TO ME, MAGNUS! MY COMPANIONS ARE HONORABLE MEN! THEY TELL ME THE WORLD--EVEN EXISTENCE ITSELF--IS AT STAKE!
AND ONLY WE CAN SAVE IT!
BUT TALPA WILL KEEP KILLING--!
A SAD LOSS! BUT YOU HAVE TO WEIGH THOSE LIVES--
--AGAINST A UNIVERSE!
YOU'RE NOT ONE TO EXAGGERATE, RAI. ALL RIGHT. IF IT'S THAT DIRE.
BUT I'LL HAVE TO RETURN THE INSTANT THE DANGER IS OVER!
AGREED.
NOT TO GET PICKY, SNOWFLAKE, BUT WE'RE TALKING WAR HERE. YOU SURE YOU WANT JUNIOR TAGGING ALONG?
I DON'T KNOW NORTH AM. WHERE WOULD HE BE SAFE?
MAY I MAKE A SUGGESTION...?
FELINA'S ORPHANAGE, LEV ONE.
MAGNUS STAYED WHOLE MINUTE --NEW RECORD!
YOU ARE CUTE CRYKID, THOUGH. KOOTCHIE!

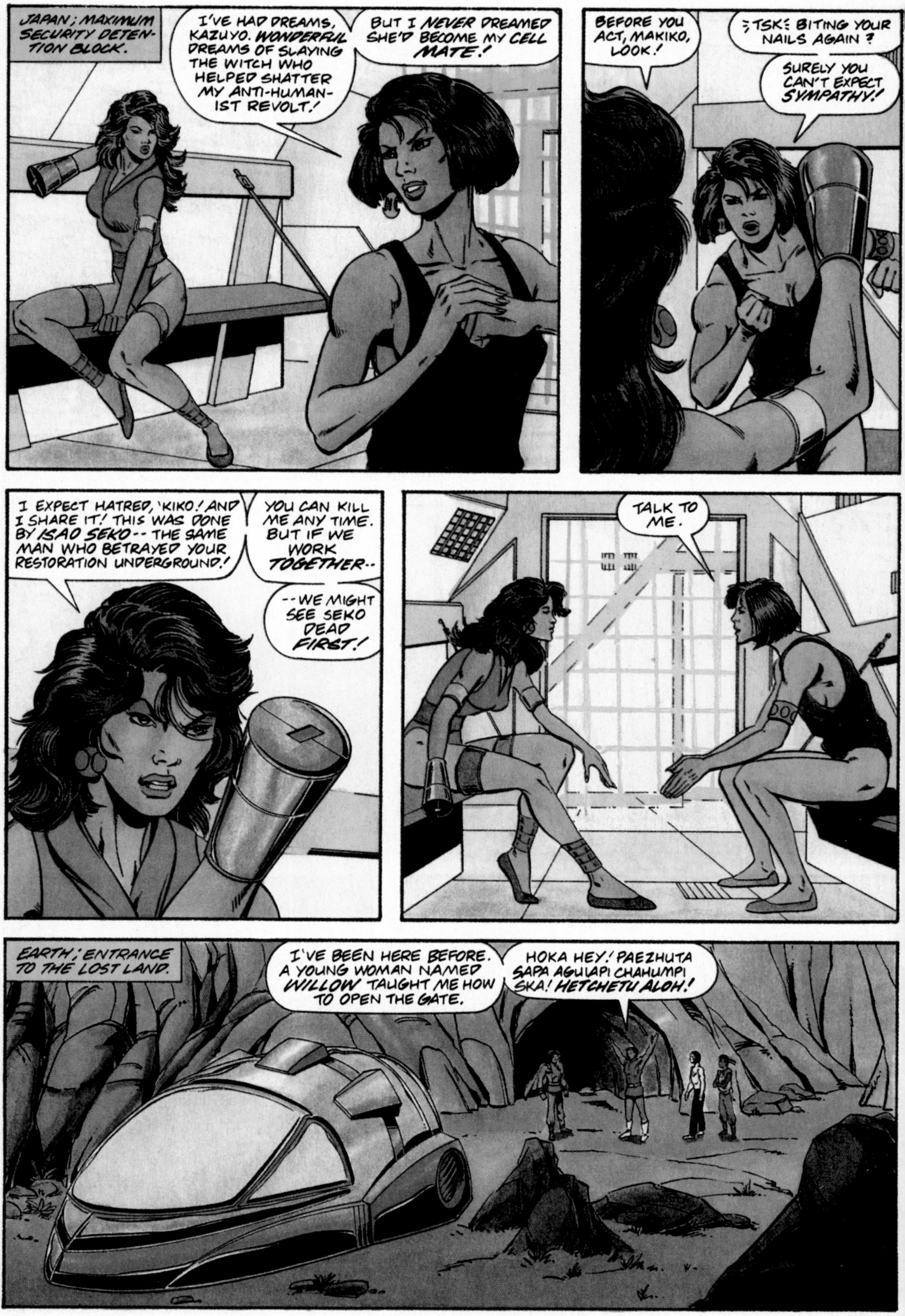
JAPAN; MAXIMUM SECURITY DETENTION BLOCK.
I'VE HAD DREAMS, KAZUYO. WONDERFUL DREAMS OF SLAYING THE WITCH WHO HELPED SHATTER MY ANTI-HUMANIST REVOLT.!
BUT I NEVER DREAMED SHE'D BECOME MY CELL MATE!
BEFORE YOU ACT, MAKIKO, LOOK!
;TSK; BITING YOUR NAILS AGAIN?
SURELY YOU CAN'T EXPECT SYMPATHY!
I EXPECT HATRED, 'KIKO! AND I SHARE IT! THIS WAS DONE BY ISAO SEKO -- THE SAME MAN WHO BETRAYED YOUR RESTORATION UNDERGROUND!
YOU CAN KILL ME ANY TIME. BUT IF WE WORK TOGETHER--
--WE MIGHT SEE SEKO DEAD FIRST!
TALK TO ME.
EARTH; ENTRANCE TO THE LOST LAND.
I'VE BEEN HERE BEFORE. A YOUNG WOMAN NAMED WILLOW TAUGHT ME HOW TO OPEN THE GATE.
HOKA HEY! PAEZHUTA SAPA AGUIAPI CHAHUMPI SKA! HETCHETU ALOH!

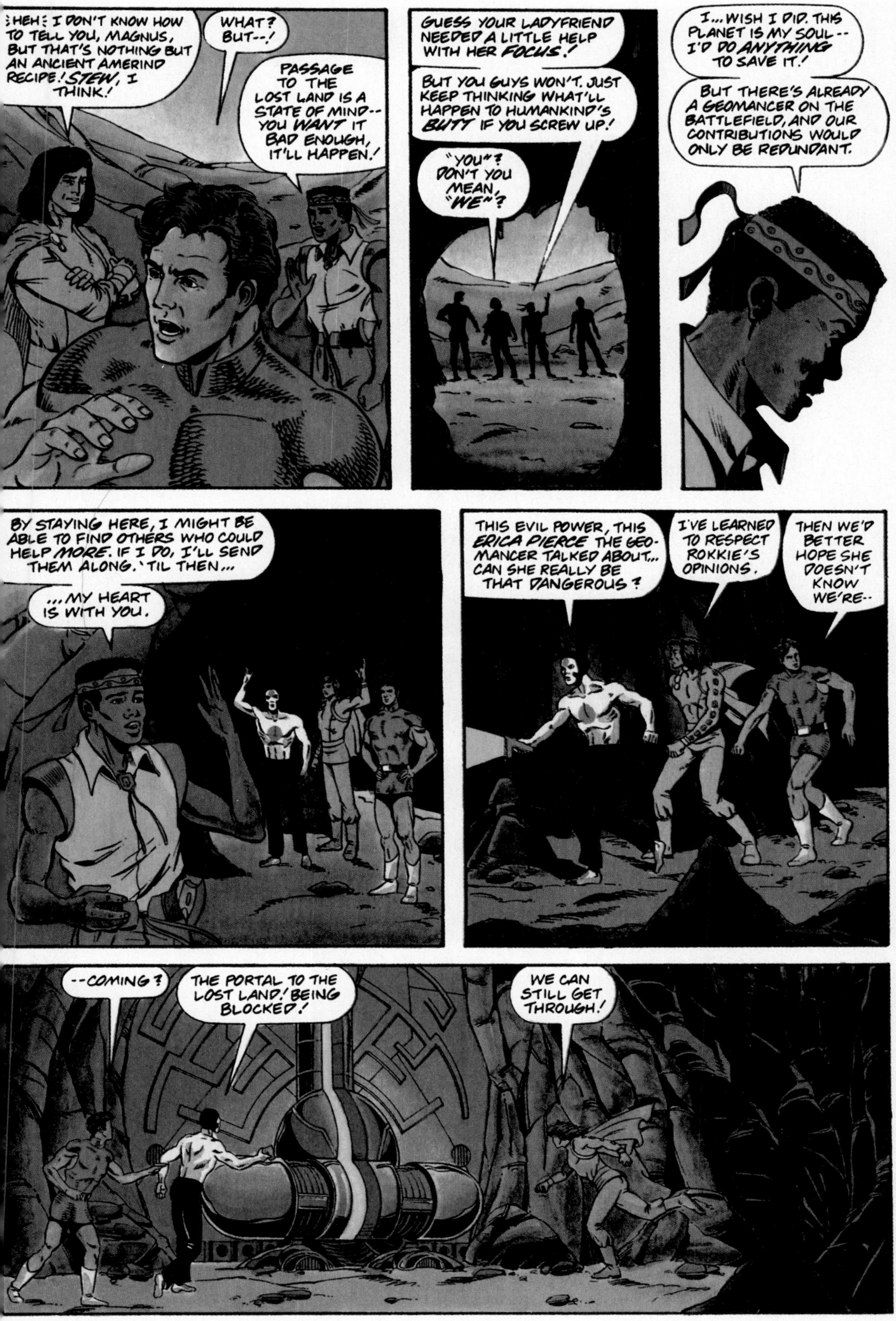
HEH! I DON'T KNOW HOW TO TELL YOU, MAGNUS, BUT THAT'S NOTHING BUT AN ANCIENT AMERIND RECIPE! STEW, I THINK!
WHAT? BUT--!
PASSAGE TO THE LOST LAND IS A STATE OF MIND-- YOU WANT IT BAD ENOUGH, IT'LL HAPPEN!
GUESS YOUR LADYFRIEND NEEDED A LITTLE HELP WITH HER FOCUS!
BUT YOU GUYS WON'T. JUST KEEP THINKING WHAT'LL HAPPEN TO HUMANKIND'S BUTT IF YOU SCREW UP!
"YOU"? DON'T YOU MEAN, "WE"?
I... WISH I DID. THIS PLANET IS MY SOUL-- I'D DO ANYTHING TO SAVE IT!
BUT THERE'S ALREADY A GEOMANCER ON THE BATTLEFIELD, AND OUR CONTRIBUTIONS WOULD ONLY BE REDUNDANT.
BY STAYING HERE, I MIGHT BE ABLE TO FIND OTHERS WHO COULD HELP MORE. IF I DO, I'LL SEND THEM ALONG. 'TIL THEN...
...MY HEART IS WITH YOU.
THIS EVIL POWER, THIS ERICA PIERCE THE GEOMANCER TALKED ABOUT... CAN SHE REALLY BE THAT DANGEROUS?
I'VE LEARNED TO RESPECT ROKKIE'S OPINIONS.
THEN WE'D BETTER HOPE SHE DOESN'T KNOW WE'RE--
--COMING?
THE PORTAL TO THE LOST LAND! BEING BLOCKED!
WE CAN STILL GET THROUGH!

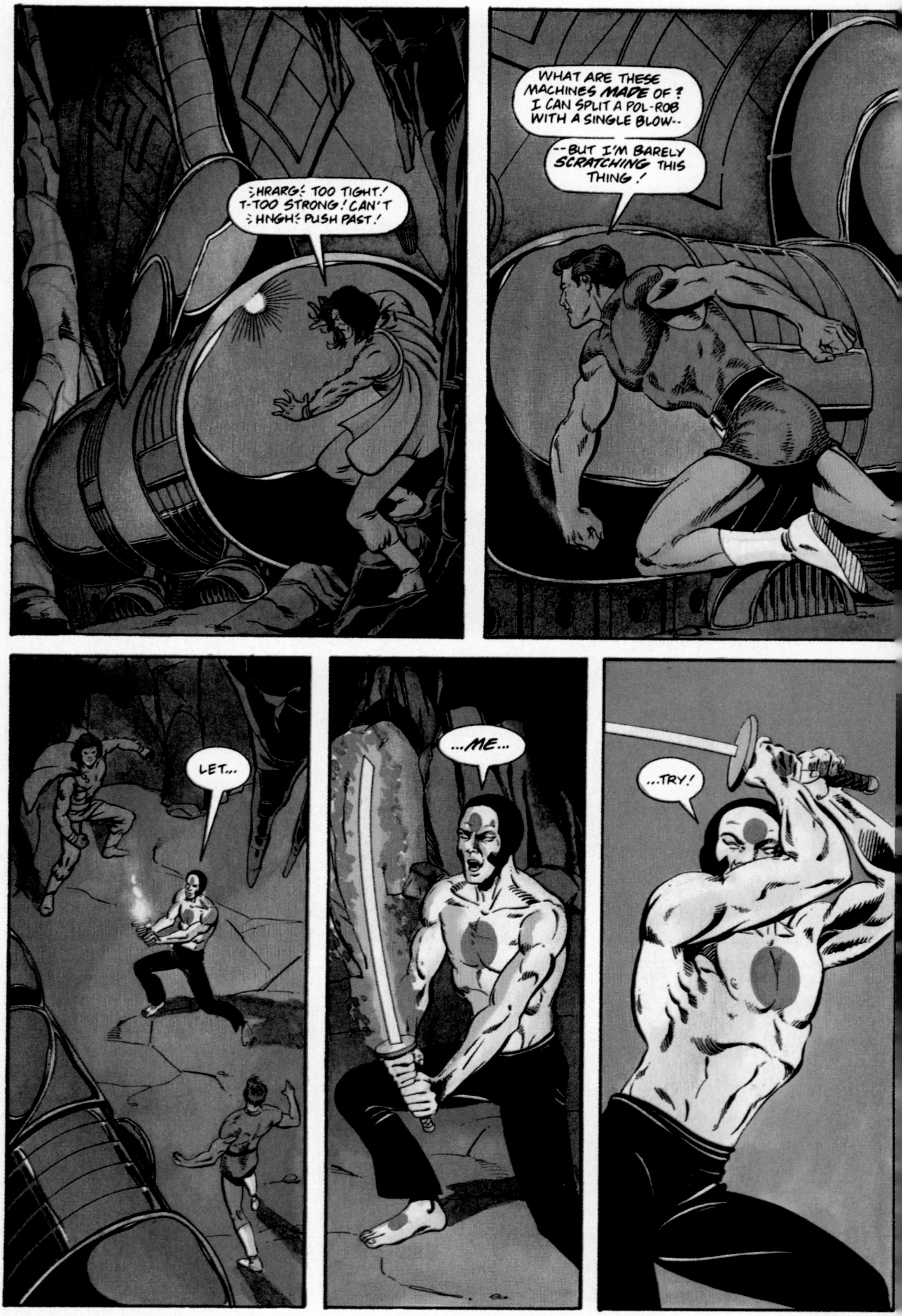

HRARG TOO TIGHT! T-TOO STRONG! CAN'T HNGH PUSH PAST!
WHAT ARE THESE MACHINES MADE OF? I CAN SPLIT A POL-ROB WITH A SINGLE BLOW--
--BUT I'M BARELY SCRATCHING THIS THING!
LET...
...ME...
...TRY!

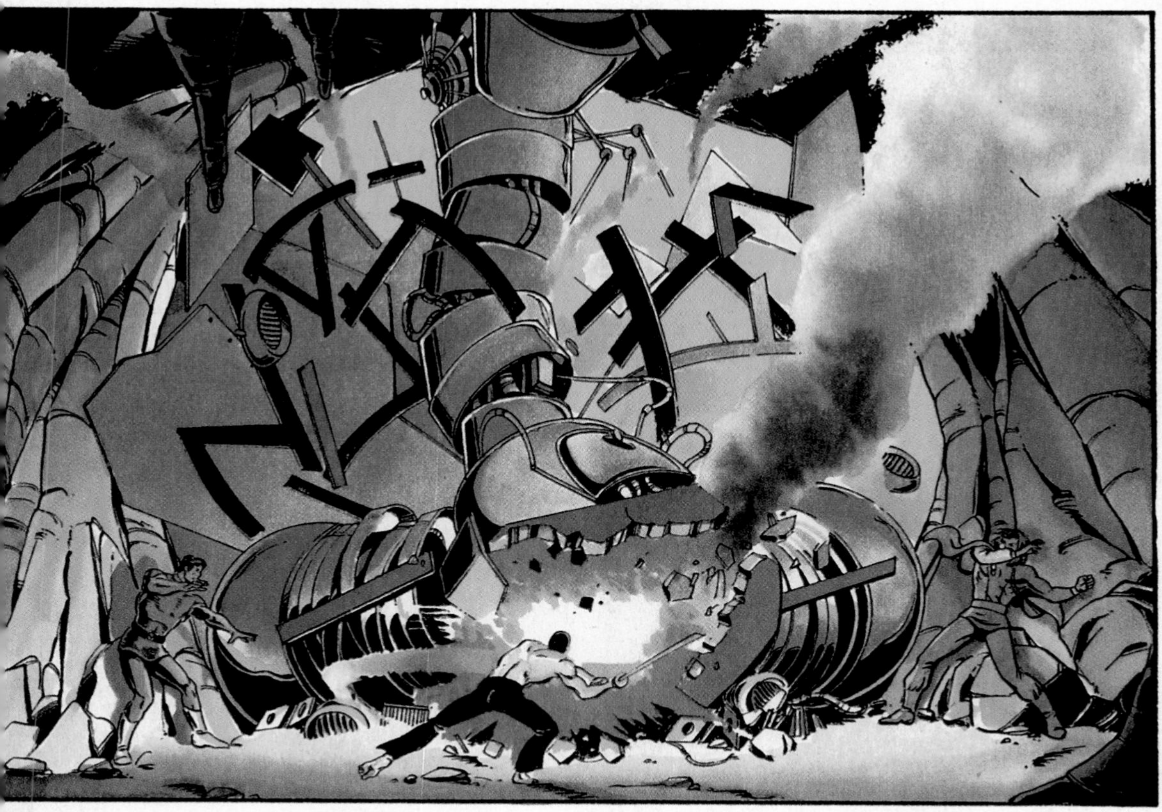

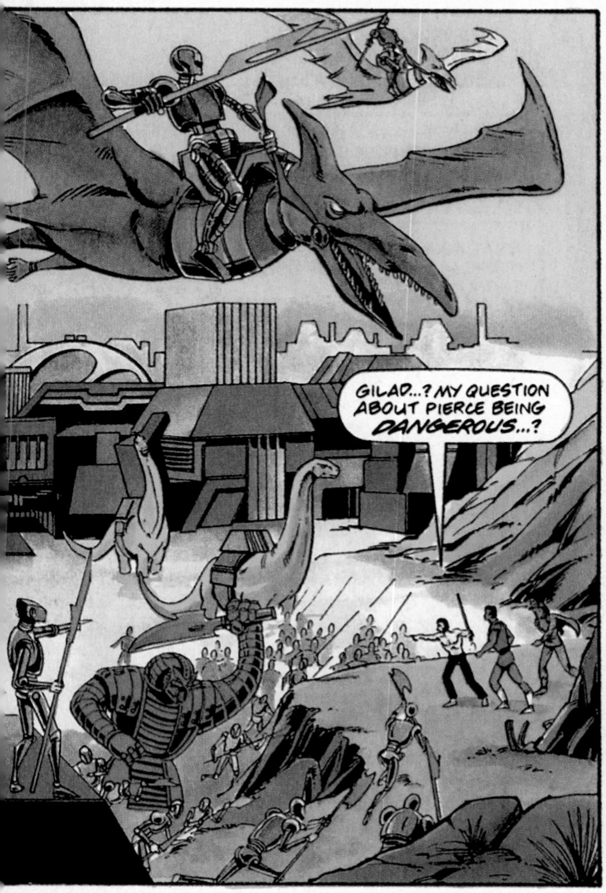
GILAD...? MY QUESTION ABOUT PIERCE BEING DANGEROUS...?

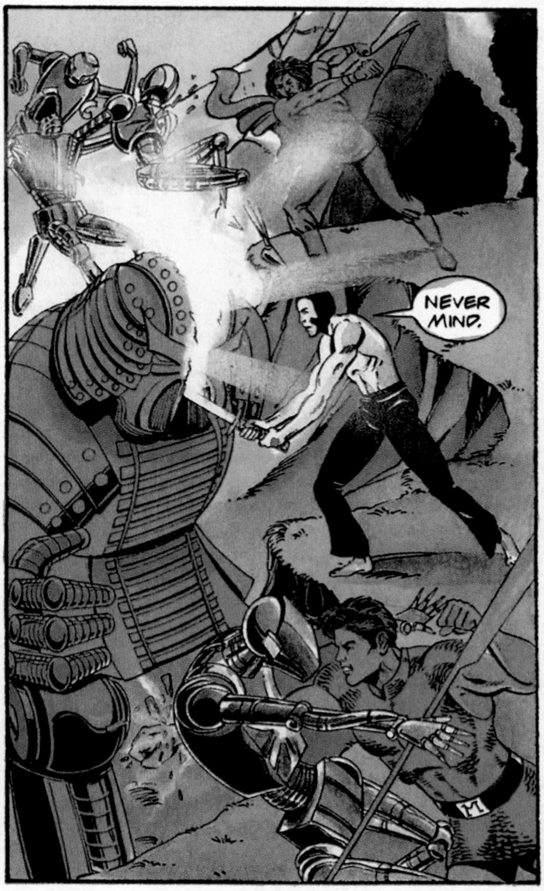
NEVER MIND.

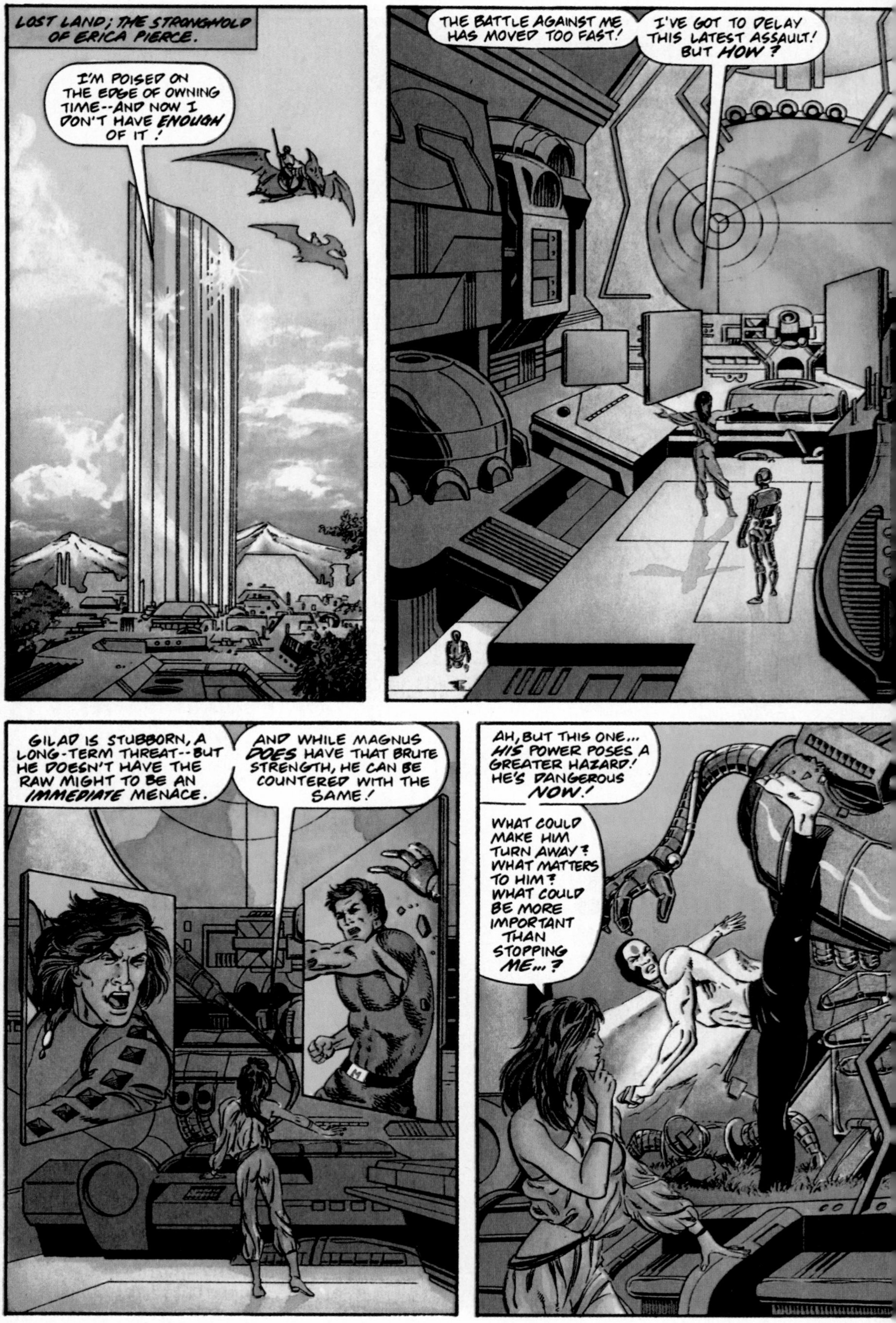
LOST LAND; THE STRONGHOLD OF ERICA PIERCE.
I'M POISED ON THE EDGE OF OWNING TIME--AND NOW I DON'T HAVE ENOUGH OF IT!
THE BATTLE AGAINST ME HAS MOVED TOO FAST!
I'VE GOT TO DELAY THIS LATEST ASSAULT! BUT HOW?
GILAD IS STUBBORN, A LONG-TERM THREAT--BUT HE DOESN'T HAVE THE RAW MIGHT TO BE AN IMMEDIATE MENACE.
AND WHILE MAGNUS DOES HAVE THAT BRUTE STRENGTH, HE CAN BE COUNTERED WITH THE SAME!
AH, BUT THIS ONE... HIS POWER POSES A GREATER HAZARD! HE'S DANGEROUS NOW!
WHAT COULD MAKE HIM TURN AWAY? WHAT MATTERS TO HIM? WHAT COULD BE MORE IMPORTANT THAN STOPPING ME...?

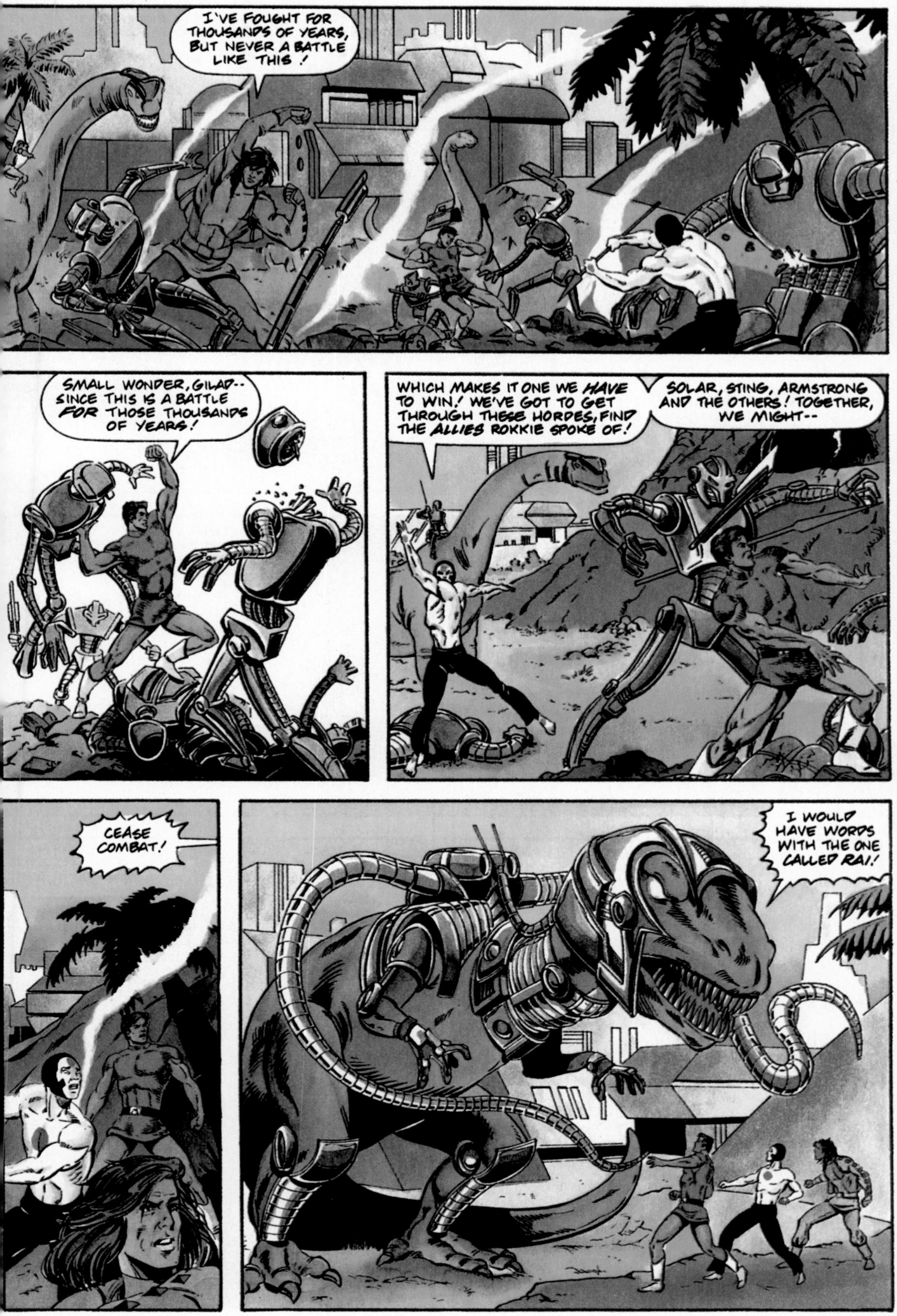
I'VE FOUGHT FOR THOUSANDS OF YEARS, BUT NEVER A BATTLE LIKE THIS!
SMALL WONDER, GILAD-- SINCE THIS IS A BATTLE FOR THOSE THOUSANDS OF YEARS!
WHICH MAKES IT ONE WE HAVE TO WIN! WE'VE GOT TO GET THROUGH THESE HORDES, FIND THE ALLIES ROKKIE SPOKE OF!
SOLAR, STING, ARMSTRONG AND THE OTHERS! TOGETHER, WE MIGHT--
CEASE COMBAT!
I WOULD HAVE WORDS WITH THE ONE CALLED RAI!

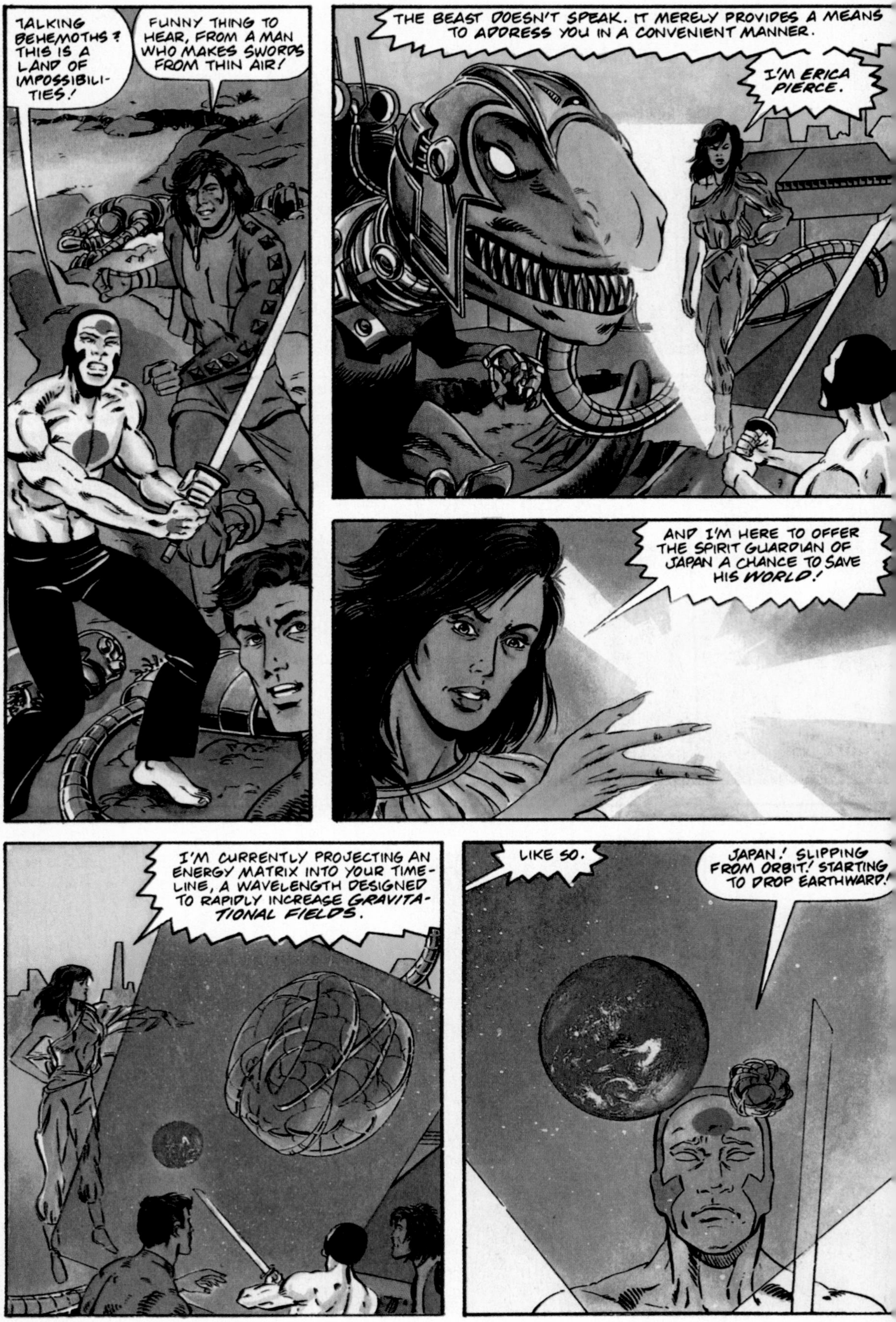
TALKING BEHEMOTHS? THIS IS A LAND OF IMPOSSIBILITIES!
FUNNY THING TO HEAR, FROM A MAN WHO MAKES SWORDS FROM THIN AIR!
THE BEAST DOESN'T SPEAK. IT MERELY PROVIDES A MEANS TO ADDRESS YOU IN A CONVENIENT MANNER.
I'M ERICA PIERCE.
AND I'M HERE TO OFFER THE SPIRIT GUARDIAN OF JAPAN A CHANCE TO SAVE HIS WORLD!
I'M CURRENTLY PROJECTING AN ENERGY MATRIX INTO YOUR TIME-LINE, A WAVELENGTH DESIGNED TO RAPIDLY INCREASE GRAVITATIONAL FIELDS.
LIKE SO.
JAPAN! SLIPPING FROM ORBIT! STARTING TO DROP EARTHWARD!

KYOTO PLEXUS.

WH-WHAT'S HAPPENING?!

SUSPENSION SUPPORT ARMS! DEPLOYING AUTOMATICALLY!

TAKE THIS ROD, GUARDIAN. PRESSING THE TOP STUD WILL INSTANTLY TRANSPORT YOU TO JAPAN.

AND ONCE THERE, PRESSING THE BOTTOM ONE WILL *NEGATE* THE MAG-GRAV FIELD!

I ... I-I ...

DON'T, RAI! PUSHING THOSE BUTTONS MIGHT *KILL* YOU!

I'LL TAKE THAT CHANCE-- *I HAVE* TO! I'LL COME BACK AS SOON AS MY COUNTRYMEN ARE SAFE!

BUT WHAT IF SHE'S LYING? WHY WOULD SHE POSSIBLY GIVE YOU THE MEANS TO--

THAT'S WHY!

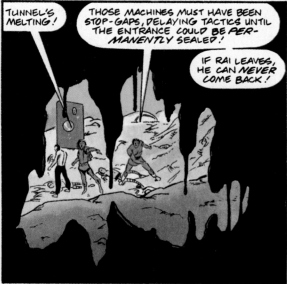

TUNNEL'S MELTING!

THOSE MACHINES MUST HAVE BEEN STOP-GAPS, DELAYING TACTICS UNTIL THE ENTRANCE COULD BE *PERMANENTLY* SEALED!

IF RAI LEAVES, HE CAN *NEVER* COME BACK!

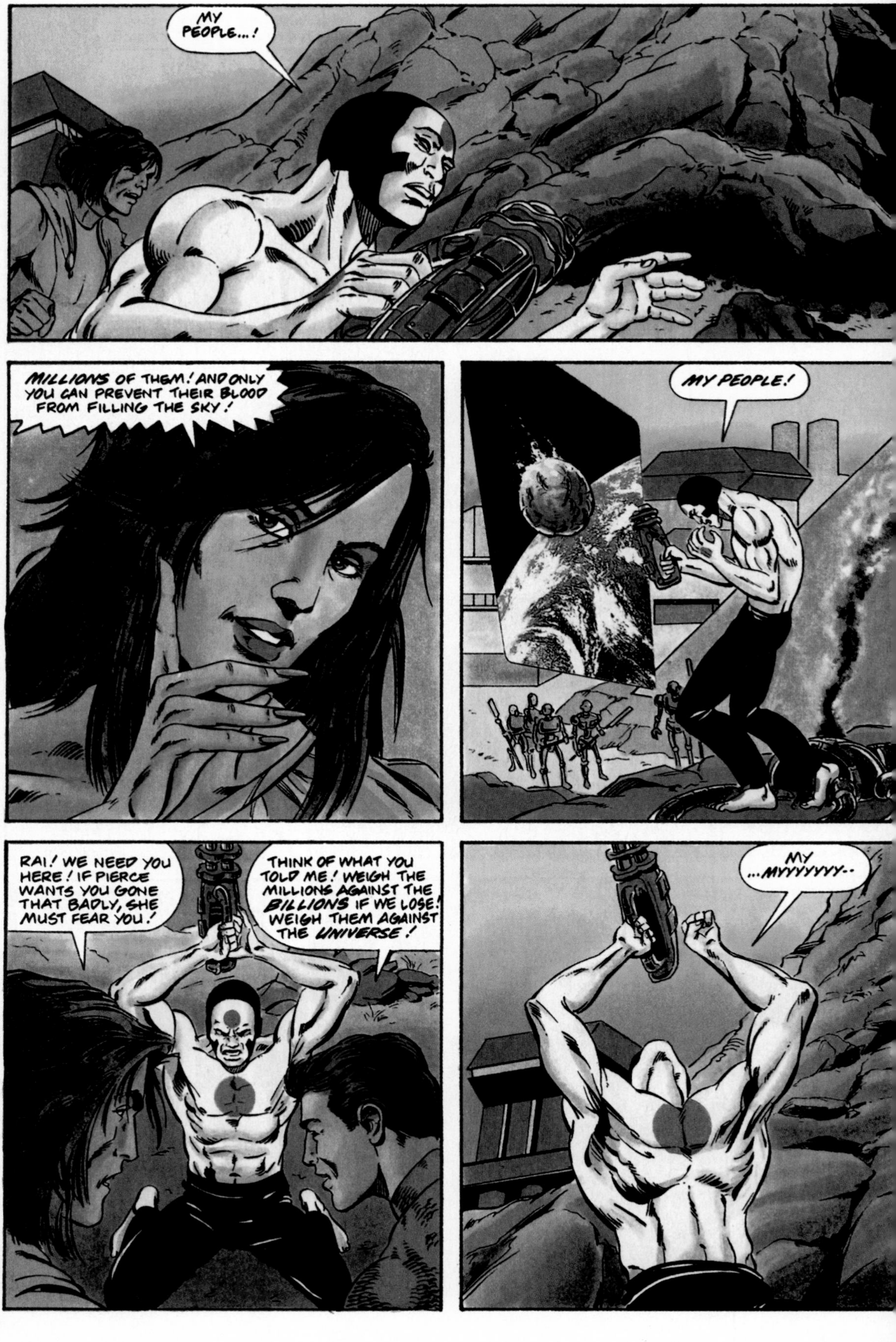
MY PEOPLE...!
MILLIONS OF THEM! AND ONLY YOU CAN PREVENT THEIR BLOOD FROM FILLING THE SKY!
MY PEOPLE!
RAI! WE NEED YOU HERE! IF PIERCE WANTS YOU GONE THAT BADLY, SHE MUST FEAR YOU!
THINK OF WHAT YOU TOLD ME! WEIGH THE MILLIONS AGAINST THE BILLIONS IF WE LOSE! WEIGH THEM AGAINST THE UNIVERSE!
MY ...MYYYYYYY..

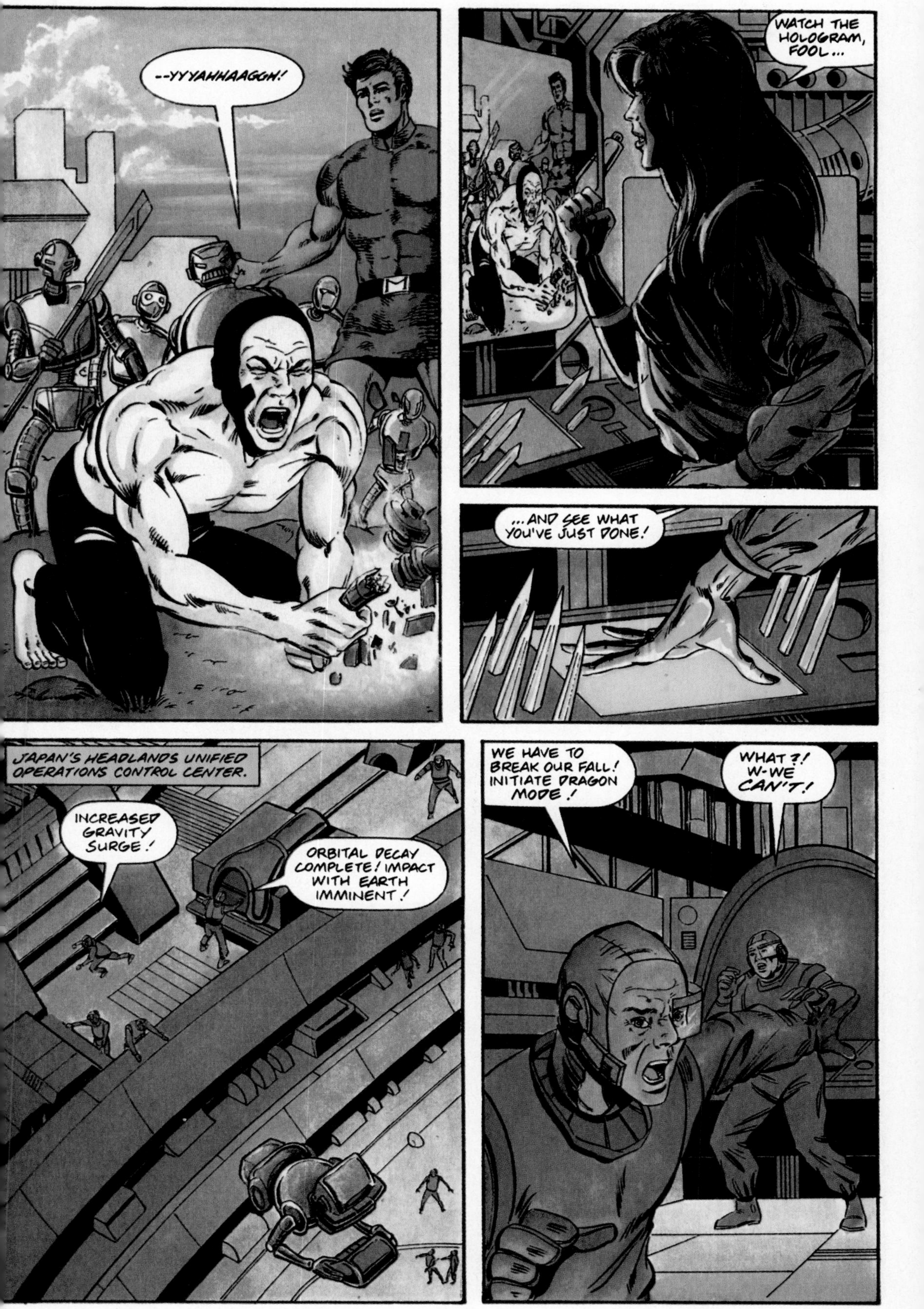
--YYYAHHAAGGH!
WATCH THE HOLOGRAM, FOOL...
...AND SEE WHAT YOU'VE JUST DONE!
JAPAN'S HEADLANDS UNIFIED OPERATIONS CONTROL CENTER.
INCREASED GRAVITY SURGE!
ORBITAL DECAY COMPLETE! IMPACT WITH EARTH IMMINENT!
WE HAVE TO BREAK OUR FALL! INITIATE DRAGON MODE!
WHAT ?! W-WE CAN'T!

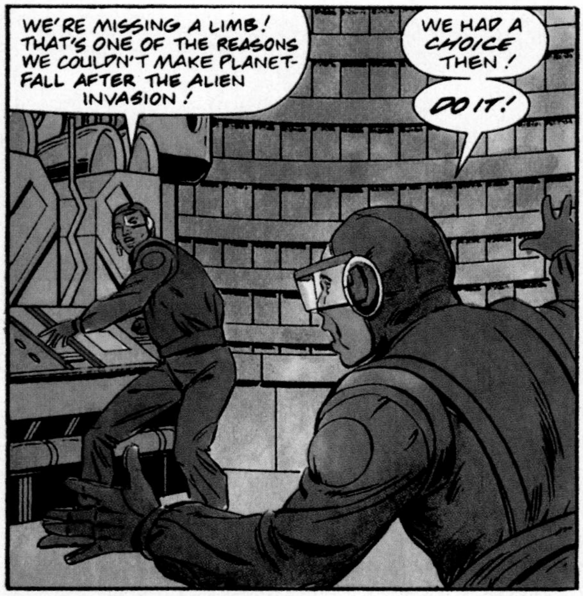
WE'RE MISSING A LIMB! THAT'S ONE OF THE REASONS WE COULDN'T MAKE PLANET-FALL AFTER THE ALIEN INVASION!
WE HAD A CHOICE THEN!
DO IT!
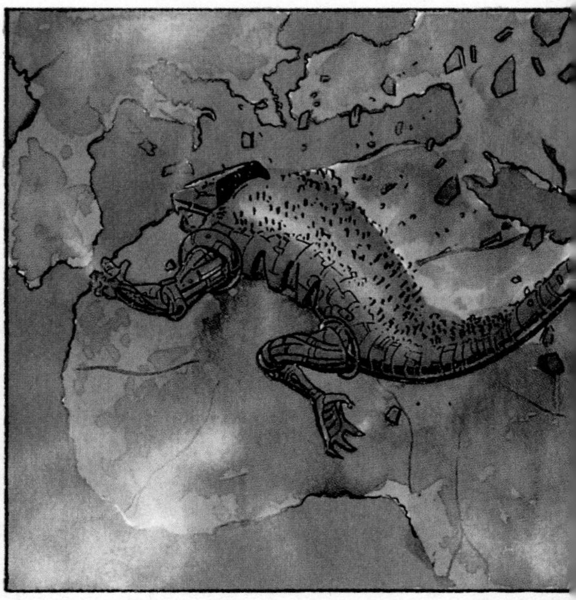
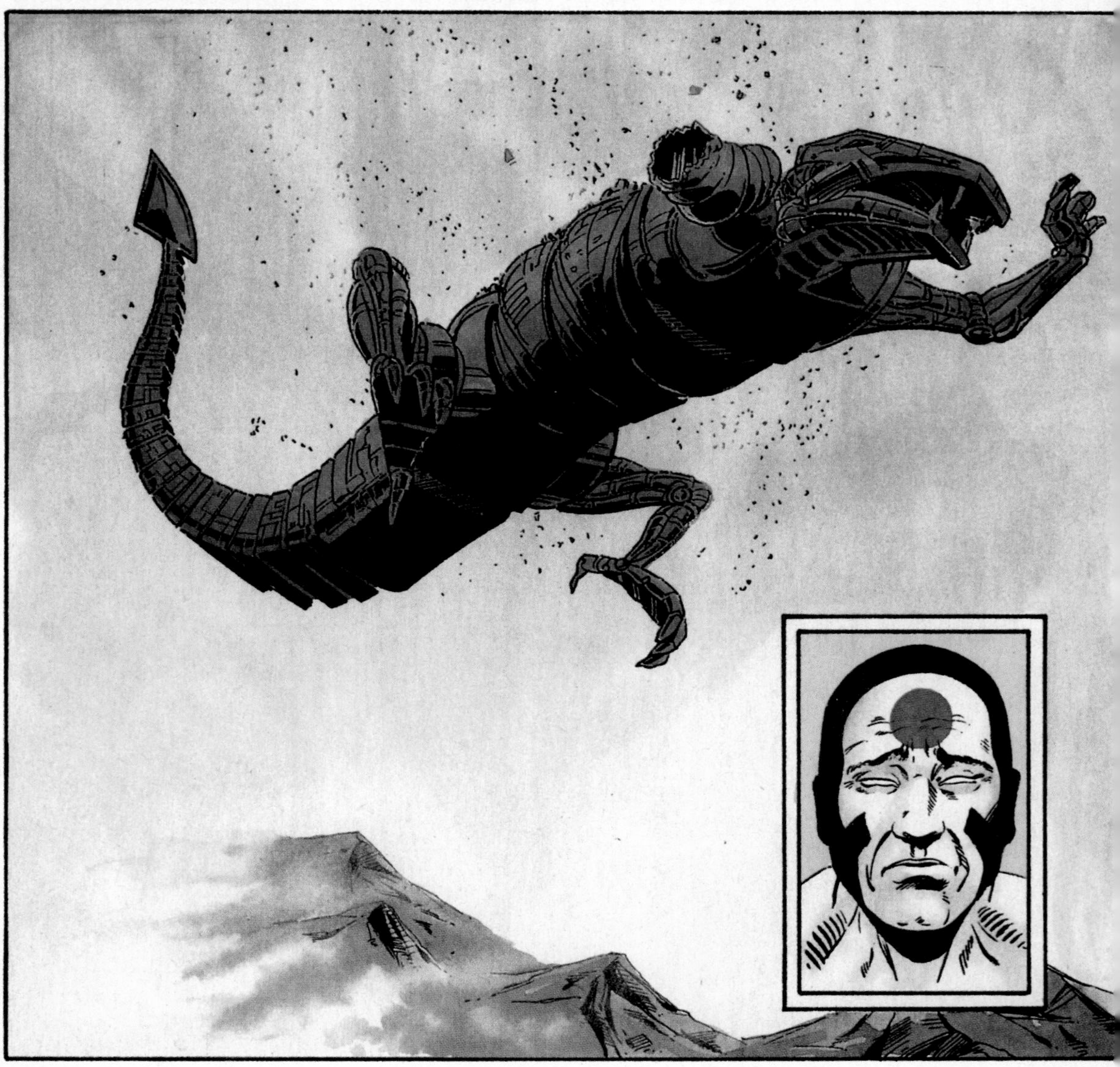

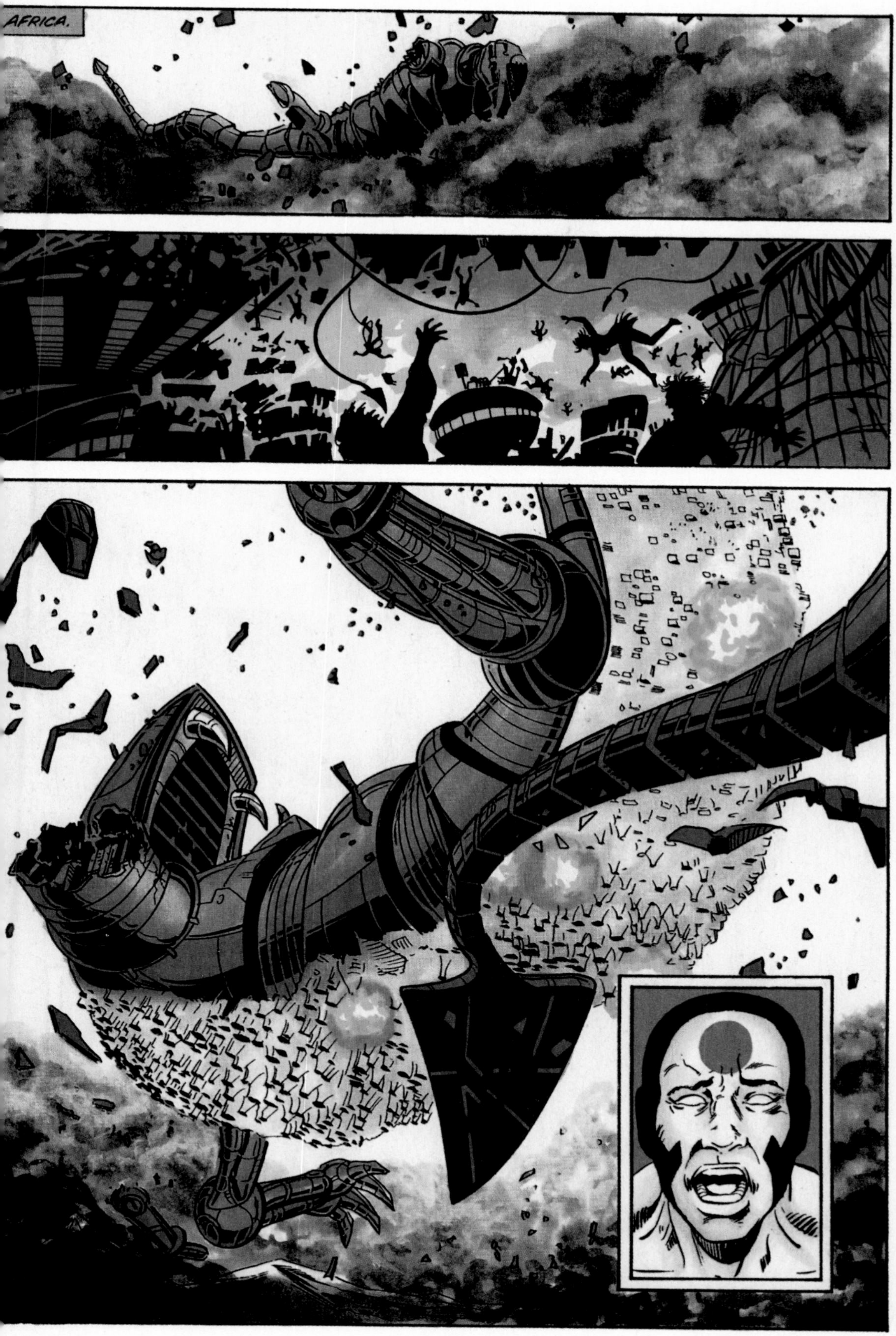
AFRICA.

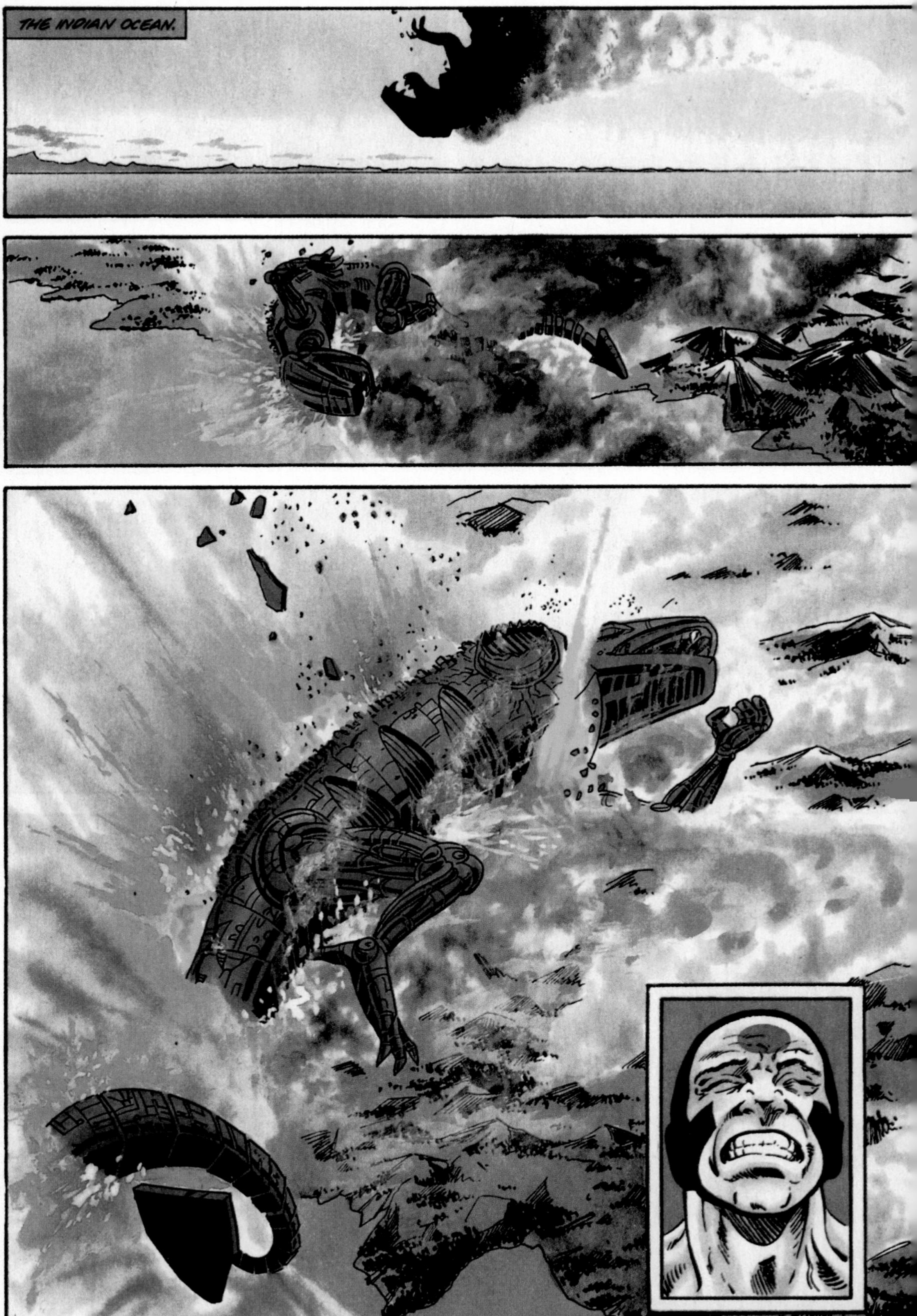
THE INDIAN OCEAN.

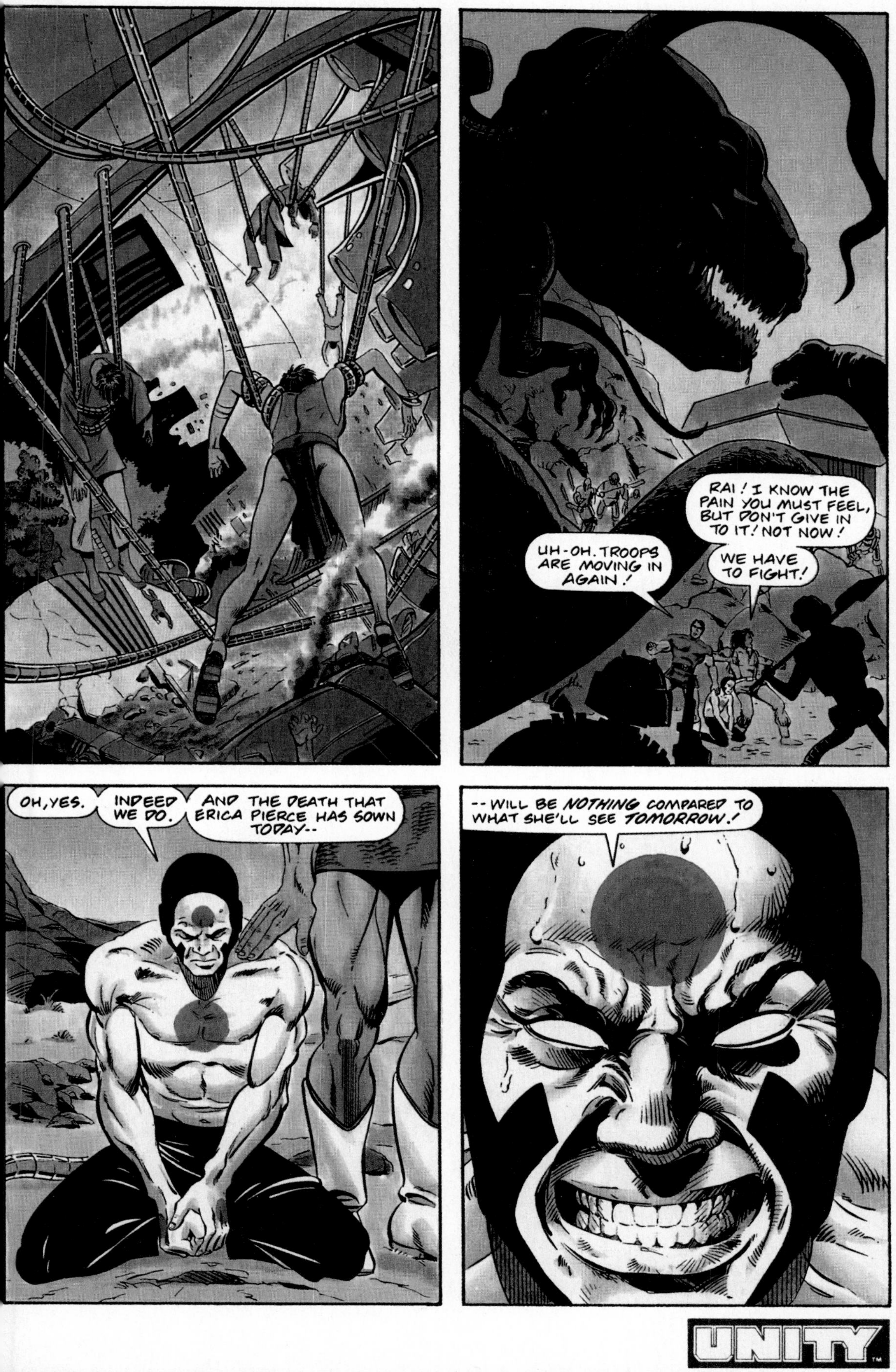
RAI! I KNOW THE PAIN YOU MUST FEEL, BUT DON'T GIVE IN TO IT! NOT NOW!
UH-OH. TROOPS ARE MOVING IN AGAIN!
WE HAVE TO FIGHT!
OH, YES.
INDEED WE DO.
AND THE DEATH THAT ERICA PIERCE HAS SOWN TODAY--
--WILL BE NOTHING COMPARED TO WHAT SHE'LL SEE TOMORROW!
UNITY™

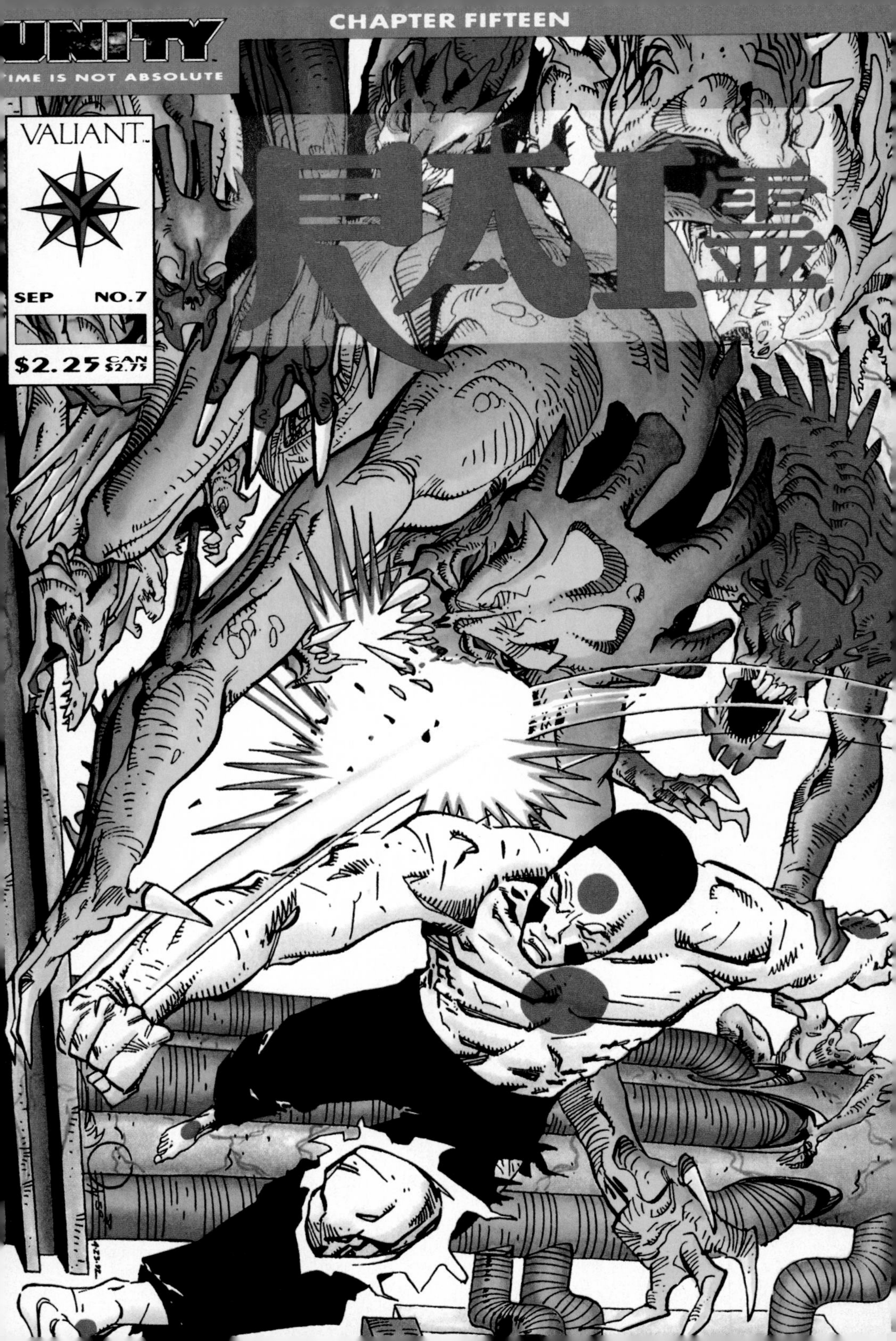
UNITY
CHAPTER FIFTEEN
TIME IS NOT ABSOLUTE
VALIANT
SEP NO.7
$2.25 CAN $2.75

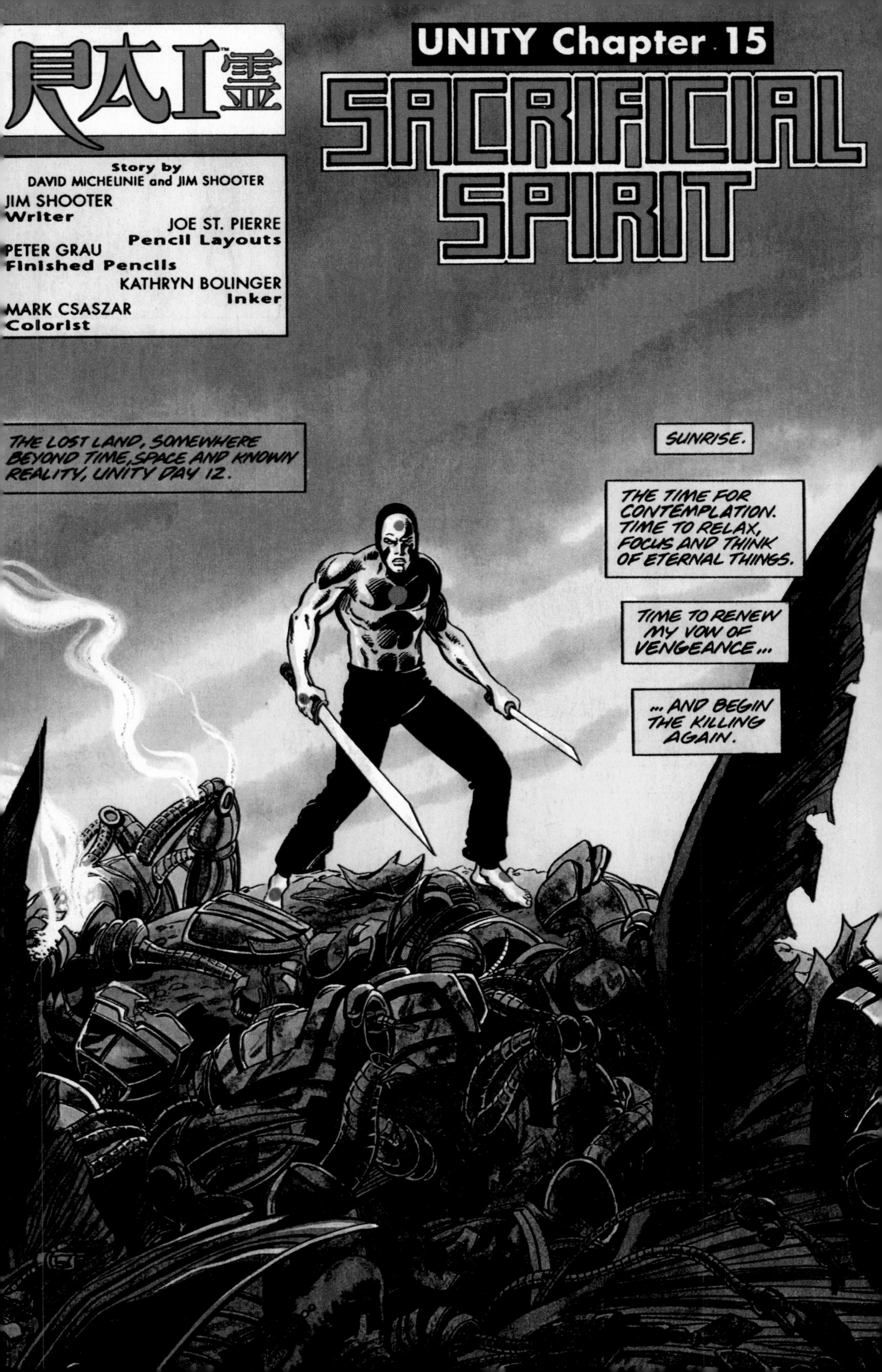

UNITY Chapter 15
SACRIFICIAL SPIRIT
Story by DAVID MICHELINIE and JIM SHOOTER
JIM SHOOTER Writer
JOE ST. PIERRE Pencil Layouts
PETER GRAU Finished Pencils
KATHRYN BOLINGER Inker
MARK CSASZAR Colorist
THE LOST LAND, SOMEWHERE BEYOND TIME, SPACE AND KNOWN REALITY, UNITY DAY 12.
SUNRISE.
THE TIME FOR CONTEMPLATION. TIME TO RELAX, FOCUS AND THINK OF ETERNAL THINGS.
TIME TO RENEW MY VOW OF VENGEANCE...
...AND BEGIN THE KILLING AGAIN.

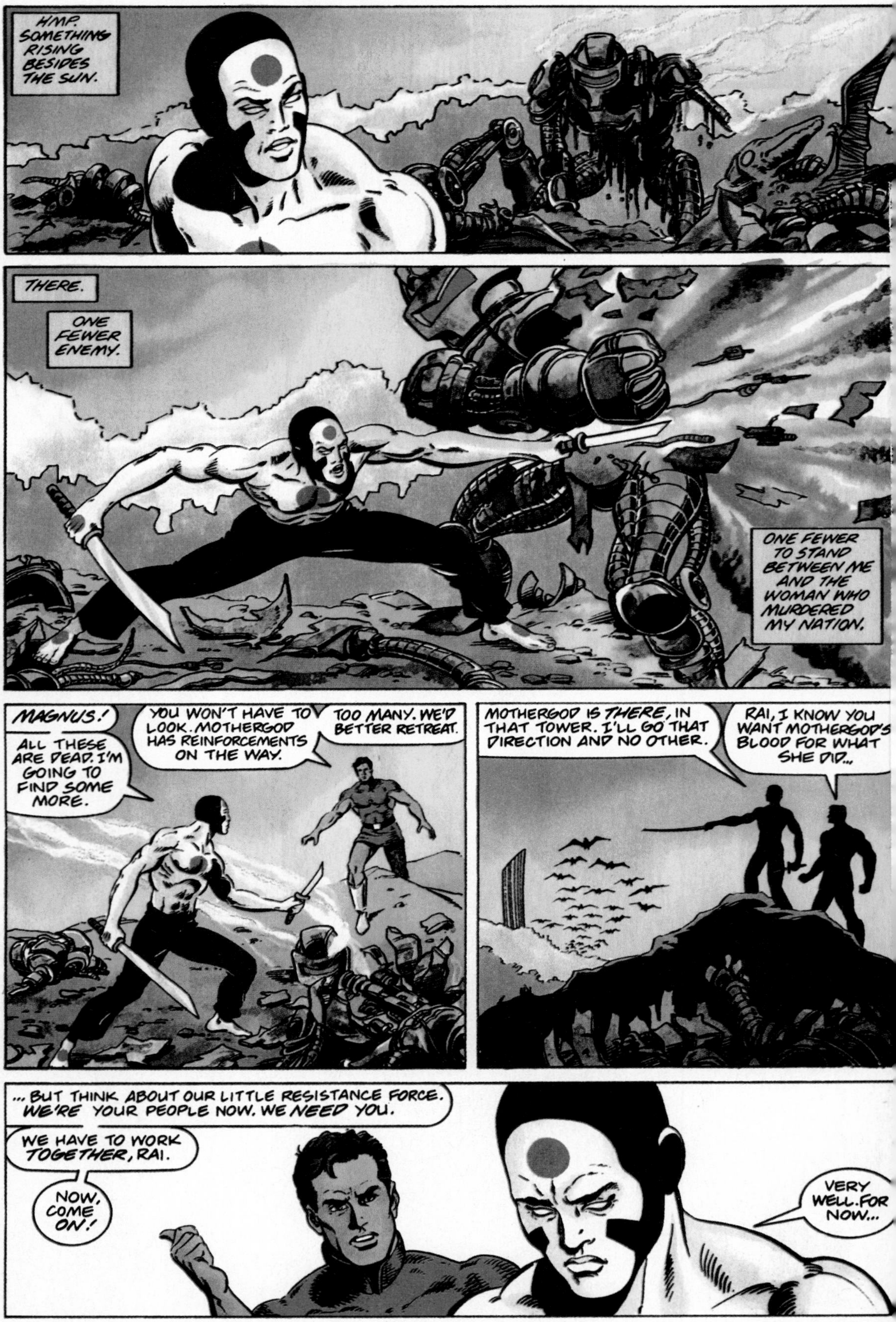
HMP. SOMETHING RISING BESIDES THE SUN.
THERE.
ONE FEWER ENEMY.
ONE FEWER TO STAND BETWEEN ME AND THE WOMAN WHO MURDERED MY NATION.
MAGNUS!
ALL THESE ARE DEAD. I'M GOING TO FIND SOME MORE.
YOU WON'T HAVE TO LOOK. MOTHERGOD HAS REINFORCEMENTS ON THE WAY.
TOO MANY. WE'D BETTER RETREAT.
MOTHERGOD IS THERE, IN THAT TOWER. I'LL GO THAT DIRECTION AND NO OTHER.
RAI, I KNOW YOU WANT MOTHERGOD'S BLOOD FOR WHAT SHE DID...
...BUT THINK ABOUT OUR LITTLE RESISTANCE FORCE. WE'RE YOUR PEOPLE NOW. WE NEED YOU.
WE HAVE TO WORK TOGETHER, RAI.
NOW, COME ON!
VERY WELL. FOR NOW...

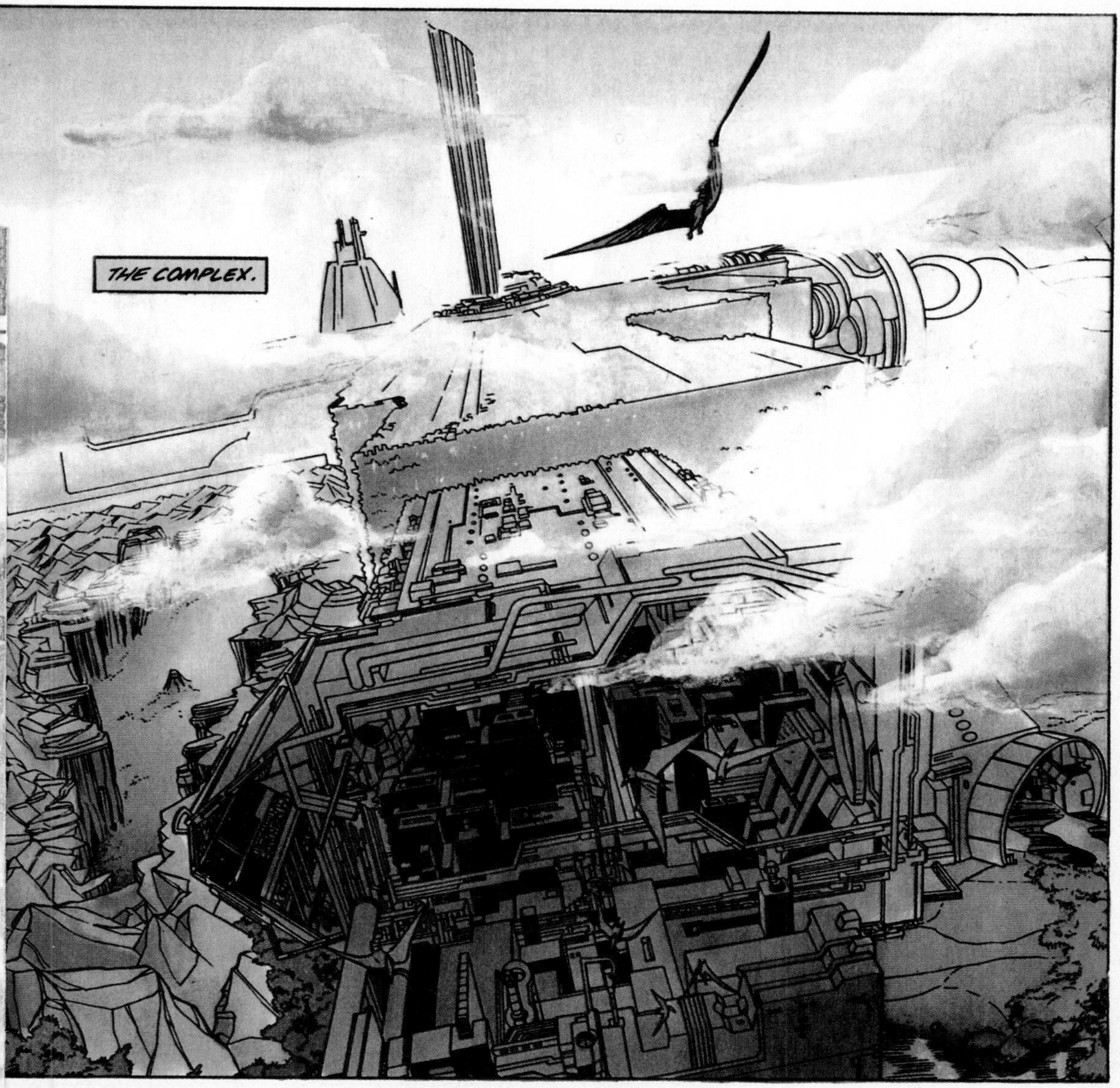
THE COMPLEX.

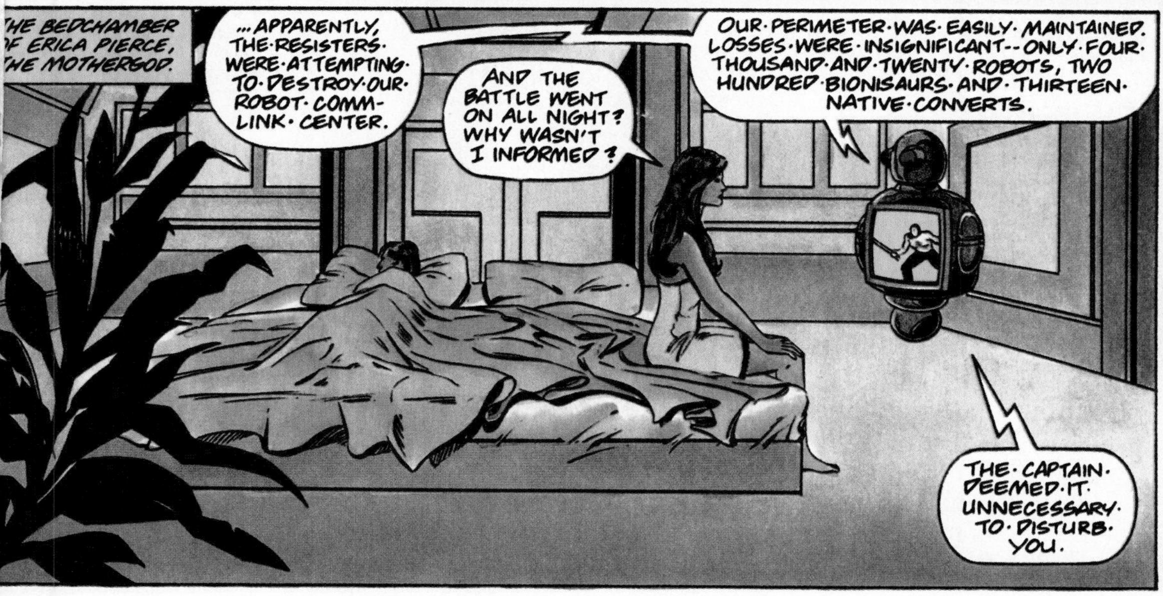
THE BEDCHAMBER OF ERICA PIERCE, THE MOTHERGOD.
...APPARENTLY, THE·RESISTERS· WERE·ATTEMPTING· TO·DESTROY·OUR· ROBOT·COMM-LINK·CENTER.
AND THE BATTLE WENT ON ALL NIGHT? WHY WASN'T I INFORMED?
OUR·PERIMETER·WAS·EASILY·MAINTAINED. LOSSES·WERE·INSIGNIFICANT--ONLY·FOUR· THOUSAND·AND·TWENTY·ROBOTS, TWO HUNDRED·BIONISAURS·AND·THIRTEEN· NATIVE·CONVERTS.
THE·CAPTAIN· DEEMED·IT· UNNECESSARY· TO·DISTURB· YOU.

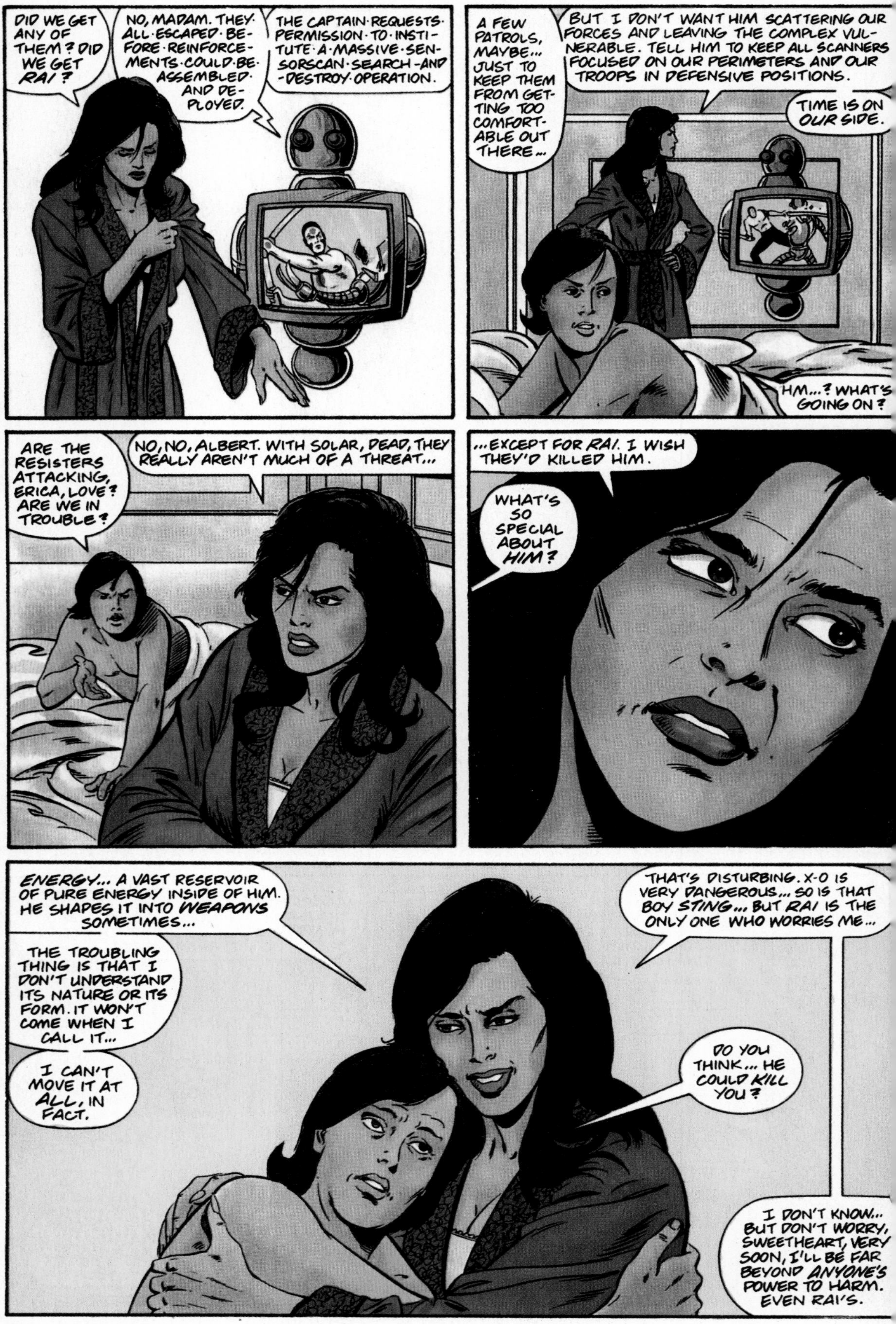

DID WE GET ANY OF THEM? DID WE GET RAI?
NO, MADAM. THEY ALL ESCAPED BEFORE REINFORCEMENTS COULD BE ASSEMBLED AND DEPLOYED.
THE CAPTAIN REQUESTS PERMISSION TO INSTITUTE A MASSIVE SENSORSCAN SEARCH-AND-DESTROY OPERATION.
A FEW PATROLS, MAYBE... JUST TO KEEP THEM FROM GETTING TOO COMFORTABLE OUT THERE...
BUT I DON'T WANT HIM SCATTERING OUR FORCES AND LEAVING THE COMPLEX VULNERABLE. TELL HIM TO KEEP ALL SCANNERS FOCUSED ON OUR PERIMETERS AND OUR TROOPS IN DEFENSIVE POSITIONS.
TIME IS ON OUR SIDE.
HM...? WHAT'S GOING ON?
ARE THE RESISTERS ATTACKING, ERICA, LOVE? ARE WE IN TROUBLE?
NO, NO, ALBERT. WITH SOLAR, DEAD, THEY REALLY AREN'T MUCH OF A THREAT...
...EXCEPT FOR RAI. I WISH THEY'D KILLED HIM.
WHAT'S SO SPECIAL ABOUT HIM?
ENERGY... A VAST RESERVOIR OF PURE ENERGY INSIDE OF HIM. HE SHAPES IT INTO WEAPONS SOMETIMES...
THE TROUBLING THING IS THAT I DON'T UNDERSTAND ITS NATURE OR ITS FORM. IT WON'T COME WHEN I CALL IT...
I CAN'T MOVE IT AT ALL, IN FACT.
THAT'S DISTURBING. X-O IS VERY DANGEROUS... SO IS THAT BOY STING... BUT RAI IS THE ONLY ONE WHO WORRIES ME...
DO YOU THINK... HE COULD KILL YOU?
I DON'T KNOW... BUT DON'T WORRY, SWEETHEART, VERY SOON, I'LL BE FAR BEYOND ANYONE'S POWER TO HARM. EVEN RAI'S.

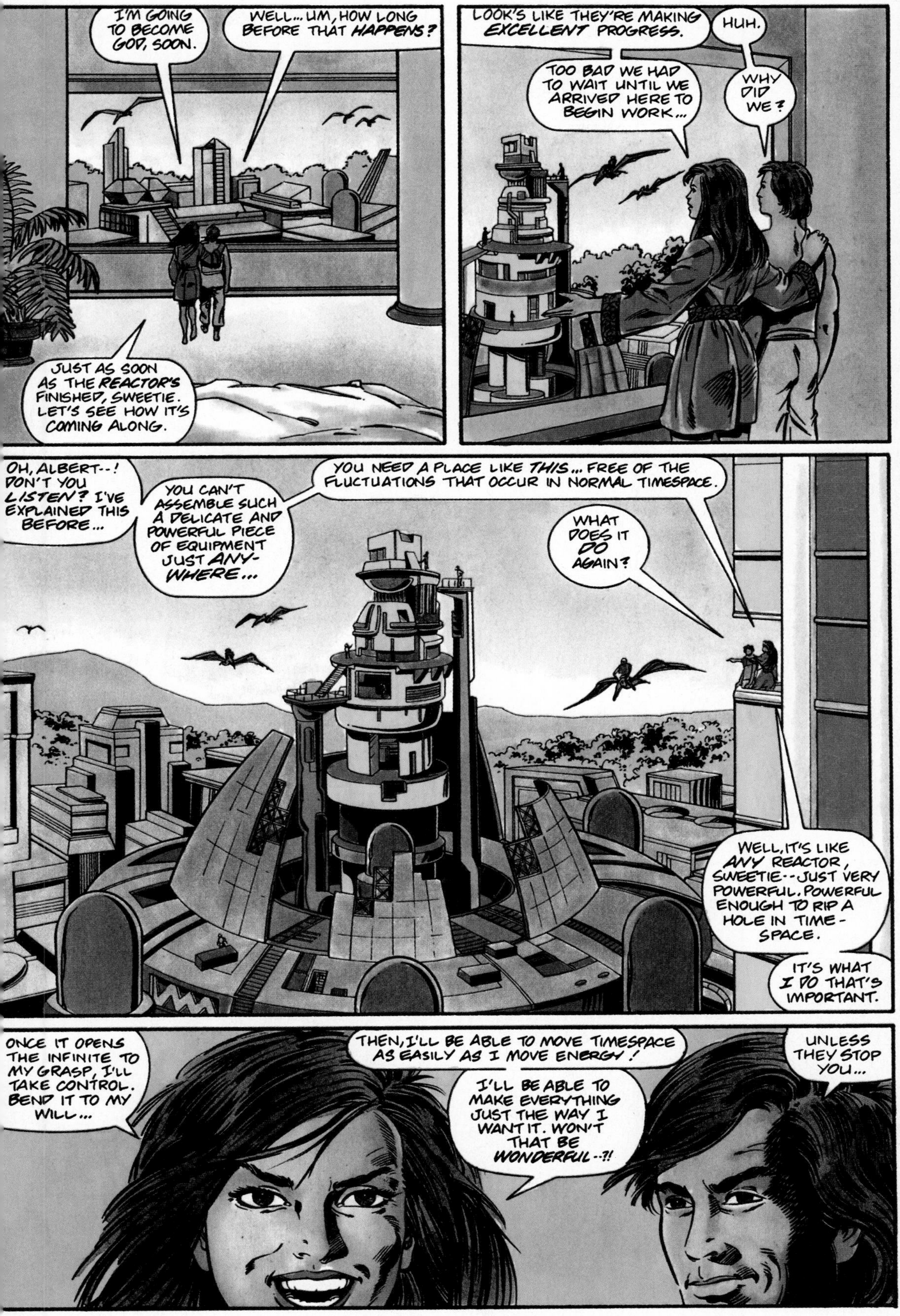
I'M GOING TO BECOME GOD, SOON.
WELL... UM, HOW LONG BEFORE THAT HAPPENS?
JUST AS SOON AS THE REACTOR'S FINISHED, SWEETIE. LET'S SEE HOW IT'S COMING ALONG.
LOOK'S LIKE THEY'RE MAKING EXCELLENT PROGRESS.
HUH.
TOO BAD WE HAD TO WAIT UNTIL WE ARRIVED HERE TO BEGIN WORK...
WHY DID WE?
OH, ALBERT--! DON'T YOU LISTEN? I'VE EXPLAINED THIS BEFORE...
YOU CAN'T ASSEMBLE SUCH A DELICATE AND POWERFUL PIECE OF EQUIPMENT JUST ANY-WHERE...
YOU NEED A PLACE LIKE THIS... FREE OF THE FLUCTUATIONS THAT OCCUR IN NORMAL TIMESPACE.
WHAT DOES IT DO AGAIN?
WELL, IT'S LIKE ANY REACTOR, SWEETIE--JUST VERY POWERFUL. POWERFUL ENOUGH TO RIP A HOLE IN TIME-SPACE.
IT'S WHAT I DO THAT'S IMPORTANT.
ONCE IT OPENS THE INFINITE TO MY GRASP, I'LL TAKE CONTROL. BEND IT TO MY WILL...
THEN, I'LL BE ABLE TO MOVE TIMESPACE AS EASILY AS I MOVE ENERGY!
I'LL BE ABLE TO MAKE EVERYTHING JUST THE WAY I WANT IT. WON'T THAT BE WONDERFUL--?!
UNLESS THEY STOP YOU...

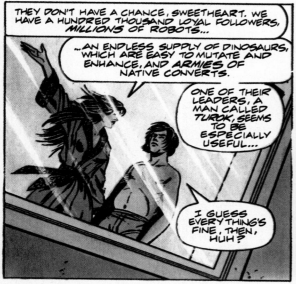

THEY DON'T HAVE A CHANCE, SWEETHEART. WE HAVE A HUNDRED THOUSAND LOYAL FOLLOWERS, *MILLIONS* OF ROBOTS...

...AN ENDLESS SUPPLY OF DINOSAURS, WHICH ARE EASY TO MUTATE AND ENHANCE, AND *ARMIES* OF NATIVE CONVERTS.

ONE OF THEIR LEADERS, A MAN CALLED *TUROK*, SEEMS TO BE ESPECIALLY USEFUL...

I GUESS EVERYTHING'S FINE, THEN, HUH?

UM-HM! IN FACT, I WAS JUST THINKING...

LET'S TAKE THE DAY OFF, SWEETS, HM? SPEND IT TOGETHER... JUST YOU AND ME...

GEE, THAT SOUNDS GREAT, LOVE... BUT I HAVE TO VISIT A FRIEND IN MED-CENTER, TODAY... I PROMISED.

SOON.

SUB-LEVEL 169.

YES?

OPEN THE DOOR AND DON'T GIVE ME THAT "WHAT'S THE PASS-WORD CRAP. YOU KNOW WHO I AM.

YES, SIR, PRINCE ALBERT.

THE UNDERGROUND INFIRMARY.

SHOULD HAVE BROUGHT HER SOME CHOCO-LUDES. OH, WELL...

INFIRMARY

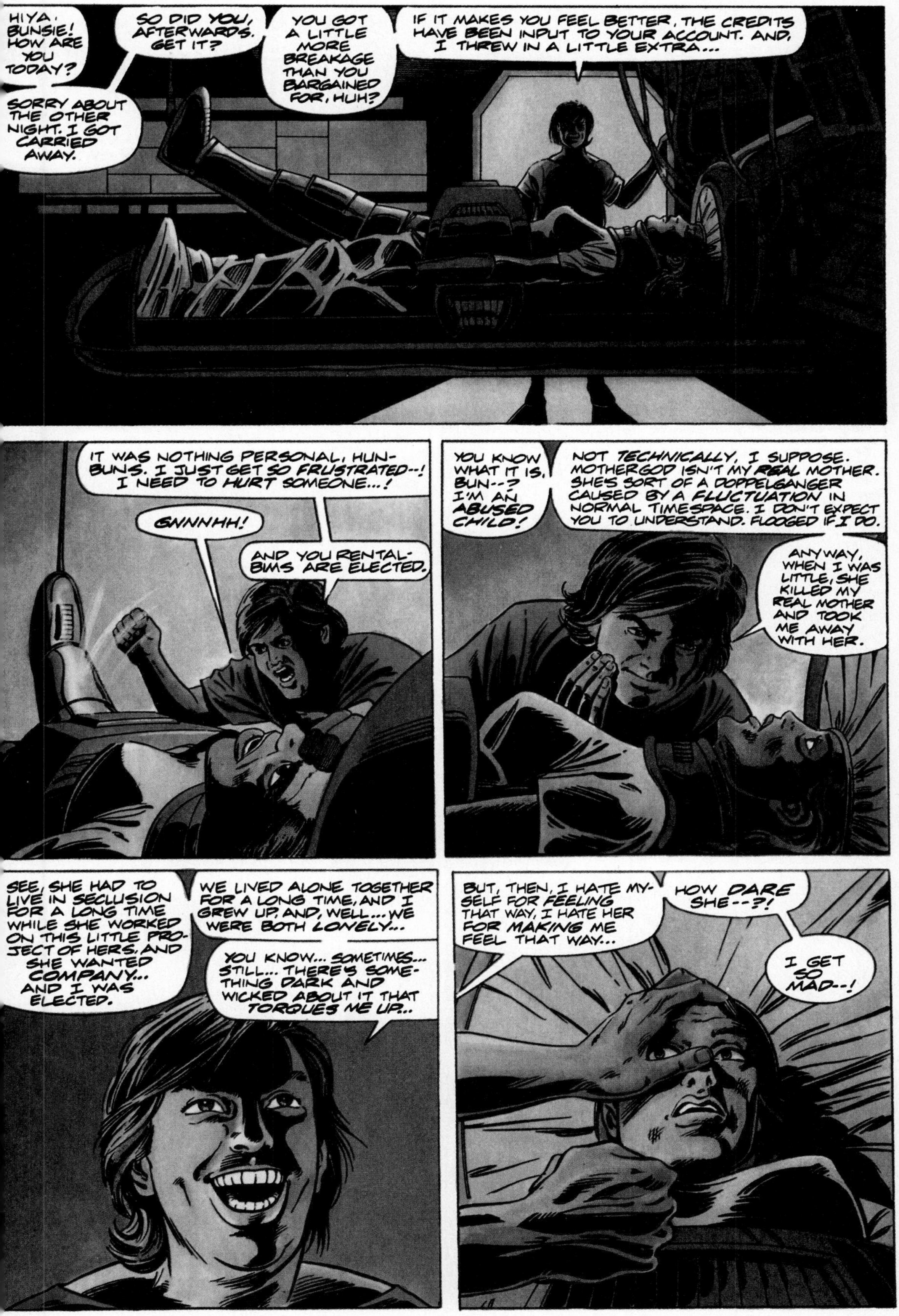
HIYA, BUNSIE! HOW ARE YOU TODAY?
SORRY ABOUT THE OTHER NIGHT. I GOT CARRIED AWAY.
SO DID YOU, AFTERWARDS. GET IT?
YOU GOT A LITTLE MORE BREAKAGE THAN YOU BARGAINED FOR, HUH?
IF IT MAKES YOU FEEL BETTER, THE CREDITS HAVE BEEN INPUT TO YOUR ACCOUNT. AND, I THREW IN A LITTLE EXTRA...
IT WAS NOTHING PERSONAL, HUN-BUNS. I JUST GET SO FRUSTRATED--! I NEED TO HURT SOMEONE...!
GNNNHH!
AND YOU RENTAL-BIMS ARE ELECTED.
YOU KNOW WHAT IT IS, BUN--? I'M AN ABUSED CHILD!
NOT TECHNICALLY, I SUPPOSE. MOTHERGOD ISN'T MY REAL MOTHER. SHE'S SORT OF A DOPPELGANGER CAUSED BY A FLUCTUATION IN NORMAL TIMESPACE. I DON'T EXPECT YOU TO UNDERSTAND. FLOOGED IF I DO.
ANYWAY, WHEN I WAS LITTLE, SHE KILLED MY REAL MOTHER AND TOOK ME AWAY WITH HER.
SEE, SHE HAD TO LIVE IN SECLUSION FOR A LONG TIME WHILE SHE WORKED ON THIS LITTLE PROJECT OF HERS, AND SHE WANTED COMPANY... AND I WAS ELECTED.
WE LIVED ALONE TOGETHER FOR A LONG TIME, AND I GREW UP, AND, WELL... WE WERE BOTH LONELY...
YOU KNOW... SOMETIMES... STILL... THERE'S SOMETHING DARK AND WICKED ABOUT IT THAT TORQUES ME UP...
BUT, THEN, I HATE MYSELF FOR FEELING THAT WAY, I HATE HER FOR MAKING ME FEEL THAT WAY...
HOW DARE SHE--?!
I GET SO MAD--!

OH, I'VE TRIED TO TALK TO HER ABOUT IT THOUSANDS OF TIMES...BUT I ALWAYS START TO GET MAD...

...AND I HAVE TO STOP BECAUSE, WHAT IF I LOSE IT AND HIT HER..?

SHE'S GOT THIS WAY WITH ENERGY. SHE MIGHT TOAST ME...! SO I JUST SHUT UP, YOU KNOW?

I REALLY NEED TO HIT HER...

SOMETIMES...WHEN I TRY TO TALK, SHE'LL START PLAYING. NEXT THING YOU KNOW SHE'S GOT ME WRAPPED AROUND HER LITTLE FINGER AGAIN...

I MEAN, I DON'T WANT TO, BUT THERE I AM...

I HATE HER. I'VE GOT TO KILL HER, BUNS, BEFORE SHE BECOMES GOD.

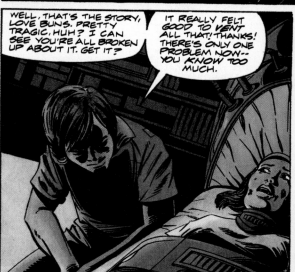

WELL, THAT'S THE STORY, LOVE BUNS. PRETTY TRAGIC, HUH? I CAN SEE YOU'RE ALL BROKEN UP ABOUT IT. GET IT?

IT REALLY FELT GOOD TO VENT ALL THAT! THANKS! THERE'S ONLY ONE PROBLEM NOW-- YOU KNOW TOO MUCH.

CAN'T HAVE YOU SPREADING VICIOUS RUMORS, CAN I?

OOPS.

ULLLGHHH...

I ACCIDENTLY TORE OUT YOUR LIFE-SUPPORT CONNEX...

YO-HEY, KNOB! THIS ONE'S DEAD.

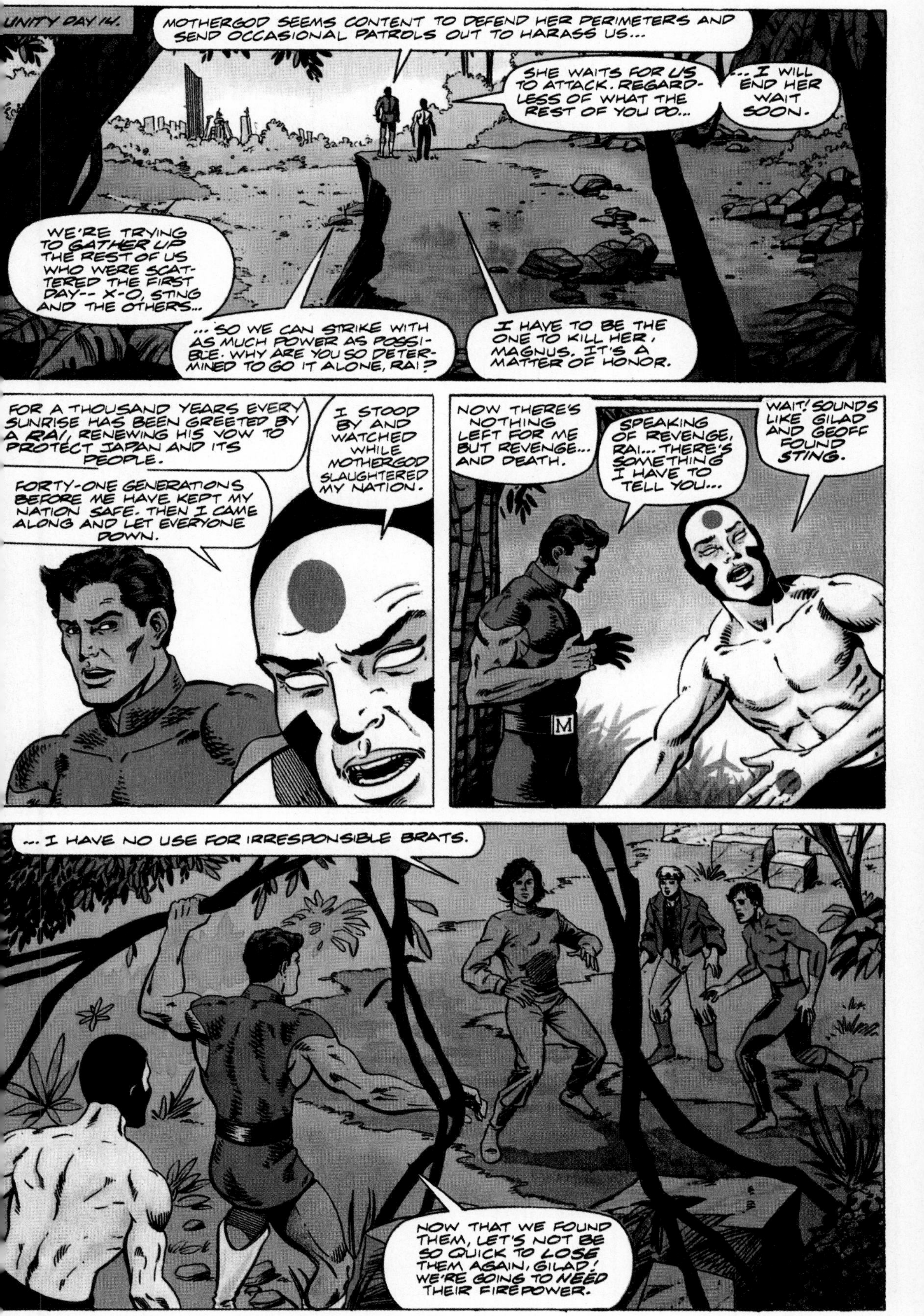
UNITY DAY 14.
MOTHERGOD SEEMS CONTENT TO DEFEND HER PERIMETERS AND SEND OCCASIONAL PATROLS OUT TO HARASS US...
SHE WAITS FOR US TO ATTACK. REGARDLESS OF WHAT THE REST OF YOU DO...
...I WILL END HER WAIT SOON.
WE'RE TRYING TO GATHER UP THE REST OF US WHO WERE SCATTERED THE FIRST DAY-- X-O, STING AND THE OTHERS...
...SO WE CAN STRIKE WITH AS MUCH POWER AS POSSIBLE. WHY ARE YOU SO DETERMINED TO GO IT ALONE, RAI?
I HAVE TO BE THE ONE TO KILL HER, MAGNUS. IT'S A MATTER OF HONOR.
FOR A THOUSAND YEARS EVERY SUNRISE HAS BEEN GREETED BY A RAI, RENEWING HIS VOW TO PROTECT JAPAN AND ITS PEOPLE.
FORTY-ONE GENERATIONS BEFORE ME HAVE KEPT MY NATION SAFE. THEN I CAME ALONG AND LET EVERYONE DOWN.
I STOOD BY AND WATCHED WHILE MOTHERGOD SLAUGHTERED MY NATION.
NOW THERE'S NOTHING LEFT FOR ME BUT REVENGE... AND DEATH.
SPEAKING OF REVENGE, RAI... THERE'S SOMETHING I HAVE TO TELL YOU...
WAIT! SOUNDS LIKE GILAD AND GEOFF FOUND STING.
M
...I HAVE NO USE FOR IRRESPONSIBLE BRATS.
NOW THAT WE FOUND THEM, LET'S NOT BE SO QUICK TO LOSE THEM AGAIN, GILAD! WE'RE GOING TO NEED THEIR FIREPOWER.

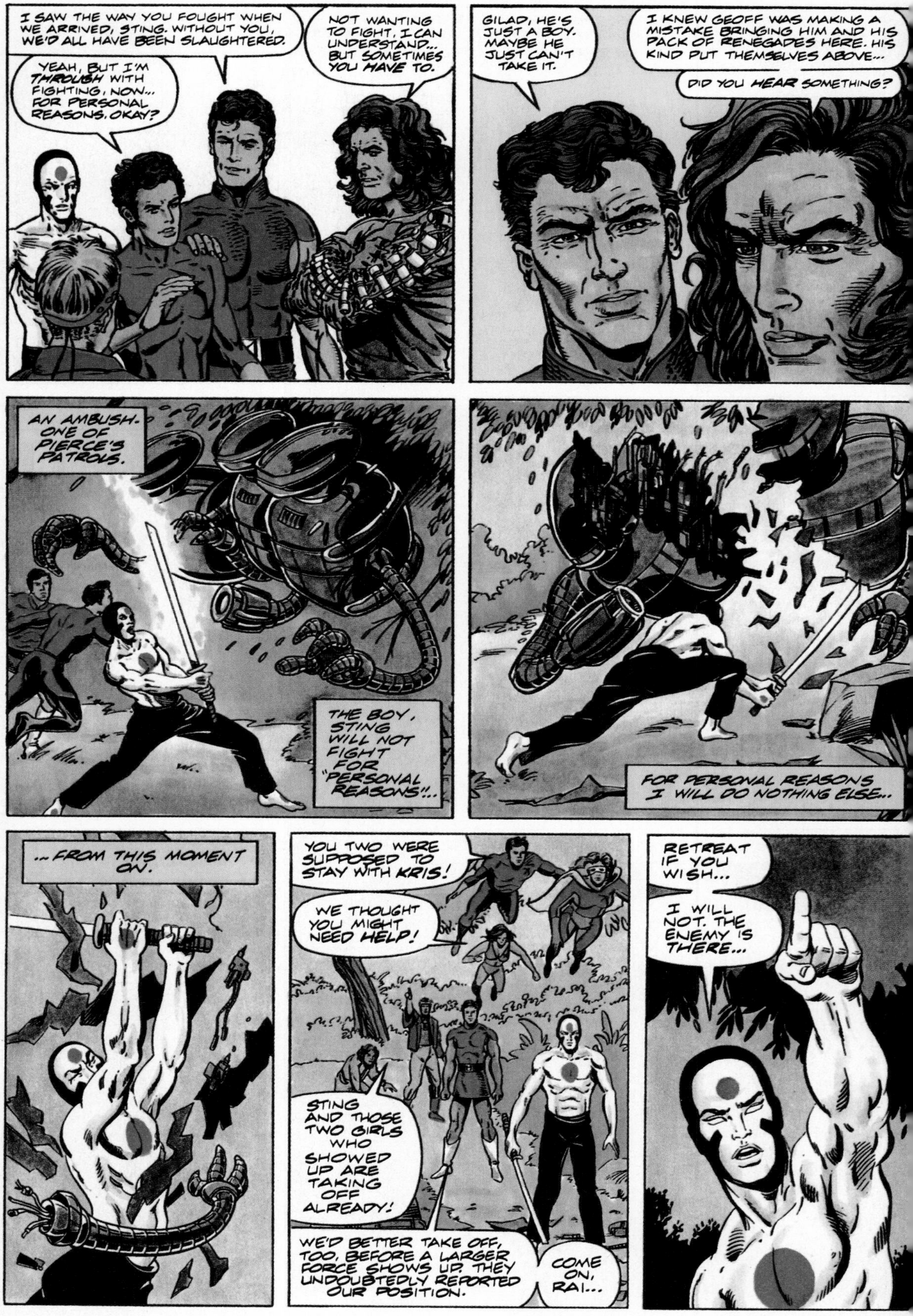
I SAW THE WAY YOU FOUGHT WHEN WE ARRIVED, STING. WITHOUT YOU, WE'D ALL HAVE BEEN SLAUGHTERED.
YEAH, BUT I'M THROUGH WITH FIGHTING, NOW... FOR PERSONAL REASONS. OKAY?
NOT WANTING TO FIGHT, I CAN UNDERSTAND... BUT SOMETIMES YOU HAVE TO.
GILAD, HE'S JUST A BOY. MAYBE HE JUST CAN'T TAKE IT.
I KNEW GEOFF WAS MAKING A MISTAKE BRINGING HIM AND HIS PACK OF RENEGADES HERE. HIS KIND PUT THEMSELVES ABOVE...
DID YOU HEAR SOMETHING?
AN AMBUSH- ONE OF PIERCE'S PATROLS.
THE BOY, STING WILL NOT FIGHT FOR "PERSONAL REASONS"...
FOR PERSONAL REASONS I WILL DO NOTHING ELSE...
...FROM THIS MOMENT ON.
YOU TWO WERE SUPPOSED TO STAY WITH KRIS!
WE THOUGHT YOU MIGHT NEED HELP!
STING AND THOSE TWO GIRLS WHO SHOWED UP ARE TAKING OFF ALREADY!
WE'D BETTER TAKE OFF, TOO, BEFORE A LARGER FORCE SHOWS UP. THEY UNDOUBTEDLY REPORTED OUR POSITION.
COME ON, RAI...
RETREAT IF YOU WISH...
I WILL NOT. THE ENEMY IS THERE...

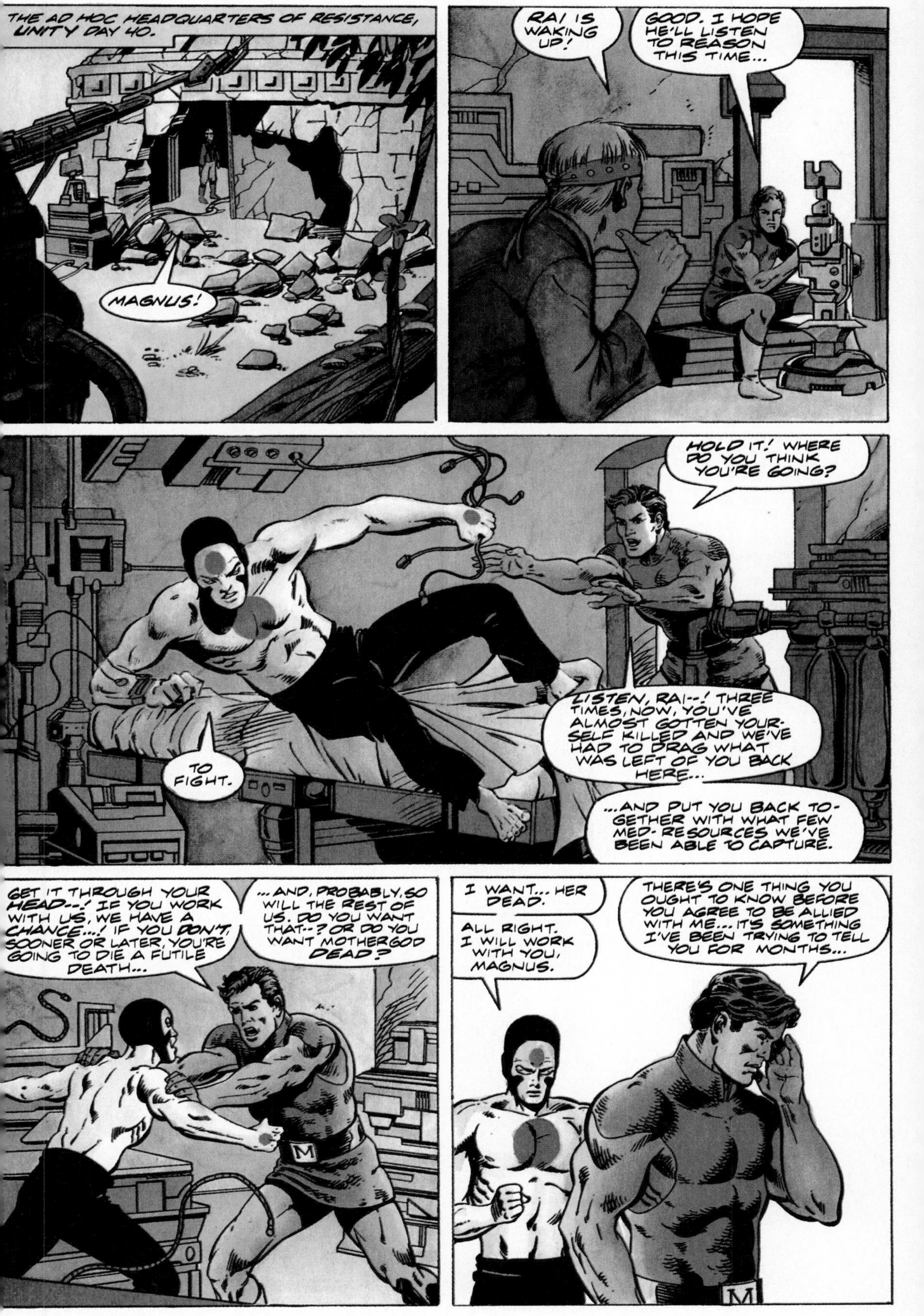
THE AD HOC HEADQUARTERS OF RESISTANCE, UNITY DAY 40.
MAGNUS!
RAI IS WAKING UP!
GOOD. I HOPE HE'LL LISTEN TO REASON THIS TIME...
HOLD IT! WHERE DO YOU THINK YOU'RE GOING?
TO FIGHT.
LISTEN, RAI--! THREE TIMES, NOW, YOU'VE ALMOST GOTTEN YOURSELF KILLED AND WE'VE HAD TO DRAG WHAT WAS LEFT OF YOU BACK HERE...
...AND PUT YOU BACK TOGETHER WITH WHAT FEW MED-RESOURCES WE'VE BEEN ABLE TO CAPTURE.
GET IT THROUGH YOUR HEAD--! IF YOU WORK WITH US, WE HAVE A CHANCE...! IF YOU DON'T, SOONER OR LATER, YOU'RE GOING TO DIE A FUTILE DEATH...
...AND, PROBABLY, SO WILL THE REST OF US. DO YOU WANT THAT--? OR DO YOU WANT MOTHERGOD DEAD?
I WANT... HER DEAD.
ALL RIGHT. I WILL WORK WITH YOU, MAGNUS.
THERE'S ONE THING YOU OUGHT TO KNOW BEFORE YOU AGREE TO BE ALLIED WITH ME... IT'S SOMETHING I'VE BEEN TRYING TO TELL YOU FOR MONTHS...

SHORTLY BEFORE WE CAME HERE, I HAD A... CONFRONTATION WITH GRAND ONE...

...THAT ENDED IN HER DEATH.

IT WAS UNAVOIDABLE. I'LL TELL YOU THE WHOLE STORY SOMEDAY...

GRAND ONE IS DEAD?

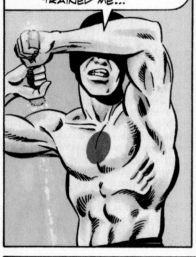

THEN... MY LOSSES ARE COMPLETE--MY NATION... MY PEOPLE... AND EVEN THE ONE WHO TRAINED ME...

SO, I HAVE ONE MORE TO AVENGE...

...AND NO ONE LEFT TO APOLOGIZE TO!

FOR NOW, MAGNUS, MY SWORD IS AT YOUR SERVICE.

AFTER MOTHERGOD HAS BEEN DEALT WITH, I WILL KILL YOU.

AND, THEN I WILL KILL MYSELF.

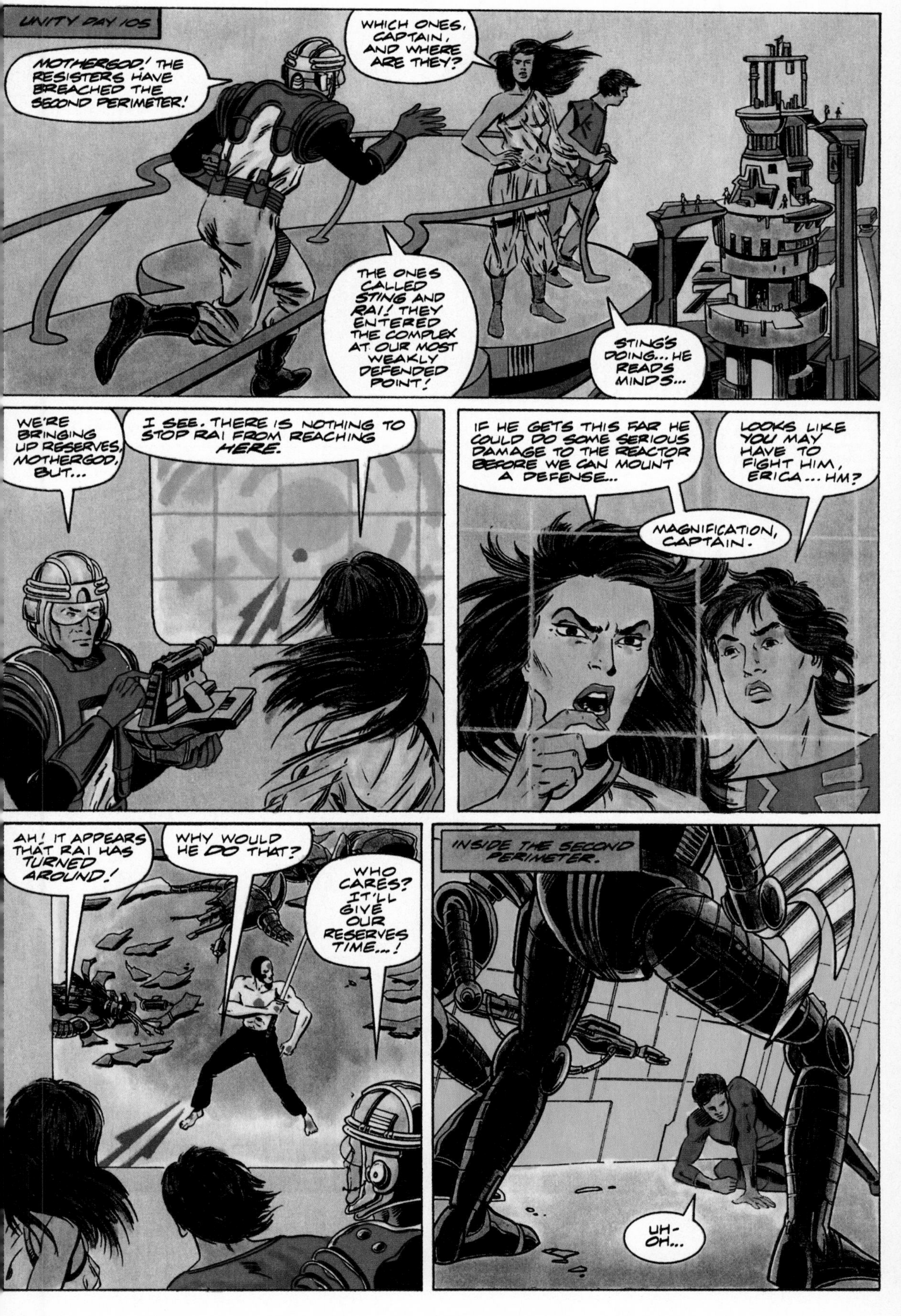
UNITY DAY 105
MOTHERGOD! THE RESISTERS HAVE BREACHED THE SECOND PERIMETER!
WHICH ONES, CAPTAIN, AND WHERE ARE THEY?
THE ONES CALLED STING AND RAI! THEY ENTERED THE COMPLEX AT OUR MOST WEAKLY DEFENDED POINT!
STING'S DOING... HE READS MINDS...
WE'RE BRINGING UP RESERVES, MOTHERGOD, BUT...
I SEE. THERE IS NOTHING TO STOP RAI FROM REACHING HERE.
IF HE GETS THIS FAR HE COULD DO SOME SERIOUS DAMAGE TO THE REACTOR BEFORE WE CAN MOUNT A DEFENSE...
MAGNIFICATION, CAPTAIN.
LOOKS LIKE YOU MAY HAVE TO FIGHT HIM, ERICA... HM?
AH! IT APPEARS THAT RAI HAS TURNED AROUND!
WHY WOULD HE DO THAT?
WHO CARES? IT'LL GIVE OUR RESERVES TIME...!
INSIDE THE SECOND PERIMETER.
UH-OH...

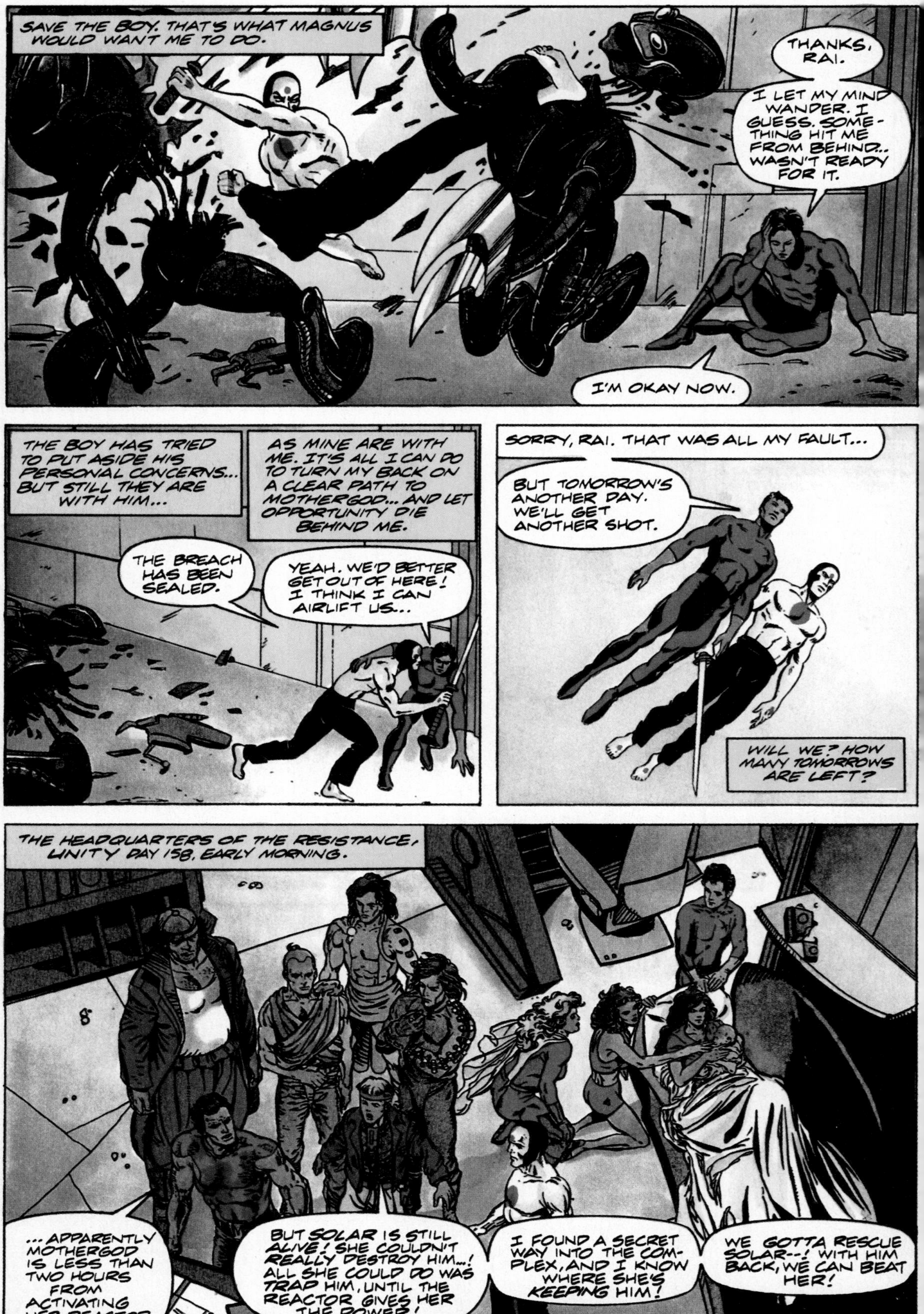
SAVE THE BOY. THAT'S WHAT MAGNUS WOULD WANT ME TO DO.
THANKS, RAI.
I LET MY MIND WANDER, I GUESS. SOMETHING HIT ME FROM BEHIND... WASN'T READY FOR IT.
I'M OKAY NOW.
THE BOY HAS TRIED TO PUT ASIDE HIS PERSONAL CONCERNS... BUT STILL THEY ARE WITH HIM...
AS MINE ARE WITH ME. IT'S ALL I CAN DO TO TURN MY BACK ON A CLEAR PATH TO MOTHERGOD... AND LET OPPORTUNITY DIE BEHIND ME.
THE BREACH HAS BEEN SEALED.
YEAH. WE'D BETTER GET OUT OF HERE! I THINK I CAN AIRLIFT US...
SORRY, RAI. THAT WAS ALL MY FAULT...
BUT TOMORROW'S ANOTHER DAY. WE'LL GET ANOTHER SHOT.
WILL WE? HOW MANY TOMORROWS ARE LEFT?
THE HEADQUARTERS OF THE RESISTANCE, UNITY DAY 158, EARLY MORNING.
...APPARENTLY MOTHERGOD IS LESS THAN TWO HOURS FROM ACTIVATING HER REACTOR.
BUT SOLAR IS STILL ALIVE! SHE COULDN'T REALLY DESTROY HIM...! ALL SHE COULD DO WAS TRAP HIM, UNTIL THE REACTOR GIVES HER THE POWER!
I FOUND A SECRET WAY INTO THE COMPLEX, AND I KNOW WHERE SHE'S KEEPING HIM!
WE GOTTA RESCUE SOLAR--! WITH HIM BACK, WE CAN BEAT HER!

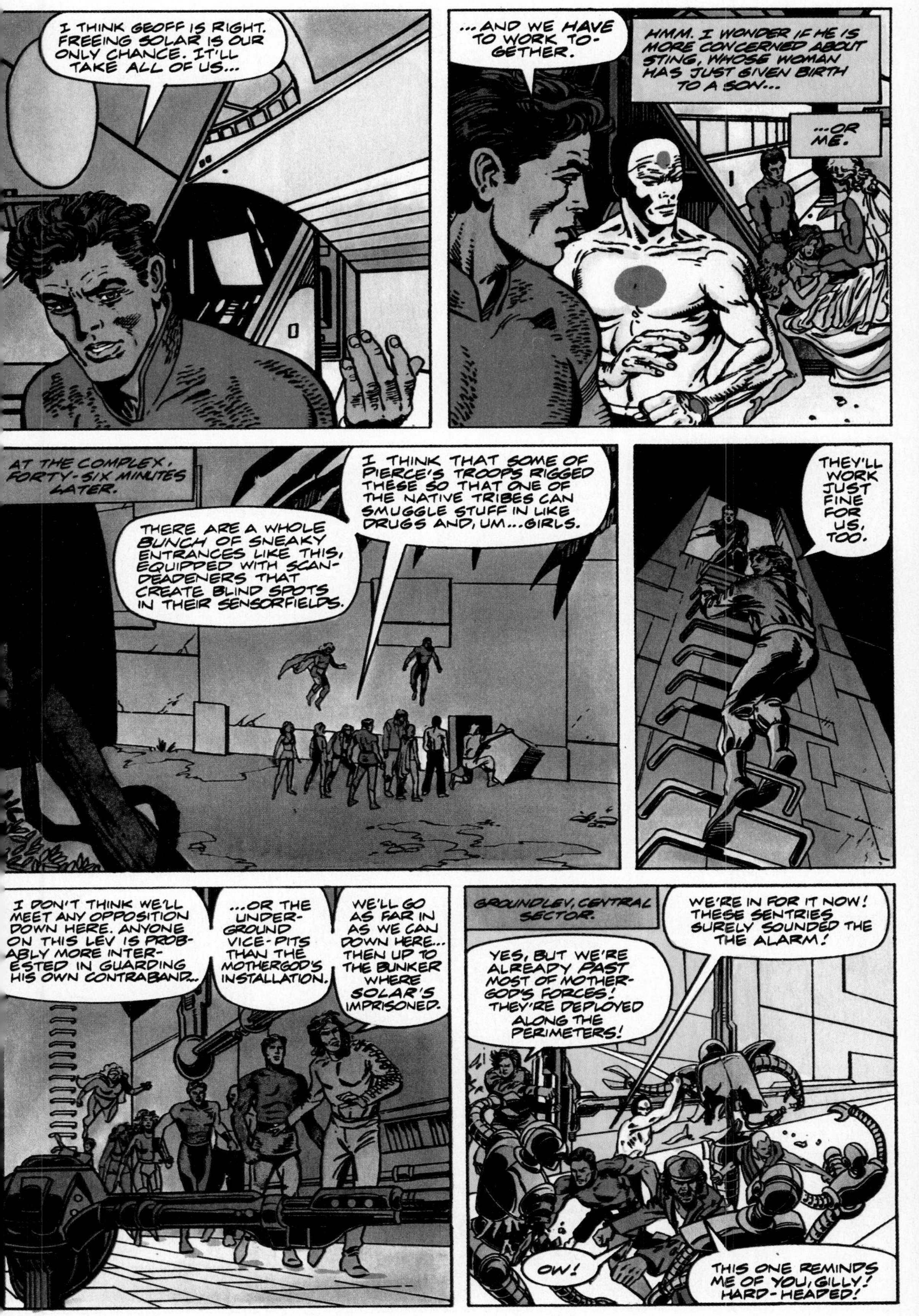

I THINK GEOFF IS RIGHT. FREEING SOLAR IS OUR ONLY CHANCE. IT'LL TAKE ALL OF US...
...AND WE HAVE TO WORK TOGETHER.
HMM. I WONDER IF HE IS MORE CONCERNED ABOUT STING, WHOSE WOMAN HAS JUST GIVEN BIRTH TO A SON...
...OR ME.
AT THE COMPLEX, FORTY-SIX MINUTES LATER.
THERE ARE A WHOLE BUNCH OF SNEAKY ENTRANCES LIKE THIS, EQUIPPED WITH SCAN-DEADENERS THAT CREATE BLIND SPOTS IN THEIR SENSORFIELDS.
I THINK THAT SOME OF PIERCE'S TROOPS RIGGED THESE SO THAT ONE OF THE NATIVE TRIBES CAN SMUGGLE STUFF IN LIKE DRUGS AND, UM...GIRLS.
THEY'LL WORK JUST FINE FOR US, TOO.
I DON'T THINK WE'LL MEET ANY OPPOSITION DOWN HERE. ANYONE ON THIS LEV IS PROBABLY MORE INTERESTED IN GUARDING HIS OWN CONTRABAND...
...OR THE UNDERGROUND VICE-PITS THAN THE MOTHERGOD'S INSTALLATION.
WE'LL GO AS FAR IN AS WE CAN DOWN HERE... THEN UP TO THE BUNKER WHERE SOLAR'S IMPRISONED.
GROUNDLEV, CENTRAL SECTOR.
WE'RE IN FOR IT NOW! THESE SENTRIES SURELY SOUNDED THE THE ALARM!
YES, BUT WE'RE ALREADY PAST MOST OF MOTHER-GOD'S FORCES! THEY'RE DEPLOYED ALONG THE PERIMETERS!
OW!
THIS ONE REMINDS ME OF YOU, GILLY! HARD-HEADED!

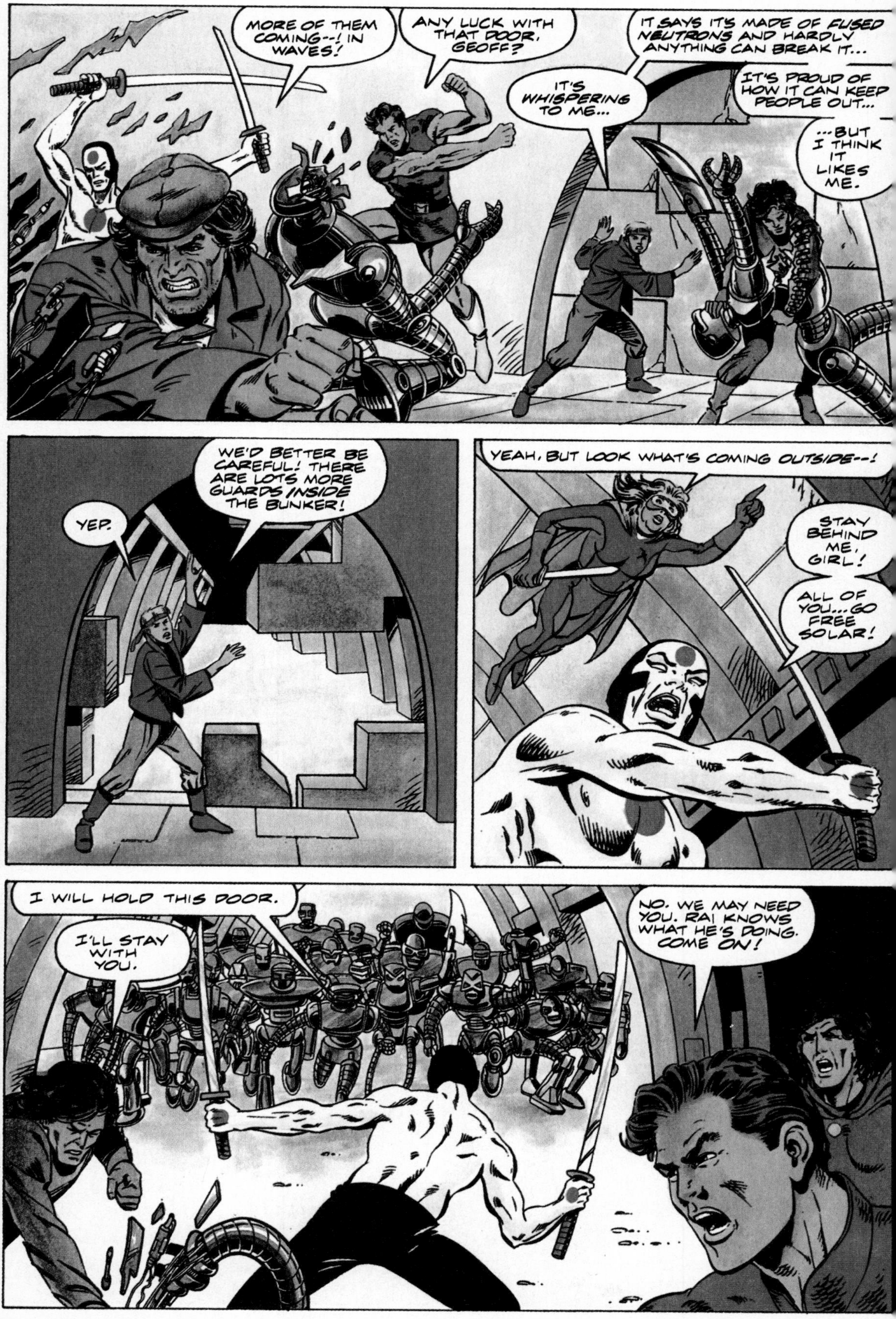
MORE OF THEM COMING--! IN WAVES!
ANY LUCK WITH THAT DOOR, GEOFF?
IT'S WHISPERING TO ME...
IT SAYS IT'S MADE OF FUSED NEUTRONS AND HARDLY ANYTHING CAN BREAK IT...
IT'S PROUD OF HOW IT CAN KEEP PEOPLE OUT...
...BUT I THINK IT LIKES ME.
YEP.
WE'D BETTER BE CAREFUL! THERE ARE LOTS MORE GUARDS INSIDE THE BUNKER!
YEAH, BUT LOOK WHAT'S COMING OUTSIDE--!
STAY BEHIND ME, GIRL!
ALL OF YOU... GO FREE SOLAR!
I WILL HOLD THIS DOOR.
I'LL STAY WITH YOU.
NO. WE MAY NEED YOU. RAI KNOWS WHAT HE'S DOING. COME ON!

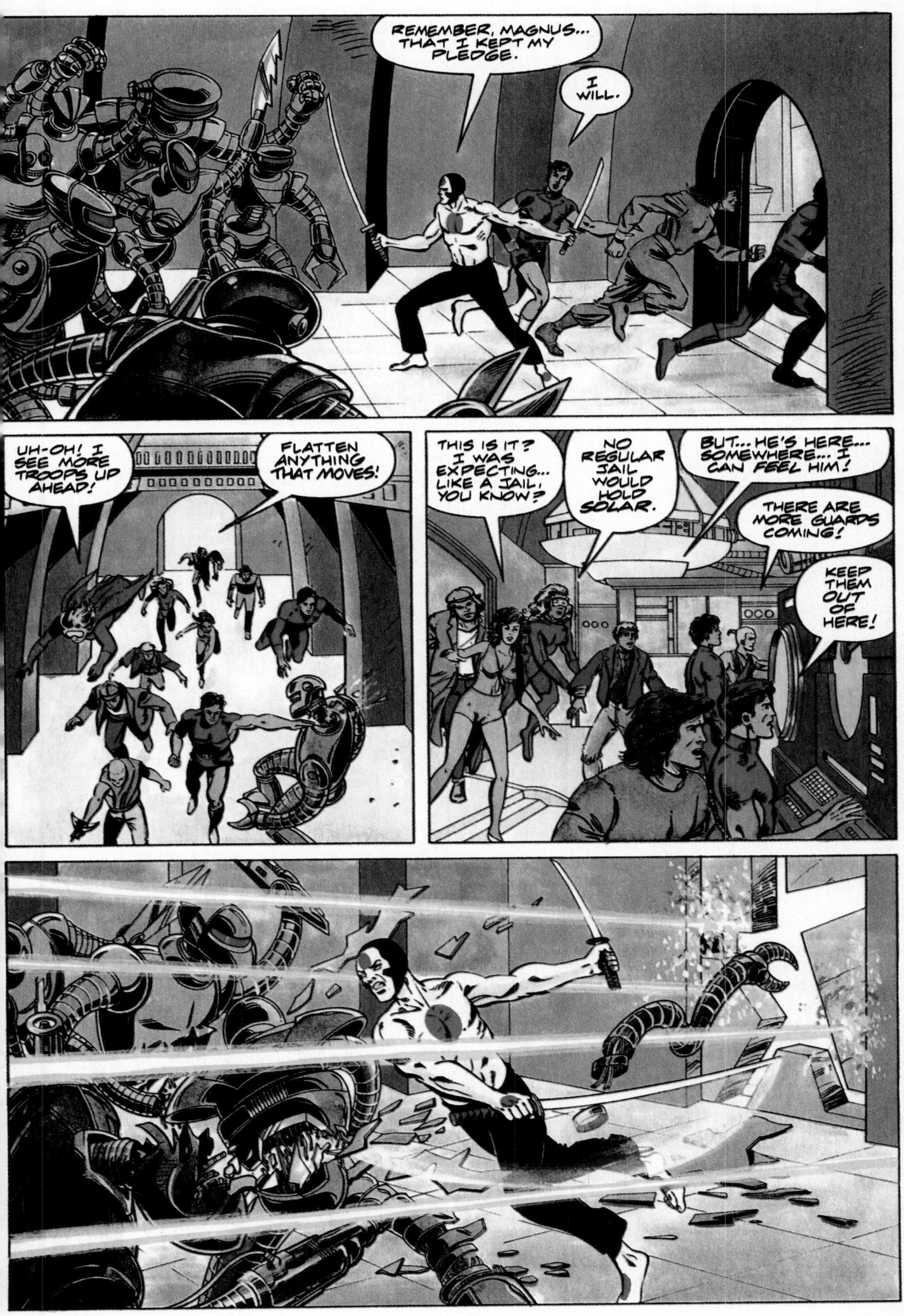
REMEMBER, MAGNUS... THAT I KEPT MY PLEDGE.
I WILL.
UH-OH! I SEE MORE TROOPS UP AHEAD!
FLATTEN ANYTHING THAT MOVES!
THIS IS IT? I WAS EXPECTING... LIKE A JAIL, YOU KNOW?
NO REGULAR JAIL WOULD HOLD SOLAR.
BUT... HE'S HERE... SOMEWHERE... I CAN FEEL HIM!
THERE ARE MORE GUARDS COMING!
KEEP THEM OUT OF HERE!

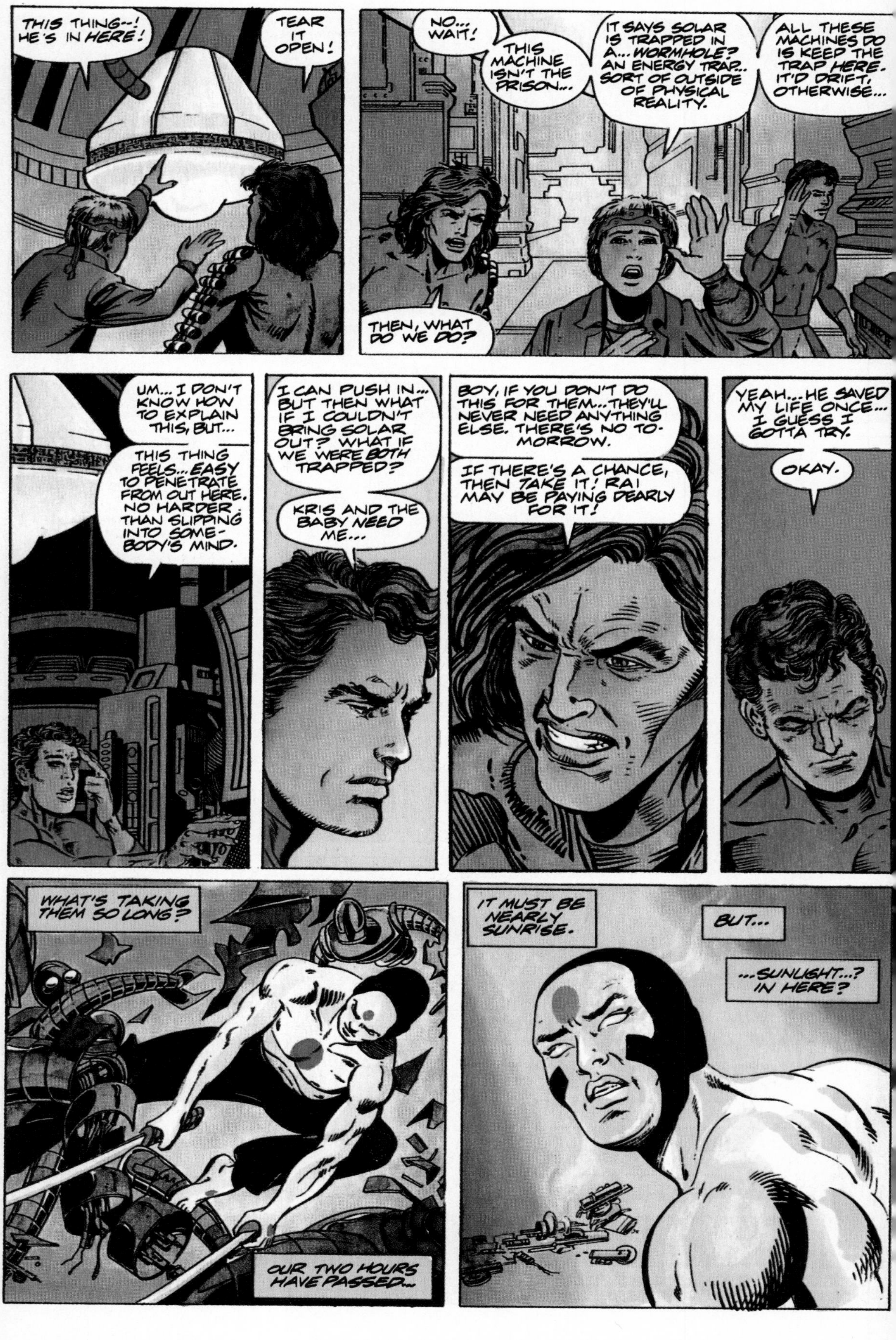
THIS THING--! HE'S IN HERE!
TEAR IT OPEN!
NO... WAIT!
THIS MACHINE ISN'T THE PRISON...
IT SAYS SOLAR IS TRAPPED IN A... WORMHOLE? AN ENERGY TRAP.. SORT OF OUTSIDE OF PHYSICAL REALITY.
ALL THESE MACHINES DO IS KEEP THE TRAP HERE. IT'D DRIFT, OTHERWISE...
THEN, WHAT DO WE DO?
UM... I DON'T KNOW HOW TO EXPLAIN THIS, BUT...
THIS THING FEELS... EASY TO PENETRATE FROM OUT HERE. NO HARDER THAN SLIPPING INTO SOME-BODY'S MIND.
I CAN PUSH IN... BUT THEN WHAT IF I COULDN'T BRING SOLAR OUT? WHAT IF WE WERE BOTH TRAPPED?
KRIS AND THE BABY NEED ME...
BOY, IF YOU DON'T DO THIS FOR THEM... THEY'LL NEVER NEED ANYTHING ELSE. THERE'S NO TO-MORROW.
IF THERE'S A CHANCE, THEN TAKE IT! RAI MAY BE PAYING DEARLY FOR IT!
YEAH... HE SAVED MY LIFE ONCE... I GUESS I GOTTA TRY.
OKAY.
WHAT'S TAKING THEM SO LONG?
OUR TWO HOURS HAVE PASSED...
IT MUST BE NEARLY SUNRISE.
BUT...
...SUNLIGHT...? IN HERE?

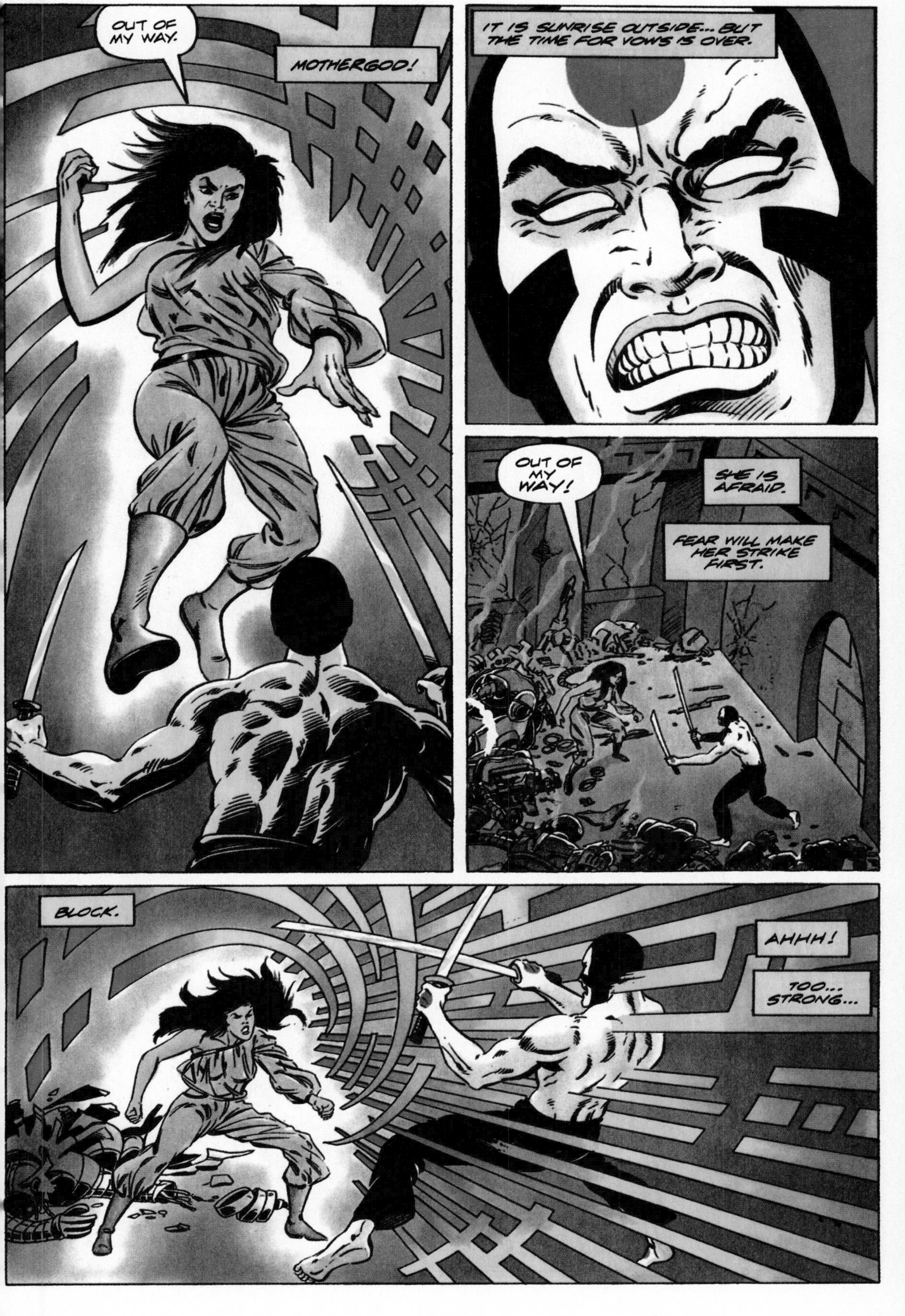
OUT OF MY WAY.
MOTHERGOD!
IT IS SUNRISE OUTSIDE... BUT THE TIME FOR VOWS IS OVER.
OUT OF MY WAY!
SHE IS AFRAID.
FEAR WILL MAKE HER STRIKE FIRST.
BLOCK.
AHHH!
TOO... STRONG...

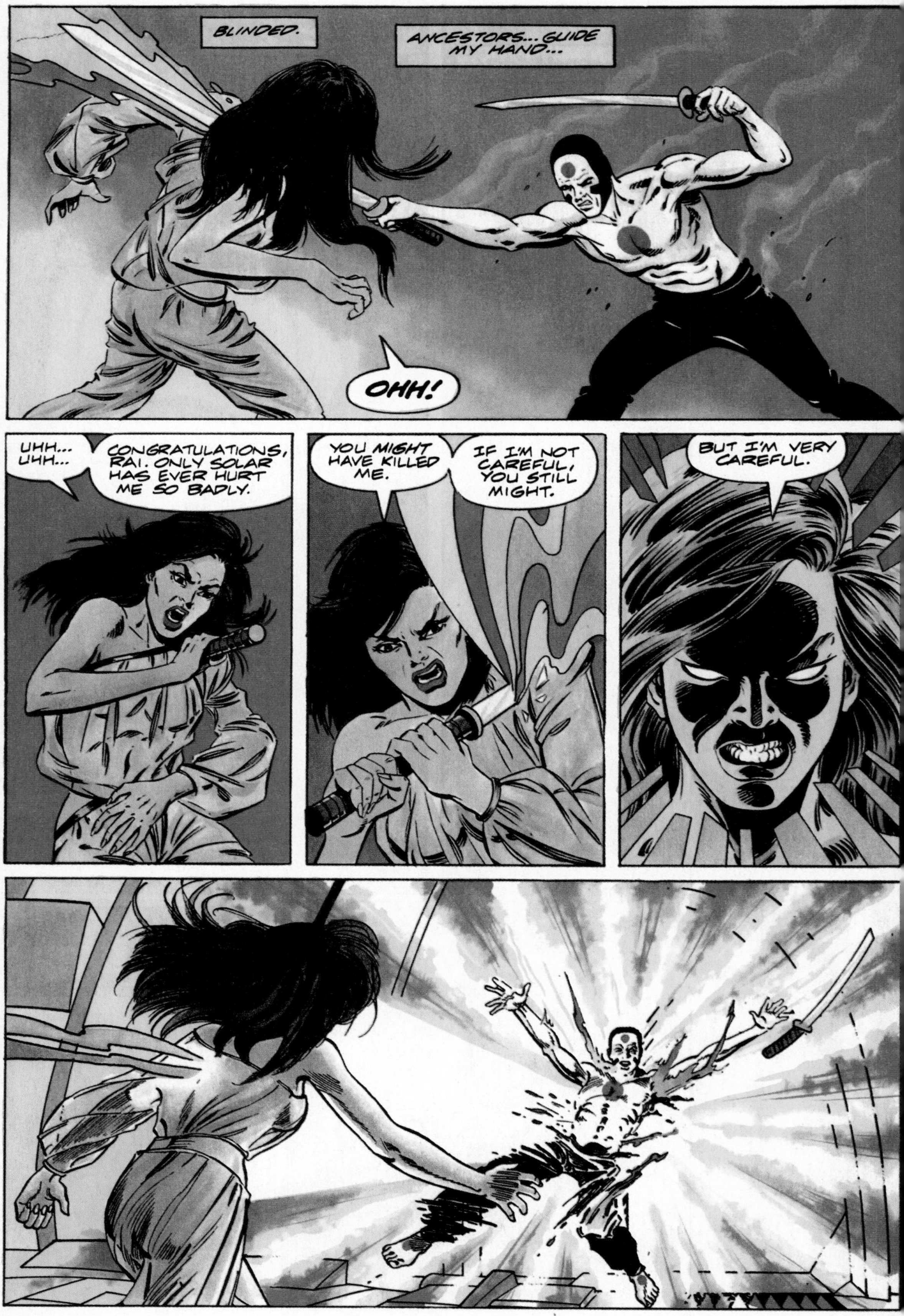
BLINDED.
ANCESTORS... GUIDE MY HAND...
OHH!
UHH... UHH...
CONGRATULATIONS, RAI. ONLY SOLAR HAS EVER HURT ME SO BADLY.
YOU MIGHT HAVE KILLED ME.
IF I'M NOT CAREFUL, YOU STILL MIGHT.
BUT I'M VERY CAREFUL.

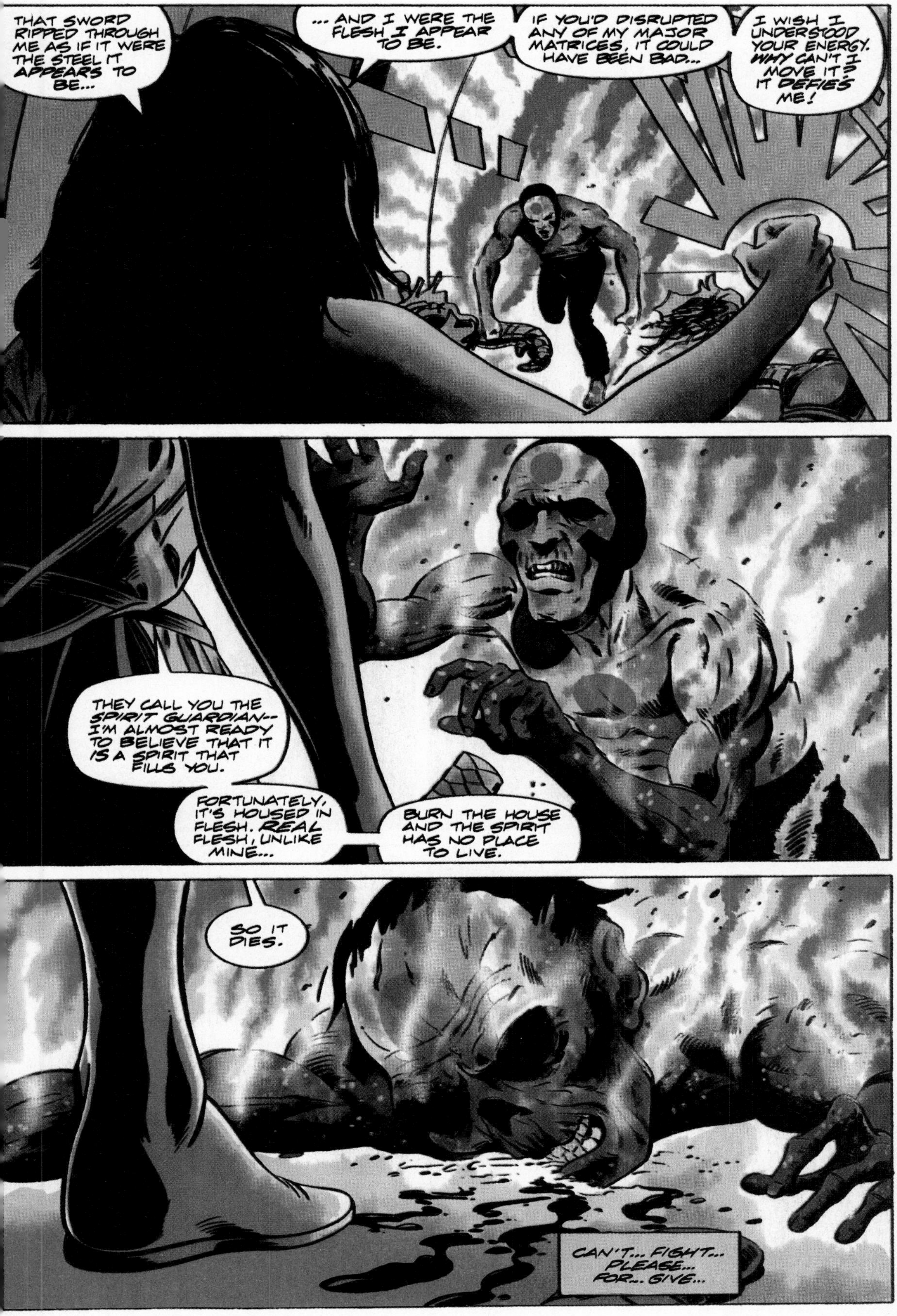
THAT SWORD RIPPED THROUGH ME AS IF IT WERE THE STEEL IT APPEARS TO BE...
... AND I WERE THE FLESH I APPEAR TO BE.
IF YOU'D DISRUPTED ANY OF MY MAJOR MATRICES, IT COULD HAVE BEEN BAD...
I WISH I UNDERSTOOD YOUR ENERGY. WHY CAN'T I MOVE IT? IT DEFIES ME!
THEY CALL YOU THE SPIRIT GUARDIAN-- I'M ALMOST READY TO BELIEVE THAT IT IS A SPIRIT THAT FILLS YOU.
FORTUNATELY, IT'S HOUSED IN FLESH. REAL FLESH, UNLIKE MINE...
BURN THE HOUSE AND THE SPIRIT HAS NO PLACE TO LIVE.
SO IT DIES.
CAN'T... FIGHT... PLEASE... FOR... GIVE...

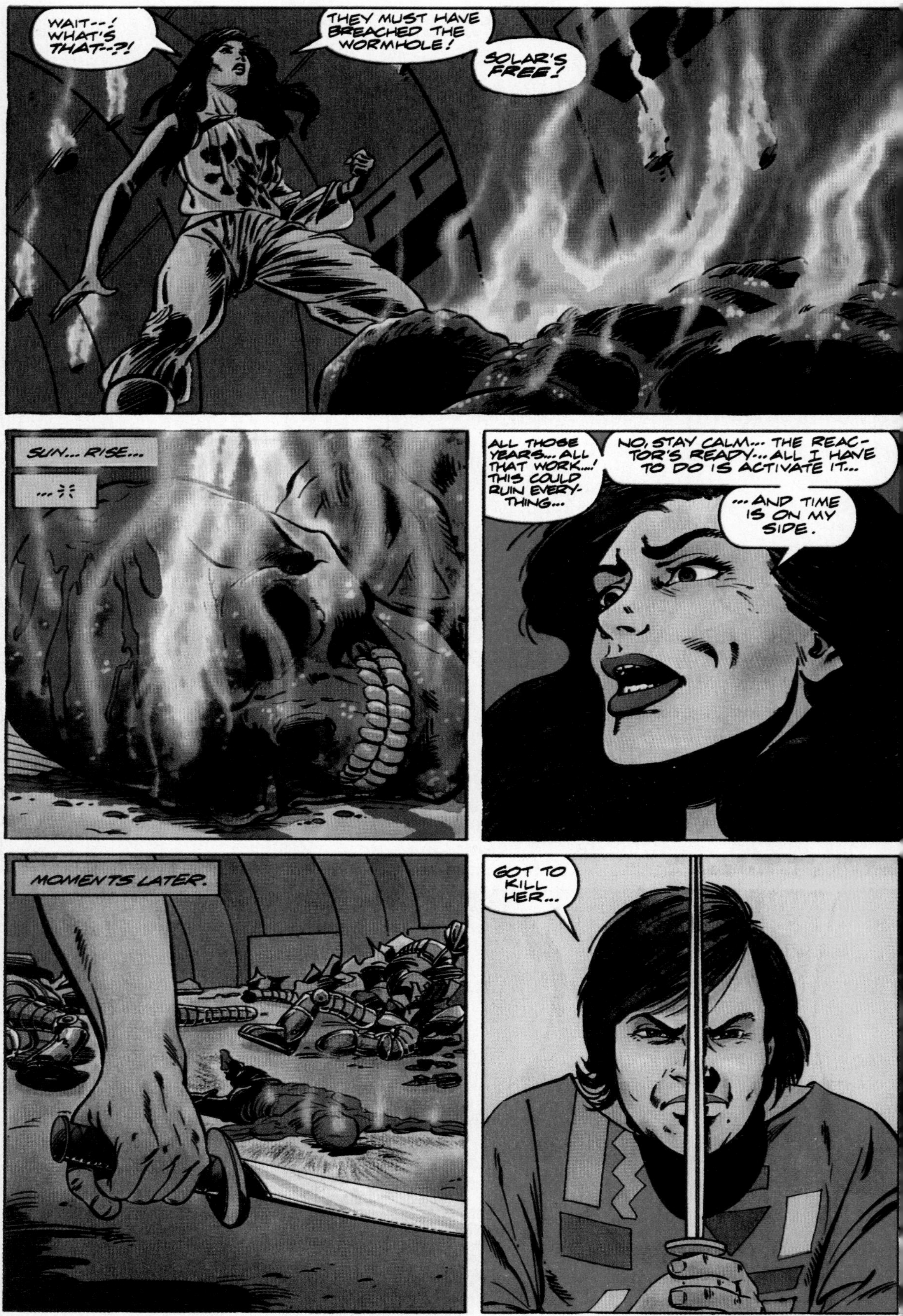
WAIT--! WHAT'S THAT--?!
THEY MUST HAVE BREACHED THE WORMHOLE!
SOLAR'S FREE!
SUN... RISE...
...
ALL THOSE YEARS... ALL THAT WORK...! THIS COULD RUIN EVERYTHING...
NO, STAY CALM... THE REACTOR'S READY... ALL I HAVE TO DO IS ACTIVATE IT...
...AND TIME IS ON MY SIDE.
MOMENTS LATER.
GOT TO KILL HER...

UNITY

TIMELINE

AUGUST 4001 After years of searching, Rokland Tate, now a full-fledged Geomancer, manages to locate Gilad, the Eternal Warrior. Though Gilad's mind had been probed many times, Rokkie manages to awaken the spark of who Gilad really is. They set out together to stop Unity.

On the verge of defeat at the hands of Talpa, Magnus is saved at the last moment by the intervention of Rai (Tohru Takashi). Rokkie Tate has recruited Rai, Gilad 4001, and now Magnus to help stop Erica Pierce and Unity.

Erica Pierce moves her San Gabriel facility to the Lost Land.

UNITY DAY 1 Magnus, Rai, and Gilad 4001 arrive. Erica, fearing Rai's power, attempts to force his retreat, threatening Japan if he does not withdraw. He refuses and, in 4001, Japan crashes from orbit into the Indian Ocean.

Seeing them, Solar joins the 4001 team. Magnus and Rai recognize Solar, but this Solar (from 1992) does not know them. Rai sights the 1992 team and they meet up.

Erica spots the teams and mounts an attack. The teams split up.

While battling pteradons, X-O is attacked from behind and falls into a cell with slaves who are to be fed to the bionisaurs. Aric rescues them and proclaims himself their leader. They escape and head for the mountains.

Shadowman arrives in the Lost Land and incorrectly assumes that Solar is the threat. He meets and quickly befriends Elya, who takes him to the Central Tower.

Archer, Armstong, and Gilad 1992 break off from the main group and begin attacking robots. Gilad, Archer, and Armstrong are separated.

Solar blasts his way through the Central Tower and confronts Erica one-on-one. Seeing the attack, Shadowman leaps to Erica's aid, nearly killing himself in the process. Erica uses the diversion to trap Solar in a cincture wormhole.

Sting can no longer sense Solar and assumes him dead. Erica's counterattack drives back and scatters her enemies. Archer and Armstrong are captured by Section Prelate Rejj.

Gilad 1992 and Geoff meet up with Gilad 4001. They set off to find their allies.

DAY 2 Kris informs Sting that she is pregnant. Sting decides to sit out the war for Kris' safety.

Archer is questioned by Rejj, who is a devotee of Archer's philosophies. Meanwhile, Armstrong succeeds at a daring escape involving natural camouflage.

Geoff, Rai, Magnus, and the two Gilads meet and regroup.

DAY 3 X-O and his new followers arrive in the mountains and set up camp in a series of caves.

DAY 6 An infatuated Elya searches the history archives for information on Shadowman.

DAY 12 Rai and Magnus attack the robot commlink sector of Erica's fortress. The attack fails, and they are forced to withdraw.

Albert visits Bunsie in the infirmary and kills her.

DAY 15 Armstrong discovers the Speakeasy and begins drinking heavily. Armstrong meets Prince Albert in the Speakeasy.

DAY 16 Rai goes on a solo mission to the fortress. Gilad 4001 and Magnus must race to save him.

Albert prevents Archer's execution and returns his crossbow. He provides Archer and Armstrong an opportunity to kill Erica, which fails.

X-O attacks the complex and accidentally gives Archer and Armstrong their chance to escape.

DAY 17 Erica dispatches Turok to kill Archer and Armstrong. However, Turok decides their cause is just and quits Erica's service.

DAY 31 Elya visits Shadowman in the medi-center.

DAY 36 Rai attempts a third solo attack on Erica's complex. This time he is severely injured and is saved only by the intervention of the resistance.

DAY 40 Rai awakens in the hastily constructed med-center at the resistance headquarters. He immediately attempts to leave for another attack, but Magnus convinces Rai to fight alongside the resistance.

DAY 45 The Harbinger team discovers an abandoned building. Sting decides it will suffice as a hideout where they can wait out the war in safety.

DAY 60 Shadowman is removed from the reconstruction vessel. Elya visits him again.

DAY 91 Magnus, Rai, and Gilad 4001 stage an assault on Erica's complex. Shortly afterwards, Magnus comes to the Harbinger team and asks for Sting's help in an attack the next morning. Sting agrees, reluctantly. Sting discovers that Kris' baby is not his, but Torque's.

DAY 92 Enraged, Sting attacks the complex alone. Erica and Sting battle, and only a last-minute appearance by X-O and the others saves his life. Erica withdraws.

DAY 101 Shadowman is discharged from the med-center, into Elya's custody.

TIMELINE

DAY 105 Sting and Rai mount an attack on Erica's complex, but are forced to retreat when Sting is injured.

DAY 150 X-O and his men attack Erica's complex and capture a power converter. He plans to ransom it back, but Magnus and Rai convince him to destroy it.

DAY 153 Erica comes to X-O's camp with tribute. While Aric is distracted, Erica takes control of the X-O armor. On cue, a bionisaur attacks, nearly biting him in two. The armor returns to Aric, encasing him and saving his life. However, X-O falls in battle and is left for dead.

DAY 157 Rai, Magus, and the two Gilads mount a diversionary attack on the citadel. Archer and Armstrong sneak into the complex to plant a bomb to blow up the main power station.

Back at resistance headquarters, the Harbinger team arrives. Geoff tries to check on the baby and discovers it will grow up to be Magnus.

Elya is called away to defend the complex and Shadowman breaks out of Elya's quarters to lend aid. He then manages to thwart Archer and Armstong's bombing plans, forcing them to return to their headquarters.

Geoff then enters the complex to reason with Erica, but is captured near the Speakeasy. The heroes then set off to rescue Geoff, leaving Armstrong behind to deliver Kris' baby. The two Gilads break into the control center to save Geoff. Erica unleashes an energy bolt, seemingly killing him.

Back at resistance headquarters, Kris has gone into labor, and the Gilads, assuming their mission has failed, are forced to retreat.

Magnus is caught under a collapsing support column and presumed killed, but he survives and manages to make his way through the citadel without a fight. Along the way he finds Geoff, who escaped Erica's blast through a secret door. Geoff has learned that Solar is not dead, but imprisoned.

Albert initiates a search for Shadowman, then sneaks off to the Speakeasy. Shadowman follows.

Kris gives birth to a son, as Zephyr returns and tells of the loss of Magnus. Kris begs Sting to find him.

Magnus attacks Erica in her control center, wounding her while her guard is down. Sting manages to locate Magnus and Geoff and the three escape.

After seeing Albert murder a bim in the Speakeasy, Shadowman learns the truth about Unity and drags Albert with him to confront Erica. Elya cannot bring herself to do her duty and shoot Shadowman.

DAY 158 While the resistance launches a final all-out assault on Erica's fortress, their own headquarters are attacked and Kris and the baby are taken prisoner. Shadowman encounters Archer and Armstrong again and ends up injured and trapped. Albert escapes.

The resistance breaks into the prison bunker, leaving Rai to defend the resistance from reinforcements. When Erica appears, Rai fights a desperate last battle, but dies.

His sacrifice buys the others time to find Solar's cage. Sting uses his powers to free Solar. Aware that Solar is free, Erica rushes back to the control center to activate the reactor. Albert picks up one of Rai's energy swords.

Solar, exhausted, is helped from the complex by Sting as Erica activates the main reactor.

X-O appears and joins in a last-ditch attack on the main reactor. Sting, realizing that Kris has been captured, leads the Harbinger team to her rescue.

Albert uses Rai's energy sword to stab Erica in the back. She is not killed, but her concentration is broken long enough for Solar to dive past her defenses and confront her face-to-face.

Shadowman awakens just in time to see the huge column of energy from the reactor and realizes he is too late. He searches for Elya, and a means of escape.

Solar defeats Erica and traps her in the wormhole as Geoff convinces Kris to give him the baby. As the universe collapses around them, Erica's men try to flee, but the robots continue to fight.

Shadowman finds Elya and together they try to return to 1992 via the portal through which he entered. Solar returns most of the people and creatures of the Lost Land to their respective times. Albert is killed by Speakeasy bims.

Shadowman escapes, but Elya is torn from his grasp by Solar's power. The reactor becomes a black hole, which Solar is barely able to destroy.

UNITY CONCLUDES ■

UNITY
CHAPTER FIVE
VALIANT.
AUG NO.1
$2.25
X-O
MANOWAR

UNITY
CHAPTER THREE
VALIANT.
AUG NO.1
$2.25
Archer &
Armstrong

UNITY
CHAPTER EIGHT
VALIANT.
AUG NO.8
$2.50
HARBINGER

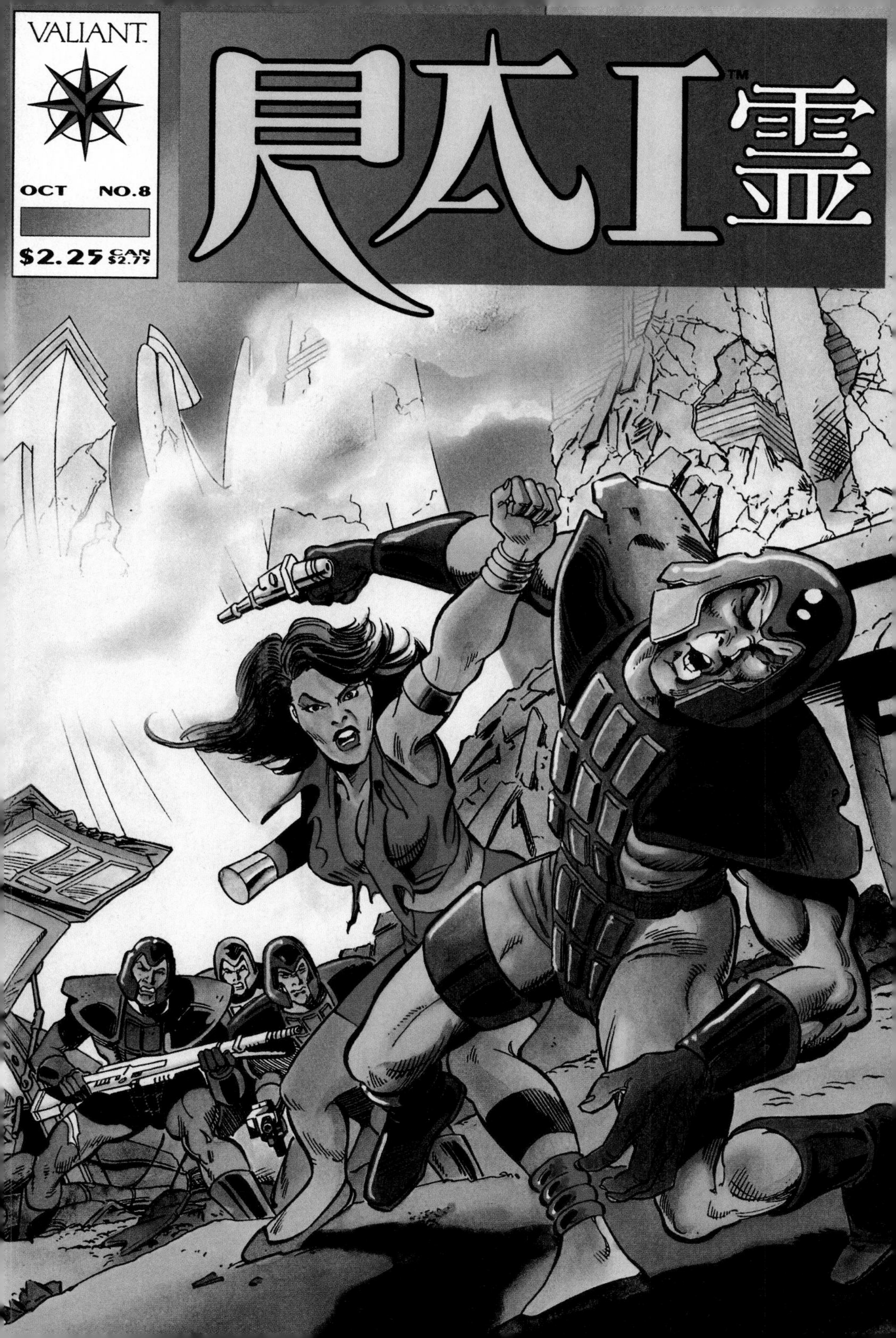

VALIANT.
OCT NO.8
$2.25 CAN $2.75
RAI™
霊

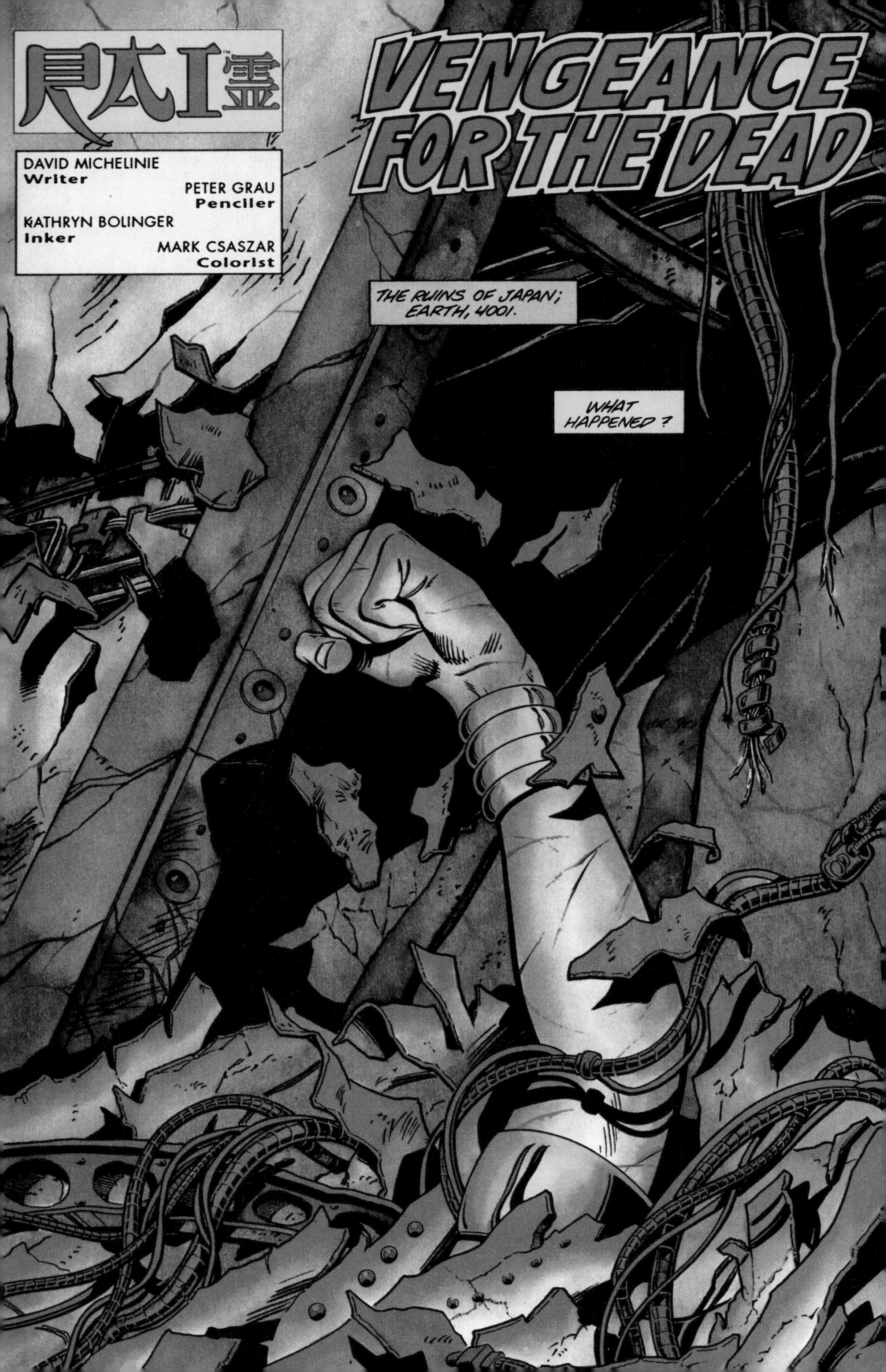
VENGEANCE FOR THE DEAD
DAVID MICHELINIE
Writer
PETER GRAU
Penciler
KATHRYN BOLINGER
Inker
MARK CSASZAR
Colorist
THE RUINS OF JAPAN; EARTH, 4001.
WHAT HAPPENED?

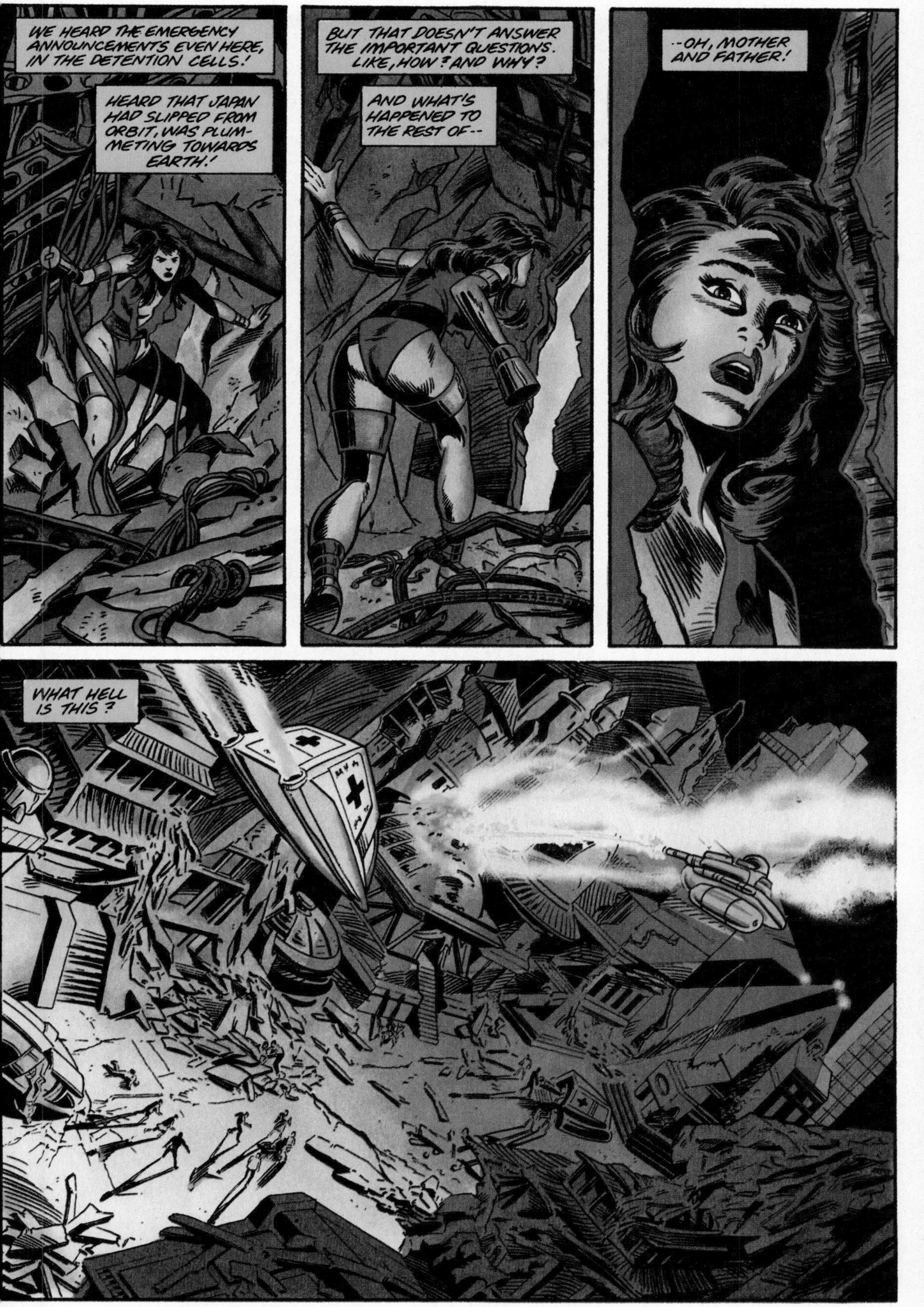
WE HEARD THE EMERGENCY ANNOUNCEMENTS EVEN HERE, IN THE DETENTION CELLS!
HEARD THAT JAPAN HAD SLIPPED FROM ORBIT, WAS PLUMMETING TOWARDS EARTH!
BUT THAT DOESN'T ANSWER THE IMPORTANT QUESTIONS. LIKE, HOW? AND WHY?
AND WHAT'S HAPPENED TO THE REST OF--
--OH, MOTHER AND FATHER!
WHAT HELL IS THIS?

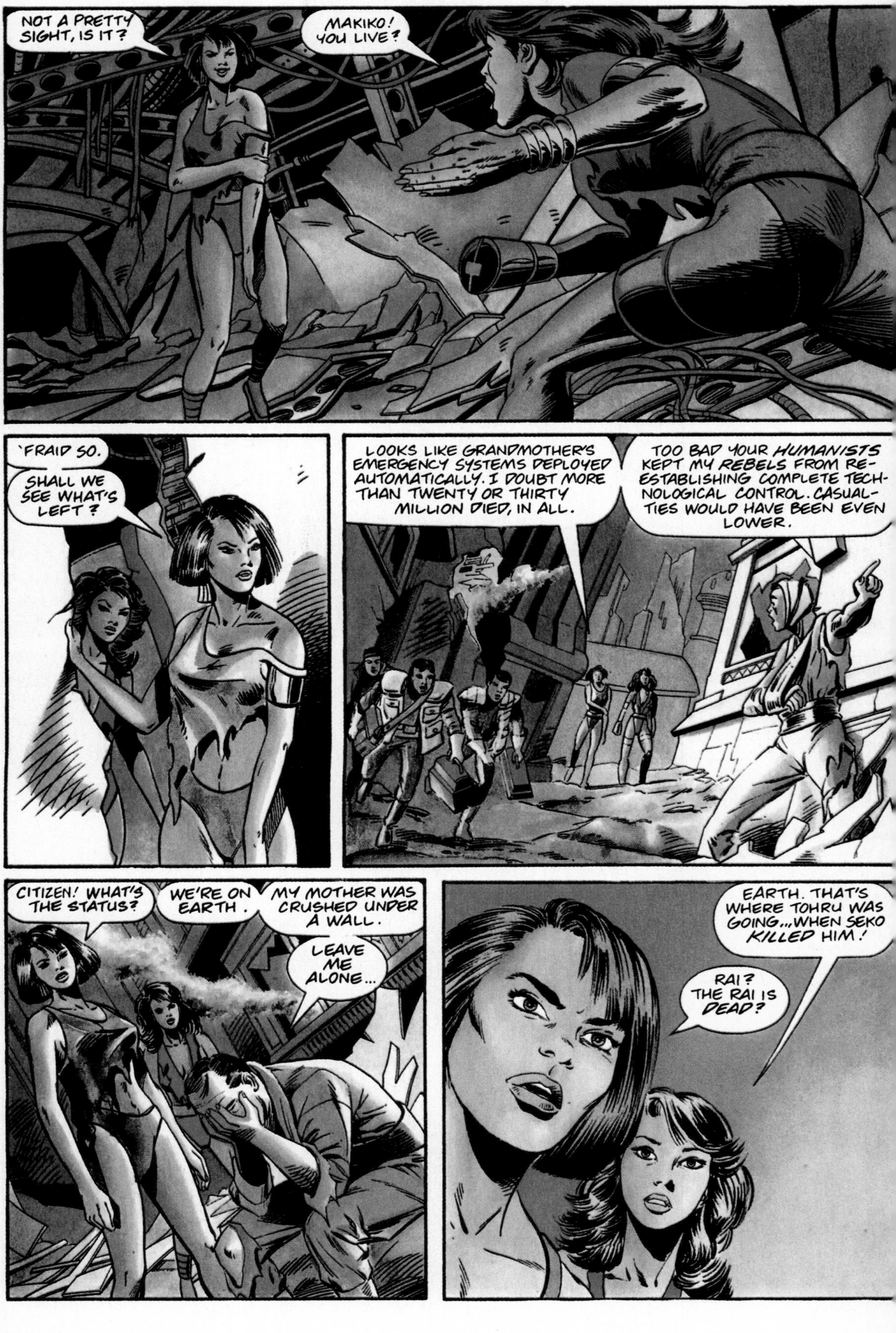
NOT A PRETTY SIGHT, IS IT?
MAKIKO! YOU LIVE?
'FRAID SO.
SHALL WE SEE WHAT'S LEFT?
LOOKS LIKE GRANDMOTHER'S EMERGENCY SYSTEMS DEPLOYED AUTOMATICALLY. I DOUBT MORE THAN TWENTY OR THIRTY MILLION DIED, IN ALL.
TOO BAD YOUR HUMANISTS KEPT MY REBELS FROM RE-ESTABLISHING COMPLETE TECHNOLOGICAL CONTROL. CASUALTIES WOULD HAVE BEEN EVEN LOWER.
CITIZEN! WHAT'S THE STATUS?
WE'RE ON EARTH.
MY MOTHER WAS CRUSHED UNDER A WALL.
LEAVE ME ALONE...
EARTH. THAT'S WHERE TOHRU WAS GOING... WHEN SEKO KILLED HIM!
RAI? THE RAI IS DEAD?

I FORGET YOU WERE IMPRISONED LONGER THAN I. MY HUSBAND WAS EXILED TO EARTH.

BUT HE DIDN'T KNOW THAT POWER-MAD WEASEL, SEKO, RIGGED HIS SHUTTLE TO VEER INTO INFINITE SPACE INSTEAD!

OUR SON, TAKASHI, WAS WITH HIM...!

I HAVE TO KNOW IF SEKO SURVIVED--

--SO I CAN KILL HIM!

BUT I'LL NEED MY LIVING ARMOR! AND THE CONTROL RING ON MY SEVERED HAND, THE ONE SEKO KEEPS AS A TROPHY!

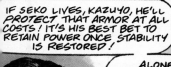

IF SEKO LIVES, KAZUYO, HE'LL PROTECT THAT ARMOR AT ALL COSTS! IT'S HIS BEST BET TO RETAIN POWER ONCE STABILITY IS RESTORED!

ALONE, UNARMED, GETTING TO HIM COULD BE IMPOSSIBLE!

GOOD LUCK!

SEKO BETRAYED 'KIKO'S REBELLION! SHE HAS AS MUCH REASON TO HATE HIM AS I DO!

SHE MUST HATE ME EVEN MORE...!

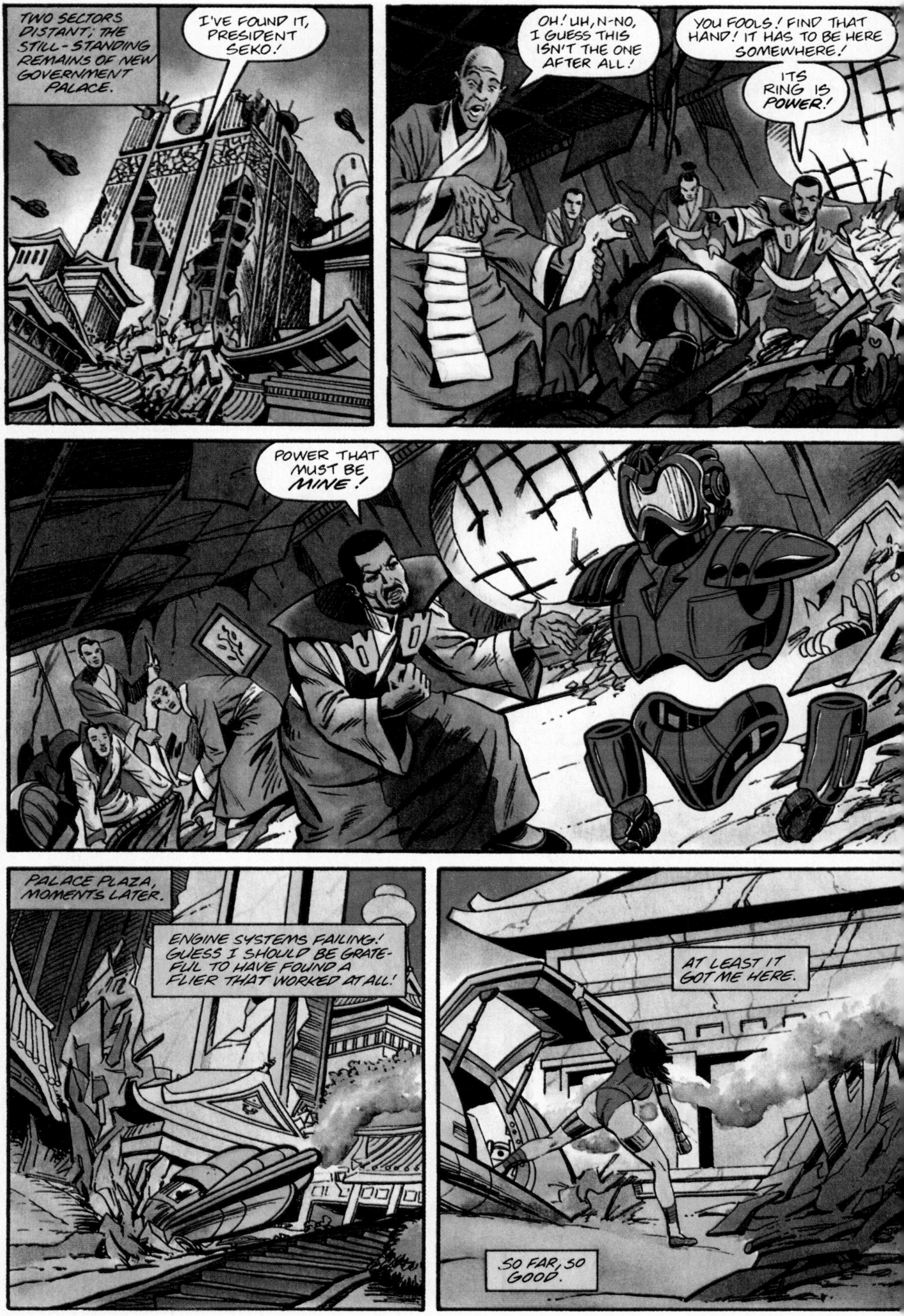
TWO SECTORS DISTANT; THE STILL-STANDING REMAINS OF NEW GOVERNMENT PALACE.
I'VE FOUND IT, PRESIDENT SEKO!
OH! UH, N-NO, I GUESS THIS ISN'T THE ONE AFTER ALL!
YOU FOOLS! FIND THAT HAND! IT HAS TO BE HERE SOMEWHERE!
ITS RING IS POWER!
POWER THAT MUST BE MINE!
PALACE PLAZA, MOMENTS LATER.
ENGINE SYSTEMS FAILING! GUESS I SHOULD BE GRATE-FUL TO HAVE FOUND A FLIER THAT WORKED AT ALL!
AT LEAST IT GOT ME HERE.
SO FAR, SO GOOD.

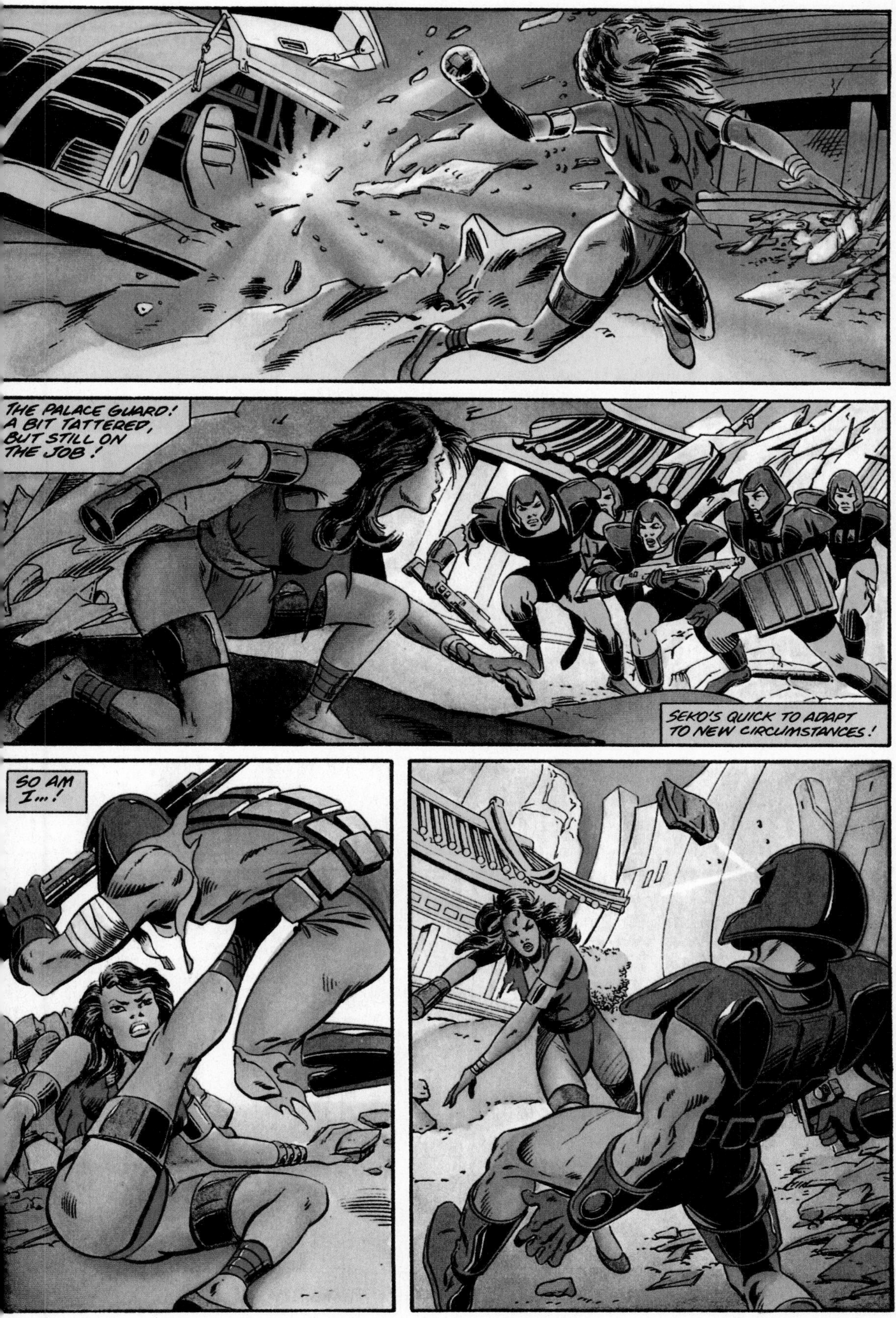
THE PALACE GUARD! A BIT TATTERED, BUT STILL ON THE JOB!
SEKO'S QUICK TO ADAPT TO NEW CIRCUMSTANCES!
SO AM I...!

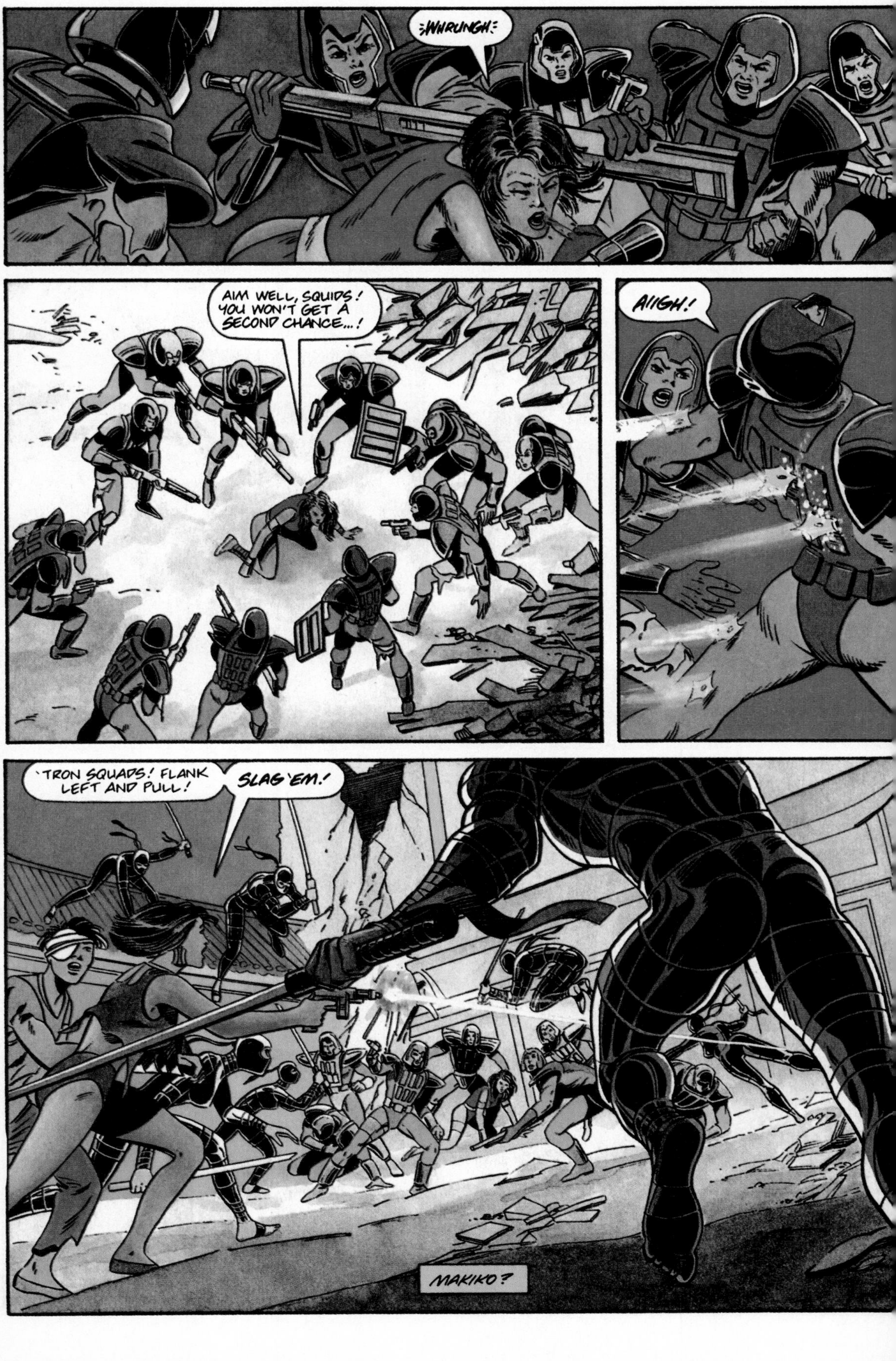
:WHRUNGH:
AIM WELL, SQUIDS! YOU WON'T GET A SECOND CHANCE...!
AIIGH!
`TRON SQUADS! FLANK LEFT AND PULL!
SLAG 'EM!
MAKIKO?

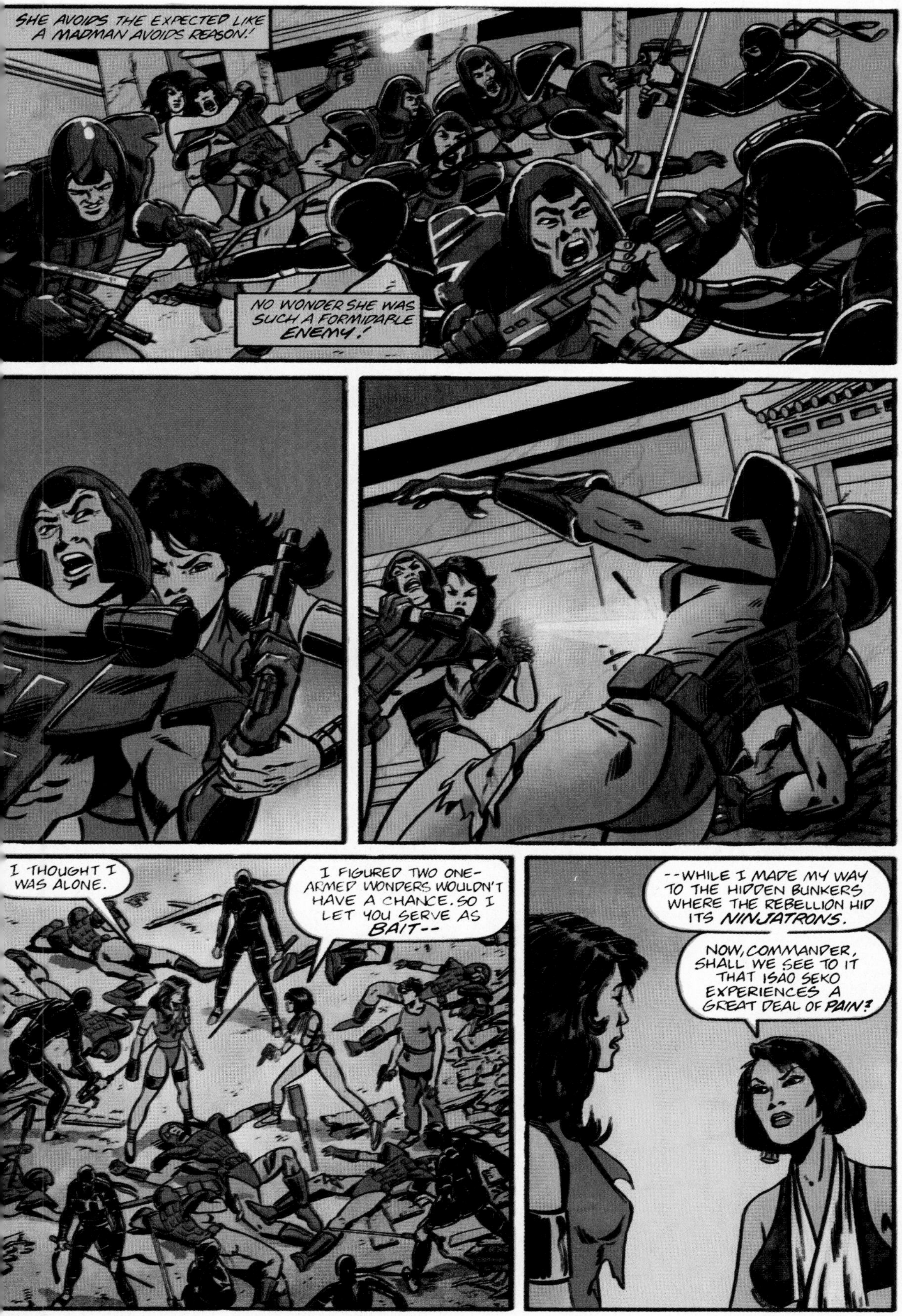
SHE AVOIDS THE EXPECTED LIKE A MADMAN AVOIDS REASON!
NO WONDER SHE WAS SUCH A FORMIDABLE ENEMY!
I THOUGHT I WAS ALONE.
I FIGURED TWO ONE-ARMED WONDERS WOULDN'T HAVE A CHANCE. SO I LET YOU SERVE AS BAIT--
--WHILE I MADE MY WAY TO THE HIDDEN BUNKERS WHERE THE REBELLION HID ITS NINJATRONS.
NOW, COMMANDER, SHALL WE SEE TO IT THAT ISAO SEKO EXPERIENCES A GREAT DEAL OF PAIN?

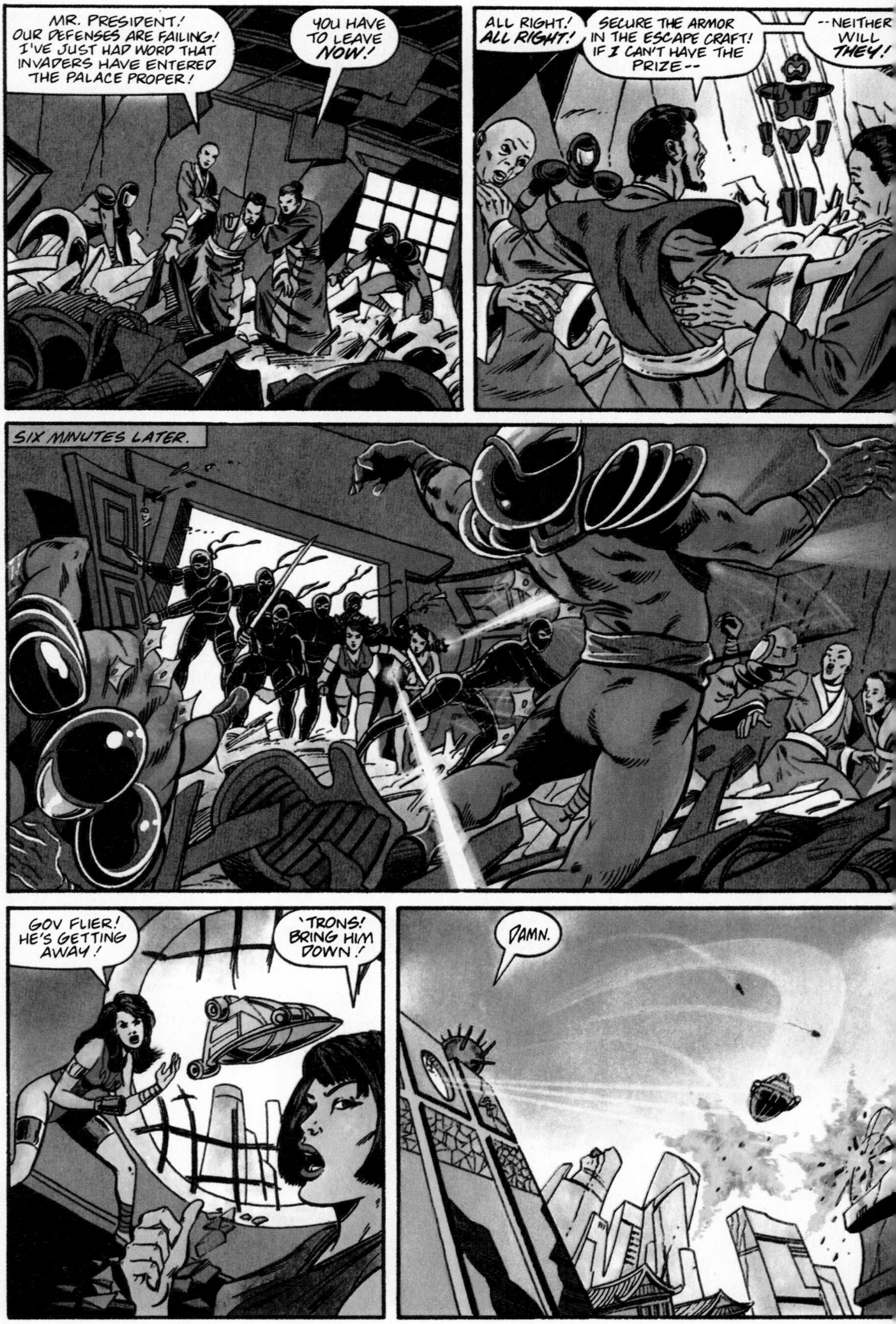
MR. PRESIDENT! OUR DEFENSES ARE FAILING! I'VE JUST HAD WORD THAT INVADERS HAVE ENTERED THE PALACE PROPER!
YOU HAVE TO LEAVE NOW!
ALL RIGHT! ALL RIGHT!
SECURE THE ARMOR IN THE ESCAPE CRAFT! IF I CAN'T HAVE THE PRIZE--
--NEITHER WILL THEY!
SIX MINUTES LATER.
GOV FLIER! HE'S GETTING AWAY!
'TRONS! BRING HIM DOWN!
DAMN.

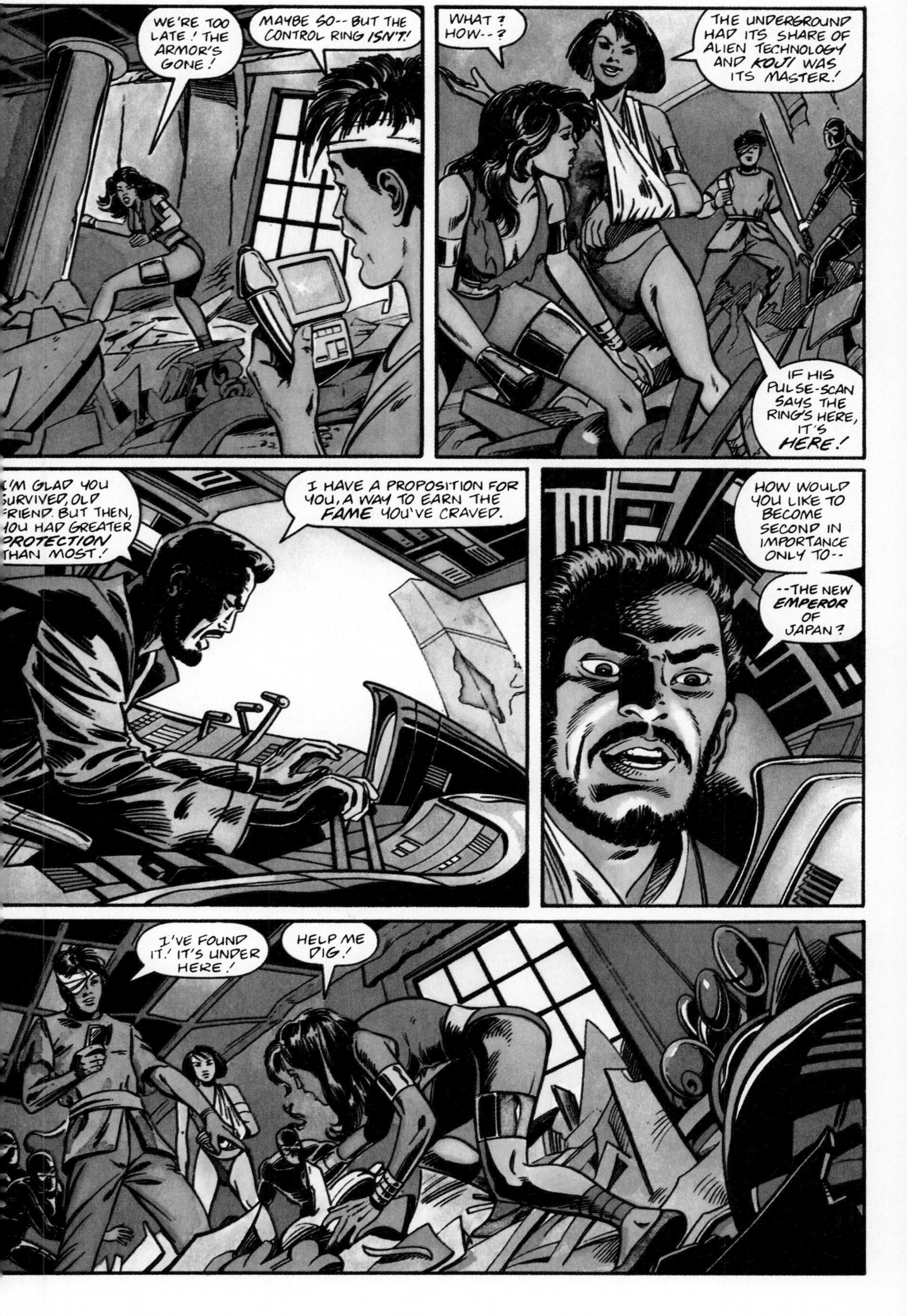

WE'RE TOO LATE! THE ARMOR'S GONE!
MAYBE SO-- BUT THE CONTROL RING *ISN'T*!
WHAT? HOW--?
THE UNDERGROUND HAD ITS SHARE OF ALIEN TECHNOLOGY AND *KOJI* WAS ITS MASTER!
IF HIS PULSE-SCAN SAYS THE RING'S HERE, IT'S *HERE*!
I'M GLAD YOU SURVIVED, OLD FRIEND. BUT THEN, YOU HAD GREATER *PROTECTION* THAN MOST!
I HAVE A PROPOSITION FOR YOU, A WAY TO EARN THE *FAME* YOU'VE CRAVED.
HOW WOULD YOU LIKE TO BECOME SECOND IN IMPORTANCE ONLY TO--
--THE NEW *EMPEROR* OF JAPAN?
I'VE FOUND IT! IT'S UNDER HERE!
HELP ME DIG!

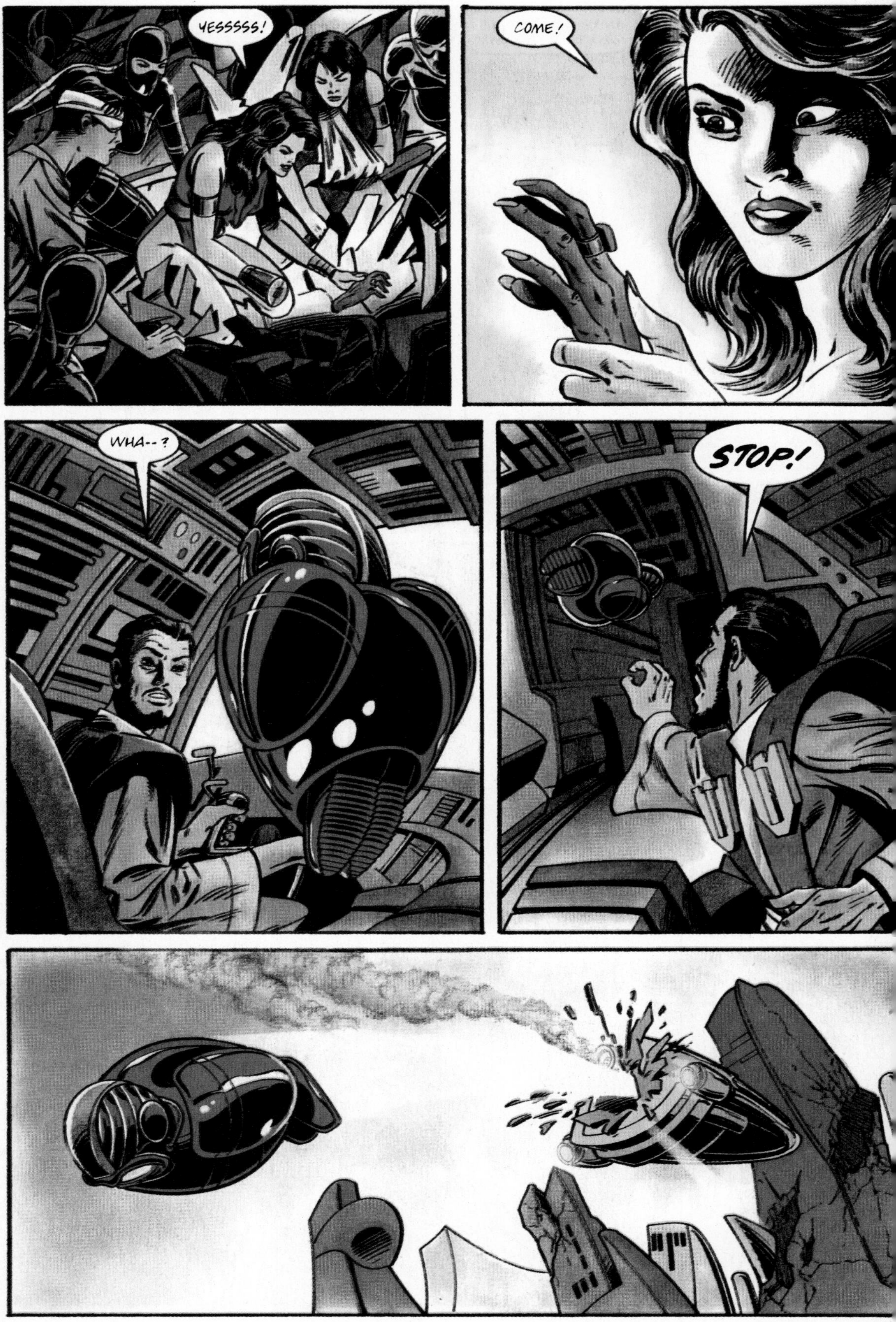
YESSSSS!
COME!
WHA--?
STOP!

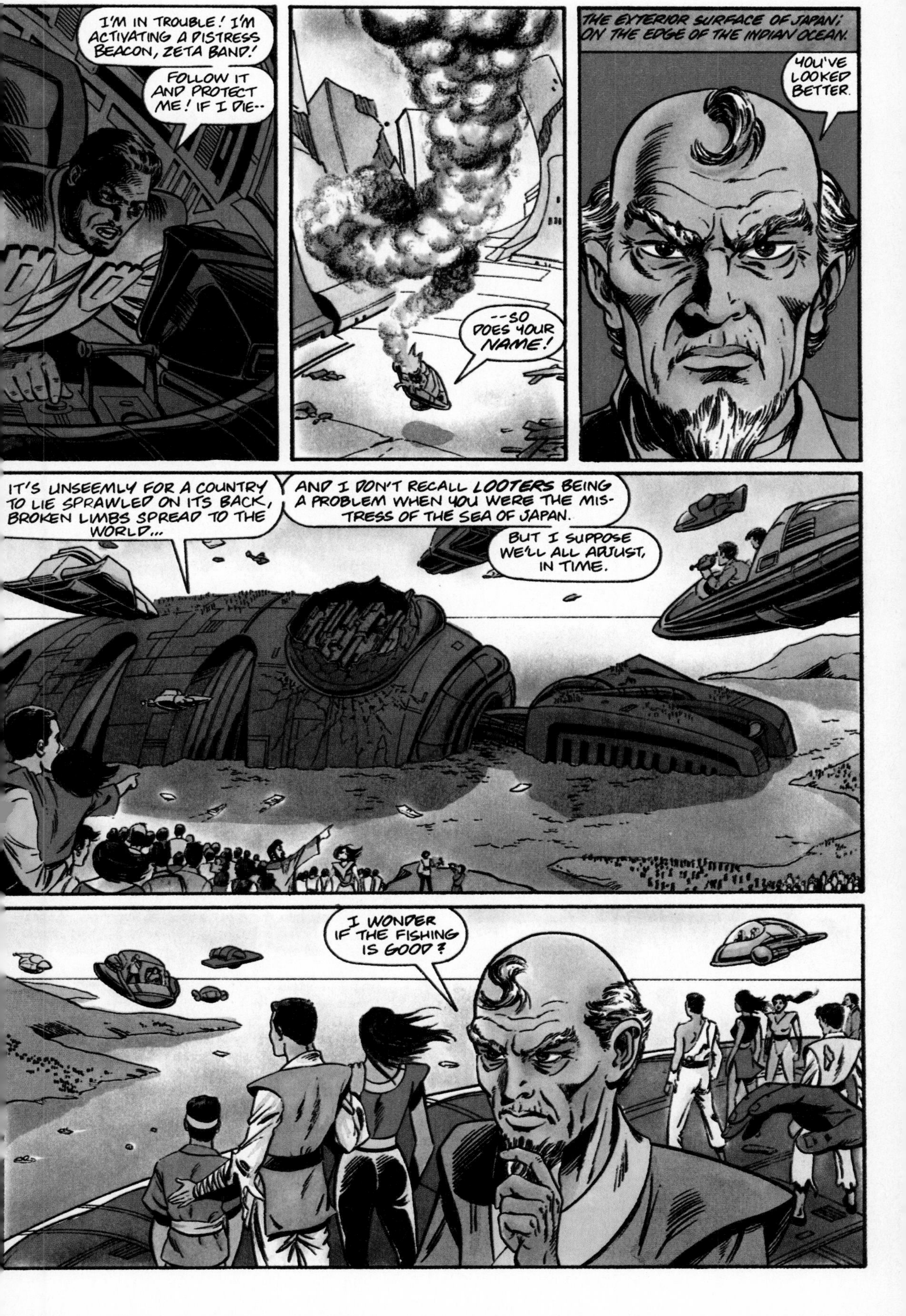
I'M IN TROUBLE! I'M ACTIVATING A DISTRESS BEACON, ZETA BAND!
FOLLOW IT AND PROTECT ME! IF I DIE--
--SO DOES YOUR NAME!
THE EXTERIOR SURFACE OF JAPAN; ON THE EDGE OF THE INDIAN OCEAN.
YOU'VE LOOKED BETTER.
IT'S UNSEEMLY FOR A COUNTRY TO LIE SPRAWLED ON ITS BACK, BROKEN LIMBS SPREAD TO THE WORLD...
AND I DON'T RECALL LOOTERS BEING A PROBLEM WHEN YOU WERE THE MISTRESS OF THE SEA OF JAPAN.
BUT I SUPPOSE WE'LL ALL ADJUST, IN TIME.
I WONDER IF THE FISHING IS GOOD?

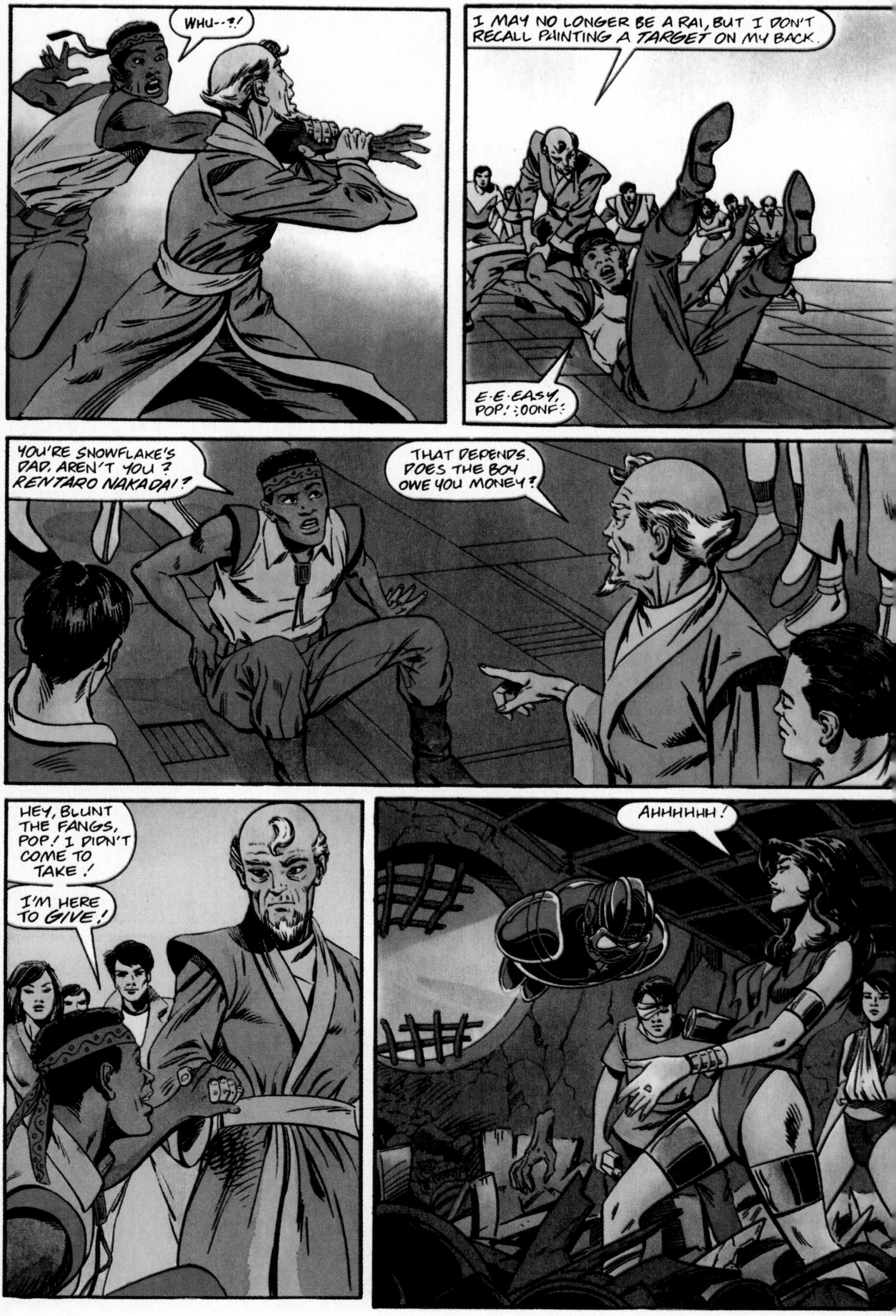
WHU--?!
I MAY NO LONGER BE A RAI, BUT I DON'T RECALL PAINTING A TARGET ON MY BACK.
E-E-EASY, POP! OONF!
YOU'RE SNOWFLAKE'S DAD, AREN'T YOU? RENTARO NAKADAI?
THAT DEPENDS. DOES THE BOY OWE YOU MONEY?
HEY, BLUNT THE FANGS, POP! I DIDN'T COME TO TAKE!
I'M HERE TO GIVE!
AHHHHHH!

IT'S BEEN TOO LONG! I'VE MISSED YOU.

A SURROGATE HAND?

NOW, WE TRULY ARE WHOLE!

I TOOK A CHANCE HELPING YOU, KAZUYO. YOU WERE AS DETERMINED THAT YOUR HUMANISTS SHOULD RULE AS I WAS THAT MY TECHNO-REBELLION SHOULD TAKE OVER!

AND ISAO SEKO IS YOUR STRONGEST LEADER, YOUR BEST HOPE OF HOLDING POWER ONCE THIS CHAOS HAS PASSED!

I HAVE TO KNOW: WHEN THE FINAL SWORD IS DRAWN ...WILL YOU KILL HIM?

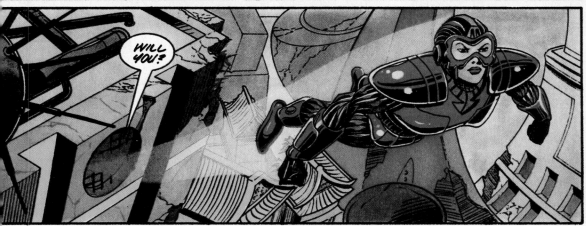

WILL YOU!?

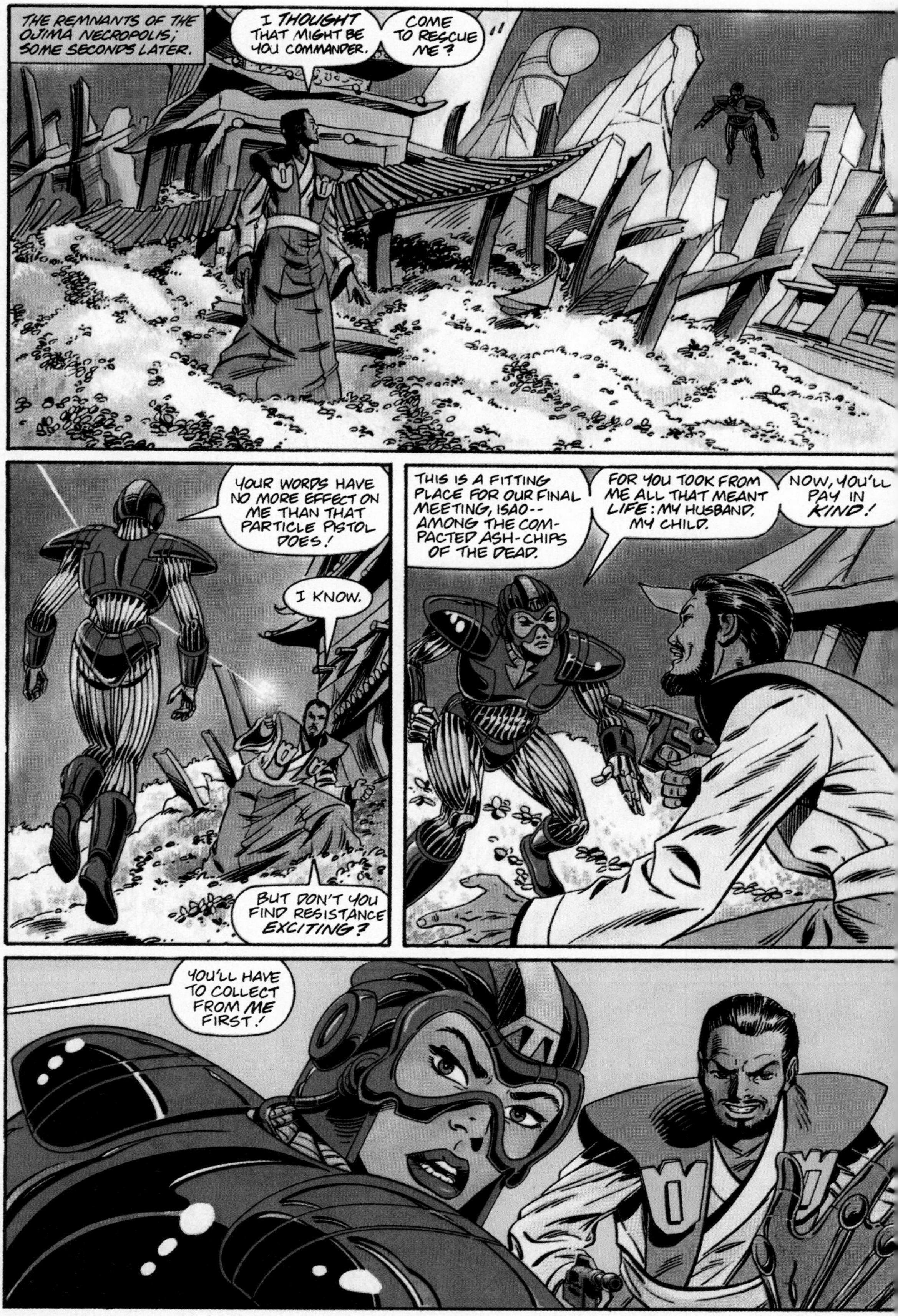
THE REMNANTS OF THE OJIMA NECROPOLIS; SOME SECONDS LATER.
I THOUGHT THAT MIGHT BE YOU COMMANDER.
COME TO RESCUE ME?
YOUR WORDS HAVE NO MORE EFFECT ON ME THAN THAT PARTICLE PISTOL DOES!
I KNOW.
BUT DON'T YOU FIND RESISTANCE EXCITING?
THIS IS A FITTING PLACE FOR OUR FINAL MEETING, ISAO-- AMONG THE COMPACTED ASH-CHIPS OF THE DEAD.
FOR YOU TOOK FROM ME ALL THAT MEANT LIFE: MY HUSBAND, MY CHILD.
NOW, YOU'LL PAY IN KIND!
YOU'LL HAVE TO COLLECT FROM ME FIRST!

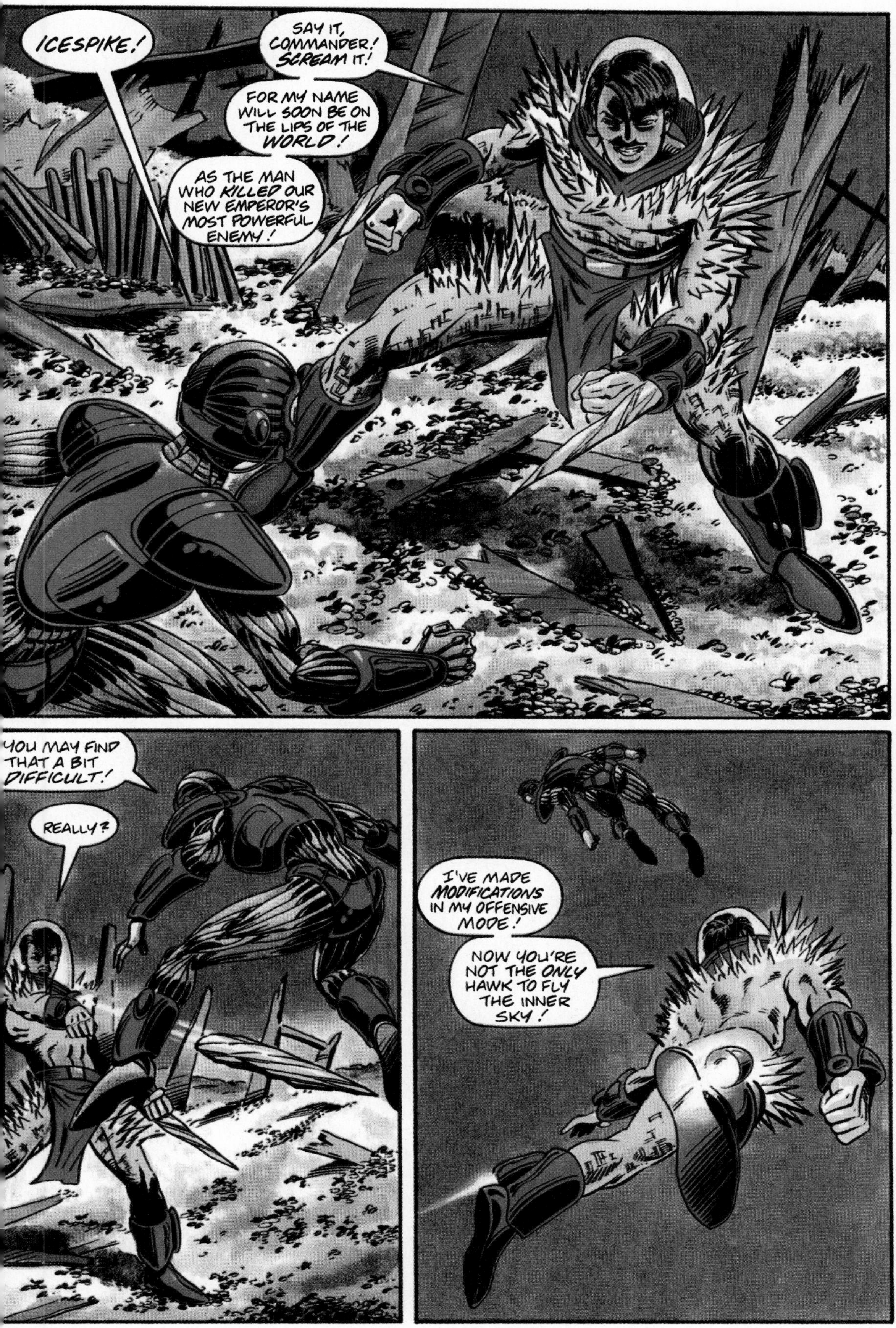
ICESPIKE!
SAY IT, COMMANDER! SCREAM IT!
FOR MY NAME WILL SOON BE ON THE LIPS OF THE WORLD!
AS THE MAN WHO KILLED OUR NEW EMPEROR'S MOST POWERFUL ENEMY!
YOU MAY FIND THAT A BIT DIFFICULT!
REALLY?
I'VE MADE MODIFICATIONS IN MY OFFENSIVE MODE!
NOW YOU'RE NOT THE ONLY HAWK TO FLY THE INNER SKY!

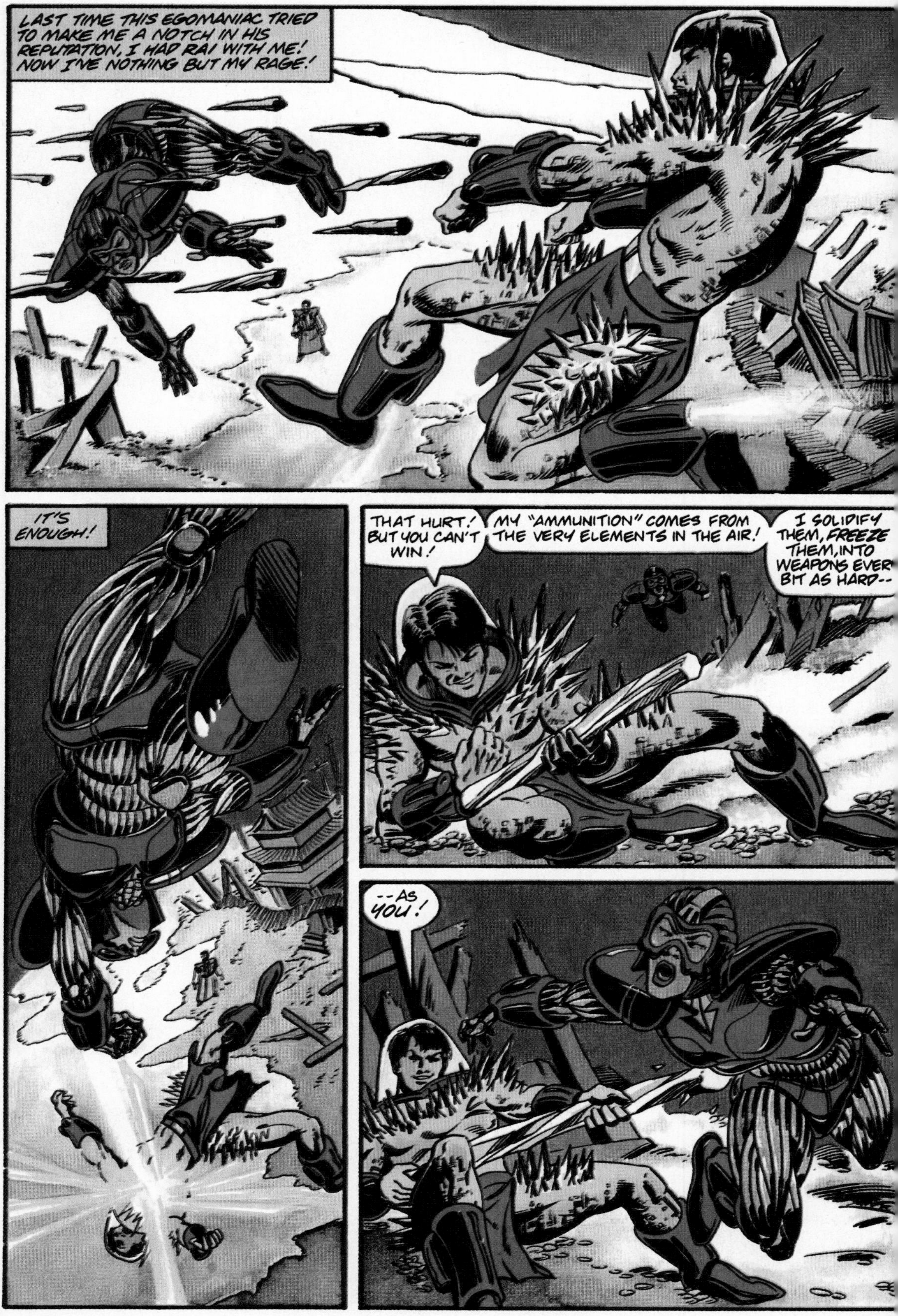
LAST TIME THIS EGOMANIAC TRIED TO MAKE ME A NOTCH IN HIS REPUTATION, I HAD RAI WITH ME! NOW I'VE NOTHING BUT MY RAGE!
IT'S ENOUGH!
THAT HURT! BUT YOU CAN'T WIN!
MY "AMMUNITION" COMES FROM THE VERY ELEMENTS IN THE AIR!
I SOLIDIFY THEM, FREEZE THEM, INTO WEAPONS EVER BIT AS HARD--
--AS YOU!

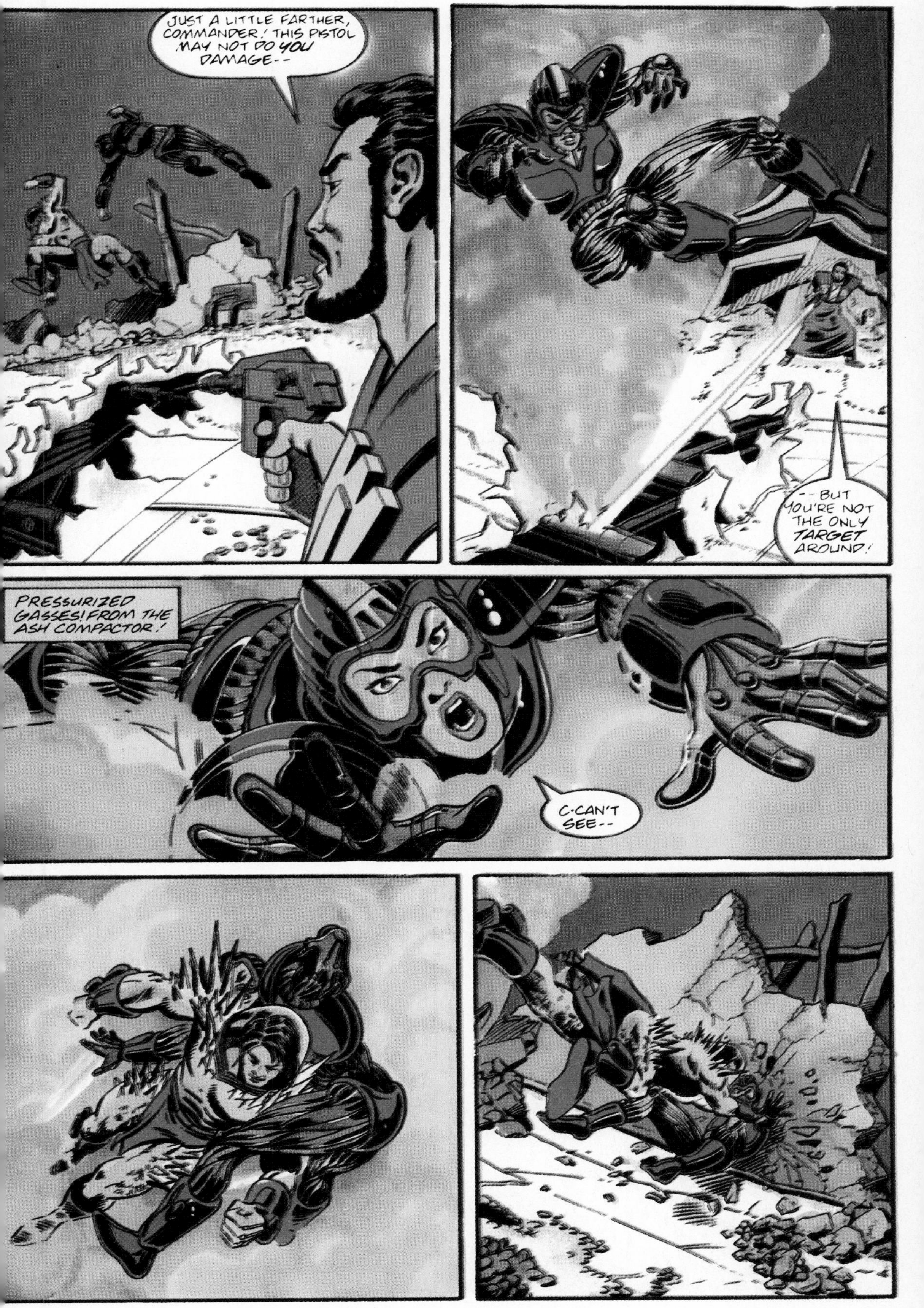
JUST A LITTLE FARTHER, COMMANDER! THIS PISTOL MAY NOT DO YOU DAMAGE--
--BUT YOU'RE NOT THE ONLY TARGET AROUND!
PRESSURIZED GASSES! FROM THE ASH COMPACTOR!
C-CAN'T SEE--

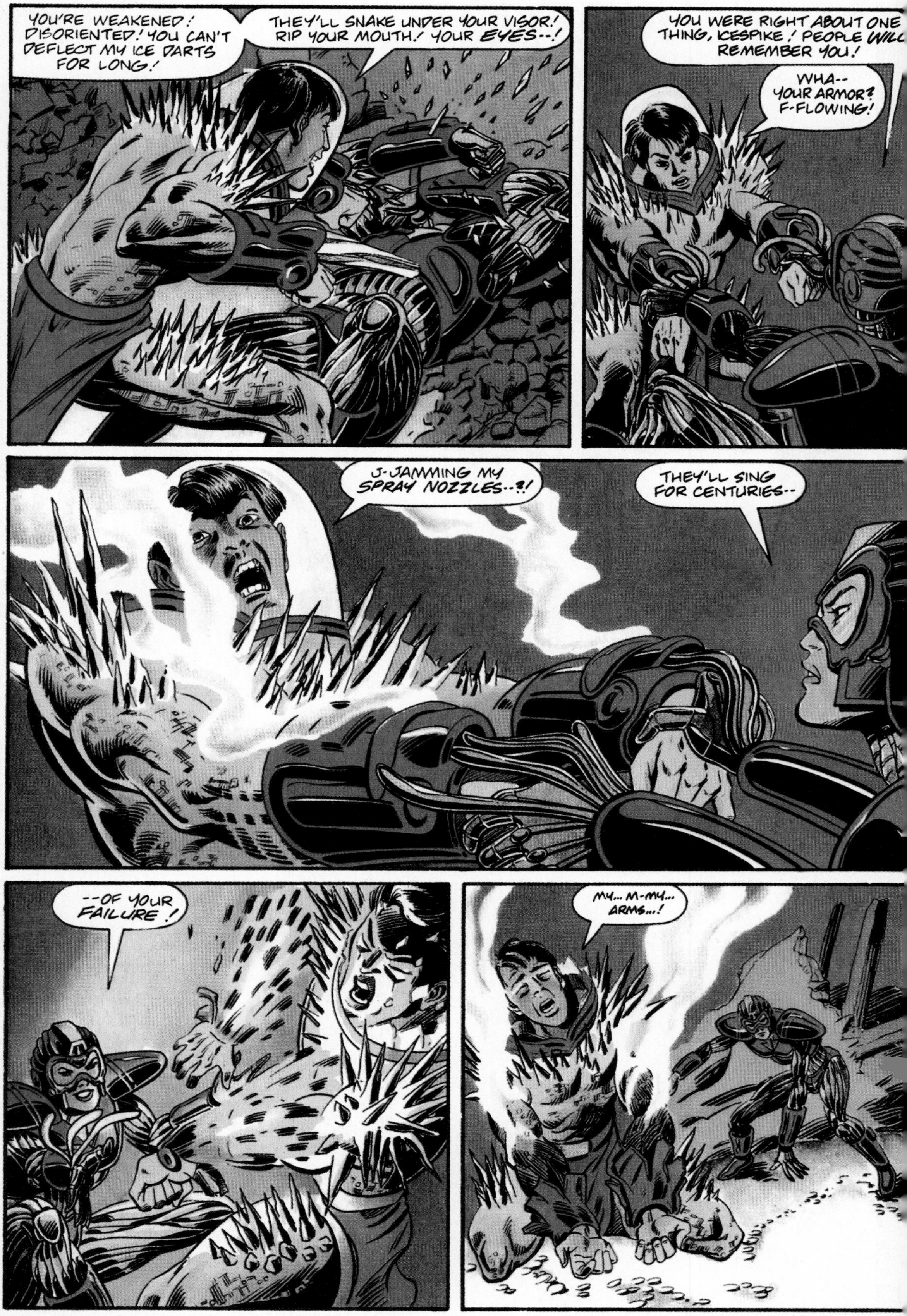
YOU'RE WEAKENED! DISORIENTED! YOU CAN'T DEFLECT MY ICE DARTS FOR LONG!
THEY'LL SNAKE UNDER YOUR VISOR! RIP YOUR MOUTH! YOUR EYES--!
YOU WERE RIGHT ABOUT ONE THING, ICESPIKE! PEOPLE WILL REMEMBER YOU!
WHA-- YOUR ARMOR? F-FLOWING!
J-JAMMING MY SPRAY NOZZLES--?!
THEY'LL SING FOR CENTURIES--
--OF YOUR FAILURE!
MY... M-MY... ARMS...!

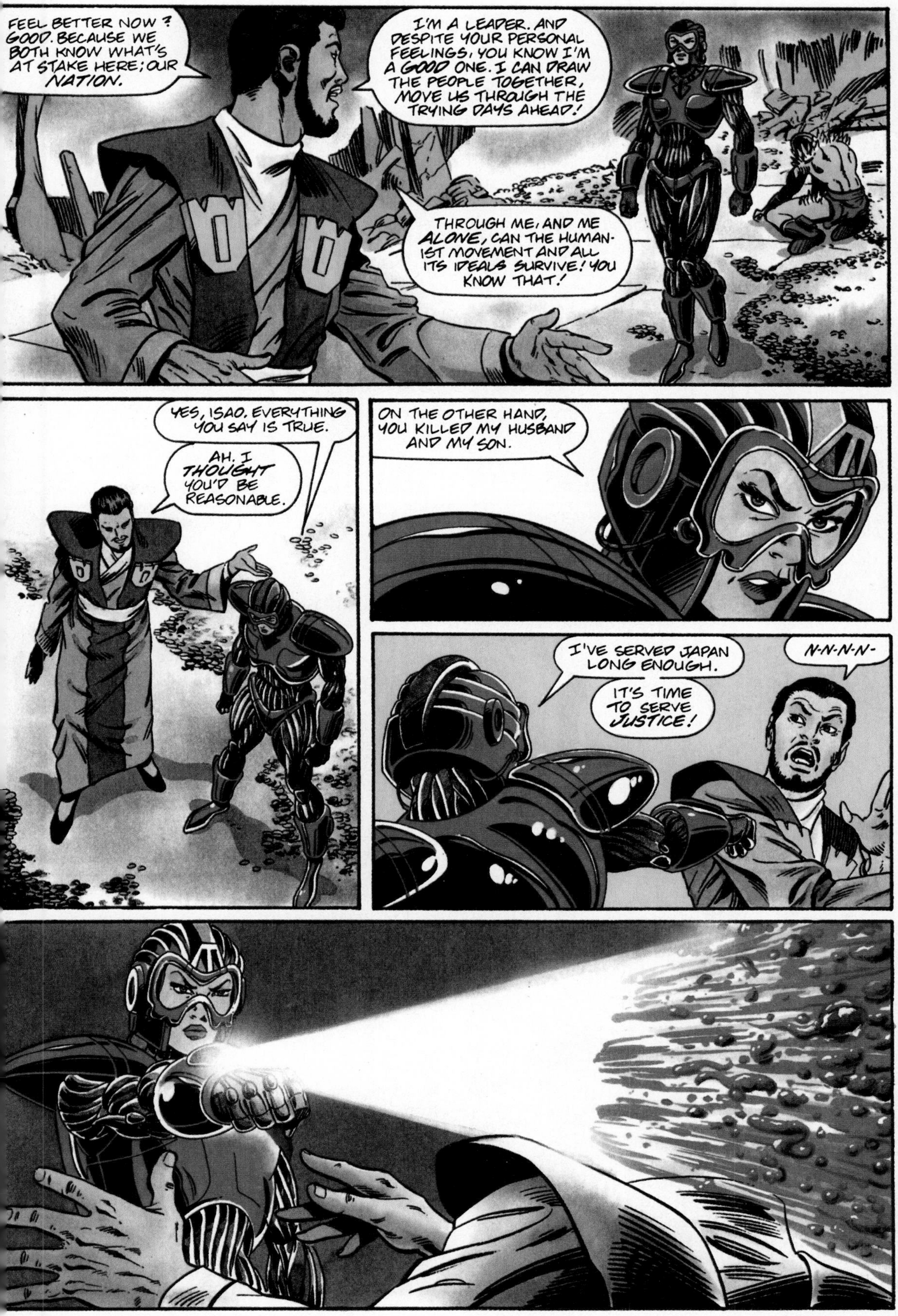
FEEL BETTER NOW? GOOD. BECAUSE WE BOTH KNOW WHAT'S AT STAKE HERE; OUR NATION.
I'M A LEADER. AND DESPITE YOUR PERSONAL FEELINGS, YOU KNOW I'M A GOOD ONE. I CAN DRAW THE PEOPLE TOGETHER, MOVE US THROUGH THE TRYING DAYS AHEAD!
THROUGH ME, AND ME ALONE, CAN THE HUMANIST MOVEMENT AND ALL ITS IDEALS SURVIVE! YOU KNOW THAT!
YES, ISAO. EVERYTHING YOU SAY IS TRUE.
AH. I THOUGHT YOU'D BE REASONABLE.
ON THE OTHER HAND, YOU KILLED MY HUSBAND AND MY SON.
I'VE SERVED JAPAN LONG ENOUGH.
IT'S TIME TO SERVE JUSTICE!
N-N-N-N-

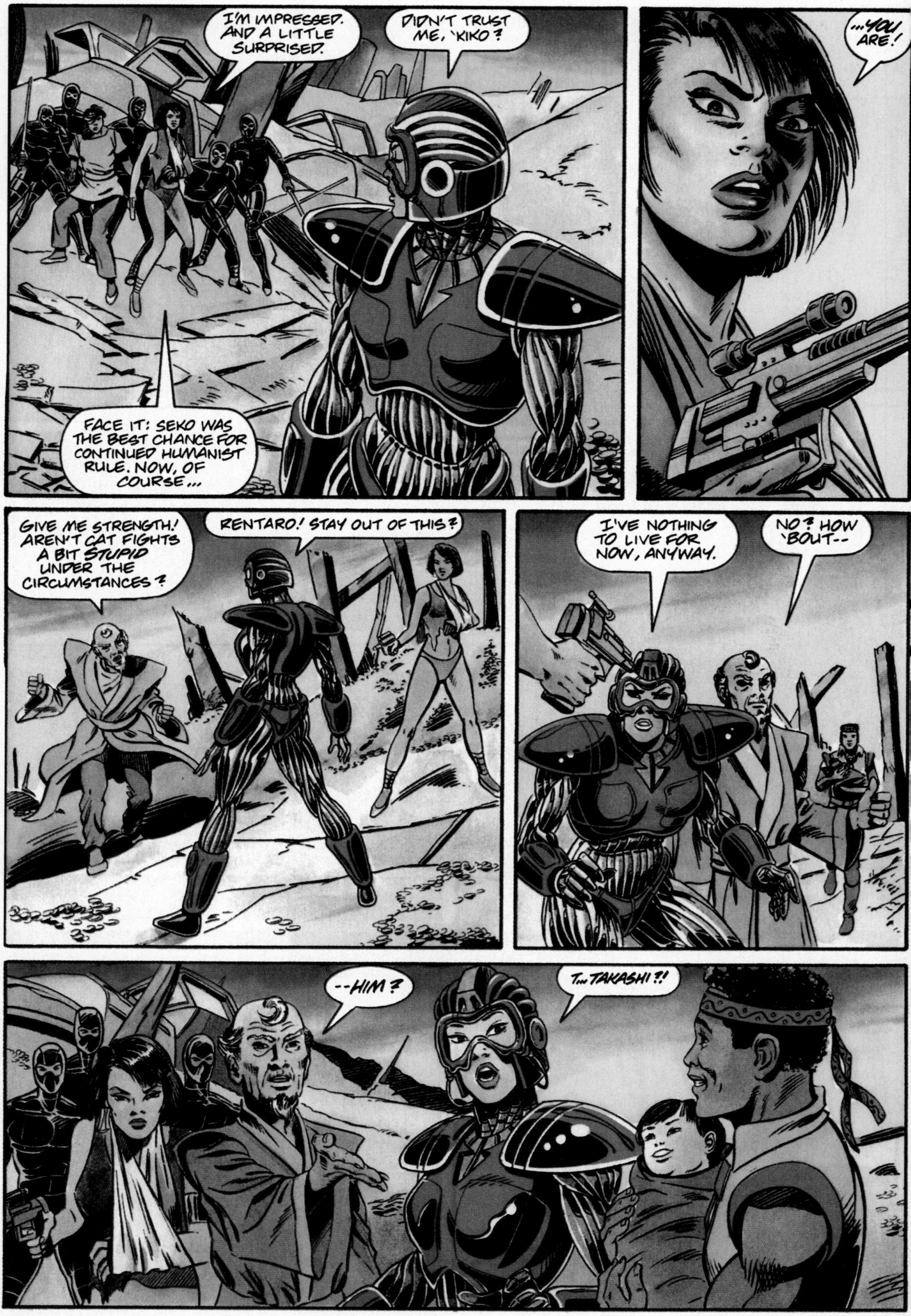
I'M IMPRESSED. AND A LITTLE SURPRISED.
DIDN'T TRUST ME, 'KIKO?
FACE IT: SEKO WAS THE BEST CHANCE FOR CONTINUED HUMANIST RULE. NOW, OF COURSE...
...YOU ARE!
GIVE ME STRENGTH! AREN'T CAT FIGHTS A BIT STUPID UNDER THE CIRCUMSTANCES?
RENTARO! STAY OUT OF THIS?
I'VE NOTHING TO LIVE FOR NOW, ANYWAY.
NO? HOW 'BOUT--
--HIM?
T...TAKASHI?!

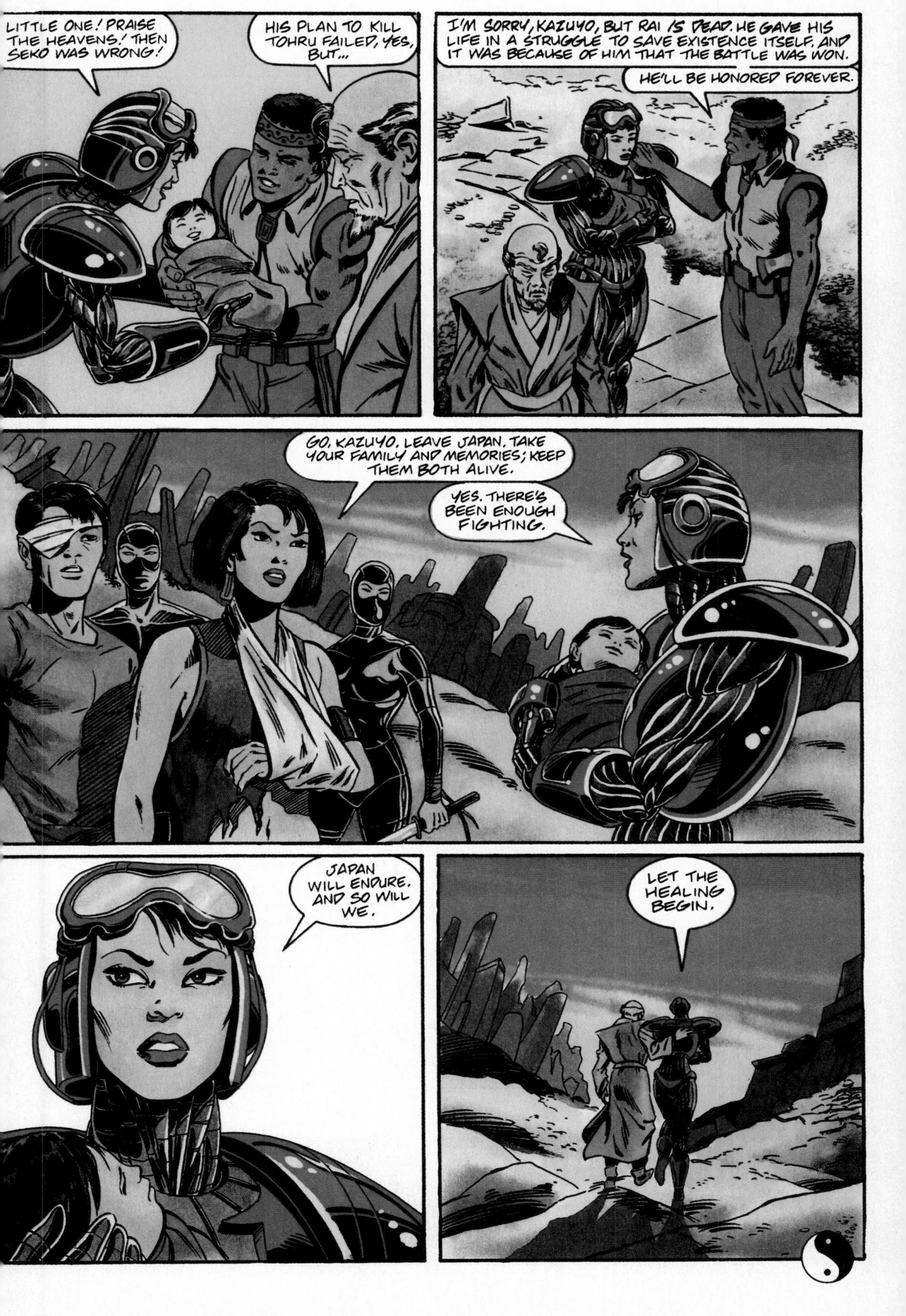
LITTLE ONE! PRAISE THE HEAVENS! THEN SEKO WAS WRONG!
HIS PLAN TO KILL TOHRU FAILED, YES, BUT...
I'M SORRY, KAZUYO, BUT RAI IS DEAD. HE GAVE HIS LIFE IN A STRUGGLE TO SAVE EXISTENCE ITSELF, AND IT WAS BECAUSE OF HIM THAT THE BATTLE WAS WON.
HE'LL BE HONORED FOREVER.
GO, KAZUYO. LEAVE JAPAN. TAKE YOUR FAMILY AND MEMORIES; KEEP THEM BOTH ALIVE.
YES. THERE'S BEEN ENOUGH FIGHTING.
JAPAN WILL ENDURE. AND SO WILL WE.
LET THE HEALING BEGIN.

RAI 2, pg 2

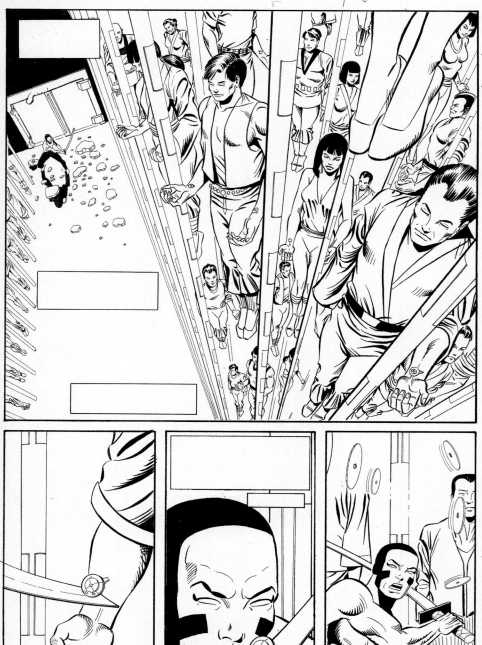

RAI #2

RAI #2 P.3

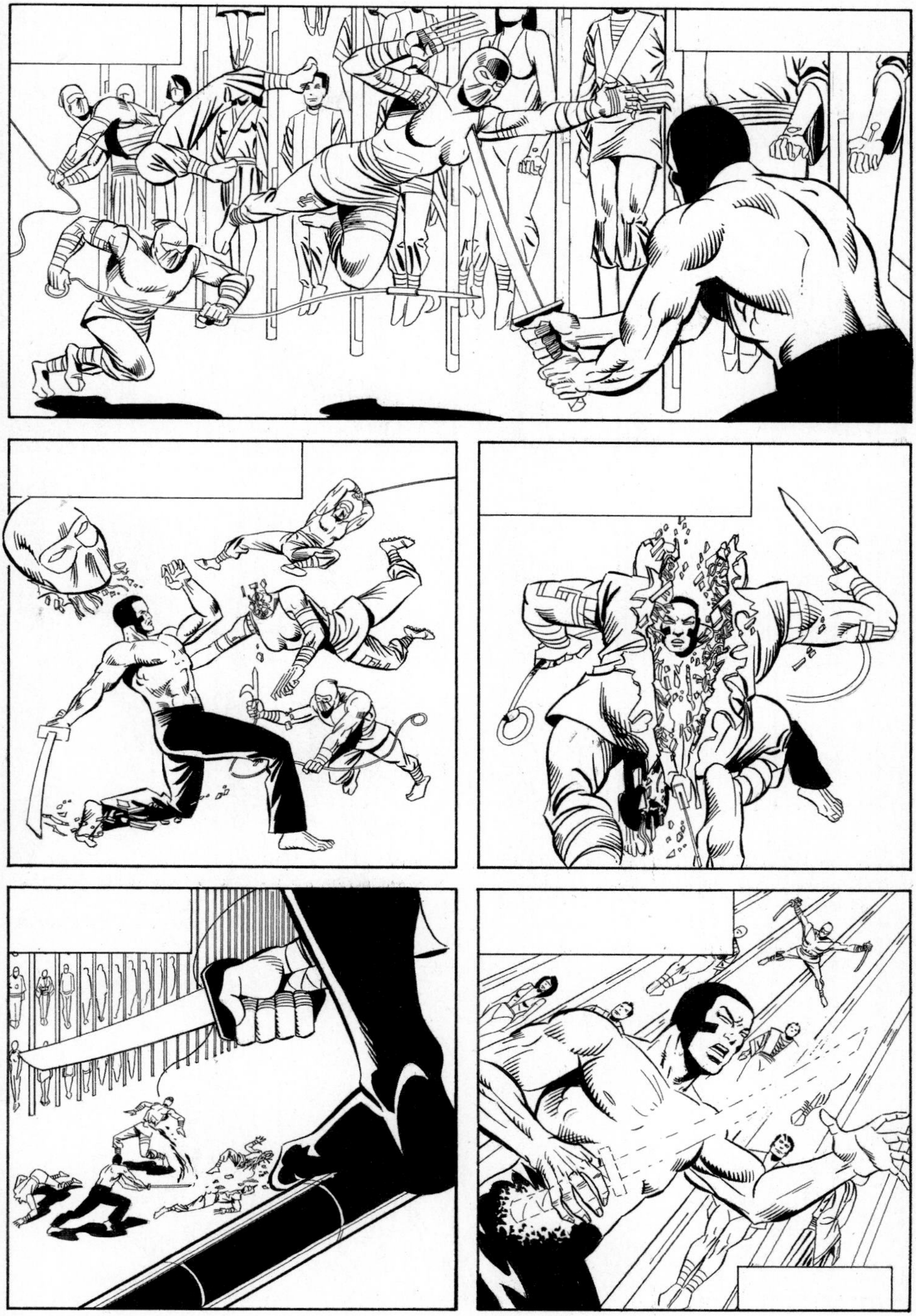

5.91

RAI #2 pg 4

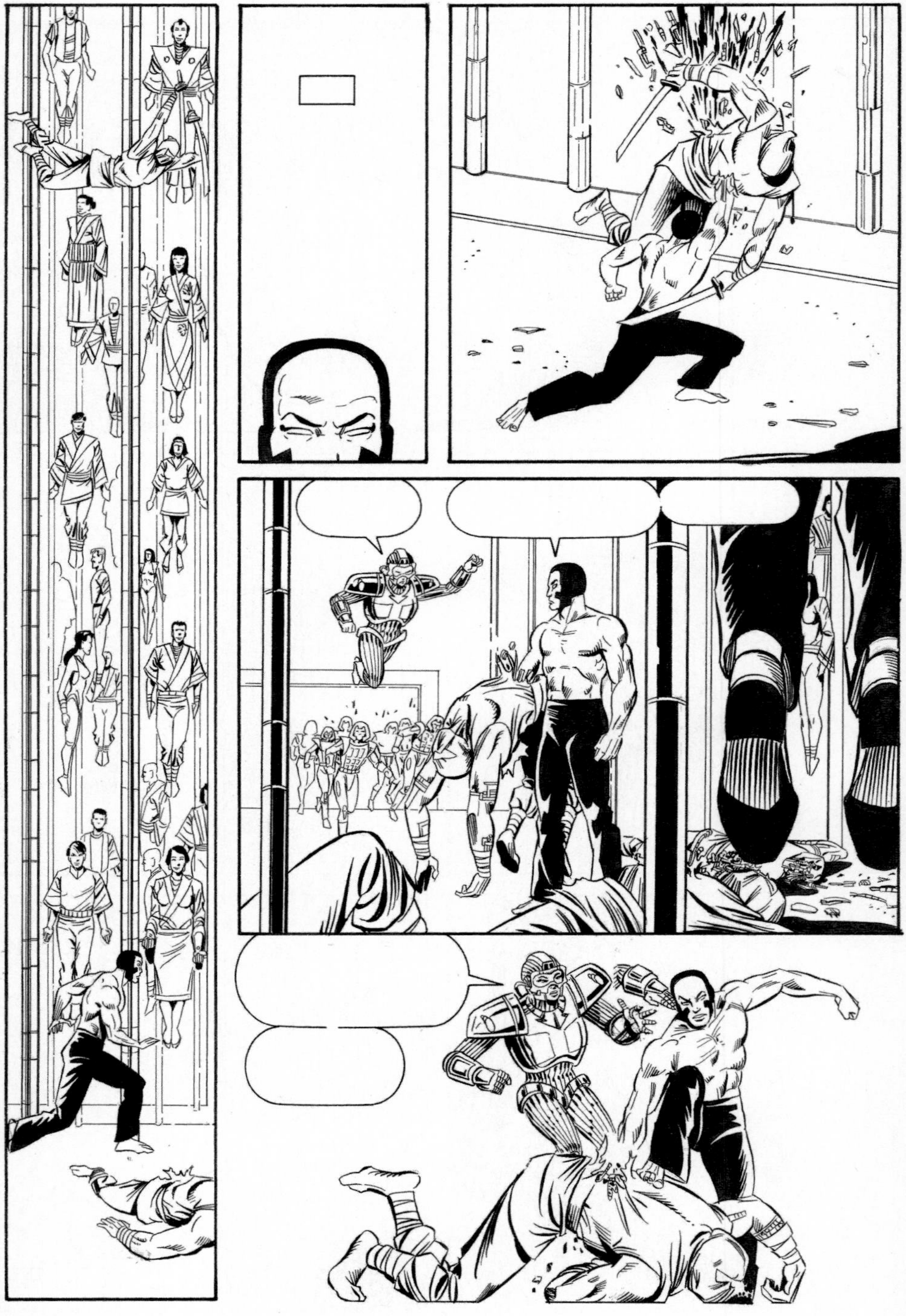

COLOR BOY:

RAI #2 pg. 22

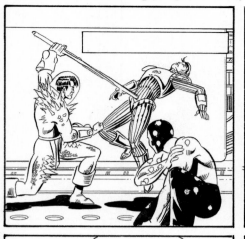

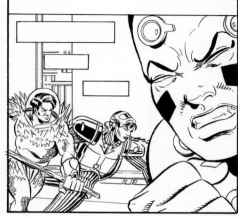

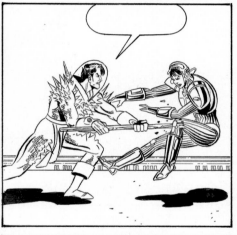

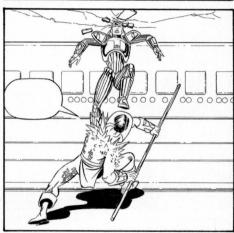

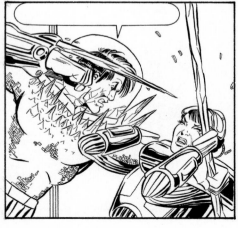

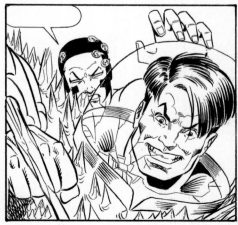

RAI #2 P. 23

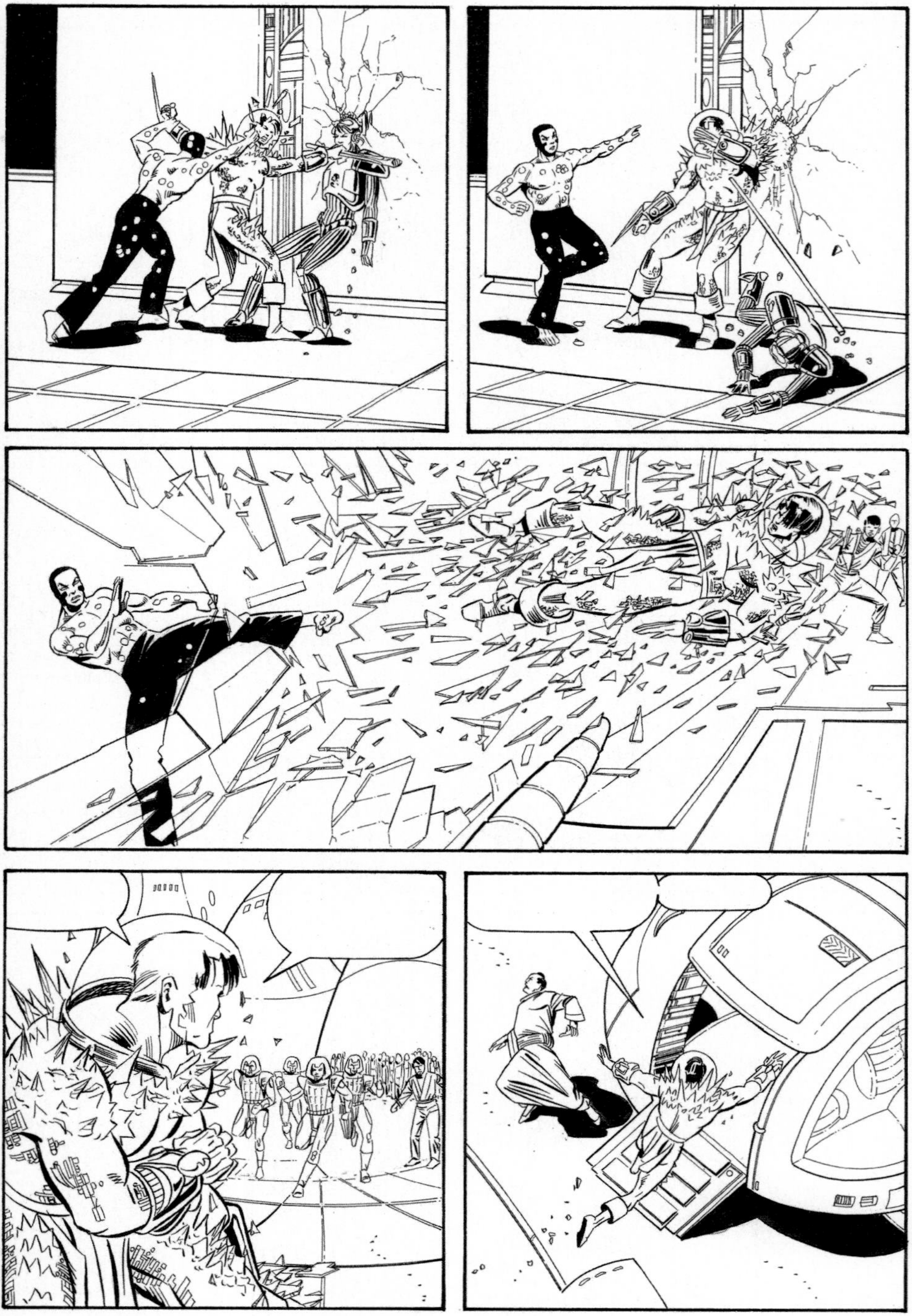

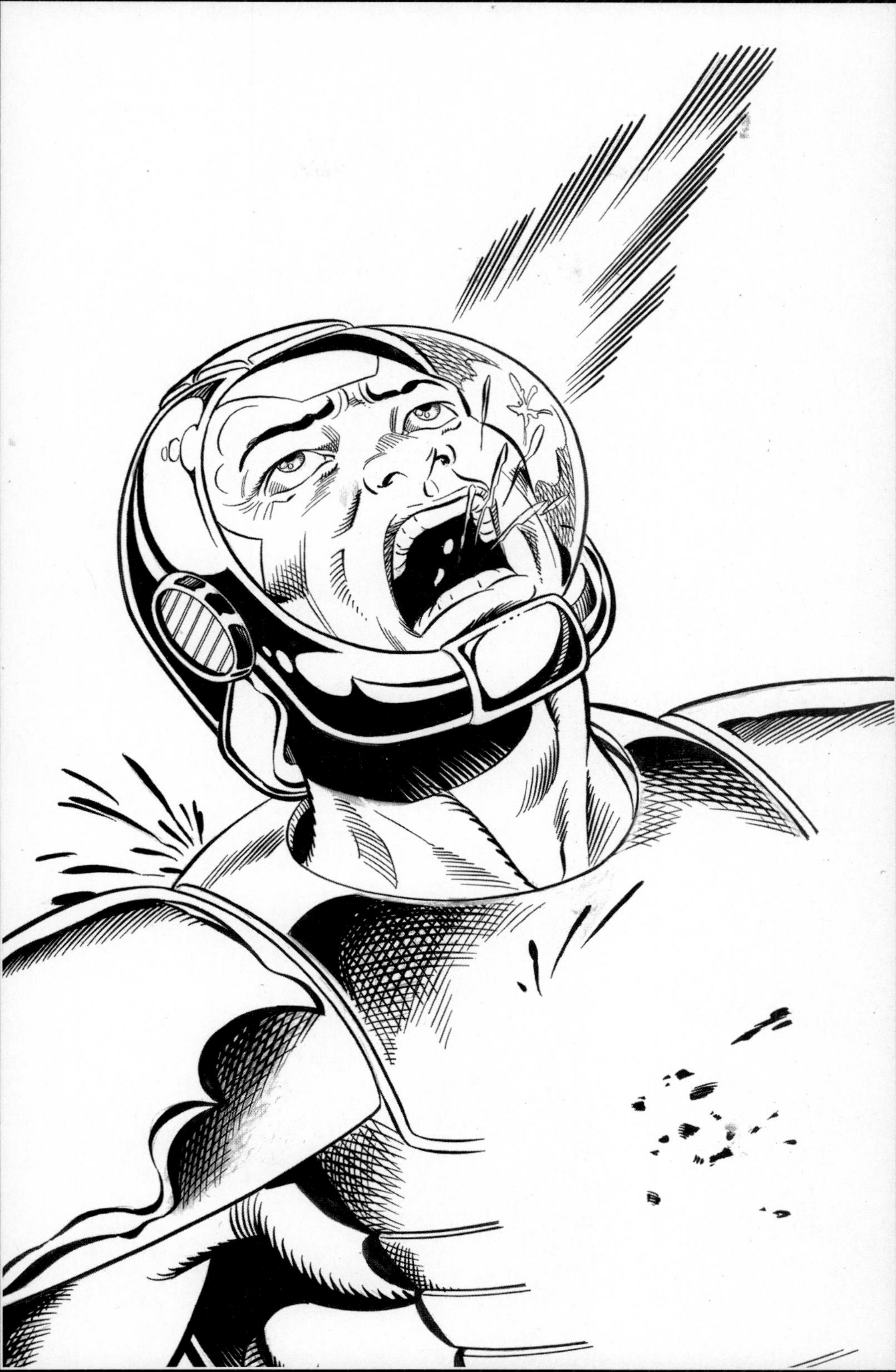

Rai #3, p.1
Layout by JOE ST. PIERRE
Pencils by SAL VELUTTO
Inks by CHARLES BARNETT III

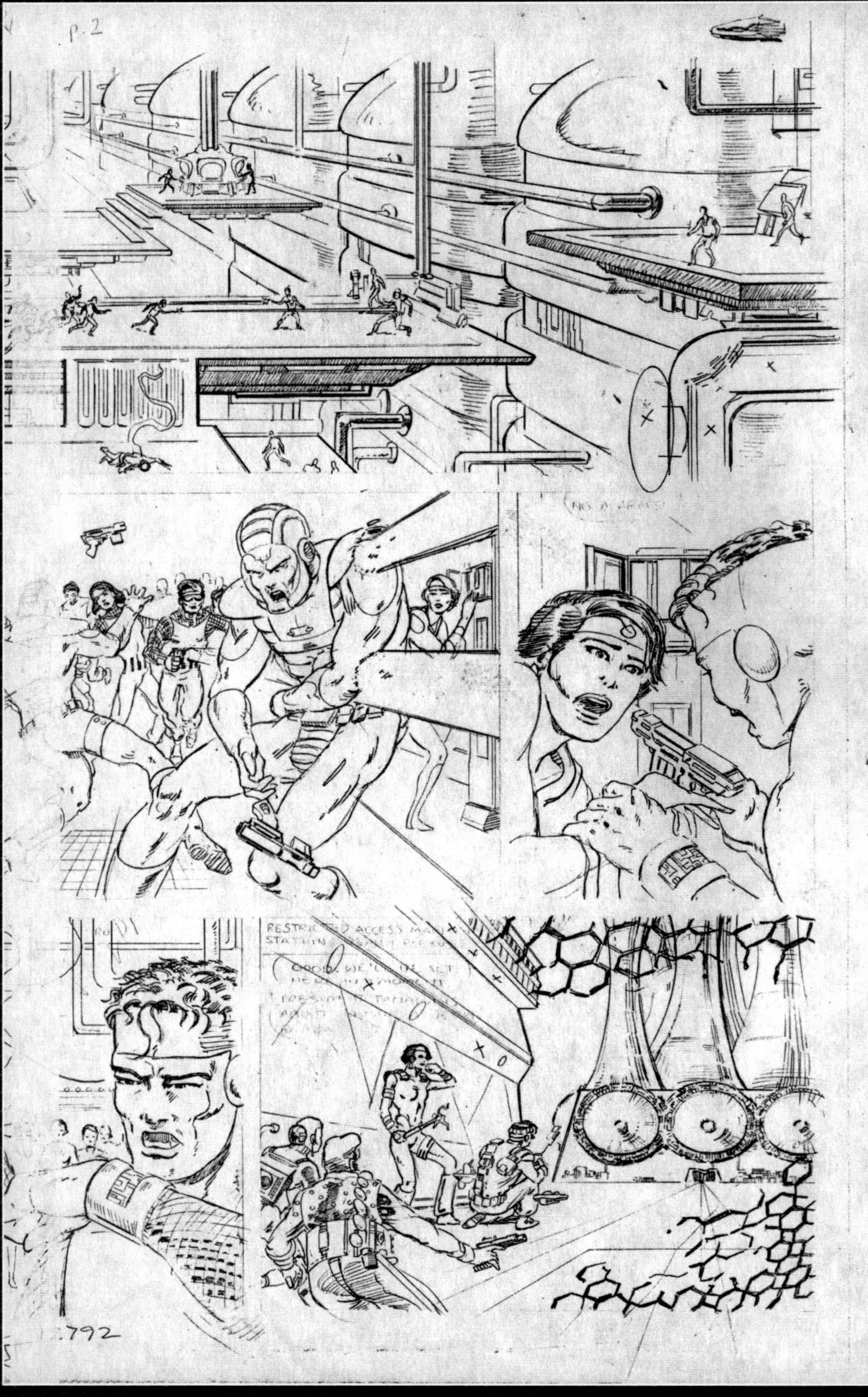
p.2
792

Rai #3, p.2

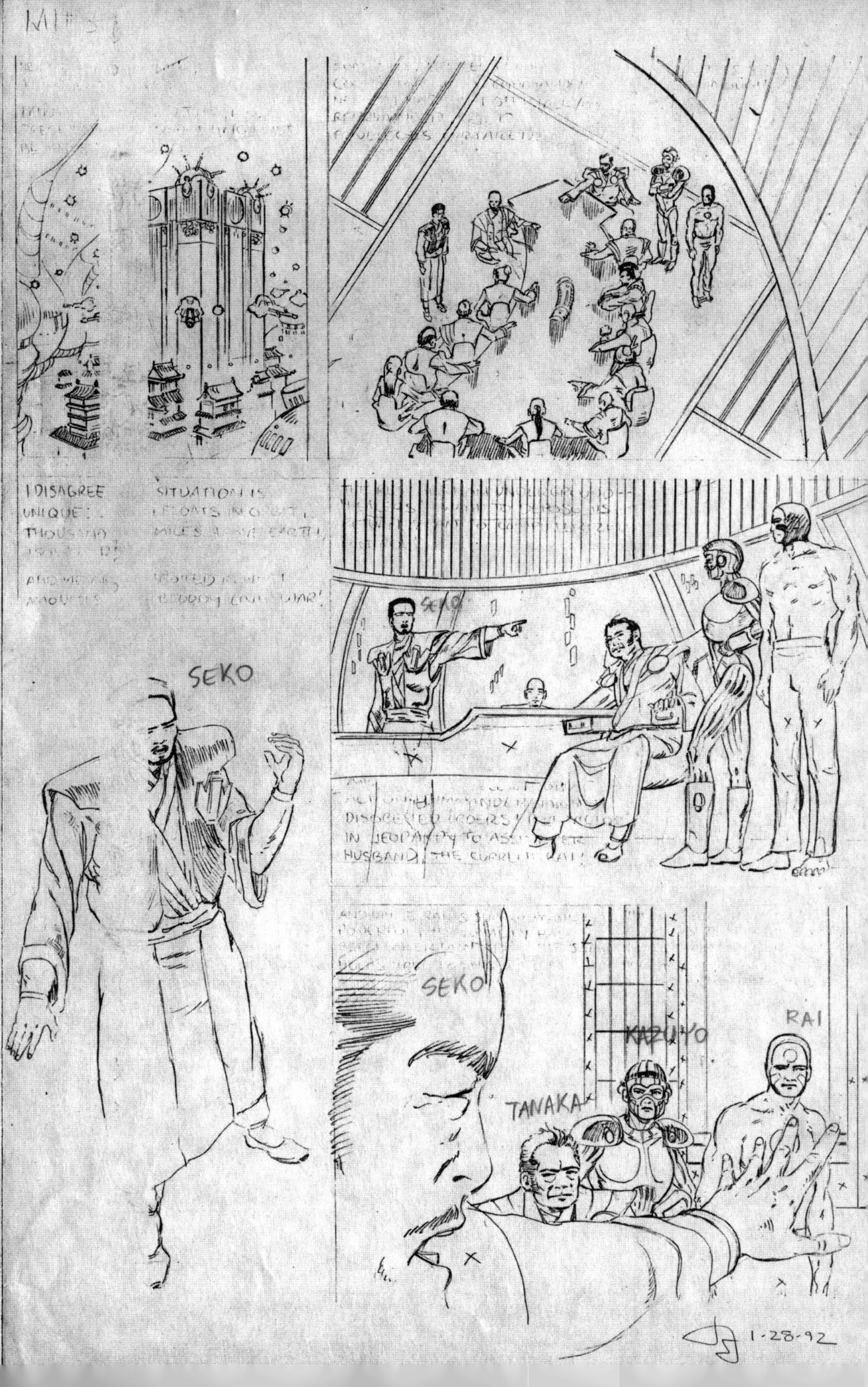
I DISAGREE
UNIQUE
SITUATION IS
SEKO
SEKO
IN JEOPARDY
HUSBAND
SEKO
KAZUYO
RAI
TANAKA
1-28-92

RAI # 3 , PAGE 4

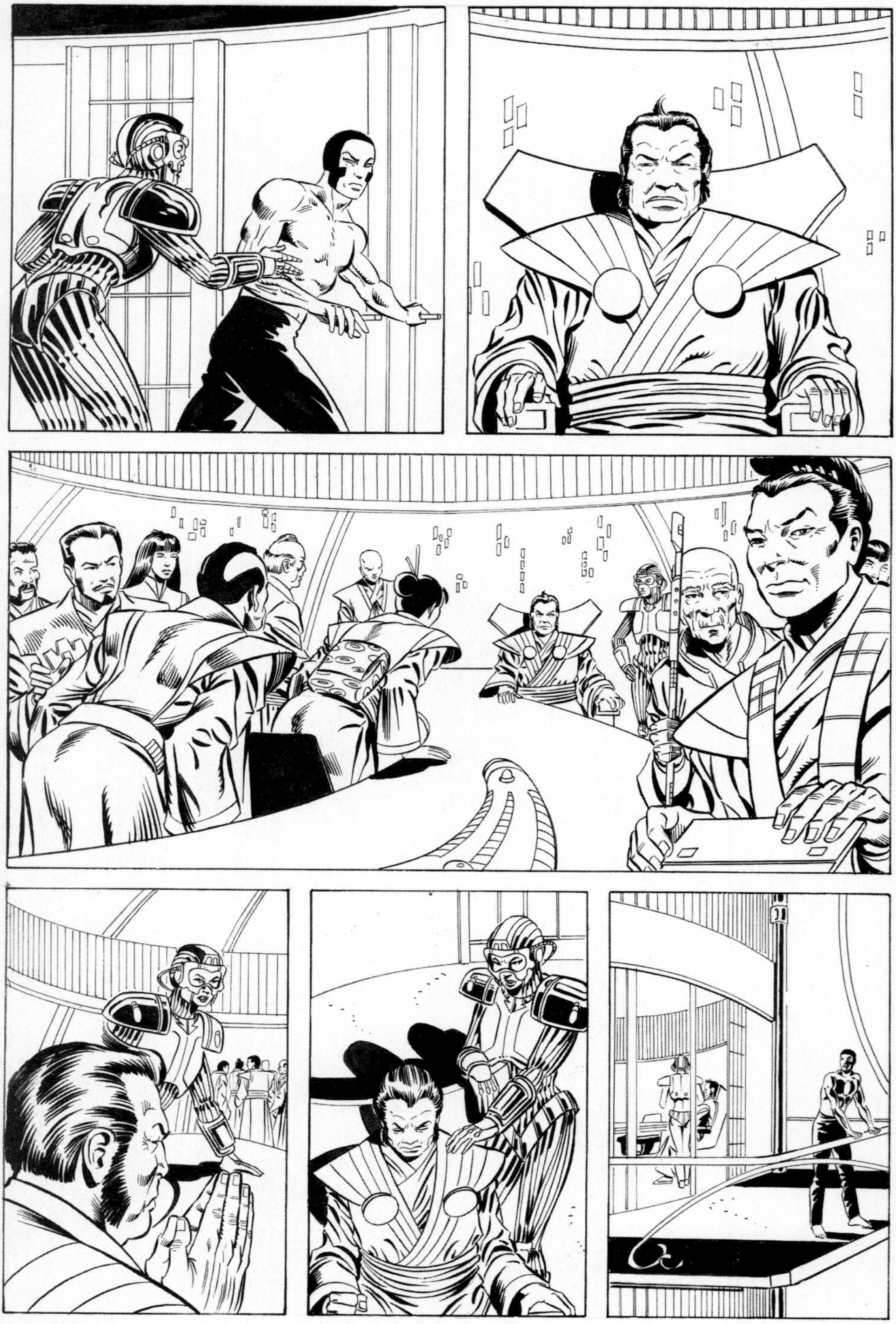

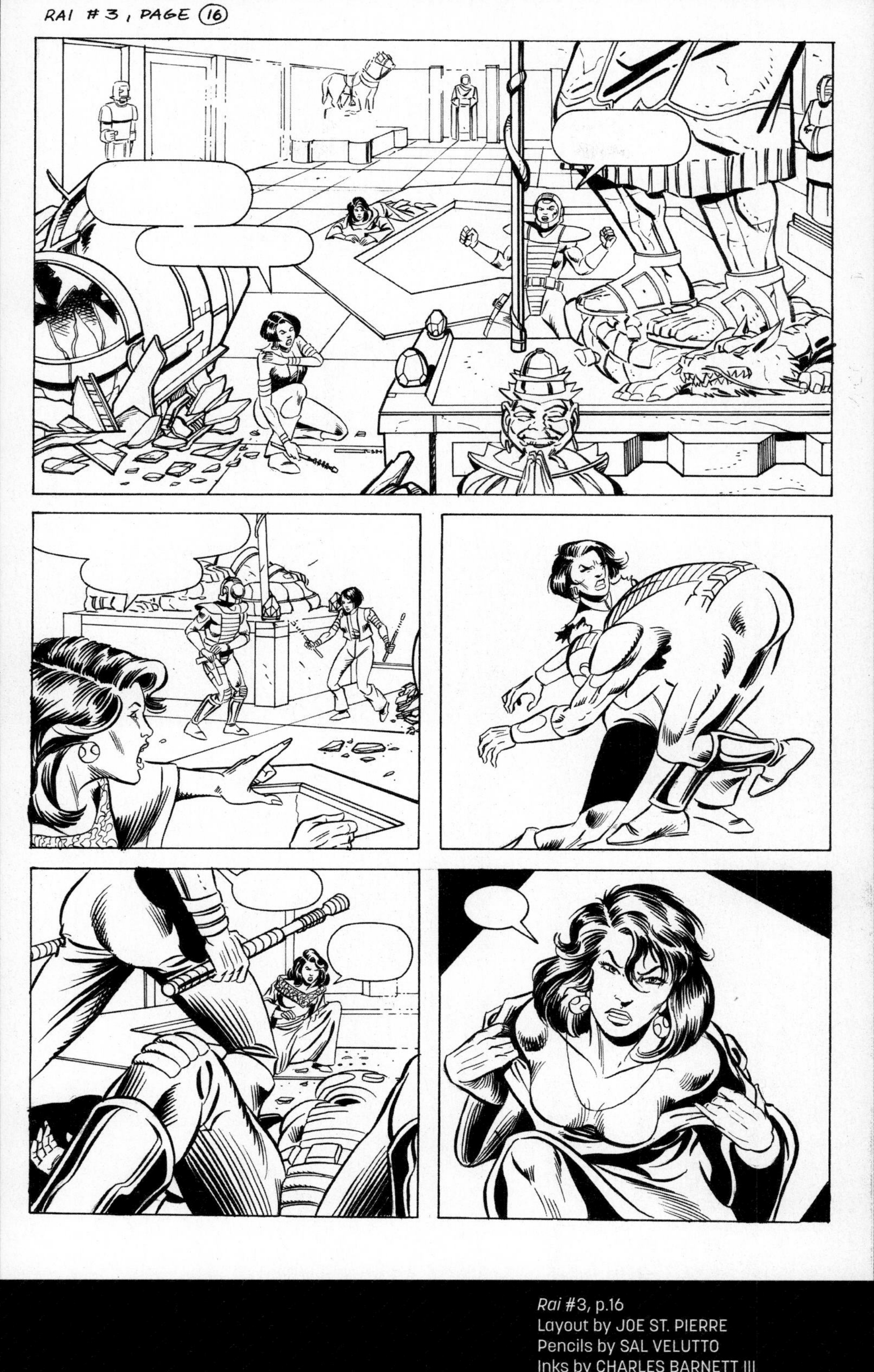
RAI #3, PAGE 16

Rai #3, p.16
Layout by JOE ST. PIERRE
Pencils by SAL VELUTTO
Inks by CHARLES BARNETT III

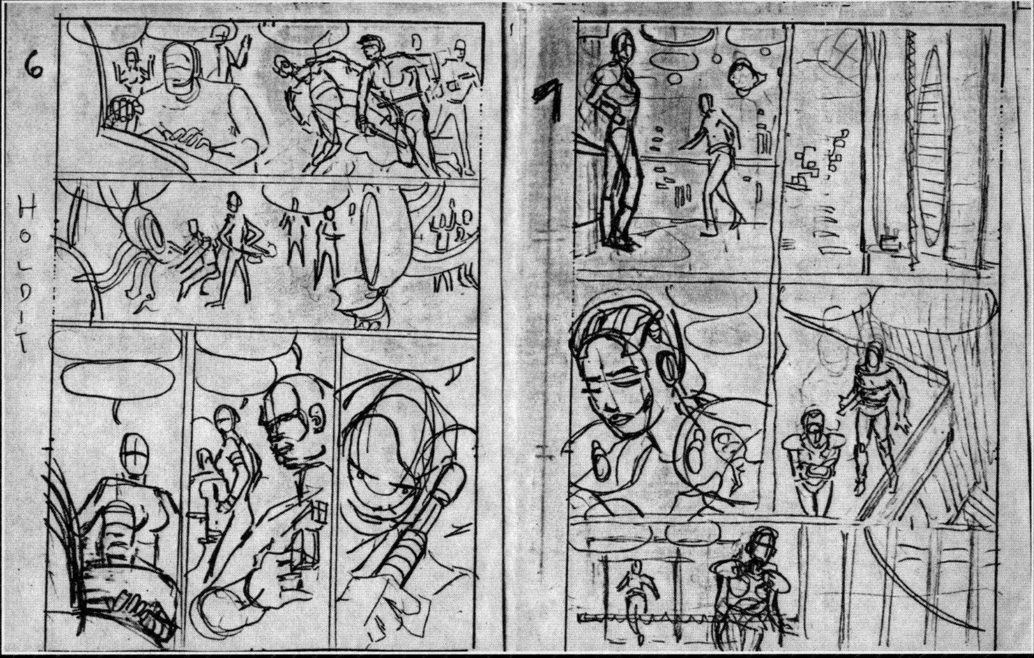
6
HOLD IT
7

Rai #3
Layouts by JOE ST. PIERRE

Rai #3, p.5
Pencils by JOE ST. PIERRE
Inks by CHARLES BARNETT III
Colors by KNOB ROW

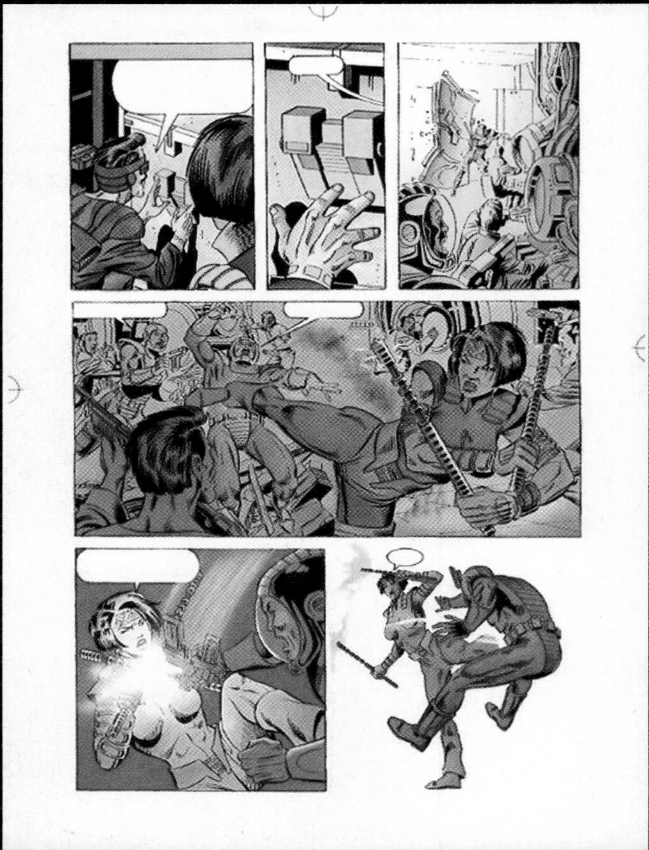

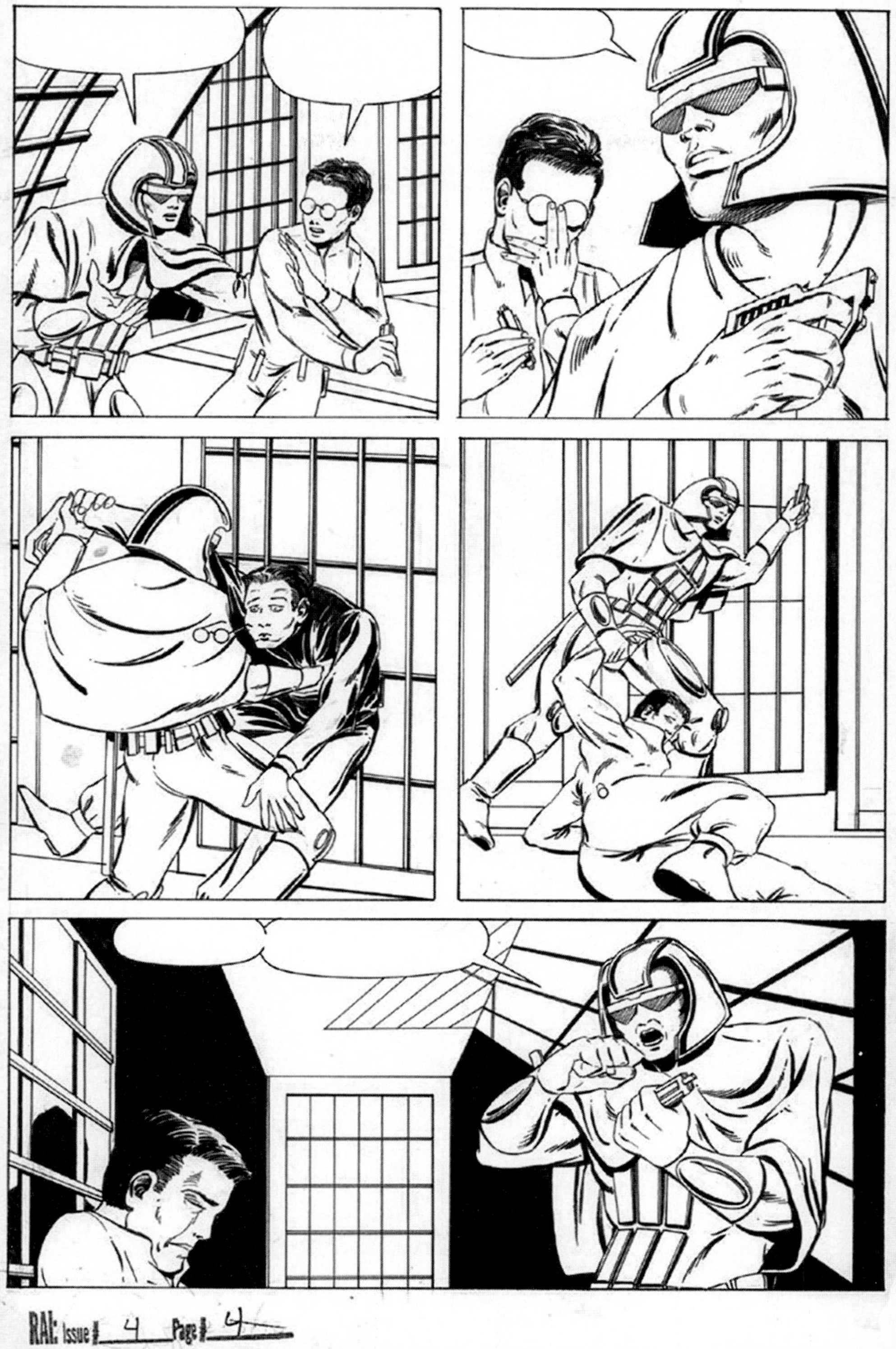
RAI: Issue # 4 Page # 4

Rai #4, p.4
Pencils by JOE ST. PIERRE
Inks by KATHRYN BOLINGER

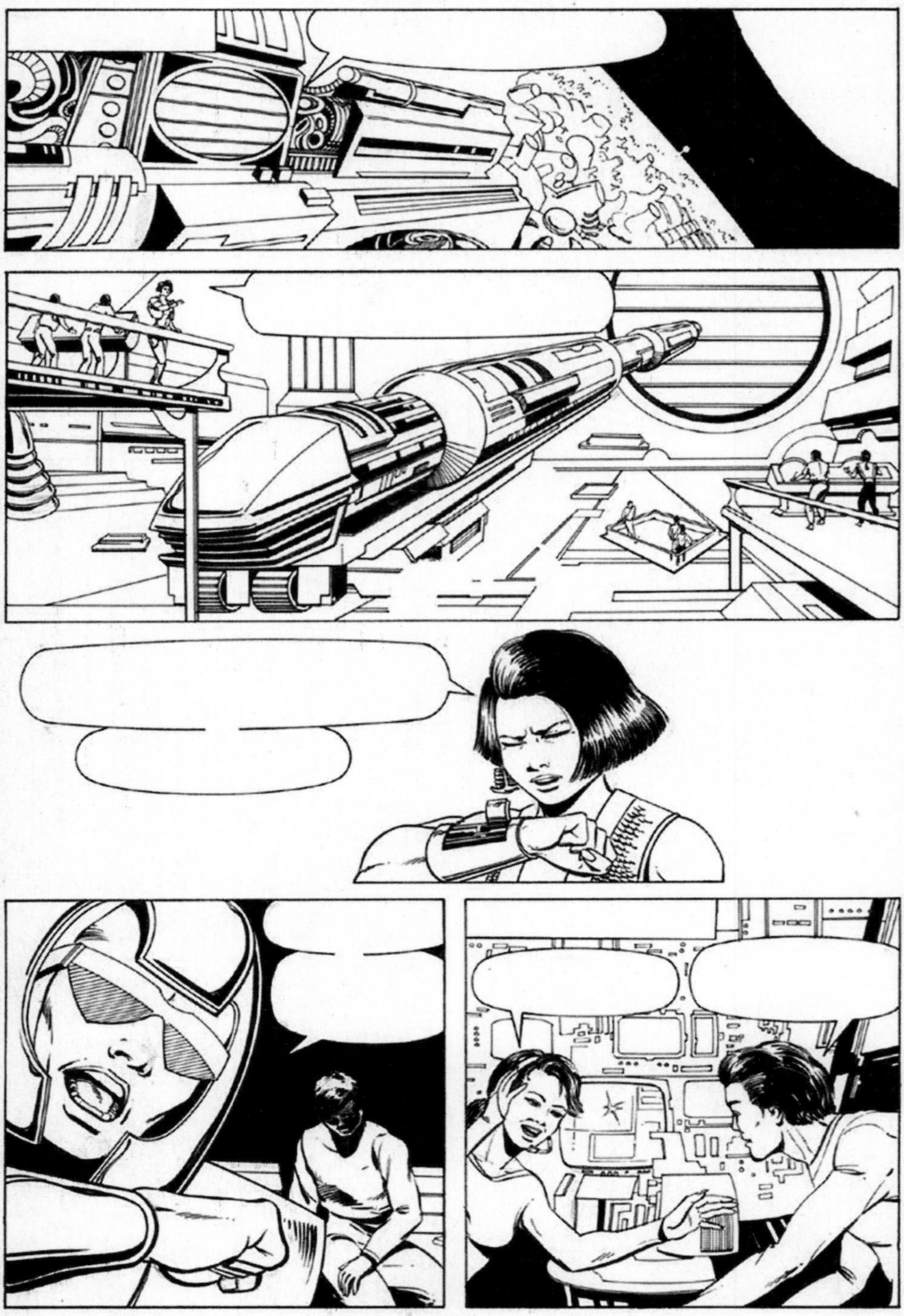

RAI: Issue # 4 Page # 5

Rai #4, p.5
Pencils by JOE ST. PIERRE
Inks by KATHRYN BOLINGER

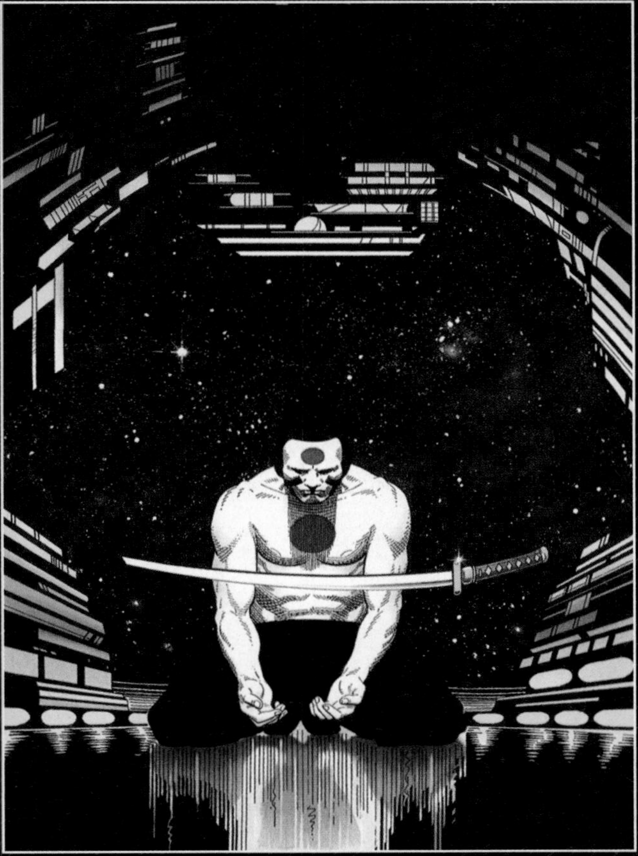

Rai #5
Cover by JOE ST. PIERRE and RALPH REESE

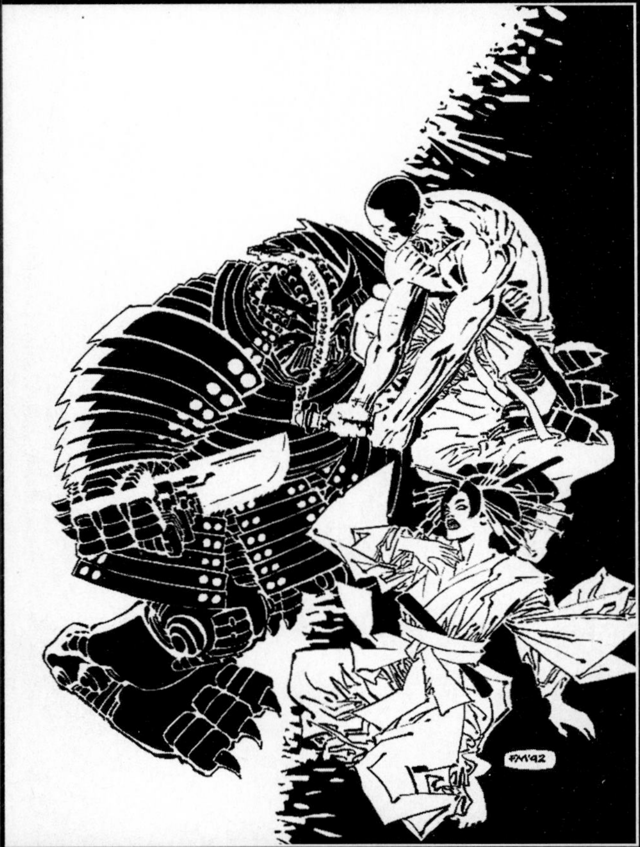

Rai #6
Cover by FRANK MILLER

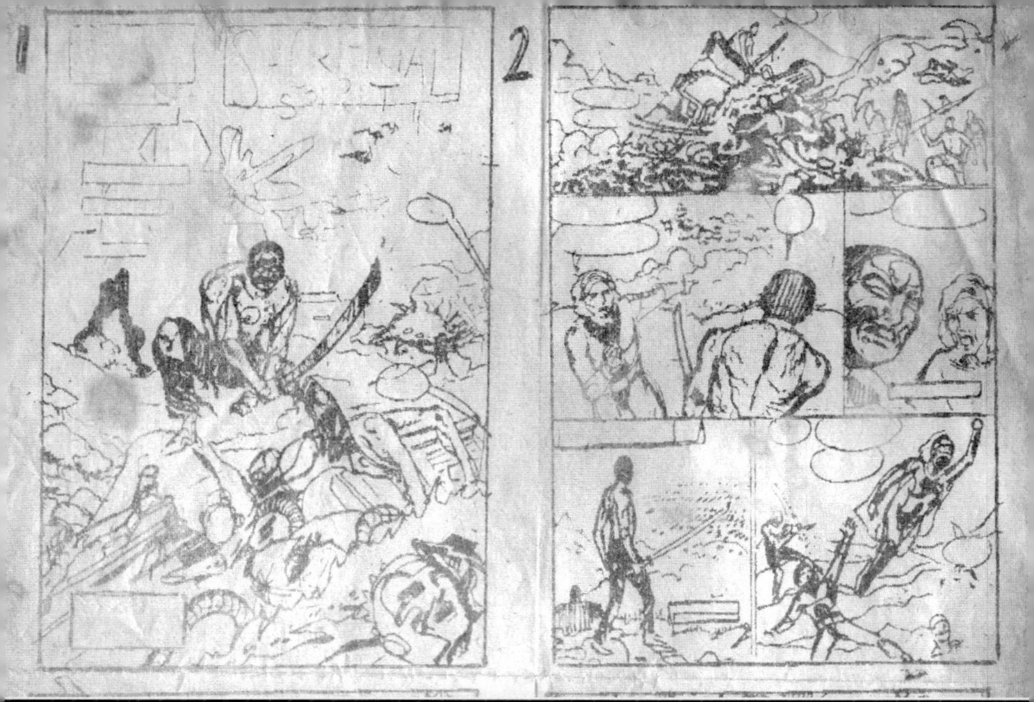

Rai #7
Layouts by JOE ST. PIERRE

Rai #8
Cover by PETER GRAU and
KATHRYIN BOLINGER

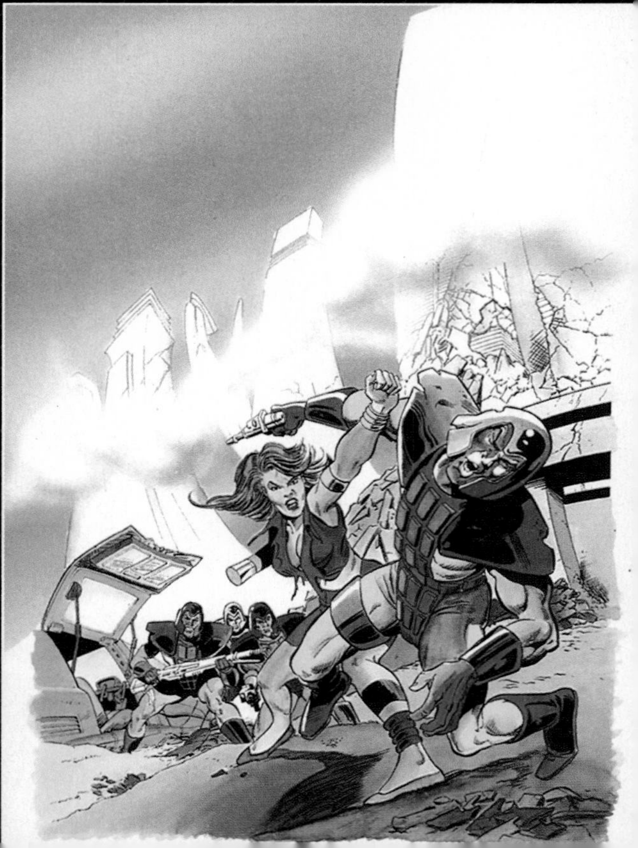